Women's and Gender Studies

Intersectional Voices

Preliminary Edition

Edited by Joanna Hadjicostandi-Anang

The University of Texas Permian Basin

cognella®
SAN DIEGO

Bassim Hamadeh, CEO and Publisher
John Remington, Executive Editor
Gem Rabanera, Project Editor
Jeanine Rees, Production Editor
Asfa Arshi, Graphic Designer
Kylie Bartolome, Licensing Coordinator
Natalie Piccotti, Director of Marketing
Kassie Graves, Vice President of Editorial
Jamie Giganti, Director of Academic Publishing

3970 Sorrento Valley Blvd., Ste. 500, San Diego, CA 92121

Dedicated to my daughters for brightening my life, giving me their love and support and for living their lives with feminist courage, strength, and integrity!

Contents

Unit VIII. Activism, Change, and Feminist Futures

Preface

Women's and Gender Studies: Intersectional Voices provides a crucial introduction to key approaches, topics and concerns of the field. It explores the gender spectrum, including people who identify as women, men, non-binary and gender expansive individuals who challenge and expand these categorizations. This anthology celebrates a diversity of influential feminist thought and focuses on a broad range of topics using analyses sensitive to the intersections of gender, race, white privilege, ability, class, age and queer representations and experiences in diverse social spaces. Within these analyses, Sociology will often provide the theoretical basis in regard to how gender issues are explored in a diverse and intersectional platform.

The book includes essays, narratives, poems and other contributions to enhance the interest and knowledge on how individuals perceive gender differences. It is intended for use as an introduction to the field in undergraduate Women's and Gender Studies courses. You may find the book useful for its examination of gender-role socialization, women's work in and out of the home, the limitations of traditional gender roles, the role of white privilege and antiracism, queer politics, gender-based crime and violence in the U.S. and internationally.

My hope is that the chapters and the introductions to the various sections will encourage you the students to look in depth at society around you and the multiple issues that arise with our involvement in everyday life with our families, jobs, schools, entertainment, and overall quality. To what extent are these personal issues connected to public issues and how do they affect each other? Academic inquiry of these topics is only one small part of the global arena and applying these concepts plays a serious part in global socioeconomic structures. Although we would not claim to be changing the world in one semester, I invite you to delve into the multiple topics and together attempt to work towards social justice, while getting involved into a meaningful analysis and restructuring of our book.

Unit I. Why an Intersectional Feminist Sociological Perspective?

I Am Rose

Loretta Diane Walker

This is what you'll find if you unzip history,
music pulsing in the cage of my ribs.
In the dark pipe of his longing,
my man makes a song for me.
White notes burst in his belly
when he thinks about the full nectar of my lips.

He keeps my name in the pocket of his tongue,
calls me his "yellow girl."
Anonymity doesn't keep me safe
from the long arms of lust.
My beauty is a magnet.

He sings of diamonds and dew;
the hard light of my eyes is a hammer
drumming against hungry hands
reaching to lift the skirt of my womanhood.

Heat climbs down the ladder of morning
three rungs at a time, descends on the day
with a heavy foot; he tells me he's leaving.
I listen to his reasons, promises of return.
My face waters with sweat, tears, knowing
I will not take him back into the folds of my love.

This quiet dusk I watch the sky float in the Rio Grande,
dream of the waves of muscles swelling
across his broad back, the camber of his mouth,
hard handsome face softening when he backs
away from me. I remember our fingers sliding
off the cliff of our grasp, the cavern of emptiness.

I shudder; the next touch will not be his.
I feel the petals of my want withering
along the pebbled-stone of distance.

The plaintive courtship-themed 1853 lyrics of "The Yellow Rose of Texas" fit the minstrel genre by depicting an African-American singer, who is longing to return to "a yellow girl," a term used to describe a mulatto, or mixed-race female born of African-American and white progenitors This iconic song of modern Texas and a popular traditional American tune, has experienced several transformations of its lyrics and periodic revivals in popularity since its appearance in the 1850s. —The Hand book of the Texas Historical Association

SEX AND GENDER

Barbara Gurr and Nancy A. Naples

The intellectual history and topics of interest in the sociology of sex and gender are tied intimately to human rights scholarship and activism. The field was generated through the advocacy of activists inside and outside the discipline inspired by the women's movement of the late 1960s and early 1970s (Fox 1995). Recognizing that women's knowledge and experience had been either erased or diminished in importance by a discipline dominated by men and fueled by patriarchal assumptions of what counts as knowledge and who should be the primary conveyers of sociological insights, women sociologists challenged the gendered assumptions of the field (Smith 1987). In 1969, Alice Rossi, who would become one of the first women presidents of the American Sociological Association (ASA) in 1983, presented data at a business meeting demonstrating the underrepresentation of women and the discrimination they faced in the discipline. As a consequence, in 1971, feminist sociologists formed their own association, Sociologists for Women in Society (SWS), and produced a separate journal, *Gender & Society*, which is now one of the leading journals in interdisciplinary gender studies. SWS dedicated itself to establishing the importance of sex and gender research for sociology; ensuring that women's contributions to knowledge and other aspects of social, economic, political, and cultural life were acknowledged in academic literature; challenging sexist language in sociology journals; and increasing women's visibility in the ASA (Fox 1995). The ASA's Sex and Gender Section was formed in 1973 and is now one of the largest sections of the ASA. SWS members hold prominent leadership positions in the ASA, including the presidency. Since the Sex and Gender Section's founding, three new ASA sections have been added that developed directly from the feminist scholarship on sex and gender.

The topics that are prominent in the field of sex and gender are also at the heart of human rights scholarship. They include processes of discrimination and economic inequalities, the roles of social activism and law in challenging gender inequality, the sources of violence against women, and the role of culture in shaping gendered understandings and practices. Sociologists of sex and gender also address the gendered processes of economic development and migration as well as militarization and global capitalism, among other social structural and historical processes (Fukumura and Matsuoka 2002; Mendez 2005; Salzinger 2005). In this regard, sociologists of sex and gender argue that a gender lens offers a powerful tool for uncovering the social dynamics shaping all major institutions (Brush 2003; Coltraine and Adams 2008; Lorber 2002). To capture the diversity of these experiences, sociologists of sex and gender frequently approach their work from an intersectional perspective (Baca Zinn and Dill 1996; Collins 1990; Naples 2009), paying attention to the intersections of gender, race, class, sexuality, age, culture, and other factors that differentially shape social life rather than concentrating on a single dimension.

THE SOCIOLOGY OF SEX AND GENDER

EXAMINING PROCESSES OF DISCRIMINATION AND ECONOMIC INEQUALITIES

Sociologists of sex and gender focus attention on how sex and gender shape structures of inequality and power. Their research addresses structural factors that derive from gender inequality, including the wage gaps between men and women and other forms of discrimination in the labor force (Britton 2003; England 2005); the gender gap in electoral politics (Rossi 1983); and sexist and heteronormative assumptions embedded in law and social policy (Bernstein and Reimann 2001; Naples 1991).

Another dimension of this scholarship relates to understanding the contribution of global economic restructuring for gender dynamics and economic inequalities. Sociologists of sex and gender highlight the fact that globalization is a result of particular actions taken by identifiable actors and that globalization lands in particular places (Sassen 2006, 2007). Rather than view globalization as a process that occurs at a distance from the everyday lives and activities of particular actors, they demonstrate that global economic and political change is manifest in the daily lives and struggles of women and other members of communities in different parts of the world in ways that are often hidden from view in analyses of globalization that start from the perspective of multinational corporations, transnational organizations, and international political institutions (Naples and Desai 2002, vii).

UNDERSTANDING THE ROLE OF SOCIAL ACTIVISM AND LAW FOR CHALLENGING GENDER INEQUALITY

Until sociologists of sex and gender focused attention on women's political activism, especially the important roles they play in their communities, the extent and variety of women's political participation were ignored or unexamined (Naples 1998). Women's community work and activism, when noticed at all by academics, were understood primarily as a natural extension of their caretaking roles and as part of a maternalist politics in which women's engagement in the public sphere was justified through their identities as mothers (Koven and Michel 1993). In contrast to these assessments, women as community activists contribute countless hours of unpaid labor to campaigns to enhance the physical and environmental quality of their communities while tending to the emotional and social needs of other community members. Their approach to community development and leadership often involves collective and empowering strategies that encourage other women and other residents frequently left out of decision-making roles in formal voluntary associations and political parties to increase their political participation (Naples 2011). This scholarship also explores the role of transnational women's, LGBT, and social justice movements that challenge gender oppression, sexual violence, and other human rights violations (Adam, Duyvendak, and Krouwel 1999; Naples and Desai 2002; Tripp and Ferree 2006).

ANALYZING THE SOURCES OF VIOLENCE AGAINST WOMEN IN PUBLIC AND PRIVATE SPHERES

One of the most important issues addressed by sociologists of sex and gender involves analyzing the many ways that women, minority men, and sexually nonconforming men become targets of violence. Studies of domestic violence were noticeably missing in early sociological literature on the family. With the recognition of the ways power inequalities in marital relations contribute to women's risk of violence in the family, as well as how women become targets of sexual harassment at work and in public spaces, sociologists of sex and gender revealed the daily costs associated with gender and sexual inequalities (Baker 2007).

In considering factors that contribute to violence against women, sociologists and other feminist scholars of sex and gender also brought attention to the roles of militarization and global capitalism in increasing risks of violence against women—for example, through the development of coercive sexual labor in military zones and gendered constructions of violence in armed conflict (Enloe 1990, 2000, 2007; Fukumura and Matsuoka 2002); the use of rape as a tool of war (Allen 1996); and the international crisis of sex trafficking and forced marriage, both of which have been centralized by international human rights groups (Gill and Sundari 2011; Zheng 2010).

ASSESSING THE ROLE OF CULTURE AND DIFFERENCE IN SHAPING GENDERED UNDERSTANDINGS AND PRACTICES

A main topic in the sociology of gender focuses on examining how cultural understandings of gender shape the norms of how a feminine or a masculine body should look and act (Connell 2002; Hughs and Witz 1997; Messner 1992; Witz 2000). This contributes to the attention that feminist sociologists have paid to standards of femininity and masculinity as they apply to evaluations of appropriate body size and shape for women and men, stigma attached to those who do not adhere to these standards, and the ways in which early childhood socialization and media serve to enforce these norms (Hesse-Biber and Nagy 2006). Sociologists of sex and gender also use an intersectional approach to explore the power dynamics between women of different racial and ethnic backgrounds (Becker 1994; Kang 2003) and with different abilities (Shakespeare 2006; Zitzelsberger 2005). Feminist scholars also analyze the role of the medical profession, pharmaceutical companies, and new technologies for providing the means by which women and men can reshape their bodies to fit into narrow definitions of appropriate gender and sexuality (Haiken 1999; Loe 2006).

Feminist sociologists of science are especially interested in new reproductive technologies and their ability to challenge the notion of the "natural" mother and father as older, infertile, or same-sex couples access alternative forms of reproduction (Mamo 2007). They point out the inequities in who can access new technologies and the expansion of "reproductive tourism," where wealthy couples travel to poorer countries to purchase reproductive services, including surrogacy arrangements (Purdy 1989). The new field of transgender studies further complicates analysis of the social construction and production of gender as well as the myriad of ways that gender shapes social policy—for example, by challenging hegemonic understandings of gender as a binary system that maps onto bodies that are understood as "male" or "female" (Currah, Juang, and Miner 2007; Valentine 2007).

Sociologists of sex and gender draw insights from postcolonial and third world feminist analysts who emphasize the ways that cultural diversity and other differences, including class, race, ethnicity, country of origin, age, ability, and sexuality, contour the lives of women and men, thus contributing to their different gendered expectations and experiences (Grewal and Caplan 1994, 2000; Alexander and Mohanty 1997; Mohanty, Russo, and Torres 1991). These complexities are particularly salient, for example, when we examine the lives of poor women, who are disproportionately women of color and disproportionately shoulder the burden of the economic and social dislocation resulting from gendered, racialized, and internationalized processes (Buvinic 1998; Sanford 2003; Women's Refugee Commission 2011). This insight relates to an approach that is at the heart of contemporary feminist sociological analyses, namely, intersectionality.

The call for intersectional analyses was first heard from feminists of color who critiqued approaches that constructed women's concerns without attention to the ways that race, class, and sexuality shaped the experiences of women (Baca Zinn and Dill 1996; Collins 1990). The most powerful approaches to intersectionality also include attention to the ways in which these interactions produce contradictions and tensions across these different levels of analysis and dimensions of difference (McCall 2001, 2005; Maynard 1994).

RESEARCH METHODS FOR THE STUDY OF SEX AND GENDER

Prior to the intervention of feminist sociologists, when included at all, sex was merely considered as a variable in sociological studies. Feminists first argued for a distinction between the biological category of sex and the social construction of gender, then recognized that the biological category is also socially constructed (Lorber and Moore 2007). Beginning in the 1970s, researchers informed by a feminist call to describe women's experiences and perspectives in their own words began to make women's lives central in ethnographic and other qualitative accounts (Smith 1987). A gendered lens on men's lives and the development of men's studies was inspired by a growing sensitivity to the ways in which femininities and masculinities are coconstituted (Connell 1987, 2005; Kimmel 2005; Pascoe 2007). Since the 1980s, feminist sociologists who are influenced by postmodern analyses of power and knowledge have become particularly concerned with the role of discourse and the myriad of ways power shapes women's lives (Ferguson 1991). Differences in feminist epistemologies of knowledge influence what counts as data and how data should be analyzed; therefore, a postmodern feminist researcher would approach the collection and analysis of interviews differently from a scholar who draws on positivist or symbolic interactionist perspectives (Naples 2003).

Feminist sociologists have been particularly effective in identifying the processes by which power and "relations of ruling" are inherent in disciplinary practices (Smith 1990). Feminist sociologists have raised questions about the ethics of social research, especially as relates to power imbalances in fieldwork and interviewing (Stacey 1991; Wolf 1996). As one strategy, sociologists of sex and gender recommend addressing these inequalities through reflexive practice designed to interrogate how personal and situational factors contribute to power imbalances. For example, Nancy Naples explains that this form of reflexive practice "encourages feminist scholars to examine how gendered and racialized assumptions influence which voices and experiences are privileged in ethnographic encounters" (2003, 22). She also argues that a reflexive "approach also implies the development of more egalitarian and participatory field methods than traditionally utilized in social scientific investigations" (201).

Sociologists of sex and gender employ a number of research methods to better understand the complexities of sex and gender. Small-scale, locally focused studies such as those conducted by Patricia Richards (2005) in Chile and Vincanne Adams (1998) in Tibet often incorporate various interview methods, including in-depth interviews and focus groups, as well as observations of and, occasionally, participation in local communities, nongovernmental organizations, and state-sponsored organizations. Sociologists interested in larger demographic trends such as poverty levels, refugee status, education attainment, and maternal mortality and morbidity frequently employ statistical methods through censuses and surveys (Hafner-Burton 2005; Hafner-Burton and Tsutsui 2005; Spirer 1990). Other quantitative approaches are used to capture aggregate patterns such as wage inequality and gender division of labor in employment across different regions (McCall 2001). Sociologists of sex and gender have also turned to policy and document analysis to better understand the bureaucratic and discursive development of instruments intended to identify and meet women's human rights needs (Merry 2006; Naples 2003; Wotipka and Tsutsui 2008).

HUMAN RIGHTS AND THE SOCIOLOGY OF SEX AND GENDER

SEX AND GENDER IN HUMAN RIGHTS DOCUMENTS

The Universal Declaration of Human Rights (UDHR) affirms the "dignity and rights" of all humankind. However, the near invisibility of sex and gender as specific categories for protection in the UDHR renders addressing the rights of women problematic, particularly in a global or transnational context (Bunch 1990; Freeman 1999; Gaer 1998; Binion 1995). Largely as a result of feminist scholarship and activism, particularly since the mid-1980s, human rights abuses based on or related to sex and gender have become increasingly noted; yet there is still no clear consensus as to how to understand these categories or appropriately address violations of women's and sexual minorities' human rights in an international human rights context. This lack of clarity continues to circumscribe the ability of activists and scholars to adequately frame gender-specific abuses as human rights violations in an international legal framework and also presents challenges to those seeking redress. However, progress has been made toward delineating women's and sexual minorities' human rights and demanding that they be formally recognized and protected. Sociologists of sex and gender contribute to this work through increasingly intersectional analyses of the interactions between gender and the state, citizenship, governance structures, and local and global political economies, among other factors.

HISTORICAL PERSPECTIVE ON SEX AND GENDER IN HUMAN RIGHTS DISCOURSE

Attention to sex and gender in human rights discourse and documents can be traced to the late nineteenth century (Lockwood et. al. 1998) and is more evident in the UDHR, which was adopted in 1948. The elaboration of concern for women's rights in particular was further evident in the efforts that resulted from the United Nations Decade for Women (1976–1985), during which women from many different geographical, ethnic, racial, religious, cultural, and class backgrounds took up the task of improving the status of women transnationally. The United Nations sponsored three international women's conferences during this time: in Mexico City in 1975, Copenhagen in 1980, and Nairobi in 1985. Several important human rights documents developed out of these conferences and the efforts of feminist activists and scholars.

The 1976 International Covenant on Civil and Political Rights recognized the equal right of men and women to the enjoyment of all civil and political rights set forth in the covenant (Article 3). This right was further codified in 1979 when the UN General Assembly adopted the Convention on the Elimination of All Forms of Discrimination against Women. Some scholars note that its references to sex include sexual freedom, thereby offering protection to sexual minorities (Mittelstaedt 2008).

In 1990, following decades of concerted effort from feminist activists, organizations, and scholars, Dr. Charlotte Bunch published a foundational call for women's rights as human rights, criticizing the reluctance of states and international structures to address the needs of women and homosexuals from the legal framework of human rights. Three years later, the participants in the World Conference on Human Rights produced the Vienna Declaration and Program of Action, which specified a platform on women's human rights as inalienable from the individual and indivisible from universal human rights, noting that the eradication of sex discrimination is a priority for the international community.

The 1994 International Conference on Population and Development in Cairo featured discussions on sex, sexuality, and sexual health but linked these rights to heterosexual reproduction with no mention of freedom of sexual expression or sexual orientation. At the Fourth World Conference on Women in Beijing in 1995, sponsored by the United Nations, feminist activists finally saw the global emergence of the idea of "women's rights as human rights" (Bunch 1990). Developed by conference participants, the Beijing Platform for Action focused on removing obstacles to women's active participation in all spheres of public and private life through a full and equal share in economic, social, cultural and political decision-making. However, this platform failed to include support for the rights of lesbians and rejected the term "sexual orientation" (Bunch and Fried 1996; see also Baden and Goetz 1997).

KEY AREAS OF CONCERN FOR WOMEN'S HUMAN RIGHTS

Sociologists have identified numerous areas of concern for the development and protection of women's human rights, and they generally understand these areas as linked globally (Naples and Desai 200; Reilly 2009). We offer here three brief illustrations: economic security, gendered violence, and reproductive health.

ECONOMIC SECURITY

The United Nations asserts that women's economic security is at far greater risk than men's globally, and this is particularly true in rural areas that rely heavily on agricultural production (UNFAO 2010). Differential access to employment opportunities continues to reflect and reproduce gendered conceptualizations of women's domestic roles and to inhibit their ability to engage fully in civic life. Further, approximately 75 percent of the world's women are not entitled to property ownership and cannot receive bank loans due to underemployment, unemployment, and insecure employment (Moser 2007). These restrictions impact not only women but families and communities as well (Cagatay 2001).

GENDERED VIOLENCE

Anthropologist Sally Merry points out that "the idea that everyday violence against women is a human rights violation has not been easy to establish" (2006, 2). Part of the difficulty lies in the tensions between global and transnational institutions and local structures. The translation of human rights laws and ideologies between multiple locations is complicated by cultural differences, questions of sovereignty, and access to resources, among other potential impediments (Bunch 1990). In this context, the role of intermediary institutions such as nongovernmental organizations is pivotal. Further complicating the ability of scholars and activists to address gendered violence as a human rights violation is the continuing construction of a public-private dichotomy in which violence against women is framed as a family issue in which state actors are reluctant to intervene (Clapham 2007; Tomasevski 1995). However, there has been some progress toward understanding gendered violence as an issue that transcends public/private dichotomies, particularly when this violence occurs in the context of war. In 2008 the UN Security Council passed Resolution 1820, which formally recognized the particular vulnerabilities of women and girl children to sexual violence during armed conflict and reaffirmed states' obligations to address sexual violence against civilians.

REPRODUCTIVE HEALTH

Maternal and child health continue to be a priority for women's human rights activists in the twenty-first century. Growing attention and increased resources from local, global, and transnational institutions over the last several decades—particularly since the 1994 International Conference on Population and Development explicitly linked the reproductive health and human rights of women to global efforts to reduce poverty—have resulted in important improvements in women's access to adequate health care (WHO 2010). However, globally women experience unequal access to health care. For example, according to the World Health Organization (2000), global maternal mortality and morbidity rates are highest in developing nations.

Guang-zhen Wang and Vijayan Pillai (2001) explain that sociologists have applied two general analytical frames to reproductive health: (1) identifying social-structural factors shaping reproductive health, and (2) examining a rights-based paradigm to elucidate states' obligations to provide reproductive health care. Utilizing these frames has enabled sociologists to offer critical analyses of the interactions between health and social environments that elucidate foundational causes for the disparities in health between sexes, genders, geographic locations, socioeconomic locations, and racial-ethnic identities, among other key factors (Doyal 1995, 2001; Warner-Smith, Bryson, and Byles 2004).

KEY SOCIOLOGICAL QUESTIONS AND INSIGHTS IN THE STUDY OF WOMEN'S HUMAN RIGHTS

A primary question emerging from the feminist sociological study of human rights is, What obstacles challenge universal recognition of women's human rights and prevent a comprehensive consideration of gender within the prevailing human rights frameworks? Findings in response to this question vary but often include the influence of religious groups, social and political constructions of a public-private gendered dichotomy, masculinized notions of citizenship, and the fact that the concept of "universal" human rights tends to mask the multiple dimensions of difference emerging from racial-ethnic, class, and cultural locations, as well as sex and gender differences, and to impose a Western conceptualization of individual rights.

The lack of women's voices in the development of religious institutions and the concurrent influence of religious doctrine on state practices impose multiple and, at times, severe restrictions on women's freedoms (European Women's Lobby 2006; Winter 2006). For example, at the time of the Beijing Conference for Women, Roman Catholic authorities rejected what they considered the ambiguity of the term "gender" and noted that they understood "gender" to be "grounded in biological sexual identity" (UN Report 1995, 165), thus reinscribing an essentialist role for women that curtails women's opportunities (European Women's Lobby 2006). The role of religious doctrine in determining women's rights is complicated by these essentialist ideas about gender as they intersect with issues of cultural relativism and fundamental human rights (Sunder 2003; Winter 2006). These complications have led many scholars, such as Madhavi Sunder, to assert that "human rights law has a problem with religion" (2003, 1401; see also Reilly 2009).

EXAMINING THE PERSISTENCE OF THE PUBLIC-PRIVATE DICHOTOMY IN HUMAN RIGHTS DISCOURSE

Sociologists of sex and gender interrogate the social construction of a public-private dichotomy in which some aspects of human lives are conceptualized as occurring or belonging in a public sphere and others are deemed private and thus, in some measure, protected from surveillance or state control (Collins 1994; Okin 1989). Many violations of women's human rights, such as domestic violence, forms of sexual slavery, and child-preference practices that disadvantage girl children, are often considered "private" matters in which global and local states are reluctant to intervene (Bunch 1990; Freeman 1999; MacKinnon 1993). The occurrence of these and similarly gendered phenomena in what is constructed as the "privacy" of family and home constructs boundaries around how these issues are addressed and inhibits the abilities of international systems to intervene in such rights violations.

GENDERING HUMAN RIGHTS DISCOURSE AND PRACTICE

Sociologists of sex and gender point out that the dominant image of the political actor is male (Haney 2000; Bunch 1990; Yuval-Davis 1997), and most human rights institutions are male dominated (Freeman 1999). Therefore, women are largely invisible as human rights institutions deal with human rights violations on a large, public scale (for example, through the institution of democracies, fair housing, and economic security); "it is assumed that women benefit" (Freeman 1999, 515) as members of the larger populace. Failure to specify the needs of women as women presents an obstacle to recognizing the many ways their human rights can be and are violated through an imposed public-private dichotomy (Bunch 1990; MacKinnon 1993). Within this dichotomy, notions of citizenship become conflated with the presumably male political actor (Yuval-Davis 1997), and the human rights of women are subsumed or delegitimized under this rubric of masculinized citizenship.

UNIVERSALIZING NOTIONS OF HUMAN RIGHTS AND OF WOMEN

Citizenship for women is further complicated by political and cultural location, as the women's-rights-as-human-rights frame potentially implies a universalizing notion of women and of rights derived from Western conceptions of citizenship and the state. Sociological perspectives point out the ways in which this runs the risk of further masking local structures and institutions such as diverse family forms, law-enforcement practices, and religious beliefs (Bonnin 1995; Chow 1996; Howard and Allen 1996; Ray and Korteweg 1999). When theoretical space is allotted for the recognition of women outside a Western paradigm, it is often limited in scope. For example, as Chandra Talpade Mohanty argues, "Assumptions of privilege and ethnocentric universality (can) lead to the construction of a … reductive and homogeneous notion of '… Third World difference'" (2006, 19), wherein third world and postcolonial women and U.S. women of color are produced as a "composite, singular 'Third World Woman'" (Narayan 1997). Women's human rights, therefore, potentially work from a binary framework of "West/not West" as well as "male/not male."

REDEFINING THE HUMAN RIGHTS PARADIGM FROM A FEMINIST PERSPECTIVE

Gender requires a revisioning of human rights as a universal concept as well as a reconstruction of the systems used to create and ensure the sanctity of women's human rights (Staudt 1997; Binion 1995). This includes a blurring of imposed boundaries around "public" and "private" and recognition of the inherently political nature of the "private" lives of women, including domestic lives, religious beliefs and practices, and sexualities. Sociologists recognize that political borders are blurred in the transnational context of global economy, migration, and armed conflict (Freeman 1999; Naples and Desai 2002). Therefore, a feminist and intersectional sociological study of relevant social structures includes, but is not limited to, family and community; local, regional, and global political economies; culture, religion, law, and education; and national and transnational governance, including nongovernmental organizations.

Just as political boundaries are not permanently fixed, a human rights framework is not a static paradigm, as our local and global conceptualizations of what counts as human rights issues and what they require continue to evolve. Feminist sociologists' particular perspective on the intersections of social institutions and structures, such as the family, state, economy, and religion, and individual experiences of power and inequality renders visible the links between the lives of women and sexual minorities, violations of their human rights, and opportunities for protection and redress.

Sociological inquiry into gender and gendered structures and institutions has helped to reveal the ways in which definitions of citizenship; local, national, and transnational institutions and structures; and even the law itself are frequently informed by gendered notions of masculinity that exclude women and their experiences. Sociological analyses of gender thereby offer theoretical tools with which to understand, highlight, and advance an agenda of women's rights as human rights. Emerging emphases in feminist sociological work on the intersections of gender with race, class, sexuality, and other social and political locations (Collins 1994; Richards 2005) provide still greater space for consideration of women's diverse lived experiences under the rubric of human rights, allowing human rights scholars and activists greater opportunity to avoid essentializing women and imposing inadequate Western concepts of "rights."

WHERE DO WE GO FROM HERE?

Recognizing the diversity of women's and men's lives, yet striving to understand "women" and "men" as universal categories, produces a theoretical tension for sociology and for human rights praxis. Women constitute a "group" that exists everywhere; yet they are often differentiated by political, cultural, racial, economic, ethnic, religious, and other considerations. The specific needs of women and non-gender-conforming men for recognition and protection of their human rights share some similarities but vary in many ways. Sensitivity to the differences among women requires nuanced, locally grounded analyses of women's and men's diverse lived experiences; yet, as Gayle Binion asserts, "The facts and conditions of cultural diversity among societies cannot, from a feminist perspective, justify a failure to rectify the conditions in which women live worldwide" (1995, 522), conditions that include gendered violence, economic insecurity, and reproductive health concerns. The international instruments of human rights retain an uncomfortable relationship with culture and gender that requires ongoing reflexive practice and attention to local structures and cultural diversity as well as global economic and political processes that shape everyday life in different parts of the world.

Empowered: Popular Feminism and Popular Misogyny

Sarah Banet-Weiser

INTRODUCTION

In 2018, we are living in a moment in North America and Europe in which feminism has become, somewhat incredibly, *popular*. It feels as if everywhere you turn, there is an expression of feminism—on a T-shirt, in a movie, in the lyrics of a pop song, in an inspirational Instagram post, in an awards ceremony speech. Feminism is "popular" in at least three senses: One, feminism manifests in discourses and practices that are circulated in popular and commercial media, such as digital spaces like blogs, Instagram, and Twitter, as well as broadcast media. As such, these discourses have an accessibility that is not confined to academic enclaves or niche groups. Two, the "popular" of popular feminism signifies the condition of being liked or admired by like-minded people and groups, as *popularity*. And three, for me the "popular" is, as cultural theorist Stuart Hall (1998) argued, a terrain of struggle, a space where competing demands for power battle it out. This means that there are many different feminisms that circulate in popular culture in the current moment, and some of these feminisms become more visible than others. Popular feminism is networked across all media platforms, some connecting with synergy, others struggling for priority and visibility. Popular feminism has, in many ways, allowed us to imagine a culture in which feminism, in every form, doesn't have to be defended; it is accessible, even admired.

But feminism isn't the only popular phenomenon we need to contend with in the early twenty-first century. Each time I began to investigate a popular feminist practice or expression, there was always an accompanying hostile rejoinder or challenge, regardless of the mediated space in which it occurred—whether that was social media, the legal realm, or corporate culture. For every Tumblr page dedicated to female body positivity, there were fat-shaming and body-shaming online comments. For every confidence organization for girls, there was yet another men's rights organization claiming that men are the "real" victims. For many women—and more than a few men—a broader acceptance of feminism as an identity, concept, and practice is exhilarating; yet, for those who find feminism to be a threat, this acceptance also stimulates fear, trepidation, aggression, and violence. When feminism is "in the water," so to speak, as it is in popular culture today, it is not surprising to witness a backlash from patriarchal culture. It is not surprising because opposition to feminism is not new. There is clearly a relationship between the creation and expression of popular feminism and what I began to call "popular misogyny."

Misogyny is popular in the contemporary moment for the same reasons feminism has become popular: it is expressed and practiced on multiple media platforms, it attracts other like-minded groups and individuals, and it manifests in a terrain of struggle, with competing demands for power. For me, popular misogyny in some ways follows a conventional definition of misogyny: a hatred of women. But I also want to make a more nuanced case for popular misogyny: it is the instrumentalization of women as objects, where women are a means to an end: a systematic devaluing and dehumanizing of women. Popular misogyny is also, like popular feminism, networked, an interconnection of nodes in all forms of media and everyday practice. Of course, misogyny is not only expressed and practiced by men; women are also part of this formation. Misogyny is also challenged and critiqued by many, even as it is often expressed as an invisible norm.

The relationship between popular feminism and popular misogyny is deeply entwined: popular feminism and popular misogyny battle it out on the contemporary cultural landscape, living side by side as warring, constantly moving contexts in an economy of visibility. This economy of visibility, as I elaborate later, is a media landscape that is many things at once: a technological and economic context devoted to the accumulation of views, clicks, "likes," etcetera; a backdrop for popular feminism and popular misogyny; the battlefield for the struggles between them; a set of tactics used by some feminisms and some misogynies to move into the spotlight with more ease than others. Both feminism and misogyny deploy the popular, albeit in different ways. The sheer popularity of popular feminism provides spaces for a specific kind of political action along themes that resonate within an economy of visibility, such as empowerment, confidence, capacity, and competence. As such, popular feminism is *active* in shaping culture. However, the "popular" of popular misogyny is *reactive*.

The contemporary networked media context in which popular feminism and popular misogyny are expressed makes for a particular manifestation of the struggle between feminism and misogyny that has existed for centuries. While networked culture has provided a context for a transfigured feminist politics, it has also provided a context for misogyny to twist and distort the popular in ways that seem new to the contemporary era. Because popular misogyny is reactive, it doesn't have the same consistency, history, and political motion as popular feminism. Clearly, the intensification of misogyny in the contemporary moment is in part a reaction to the culture-wide circulation and embrace of feminism. Every time feminism gains broad traction—that is, every time it spills beyond what are routinely dismissed as niched feminist enclaves—the forces of the status quo position it as a peril, and skirmishes ensue between those determined to challenge the normative and those determined to maintain it. This happened with suffrage and abolition, with the US civil rights movement and the liberal feminist movement of the 1960s and '70s. It happened in the 1980s, as Susan Faludi (1991) and others have documented, and these challenges continue into the current moment, where among other things, US states such as Texas and Arkansas, in their fight to eliminate abortion rights for women, have decimated women's health care in general. Feminism is framed, by media and society alike, as a set of risks—risks that emerge anywhere and everywhere: feminism threatens conventional definitions and performances of masculinity; it threatens work culture, especially perilous in a global recession because when women have jobs this is somehow seen as taking away a man's natural right to have a job; and it threatens conventional performances of heteronormative femininity, particularly in the ways that femininity functions to reassure men of their dominant position.[1] Such efforts to dismantle and delegitimize feminism have been occurring at regular intervals for centuries. Misogyny has certainly long existed as a norm, built into our structures, laws, policies, and normative behavior. As such, it has been relatively invisible as a politics, existing rather as common sense, the "way things are." But the contemporary version of misogyny is also a new outgrowth of its reactive nature. The contemporary networked visibility of popular feminism, available across multiple media platforms, has stimulated a reaction, mobilizing misogyny to compete for visibility within these same mediated networks.

In the following pages I contend with how, and in what ways, the rise of popular feminism has encouraged both a response and an intensification of popular misogyny. I attempt to show some of the social, cultural, and economic conditions that define and describe particularly visible forms of popular feminism and popular misogyny. *Empowered* is organized around some of the key themes I have recognized within popular feminism: *shame*, *confidence*, and *competence*. These are also themes that are then taken up by popular misogyny, though the meaning of them is distorted, and deflects attention away from women and toward men, and is then targeted actively *against* women. In turn, each of these themes is dependent on a logic that revolves around the twinned discourses of *capacity* and *injury*. By this I mean that both popular feminism and popular misogyny tap into a neoliberal notion of individual capacity (for work, for confidence, for economic success), but both also position injury—for women, the injury of sexism; for men, the injury of feminism and "multiculturalism"—as a key obstacle to realizing this capacity. I also situate popular feminism and popular misogyny as practices that are simultaneously residual and emergent: there are clear ways that both feminism and misogyny have been engaged in a particular dynamic for centuries—just as it is clear that the current networked moment shifts this dynamic in important ways.

Popular feminism exists along a continuum, where spectacular, media-friendly expressions such as celebrity feminism and corporate feminism achieve more visibility, and expressions that critique patriarchal structures and systems of racism and violence are more obscured (see McRobbie 2009; Gill 2011; Rottenberg 2014). Seeing and hearing a safely affirmative feminism in spectacularly visible ways often eclipses a feminist critique of structure, as well as obscures the labor involved in producing oneself according to the parameters of popular feminism. The visibility of popular feminism, where examples appear on television, in film, on social media, and on bodies, is important, but it often stops there, as if *seeing* or purchasing feminism is the same thing as changing patriarchal structures. To be clear: the popular feminism I discuss in this book focuses on media expressions and their circulation, the social, cultural, and economic conditions that provide a context for a specific version of popular feminism to emerge as highly visible. That is, this book is not about the political intentions that energize a variety of feminist practices; it is about how some of these political intentions are marshaled by institutions and structures, and what they make available and what they foreclose in terms of politics. Yet, while popular feminisms are often framed by this kind of ambivalence, popular misogyny, in contrast, frames itself in deterministic and resolute terms. The spaces that are opened up by contemporary iterations of popular misogyny are framed not in ambivalent terms but as a zero-sum game: according to popular misogyny, men are suffering because of women in general, and feminism in particular. Women are taking over space, jobs, desire, families, childrearing, and power. For popular misogynies, every space or place, every exercise of power that women deploy is understood as taking that power *away* from men. In this historical moment, popular feminism is in defense against, among other things, structural gendered inequalities. Popular misogyny is in defense against feminism and its putative gains.

The risks posed by popular feminism share some similarities with historical moments, but it is also clear to me that we are in a new era of the gender wars, an era that is marked by a dramatic increase in the visible expression and acceptance of feminism, and by a similarly vast amount of public vitriol and violence directed toward women. Both feminism and its repudiation abound online and offline, which means that our avenues for expression—indeed, our very means of expression, from emoji to the media platforms on which we type them—are radically different from the wars of generations past. Misogyny, once a social formation that was expressed primarily in enclosures (home, locker room, board room, etc.) now increases via the connection, circulation, publicness, networks, and communication across and through those enclosures.[2] But while it circulates with relative ease in digital networks, misogyny is also reified in institutional structures: the workplace (unequal pay, sexual harassment, glass ceilings); organized religions (many of which continue to denigrate women); state politics (where women remain in the vast minority, and, as we have seen in the Trump administration, are often interrupted, diminished, and outright silenced).

Because I conducted research for this book while living in the United States, many of the examples are US-based, though popular feminism is not confined to the United States. Popular feminism and popular misogyny are expressed and practiced around the world in different ways, in a variety of contexts. Indeed, not a single day has gone by in the last several years that there hasn't been new material in both popular feminism and popular misogyny across the globe; it has been difficult to determine which examples to include, and which to leave out. Ultimately, I selected some of the examples that became particulary visible within the popular, be that a social media–shared campaign, a cable reality television show, or a confidence organization that made headlines. Some of these enjoyed an especially heightened visibility, such as the Always #LikeAGirl campaign, which aired during the Super Bowl in 2015, the annual US football championship, which is one of the most watched events on American television, and one of very few broadcast events that is widely watched by diverse (rather than niche) audiences; for this reason, the event has become particularly known for the very expensive advertisements aired during the broadcast. Others, such as the #DontMancriminate campaign I discuss in chapter 1, were the creation of a small online magazine based in India. However, the images from #DontMancriminate circulated widely and swiftly on social media, and they were then picked up by popular blogs and websites—so it became quite visible as an example of popular misogyny. I do not attempt to be exhaustive with my examples, nor do I present examples that are necessarily equal in their popularity and visibility. Indeed, this variety is part of the point I am making: the examples gesture to a set of networked cultures rather than to a specific political mechanism. I use them as a lens through which we can see the active response and reactive call of popular feminism and popular misogyny operating. In other words, the examples I analyze in this book are not characterized by their specificity or uniqueness but rather by how they form a broad contemporary context, one that shares similarities with histories of feminisms and misogynies, but also one that represents a shift happening now.

Popular Feminism

I began this introduction with three senses of the "popular" in popular feminism: as media visibility and accessibility, as popularity, and as a struggle for meaning. Surely there are other meanings of "popular," but in surveying the cultural landscape over the past decade, it is these three that signify most powerfully with popular feminism; thus I will use them as a map to clarify what I mean by "popular feminism." What does popular feminism look like? How does it circulate? Who are its ideal constituents? What are its goals? These questions have been asked more and more over the past decade, as versions of popular feminism have circulated more broadly through American and European culture. A key signifying moment in popular feminism, for many girls and women, was when Beyoncé performed at the MTV Video Music Awards in 2014 with the word "feminist" lit up behind her. Despite the fact that I've spent many years investigating commodity feminism, there seemed to be something special about that moment (a specialness that was then replicated in thousands of memes and images on social media). After the performance, columnist Jessica Valenti (who is herself part of popular feminism) proclaimed in the *Guardian*, "The zeitgeist is irrefutably feminist: its name literally in bright lights" (Valenti 2014, n.p.). Earlier, in February 2014, the popular blog *Jezebel* asked, "What does it mean for feminism if feminism becomes trendy?" (Beusman 2014, n.p.). Valenti similarly wondered, "If everyone is a feminist, is anyone?" (Valenti 2014, n.p.). So while Beyoncé's performance was spectacular, it was only one of many popular feminist images and expressions within the contemporary media landscape; in asking these questions, the authors refer to popular feminist practices, from organizing marches to hashtag activism to T-shirts. Indeed, these questions have only grown more urgent, as feminist manifestos have crowded most media platforms, making a specific version of feminist subjectivity and its parent political commitments both hypervisible and normative within popular media.

Of course, the architecture of many of these popular media platforms is capitalist and corporate. As we have seen historically, specific messages of feminism are often incorporated into advertising and marketing, and contemporary popular feminism is no different. One after another, major global companies—from the technology company Verizon to the beauty corporations CoverGirl and Dove to the automobile companies Chevrolet and Audi—have churned out emotional advertising campaigns, urging us to pay closer attention to girls and the opportunities available to them (or the lack thereof). American girls, this new marketing narrative typically goes, have been excluded from a plethora of professional and personal fields, from science, technology, engineering, and math (STEM) careers to music to athletics, because they feel unqualified and have low self-esteem. However, these ads declare, an answer is at hand, and with only the right products, anything is possible.

Successful female entrepreneurs have become eager spokeswomen for the cause: Facebook's Sheryl Sandberg (2013) wrote a best-selling memoir and feminist ode, offering her own brand of motivational and aspirational

FIGURE INTRO.1. Beyoncé, MTV Video Music Awards, 2014.

corporate feminism, pleading with girls and women to overcome "imposter syndrome" and to "lean in." Girl empowerment organizations, in both US and global development, insist that focusing on gender equality is "smarter economics," and again, that girls and women need to "lean in" to be economically successful. Teaching girls and women to code in computing, as a way to address the marginalization of women in technology industries, became a hot new industry itself. Social media has exploded with feminist campaigns, from #bringbackourgirls to #solidarityisforwhitewomen to #yesallwomen to the campaign in 2016, inspired by US president Donald Trump's casual dismissal of sexual assault, #NotOkay, to the 2017 (and continuing) explosive movement about sexual harassment in the workplace, #MeToo. Blogs and websites, such as *Black Girl Dangerous*, *Feministing*, *Feminist Current*, *Crunk Feminist Collective*, and *Jezebel*, are filled with passionate defenses and celebrations of feminism and exhortations toward feminist and antiracist activism. Meanwhile, the question du jour for female (and some male) celebrities has become: "Are you a feminist?" *Cosmopolitan* magazine and the Ms. Foundation, in an unlikely partnership, announced a "top ten" list of celebrity feminists at the end of 2014, with actress Emma Watson awarded as the "celebrity feminist of the year" (Filipovic 2014). Last but certainly not least for our particular era, feminist ideology is now sartorial—and just a click away. Etsy and others offer feminist tank tops, buttons, and entire wardrobes. High fashion has also taken note: as part of collections in 2017, designer Christian Dior created a $710 T-shirt that proclaimed "We Should All Be Feminists," and Prabal Gurung's more modestly priced version (at only $195) stated "This Is What a Feminist Looks Like." The manifestations of popular feminism are numerous, from hashtag activism to corporate campaigns to intersectional political and social action. Surely an ad campaign from Dove about body positivity is seen by far more viewers than critical commentary on sexual violence toward women of color. Yet it is important to see these two manifestations of feminism as related; to consider them as completely discrete is to simplify the context that enables and propels both of them into a simultaneous existence, even if this existence is asymmetrical in terms of visibility.

In other words, there are many different feminisms that are popular in the current moment. Indeed, media platforms such as Twitter and Facebook have enabled a visibility of feminisms that have long struggled for a broader space and place in culture, which makes it often difficult to distinguish between and among them. This mediated circulation around and within different spaces is crucial to popular feminism. J. K. Gibson-Graham envisioned feminist politics as one that is about a kind of network; a "vast set of disarticulated economic 'places'—households, communities, ecosystems, workplaces, civic organizations, enterprises, public arenas, urban spaces, diasporas, regions, government agencies—related analogically rather than organizationally and connected through webs of signification" (2006, 38). Popular feminism is analogical, in that feminist practices share similar experiences and particularities, but it is also more broadly networked, connected through webs of signification. *Empowered* explores and theorizes this networked characteristic of popular feminism and locates it within a dynamic relationship with a similarly networked popular misogyny.

The Popular as Media Accessibility

It is important to analyze the "popular" in popular feminism to see how it is distinct from other feminist practices and expressions. What are its boundaries, its borders? Is it defined by its politics, its visibility, where it emanates from? The popular feminism I analyze in this book generally materializes as a kind of *media* that is widely visible and accessible. It appears on broadcast media, in television and advertising. It appears in popular music. In the contemporary context, it appears perhaps most urgently in social media, with media companies such as Instagram, Tumblr,

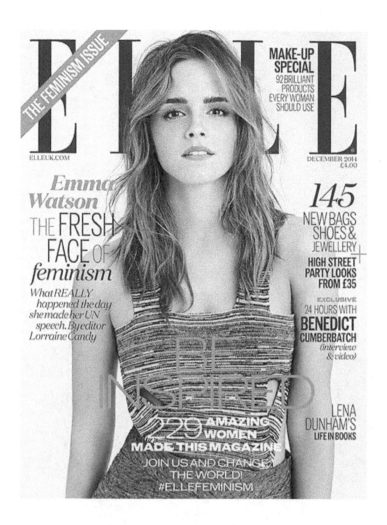

Facebook, and Twitter providing platforms for its circulation. As I expand on below, popular feminism circulates in an economy of visibility. Yet visibility is never simple. Media scholars, feminists, critical race scholars, LGBTQ scholars, and others have worked over many decades in the name of visibility; in a media context in which if you are visible, you *matter*, visibility matters indeed (e.g., Grewal 2005; Hegde 2011; Gross 2012; H. Gray 2013; Smith, Pieper, and Choueiti 2017). Part of this visibility means being accessible to a large, popular audience. As a set of practices and expressions that circulate in an economy of visibility, popular feminism is part of the larger "attention" economy, where its sheer accessibility—through shared images, "likes," clicks, followers, retweets, and so on—is a key component of its popularity. And this popularity and accessibility are measured in and through their ability to increase that visibility; popular feminism engages in a feedback loop, where it is more popular when it is more visible, which then authorizes it to create ever-increasing visibility. Visibility is not a static thing; it has to be in a constant state of growth.

But, as we also know, in a media context in which most circuits of visibility are driven by profit, competition, and consumers, simply *becoming* visible does not guarantee that identity categories such as gender, race, and sexuality will be unfettered from sexism, misogyny, and homophobia. The popular feminisms I explore in this book are typically those that become visible precisely because they do not challenge deep structures of inequities. That is, in order for some images and practices to become visible, others must be rendered invisible.

In this sense, the popular feminism I discuss throughout this book is not disruptive to capitalism or mainstream politics, but rather follows what Catherine Rottenberg (2014) has called neoliberal feminism. Rottenberg argues that neoliberal feminism is one in which the values and assumptions of neoliberalism—ever-expanding markets, entrepreneurialism, a focus on the individual—are embraced, not challenged, by feminism. In her words, "Unlike classic liberal feminism whose *raison d'être* was to pose an immanent critique of liberalism, revealing the gendered exclusions within liberal democracy's proclamation of universal equality, particularly with respect to the law, institutional access, and the full incorporation of women into the public sphere, this new feminism seems perfectly in sync with the evolving neoliberal order. Neoliberal feminism, in other words, offers no critique—immanent or otherwise—of neoliberalism" (Rottenberg 2014, 419).

While the popular feminism I analyze in this book clearly connects to neoliberal principles of individualism and entrepreneurialism, it also does, in fact, owe a debt to liberal feminism's critique of gendered exclusions in the public and corporate spheres. That is, this corporate-friendly popular feminism emanates from an increasing visibility of a gendered disparity in dominant economic spheres—a lack of female CEOs, a lack of female Hollywood directors, a lack of women in technology and media fields, and an increased awareness of sexual harassment within corporate industries such as media and technology. The popular feminisms I analyze in this book are, like liberal feminism, in many ways a call to bring more women to the table, simply because they are women. It thus has a history in what feminist historian Joan Scott has called an "add women and stir" kind of liberal feminism, in which the presence of women is sufficient to call feminism into being (Scott 1991). The inclusion of women becomes the solution for all gender problems, not just those of exclusion or absence. It is, of course, important to have bodies at the table, but their mere presence doesn't necessarily challenge the structure that supports, and builds, the table in the first place; as Scott points out, merely including women does not address "the framework of (historically contingent) dominant patterns of sexuality and the ideology that supports them" (Butler and Scott 1992, 25). In this way, popular feminism and its exhortations to simply have *more* women in various cultural, political, and economic realms is similar to liberal efforts to include people of color within a widened field of whiteness, one that continues to shape representation, work, and politics without interrogating the racism that forms the boundaries of whiteness from the ground up.

The focus on inclusion by popular feminism makes it specifically corporate friendly; it has benefited from decades of neoliberal commodity activism, in which companies have taken up women's issues, especially those that have to do with individual consumption habits, as a key selling point for products (Mukherjee and Banet-Weiser 2012). I explore many of these recent campaigns in this book and argue that there is a market for feminism; the popular feminisms I discuss mainly contribute to, rather than challenge, this market. This historical context of commodity feminism provides a backdrop for the expansion of popular feminism into other capitalist, consumerist realms. Within neoliberal brand culture, specific feminist expressions and politics are brandable, commensurate with market logics: those that focus on the individual body, those that connect social change with corporate capitalism, and those that emphasize individual attributes such as confidence, self-esteem, and competence as particularly useful to neoliberal self-reliance and capitalist success. In a capitalist, corporate economy of visibility, those feminisms that are most easily commodified and branded are those that become most visible. This means, most of the time, that the popular feminism that is most visible is that which is white, middle-class, cis-gendered, and heterosexual.

The Popular as Popularity

Popular feminism is also about specific *exclusions*, which leads to the second definition of "popular" in popular feminism: that of *popularity*. A basic definition of popularity is being admired by like-minded individuals. But a more practiced definition of popularity recalls for many of us the cliques and exclusionary practices of high school. Memorialized in films from *Grease* to *Pretty in Pink* (and the rest of the John Hughes oeuvre) to *Mean Girls*, popularity means the privilege of some to say to others, as the character Gretchen Wieners did in *Mean Girls*, "You can't sit with us." One can't sit with the popular clique unless one conforms to the norms of that group; again, the dominant culture of the popular feminism I examine in this book is primarily white, middle-class, cis-gendered, and heteronormative. This is the popular feminism that seizes the spotlight in an economy of visibility and renders other feminisms less visible. We witness this kind of exclusion in the popular feminist insistence on a universal definition of "equality" between men and women as its key definition. When feminists of color have challenged this universality, pointing out that "universal" equal rights have historically meant equal rights for white people, and insist on specificity and history as part of feminism, it is often met by popular feminism as an obstruction. In a similar move to the challenge to the Black Lives Matter movement with "All Lives Matter," or the response to LGBTQ pride of "heterosexual pride," popular feminism insists that a universal gender identity must be the central category of analysis. This is a classic liberal move, denouncing specificity, insisting on a universal definition of identity—even as this "universality" typically signifies white, middle-class, cis-gendered, and heterosexual identity. In this way, popular feminism frequently refuses intersectionality, and often erases and devalues women of color, working-class women, trans women, and non-heteronormative women, even when it claims to include all women. The Women's March in 2017, as I discuss in the conclusion, is an example of popular feminism that makes that type of all-inclusive claim.

The "popular" of popular feminism is structured by this dynamic of inclusion and exclusion. But because of its indebtedness to corporate feminism and a desire to not alienate consumers, popular feminism also depends on affectively resisting the "mean" in mean girl cliques. Despite its exclusions, popular feminism is often an *accommodating* feminism, and in particular, accommodating men (even when this appears in ironic misandrist feminism). This accommodationist strategy is not just conducive to corporate expression; it exists in part in order to become *available* to corporate expression. Popular feminism thus also emanates from an affective space: historically, the visibility of feminism in the US media has predominantly been as angry, defiant, man-hating women. The current manifestation of popular feminism directly challenges this representation; while recognizing that gendered relations of power marginalize women, this critique is expressed in a friendly, safe way. Popular feminism is decidedly not angry—indeed, anger (at sexism, racism, patriarchy, abuse) seems to be an old-fashioned vestige, a ghost of feminism's past, one not suited to the popular media context of contemporary feminism. What we see today, as Gill puts it, is a "feminism that is actually encumbered by its desire not to be angry, not to be 'difficult,' not to be 'humourless'"—a version that is implicitly "positioned against the figure of the 'feminist killjoy'" (Gill 2016b, 618).

In her book *The Promise of Happiness*, Sara Ahmed defines the feminist killjoy thus: "The feminist killjoy 'spoils' the happiness of others; she is a spoilsport because she refuses to convene, to assemble, or to meet up over happiness. In the thick sociality of everyday spaces, feminists are thus attributed as the origin of the bad feeling, as the ones who ruin the atmosphere" (2010, 65). Popular feminism is decidedly not a spoilsport, it is not the origin of bad feeling. We see this in its corporate-friendly expressions (because bad feelings are not good for marketing). We see this clearly in celebrity Emma Watson, who has become visible within popular feminism with her United Nations campaign "HeForShe," where she explicitly says that feminists need to invite men into a conversation about gender inequalities. We see this in the way that popular feminism is framed by heteronormativity and heterosexuality. To be clear, men *should* be in a conversation about gender inequalities. But popular feminism accommodates men through its heteronormativity, which is of course defined by gendered norms that already prioritize the logic of heterosexuality.

The Popular as Struggle

Finally, I theorize popular feminism through my third definition of the popular, as a terrain of struggle over meaning. As cultural theorist Stuart Hall famously said, "Popular culture is one of the sites where this struggle for and against a culture of the powerful is engaged: it is also the stake to be won or lost in that struggle. . . . It is the arena of consent and resistance" (1998, 453). The dynamic between consent and resistance is a key mobilizer within popular feminism, where it is privileged in an economy of visibility, and is firmly within the "culture of the powerful." This is a culture of racial and economic privilege. The most visible popular feminism is that within the arena of consent: it consents to heteronormativity, to the universality of whiteness, to dominant economic formations, to a trajectory of capitalist "success."

There are, of course, other feminisms that share some of the characteristics of media visibility and popularity but are positioned more within Hall's arena of resistance than consent: those that challenge and expose the whiteness of much of popular feminism; those that use the media visibility as a way to expose structural violence; those that are nonheteronormative; those that insist on intersectionality. Black Twitter, for example, as Caitlin Gunn (2015), Dayna Chatman (2017), André Brock (2012), and others have shown, has become a place for feminists of color to create campaigns for social justice. Many feminist blogs, such as *Black Girl Dangerous*, *Crunk Feminist Collective*, and *Feministing*, specifically critique the whiteness of much popular feminism and offer important intersectional analyses of gendered power relations in contemporary culture. There are popular feminist authors, such as Laurie Penny and Jessica Valenti, who write incisive critiques of gender and capitalism. In relation to these practices, popular feminism can be seen as a kind of backlash against feminism's goals of critiquing racism, capitalism, and patriarchy (and their deep relations). By commodifying and making feminism "safe," popular feminism resists structural critique.

The struggle between a consenting popular feminism and one that is more resistant became clearly evident in October 2017 in the United States, when multiple accusations of sexual harassment against Hollywood producer Harvey Weinstein were publicized; the Weinstein case mobilized, as is now well known, hundreds of other stories from women about harassment, which were manifest in the multimedia movement #MeToo (Kantor and Twohey 2017, n.p.).

As many have pointed out, the phrase "me too" was actually created in 2006 by an African American activist, Tarana Burke, a survivor of sexual assault, who wanted to share her story as a way to connect with other victims of sexual assault, especially women of color (Garcia 2017, n.p.). The fact that Burke, the originator of "me too," was largely eclipsed by the high-profile, mostly white female celebrities who came forward in the Weinstein (and Roger Ailes, and Matt Lauer, and what seems to be countless others) scandal is not insignificant. *Time* magazine's 2017 "Person of the Year" was named the "Silence Breakers," and the issue featured women who have come forward to expose sexual harassers and predators (Zacharek, Dockterman, and Sweetland Edwards 2017). Yet Burke, who created the movement, was inside the pages, not featured on the cover. The mainstream media has covered the #MeToo story expansively, which is an important move—but the stories are often about the powerful men who are accused, or the celebrity women who accuse them. Not surprisingly, there soon was a market for #MeToo, ranging from cookies to jewelry to clothing, as well as the emergence of new apps and other media technologies that attempt to document workplace sexual harassment.

In other words, while the public awareness of #MeToo has helped reveal how widespread and normative sexual harassment is, it is also more spectacularly focused on very visible public figures. This is not to dismiss the accusations in any way; rather, I want to point out that while "me too" existed in the early 2000s as a mechanism for building intersectional feminist community, it became spectacularly visible under the logics of popular feminism; this is the struggle of the popular. The #MeToo movement is expressed on those media platforms that easily lend themselves to commodification and simplification, those industries that provide platforms of visibility (entertainment, news media) already designed and scripted for *any* mode of spectacular spotlight. Some of the more spectacular #MeToo moments, such as when the celebrity components of the story distract us from systemic, structural sexism across all industries, can end up working against the calls for social change promised at its beginning, producing more and more visibility—and increasingly narrowing the discourses of that visibility in the process.

I argue that contemporary popular feminism reimagines and redirects what "empowerment" means for girls and women, and thus is restructuring feminist politics within neoliberal culture. Historically, feminisms have used "liberation" as a goal and specified this liberation as one from sexist and unequal social, political, and economic structures. Within popular feminism, empowerment is the central logic; with little to no specification as to what we want to empower women to do, popular feminism often restructures the politics of feminism to focus on the individual empowered woman. Here, the historical feminist politics of "the personal is the political" are often understood in the reverse, as "the political is the personal."

Why has popular feminism become popular now, in the twenty-first century? What are the various conditions that produce it in the current moment, that authorize its circulation? Popular feminism relies on other feminisms from the nineteenth and twentieth centuries for its gendered logics. Many of the issues popular feminism supports are not new: recognizing that women are hypersexualized and commodified in the media; identifying inequities in labor and the workplace; pointing out gendered asymmetries in individual self-esteem; and challenging the policing and regulation of the female body. The historical antecedents of popular feminism—such as antiracist movements, liberal feminism and women's liberation feminism, LGBTQ movements, third-wave feminist movements, and postfeminism—provide necessary conditions for a popular feminism to flourish in the current moment. Other feminist iterations and practices, such as intersectional feminism, queer feminism, and materialist feminism, also circulate and compete within an economy of visibility, which is organized around exclusion and inclusion. Yet popular feminism becomes the central feminism within an economy of visibility. Popular feminism is thus partly a residual movement, energized and authorized by decades of political organizing around identity issues, such as gender, race, and sexuality. But the popularity of popular feminism is also new and emergent— we see feminist slogans, messages, and practices in everyday spaces, on social media, and in afterschool programs. So what are the social, cultural, and economic conditions that need to be in place for popular feminism to flourish in this moment?

Perhaps most importantly, in order to emerge so forcefully, popular feminism needs a neoliberal capitalist context. Related to this, it needs digital media and its affordances, its commitment to capitalism, its expanded markets, its circulation capabilities. Digital media has afforded spaces and places for popular feminists to create media, voice their opinions, and launch businesses. These conditions have often been called "platform capitalism," implying the emptying or flattening out of the *content* of meaning, emphasizing instead the endless traffic and circulation of this content (see Srnicek 2016; Hearn 2017). These logics of visibility—composed of metrics, numbers, clicks, "likes," etcetera—form the social, cultural, and economic conditions for popular feminism, though the implications of these logics is not just for feminism, but also for social movements in general. The logics of platform capitalism emphasize metrics, numbers, "likes," and followers; given the predominance of digital media platforms that are predicated on the accumulation of numbers, where their business depends on these numbers, to make oneself visible or to express oneself is then also dependent on this kind of numerical accumulation. Jose van Dijck calls this the "popularity principle," where, despite differences among media platforms, these platforms are invested "in the same values or principles: popularity, hierarchical ranking, quick growth, large traffic volumes, fast turnovers, and personalized recommendations" (van Dijck 2013, n.p.).

And, as Brooke Erin Duffy (2017) details in her work about social media and aspirational labor, women largely populate many of the most visible genres of social media production, and digital media in general is crucial to the heightened visibility of popular feminism.[3] As Duffy theorizes, digital media encourages "aspirational labor," in which the successes of some women in digital spaces mobilize a general ethos where "everyone" can be creative and succeed (McRobbie 2016). The logic of aspirational labor depends on the popular feminist themes I examine in this book: self-esteem, confidence, and competence. This digital context, with its rapid circulation and loyalty to numerical accumulation, authorizes expressions and practices of popular feminism to an audience that has a wider reach than ever before. At the same time, these digital affordances also partly enable media to hyperbolize and bifurcate political positions, thus helping to generate a discursive climate of extreme views (such as misogyny).

More than any other historical influence, popular feminism emerges within the ongoing ethos and sensibility of postfeminism (Gill 2007). Postfeminism, as Rosalind Gill (2007), Angela McRobbie (2009), Diane Negra and Yvonne Tasker (2007), and others have argued, is dedicated to the recognition, and then repudiation, of feminism—and it is through this repudiation, an insistence that feminism is no longer needed as a politics, that women are empowered. Women, that is, are empowered within postfeminism precisely because feminism is seen as having done the political work needed to eradicate gender asymmetry.

In this way, postfeminism celebrates a kind of gendered "freedom" in which women are apparently free to become all they want to be. Women just have to be a "Girl Boss" or "Lean In" in order to overcome sexist history. Materially, what this means is that neoliberal values such as entrepreneurialism, individualism, and the expansion of capitalist markets are embraced and adopted by girls and women as a way to craft their selves.

These values are privileged within postfeminism, rather than feminist politics, which are seen are unproductive and obsolete. Postfeminism can be characterized as a set of ideas, elements, feelings, and emphases that operate as a kind of gendered neoliberalism. Importantly, the "post" in postfeminism is not necessarily temporal, as in a new "wave" after second- or third-wave Western feminism (Dosekun 2015). Rather, postfeminism and popular feminism are entangled together in contemporary media visibility. Postfeminism remains a dominant, visible iteration of feminism in culture, and is not displaced by popular feminism but rather bolstered by it. As Rosalind Gill points out, "New cultural trends do not simply displace older or existing ones. A momentarily visible resurgence of interest in feminism should not lead us to the false conclusion that antifeminist or postfeminist ideas no longer exist" (Gill 2016a, 2).

Yet, on the face of it, popular feminism seems quite distinct from postfeminism's disavowal of feminist politics. After all, popular feminism takes up the mantle of traditional feminist issues, pointing out that girls and women have experienced crises of gender in the twenty-first century, from low self-esteem to low numbers in leadership positions. Popular feminism asks: If the postfeminist claims of gender equality are actually true, why aren't there more female CEOs? Why are more women reporting sexual assault? Why is there such a discrepancy between women and men in technology fields? The early twenty-first century saw the emergence of a newly forged feminist avowal: popular feminism explicitly *embraces* feminist values and ideologies and is dedicated to recognizing that gender inequality still exists. Popular feminism recognizes the vulnerability of women in a sexist context, shifting away from the vague "girl power" slogan of postfeminism. The popular feminist recognition that vast gender inequities still organize our cultural, economic, and political worlds is important, and a necessary correction to the false optimism of postfeminism. Again, though, popular feminism in the current moment also shares great structural similarities with postfeminism (Gill 2016b). While postfeminism and popular feminism are oppositional on the surface, they are actually mutually sustaining. Indeed, the feminist visions that come into dominant view in the current moment are shaped by the same affective politics that shape postfeminism: entrepreneurial spirit, resilience, gumption.

The "feminist standpoint" that Nancy Hartsock theorized in 1983 was connected to a Marxist notion of a proletarian understanding of inequality—and is a perspective that emerges from struggle and collective achievement (Hartsock 1983). One doesn't just "have" a feminist standpoint simply because one is a woman, in other words. It is a political commitment, a struggle over power, an activist responsibility. There is no postfeminist or popular feminist standpoint; on the contrary, it is more a kind of attitude, a feminist weightlessness, "unencumbered by the need to have a position on anything" (Gill 2016b, 618). The success of postfeminism and popular feminism seems to begin and end with ease: you merely need to identify as female, but don't need to identify with the murky realms of gender's social construction, or with an identity that is unequal from the ground up. So despite this seeming contradiction, between disavowal and avowal of feminism, it does not necessarily mean that popular feminism critiques the roots of gender asymmetry; rather, popular feminism tinkers on the surface, embracing a palatable feminism, encouraging individual girls and women to just *be* empowered.

These discourses of post- and pop-feminist empowerment are intimately connected to cultural economies, where to be "empowered" is to be, as Angela McRobbie (2007) has pointed out, a better *economic* subject, not necessarily a better feminist subject. Post- and popular feminism utilize different subjectivities to become visible, but for both, visibility is paramount. For this, both post- and popular feminism require an economy of visibility.

NOTES

1. The "risks" of feminism can be understood as part of a larger "risk society," as theorized by Anthony Giddens and Ulrich Beck. For both theorists, risk society is a manifestation of modernity; as Beck puts it, risk society is "a systematic way of dealing with hazards and insecurities induced and introduced by modernisation itself" (Beck 1992, 21). Feminism, in this context, is also a result of modernity, and presents itself to broader society as a set of "hazards and insecurities" that garner a reactive response.

2. See Trump's comments on the released video tape, where he said that powerful men can "grab 'em [women] by the pussy." These comments were dismissed by Trump as "locker room" talk ("Transcript" 2016).

3. Of course, as Duffy argues, these genres, and the women who labor within them, rely "on historically constructed notions of femininity—particularly discourses of community, affect, and commodity-based self-expression" (Duffy 2017, 9).

Intersectionality and Decolonial Feminism

Anna Carastathis

THE PILLARS OF WHITE SUPREMACY AND
THE COLONIALITY OF GENDER

María Lugones, whose theory of intersecting, interlocking, and inter-meshed oppressions we will discuss in the next section, argues that the coloniality of power produces multiple genders on either side of the colonial divide (see Lugones 2007, 2010). A similar claim is advanced by Andrea Smith (2006, 2012), who discerns multiple and sometimes contradictory logics subtending white supremacy, resulting in differential processes of racialization and variable forms of racism targeting groups of women of color. White supremacy is not "enacted in a singular fashion; rather, white supremacy is constituted by separate and distinct, but still interrelated logics" (2012, 67; see also 2006, 67). Smith argues that the primary "pillars" of white supremacy are three and that they correspond to, or act as, "anchors" for three political-economic systems: slavery/antiblack racism, "which anchors capitalism"; genocide, "which anchors colonialism"; and orientalism, "which anchors war" (2012, 68). She uses the language of intersectionality to characterize the "intersecting" relationships among these white-supremacist logics. Her normative goal is to motivate an insurrectionary, anticolonial, antiracist coalitional politics that addresses "the intersections of settler colonialism *and* white supremacy simultaneously" (88). She contrasts this "intersectional" approach to the assumption prevalent in ethnic studies scholarship and women-of-color feminist organizing alike, that "communities of color share overlapping experiences that they can compare and organize around" (67). This presumes that white supremacy functions through a singular and coherent logic in constructing, targeting, and oppressing various racialized groups. The model of "shared victimhood" fails to capture the ways in which "we not only are victims of white supremacy but are complicit in it as well. . . . What keeps us trapped within our particular pillars of white supremacy is that we are seduced with the prospect of participating in the other pillars" (70). This recognition is crucial if "strategic alliances" are to be forged "based on where we are situated within the larger political economy"; moreover, coalitions cannot only address racial oppression: they must also address complicity (70). One implication of Smith's pillars argument is that what are conventionally understood as ethno-racial groups (an understanding that follows closely the demographic taxonomies of the racial/colonial state) may be "destabilized" by a focus on distinct and intersecting logics of white supremacy (70). She draws on Dylan Rodriguez to argue that "rather than organize around categories based on presumed cultural similarities or geographical proximities, we might organize around the differential impacts of white supremacist logics" (70). To develop a sufficiently complex analysis of white-supremacist/settler colonial power as it articulates heteropatriarchy, we must inhabit sites of resistance based not solely on similarities but also on divergences, contradictions, tensions, and complicities, through a negotiation of which we can broaden our struggles (see Cohen 1997, 483). This is not a claim for recognition or visibility but rather an argument for understanding, in terms more complex than perhaps the language of "identity" allows, how we are differentially positioned with respect to systems of power that are normatively not thought together.

However, Smith discerns in "the move to 'postidentity,'" which privileges hybridity and mixture and refuses binary logic, an unwitting appropriation of "colonized indigenous peoples as foils for the emergence of postcolonial, postmodern, diasporic, and queer subjects" (2010, 63). If Native studies is to "intersect" with queer-of-color theory, borderlands theory, and decolonial feminist critique, what is needed is an "identity plus politics": "a politic that marks all identities and their relationship to the fields of power in which they are imbricated" (63). Indeed, whereas the theories explored in the foregoing discussion "tend to be critical of binaries," Smith argues that "it is important not to have a binary analysis of binaries" (57). Indeed, "a binary analysis of the colonizer and colonized can sometimes be helpful in highlighting the current conditions of settler colonialism that continue to exist today both in the United States and in the rest of the world" (58). She suggests that "the presumption that binarism is bad and hybridity good often works against indigenous interests," often relying—as she charges Anzaldúa of doing—on a "mixed" or "hybrid" subject who is "positioned against the Native foil": "a rigid, unambiguous Indian [that] becomes juxtaposed unfavorably with the mestiza who 'can't hold concepts or ideas in rigid boundaries'" (57). This relegates Indigenous peoples to a "primitive past," constructing their identities as "premodern precursor" to mestiza identity (57). Abstracted from the settler colonial context, a "valorization of mixedness" fails to recognize how colonial law uses the genocidal logic of hyperdescent to undermine claims to Indigenous identity, citizenship, and sovereignty precisely through an equation of mixedness to inauthenticity and assimilation. The point is not, I take it, to reify the binaries that operate in settler colonial law and ideology, but rather to reveal their material operation. This supports Ferguson's (2012) claim that the stranglehold that ideologies of discreteness have over us cannot be undone at the level of language. Conceptual transformations require material transformations—not as temporally prior preconditions but as co-constitutive, multidimensional struggles. Smith's arguments in favor of reconceptualizing the structural bases of white supremacy are therefore articulated in a movement context, calling for and participating in the formation of coalitions that address the "intersections" of multiple manifestations of institutionalized, structural, systemic racisms as they articulate heteropatriarchy in ways that do not "fall back on the presumptiveness of the white-supremacist, settler state" (2012, 88). "When we no longer have to carry the burden of political and cultural purity," writes Smith, "we can be more flexible and creative in engaging multiple strategies and creating a plethora of alliances that can enable us to use the logics of settler colonialism against itself" (2010, 58).

Although Smith's insistence on the plurality of the logics of racism is astute, her analysis of the relation between white supremacy and heteropatriarchy—which tends to view the latter as a singular, homogeneous form of power—could fruitfully be complemented by Lugones's conceptualization of the modern/colonial gender system, which I believe is consistent with Smith's insight, articulated throughout her work, that the colonial imposition of heteropatriarchy on Indigenous societies not structured hierarchically served to naturalize colonial and racial hierarchies (Smith 2005, 17-18; 2006, 72; 2010, 62). Smith and Lugones offer analyses that give content to the mutual constitution claim that circulates in intersectional scholarship with respect to the relationships among what are viewed as discrete "axes" of oppression. Moreover, their conceptualizations illuminate new logics through which to problematize discreteness as a presupposition of mutual constitution on the way toward a synthetic analysis that overcomes the fragmentation of representation that intersectionality reveals.

Lugones traces the "congealing" of the modern/colonial gender system "as Europe advanced its colonial project" arguing that compulsory, violently enforced, and "consistently perverse" heterosexuality was as formative of imperial power as imperial power was of it (2007, 187, 202). Emerging during the Spanish and Portuguese colonization of the Americas in the fifteenth century, it "created different arrangements for colonized males and females than for white bourgeois colonizers" that, Lugones argues, persist into the colonial present (186). Compulsory heterosexuality engenders a division of labor that "permeates racialized patriarchal control over production, including knowledge production" (206). In some cases, the colonial gender system created categories of gender where none previously existed, as Oyèrónké Oyěwùmí (1997) has argued with respect to Yoruba society in what is now Nigeria. In other cases, European sex/gender constructs interacted in complicated ways with "local" or "indigenous" patriarchies. In all cases, gender relations were fundamentally transformed through the violent introduction of a colonial gender system that regulated the racialization of gender, creating multiple genders on the "light and dark sides" of racial binaries (Lugones 2007). Heterosexualism and its attendant gender hierarchies became powerful metaphors for racialized relations of rule, as in the mid-nineteenth-century trope of the "Family of Man" (McClintock 1995, 357–58).

The modern/colonial gender system has "light" and "dark" sides that install differential gender norms for "white" colonizers and racialized colonized people: the "light side" constructs hegemonic gender relations between white, bourgeois women and men; it constitutes the hegemonic meaning of these gender categories (Lugones 2007, 206). "The dark side of the gender system was and is thoroughly violent," writes Lugones (202). It involved the "reduction [of nonwhite people] to animality, to forced sex with white colonizers, to such deep labor exploitation that often people died working" (206). Lugones's analysis of the "dark side" of the modern/colonial gender system illuminates the economic function of gender, that is, its role in colonial dispossession, appropriation, and superexploitation of labor. Linking the appropriation and violation of bodies to that of land, Smith argues that "the project of colonial sexual violence establishes the ideology that Native bodies are inherently violable—and by extension, that Native lands are also inherently violable" (2005, 12). The two senses of "conquest"— territorial and sexual—are imbricated and historically inextricable, constructing the heteropatriarchal foundation of white-supremacist, settler colonial power. Notably, in an early article Smith critiques Crenshaw's intersectional analysis of violence against women of color (Crenshaw 1991), arguing that Crenshaw "falls short of describing how a politics of intersectionality might fundamentally shift how we analyze sexual/domestic violence" (A. Smith 2003, 71). Smith argues that to the extent that sexual violence is instrumental to colonization, "then entire communities of color" are its targets (71). Yet she agrees with Crenshaw's emphasis on the qualitative difference between racialized experiences of gendered violence and those experiences of gendered violence inflected and perhaps mitigated by racial privilege, a function of the inseparability of colonial, racial, and gender oppression (72).

DECOLONIAL INTERSECTIONALITY?

Reading the founding texts of intersectionality scholarship "against the grain" of the dominant interpretation—which arguably participates in the "categorial, dichotomous, hierarchical logic . . . central to modern, colonial, capitalist thinking about gender, race, and sexuality" (Lugones 2010, 742)—Lugones's explicit critique of the prevailing understanding of intersectionality is that it reproduces the "categorial separation" of categories based on the invisibility of women of color (2007, 192–93). Rather than making visible the experiences of women of color—as has been widely imputed to intersectionality—the intersection of these categories reveals the failure of representation, the absence of concepts adequate to the lived experience of simultaneous oppression(s). Lugones writes:

> Intersectionality reveals *what is not seen* when categories such as gender and race are conceptualized as separate from each other. . . . [T]he logic of categorial separation distorts what exists at the intersection, such as violence against women of color. . . . So, once intersectionality shows us what is missing, we have ahead of us the task of reconceptualizing the logic of the intersection so as to avoid separability. It is only when we perceive gender and race as intermeshed or fused that we actually see women of color. (2007, 192–93)

While this may be read simply as a critique of intersectionality, I think it is more productive to view it as a heterodox interpretation that delimits the scope and intent of the concept to reveal the theoretical and political work that still lies ahead. I would suggest that this is not inconsistent with Crenshaw's own characterization of the provisionality of intersectionality in her early work. The hermeneutic question here is whether intersectionality constitutes a representational theory of identity (as the dominant interpretation assumes), or whether it can be understood more fruitfully as a critique of representations that rely upon extant categorial axes of oppression. Elaborating the latter interpretation, Lugones argues:

> Modernity organizes the world ontologically in terms of atomic, homogeneous, separable categories. Contemporary women of color and third-world women's critique of feminist universalism centers the claim that the intersection of race, class, sexuality, and gender exceeds the categories of modernity. If *woman* and *black* are terms for homogeneous, atomic, separable categories, then their intersection shows us the absence of black women rather than their presence. (2010, 742)

The intersection of monistic categories reveals that they render multiplicity invisible. Insofar as it preserves these categories, intersectionality does not transcend modern/colonial cognitive limitations, although it anticipates and illuminates the task of conceptual transformation and "impure resistance." Intersectionality reveals that insofar as we are trained into perceiving and thinking through the logic of purity, we are not habituated into seeing race and gender as "intermeshed or fused"; to the extent that multiple oppressions are understood through "pure" concepts and resisted through interventions that "contest univocally along one axis of domination" (Lugones 2003, 222), social movements contribute to at least as much as they combat social fragmentation. If "the internalization of domination" produces a "dichotomizing imagination" that entraps us in "the need to control," by contrast, "impure" perception "disrupt[s] dichotomies in resistance to domination" (196). Impure resistance is curdled, coalitional resistance based on the understanding that "identifications have to be forged rather than found as natural or inevitable" (198). For "curdled beings," thick members of fragmented groups, vulnerable to the logic of purity and "susceptible to transparency," it is particularly important to stop "see[ing] split-separation from other curdled beings as sensical in our resistance to oppression" (143). "The fragmentation of perception disempowers our resistance by making deep coalitions logically impossible," writes Lugones (160), but "coalition is always the horizon that rearranges both our possibilities and the conditions of those possibilities" (ix).

Lugones proposes a distinction between intermeshed and interlocking oppressions that corresponds to the ontological difference between multiplicity and fragmentation in her account. She argues (particularly in her later work) that the concept of interlocking oppressions—an antecedent concept to "intersectionality" introduced (at least in print) by the Combahee River Collective in "*A Black Feminist Statement*" (CRC 1983)—disguises multiplicity and fragments oppressed groups and individuals (Lugones 2003, 223–24). However, this does not mean that "interlocking oppressions" is a "bad concept": Lugones clarifies that it is "not merely an ideological mechanism, but the training of human beings into homogeneous fragments" (224). At the second level of her analysis, then, Lugones argues that "interlocking oppressions" and "intermeshed oppressions" function jointly, creating "a conceptual maze that is very difficult to navigate" (224). Intermeshed oppressions are misrepresented as interlocking, both by systems of domination and by social movements that "contest univocally along one axis of domination" (222); "everywhere we turn we find the interlocking of oppressions disabling us from perceiving and resisting oppressions as intermeshed" (224), mystifying the fact that oppressed people's lives and struggles are interconnected. Finally, Lugones offers a "theory of resistance to both the interlocking of oppressions and to intermeshed oppressions" (208). This theory of resistance activates "a spatial politics that emphasizes difference," one that does not "mythify territorial enclosures and purities of peoples, languages, traditions," but instead negotiates "intersections where subaltern sense is fashioned in the tense and where ongoing crossings between multiple resistant worlds of sense are sometimes tentatively, sometimes powerfully enacted" (220).

What is interesting in Lugones's interpretation of the "intersection" metaphor is that it seems to me to restore it to its original meaning in Crenshaw's 1989 essay, liberating it from the significations that "intersectionality" has subsequently acquired. For one, the intersection is read as a space of violent reduction, of invisibility, and of desubjectification. Further, as I will argue in what follows, Lugones rejects a positivist, "identitarian" deployment of "intersectionality" that reifies axes of identity and, by implication, constructs the intersection as the site of a politics of location for multiply oppressed subjects, so that Black women, for instance, are purported to have "intersectional identities" made visible by an intersectional politics. By contrast, Lugones argues that their intersection does not *represent* women of color; rather, given the logic of purity informing the categorial construction of axes of "race" and "gender," the intersection functions as an index of their *invisibility* (2007, 193). Importantly, she concludes, "once intersectionality shows us what is missing, we have ahead of us the task of reconceptualizing the logic of the intersection," to "perceive gender and race as intermeshed or fused [so] that we actually see women of color" (193). Intersectionality is not the theoretical solution to intermeshed and interlocking oppressions, or, as it is hegemonically re-presented, the arrival of an "inclusive" feminism; rather, in "showing us what is missing" it constitutes the point of departure for a liberatory, coalitional project of "decolonizing gender" (Lugones 2007, 2010).

According to Lugones, "the interlocking of oppressions is a central feature of the process of social fragmentation, [which] requires not just shards or fragments of the social, but that each fragment be unified, fixed, atomistic, hard-edged, internally homogeneous, bounded, repellent of other equally bounded and homogeneous shards" (2003, 232n1). Intermeshed oppressions are represented as interlocking, but "representation" is not merely an ideological process: intermeshed oppressions are socially, discursively constructed—by systems of dominance and by single-axis social movements—as separable, distinct phenomena, affecting discrete groups with divergent political agendas. In other words, the interlocking of oppressions obscures the simultaneity of experiences of multiple, intermeshed oppressions and dissimulates the necessity of contesting and resisting multiple oppressions simultaneously. As Lugones writes in "Tactical Strategies of the Streetwalker/Estrategias Tácticas de la Callejera," where she more fully develops the distinction between intermeshed and interlocking oppressions,

> oppressions interlock when the social mechanisms of oppression fragment the oppressed both as individuals and collectivities. Social fragmentation in its individual and collective inhabitations is the accomplishment of the interlocking of oppressions. Interlocking is conceptually possible only if oppressions are understood as separable, as discrete, pure. Intermeshed oppressions cannot be cogently understood as fragmenting subjects either as individuals or as collectivities. Thus, the interlocking of oppressions is a mechanism of control, reduction, immobilization, disconnection that goes beyond intermeshed oppressions. It is not merely an ideological mechanism, but the categorial training of human beings into homogeneous fragments is grounded in a categorial mind frame. Interlocking is possible only if the inseparability of [intermeshed] oppressions is disguised. (2003, 223–24)

Lugones's point is not just the semantic objection to the prefix "inter-" in "interlocking," which, as Marilyn Frye apparently insisted to Lugones, implies "two entirely discrete things . . . that articulate with each other" (Lugones 2003, 146n1) but whose articulation "does not alter the monadic nature of the things interlocked" (231–32n1). After all, Lugones concedes that "intermeshed"—which shares the same prefix—implies "still too much separability" (231–32n1). By offering "intermeshed oppressions" as a new term, Lugones is not trying to "one-up" the existing concept of "interlocking oppressions" and the theorists who invoke them. On the contrary, in an earlier essay she describes her reluctance "to give up the term because it is used by other women of color theorists who write in a liberatory vein about enmeshed oppressions" (146n1). Although in her earlier work she is searching for "better images" to render the simultaneity of multiple oppressions (146n1), as her thought progresses, I think she diagnoses different political conditions requiring different conceptualizations and resistances, to be signified by different terms. It is not just that "intermeshed oppressions" is a better concept for the same phenomenon that "interlocking oppressions" names; rather, "intermeshed oppressions" signifies an ontological, existential, and social condition of multiplicity that has been discursively and materially obscured through a systematic process of social fragmentation, through the interlocking of oppressions.

In her essay "Toward a Decolonial Feminism," Lugones articulates a methodological shift from "women of color feminisms" to a "decolonial feminism" (2010, 746). She conceptualizes the modern/colonial gender system as a "resistant response to the coloniality of gender" but offers it as a problem that is "being set up rather than answered" (746). Decolonial feminism is defined here as "the possibility of overcoming the coloniality of gender," that is, "racialized, capitalist gender oppression" (747). It is a "movement toward coalition that impels us to know each other as selves that are thick, in relation, in alternative socialites, and grounded in tense, creative inhabitations of the colonial difference" (748). This possibility is intimated in the anti-, pre-, and postcolonial cosmologies, ontologies, epistemologies, and histories of resistance that inform decoloniality (749, 753).

If women-of-color feminisms have (rightly or wrongly) become synonymous with an identitarian project of intersectionality, decolonial feminism unravels the historical production of racialized gendered identities, synthesizing an intersectional awareness of multiplicity that the modern/colonial logic of purity renders invisible through categorial fragmentation with a theorization of the coloniality of power (Lugones 2007, 188–89). Intersectionality, writes Lugones, remains useful "when showing the failures of institutions" to address "discrimination or oppression against women of color" (2010, 757n9). But the emphasis of a decolonial feminism shifts from explicating the logic of domination to perceiving both oppression ("the coloniality of gender") and resistance ("the colonial difference at the fractured locus") that women of color, Indigenous women "fluent in native cultures," and women in colonized groups embody (758n9). In this respect, decolonial feminism radicalizes the generativeness of resistant perception, knowledge, and affect: it moves beyond critique to construct "a different logic"; for even when we

"unravel … the logic of the oppressor's gaze … [and] discover its irratio-
nality we are not on our way towards a resistant subjectivity" (Lugones
2003, 156). Challenging race-gender binarisms, categorial positivisms,
and colonial logics, decolonial feminism calls upon us to "intervene at
the level of meaning" (3).

Yet, Lugones advises us not to "think what [we] cannot practice," but
rather to "live differently in the present, to think and act against the grain
of oppression" (2003, 5). This requires that we historicize our epistemic
and enunciatory locations, our perceptual and cognitive schemas, and
our affective and political commitments. It requires that we attempt a
decolonial shift from received, hegemonic ways of thinking and living
to resistant ways. How each of us does this depends on tarrying with the
questions of "who and where we are," which imply differential responsibilities and relations based on this structural positioning along colonial
divides. Intersectionality can reveal the problem of colonial thinking as
it structures our perceptual-cognitive experience, the extent to which
it has become habitual and goes unquestioned—even at the very same
time as it is pronounced as having been transcended. As an analytic
sensibility, or a critical (dis)orientation toward categorial hegemony,
intersectionality can illuminate the need to resist fragmentation and
domination at the level of critical discourses, political movements, and
embodied identities. Honing our resistant perception against our being
"torture[d] … into simple fragmented identities" opens up a space for
"rearranging one's own identity, for making the complexity of one's own
subjectivity explicit, for articulating it, for making it public" (Lugones
1998, 50–52). Intermeshed oppressions, violently forged through a mod-
ern/colonial gender system, are interlocked through categorial and social
fragmentation, a process that the multiply oppressed, curdled being con-
cretely "comes to understand through a jarring vivid awareness of being
broken into fragments" (Lugones 2003, 231). For Lugones, lived experience also discloses "that the encasing by particular oppressive systems
of meaning is a process one can either consciously and critically resist
with uncertainty," through a collective, decolonial feminist coalitional
praxis, "or [one] to which one can passively abandon oneself," dwelling
invisibly in a deadly intersection (231).

In this chapter I have pursued the question of the relationship between intersectionality and decolonial feminism. Can a synthesis between a provisional concept of intersectionality and a decolonial feminist praxis serve the political project of decolonization? Such an argument must be attentive to the pitfalls, evasions, and depoliticizations of "decolonization," arguably inherent in the enunciatory location—in my case, that of an immigrant to, and naturalized citizen of, a white settler state—from which it is articulated. Specifically, I am wary of appropriative appeals to "decolonization" that increasingly seem to circulate in "critical" settler academic discourses (including feminism) without fundamentally altering non-Indigenous relationships to land, sovereignty, and power. Thus, in concluding the above discussion prefiguring a "decolonial intersectionality," I would like to avoid closure by reflecting on the ongoing debate about "decolonizing antiracism" and other critical social-justice projects, and specifically, the apparent ease with which, in recent years, the concept of "decolonization" is appropriated, often in ways that distort its actual meaning or evade its political implications for non-Indigenous groups, settlers and immigrants (see Lawrence and Dua 2005; Sharma and Wright 2008–9; Phung 2011; Sehdev 2011; Jafri 2012; Tuck and Yang 2012; Dhamoon 2015). Indeed, it is worth noting that "intersectionality" and "decolonization" circulate in not dissimilar ways in the settler academy, and are often invoked as an alibi, ostensibly to guarantee the ethical or political commitments underpinning intellectual projects, or the "inclusiveness" of curricula, academic disciplines, and institutions. In fact, such appeals avoid tarrying both with the militancy of the concepts they invoke—the normative claims they imply—and with non-Indigenous people's complicity with colonial power. Specifically, facile appeals to "decolonization" seem to evade the question of land, and the genocidal violence against Indigenous people that maintaining colonial state control over Indigenous land bases entails. Tuck and Yang observe "with growing apprehension" a metaphorical use of "decolonization" as a synonym for a range of social-justice projects, a use that serves to "domesticate" the concept (2012, 3). Being "grafted" onto or "subsumed" under existing critical frameworks is, they argue, "just another form of settler appropriation" (3):

> Decolonization as metaphor allows people to equivocate . . . because it turns decolonization into an empty signifier to be filled by any track towards liberation. In reality, however, the tracks walk all over land/people in settler contexts. . . . [I]n our view, decolonization in the settler context must involve the repatriation of land simultaneous to the recognition of how land and relations to land have always already been differently understood and enacted; that is, *all* of the land, and not just symbolically. This is precisely why decolonization is necessarily unsettling; especially across lines of solidarity. . . . Settler colonialism and its decolonization implicates and unsettles everyone. (2012, 7)

Tuck and Yang identify several "settler moves to innocence" through which the unsettling implications of decolonization are evaded as the concept is "absorbed" into settler colonial discourses (even emancipatory or transformative ones). I would like to focus here on two that seem to be particularly important for the present argument: "colonial equivocation" and "conscientization" (4). The first refers to "the homogenizing of various experiences of oppression as colonization," or "all struggles against imperialism as 'decolonizing,'" a move that, the authors argue, "creates a convenient ambiguity between decolonization and social justice work, especially among people of color, queer people, and other groups minoritized by the settler state" (17). If it is true in some sense that "we are all colonized," this claim is nevertheless "deliberately embracive and vague" and enabling of the "inference: 'None of us are settlers'" (17). Arguing for the historical salience and contemporary relevance of a tri-partite structure of power that locates Indigenous people—"those who have creation stories, not colonization stories about how we/they came to be in a particular place"—in a non-constitutive relation to settlers and descendants of enslaved people, Tuck and Yang probe how social-justice efforts may be "invested" in settler colonialism even if they are antiracist or contest white supremacy (17–18). For instance, as Lisa Kahaleole Hall has argued, "The logics of some forms of antiracist struggles paradoxically can undermine group identities by advocating for a form of social justice based on the equal treatment of individuals," resulting in the "vanishing" of Indigenous peoples from antiracist politics (as well as from feminist theory) (2008, 277). Hence, Tuck and Yang argue, "Vocalizing a 'multicultural' approach to oppressions, or remaining silent on settler colonialism while talking about colonialisms, or tacking on a gesture towards Indigenous people without addressing Indigenous sovereignty or rights, or forwarding a thesis on decolonization without regard to unsettling/deoccupying land, are equivocations" (2012, 18).

Relatedly, a second move to settler innocence Tuck and Yang describe is "conscientization," which involves focusing on "decolonizing the mind, or the cultivation of critical consciousness, as though it were the sole activity of decolonization" and a proxy for "the more uncomfortable task of relinquishing stolen land" (2012, 19). The critical reader of the literature on intersectionality may notice a similar set of evasions and equivocations with respect to its uptake. Thus, Vivian May's titular emphasis on "Unsettling Dominant Imaginaries" by "Pursuing Intersectionality" resonates here (2015). Indeed, May argues that, by resisting the "erasure or forgetting that progress narratives tend to encourage," intersectionality can "rupture stories about the nation's evolution and to unsettle its setter logics in great part because [its] both/and approach is amenable to 'apposition,'" which she describes as "a flexible and destabilizing interpretative method capable of reading time periods and multiple identities concurrently, in syntactical relation" (2015, 57). If this, most promising version of intersectionality embodies a decolonial orientation, in a not too dissimilar way to "decolonization," "intersectionality" is often used to defuse rather than to enact challenges to the prevailing material and ideological colonial, white, supremacist, heteropatriarchal orders.

Still, likely to resist such comparisons, Tuck and Yang call for "an ethic of incommensurability" infusing decolonial approaches to solidarity and coalition. They suggest that "decolonization offers a different perspective to human and civil rights approaches to justice, an unsettling one, rather than a complementary one. Decolonization is not an 'and.' It is an elsewhere" (2012, 36). If this is true, then an attempt to "merge" an intersectional analytic sensibility with a decolonial politics could be still another evasion of the difficult realizations that the latter entails. But what if an intersectional sensibility could enable us to realize precisely the praxical orientation to solidarity between groups situated in diametrically opposed yet structurally intertwined ways that Tuck and Yang identify? What if it enables us to grasp and embody the conditions of possibility for "solidarity . . . in what is incommensurable rather than [in] what is common" (28)? As Andrea Smith and J. Kehaulani Kauanui suggest, decolonization projects are falsely separated from efforts to realize gender justice (A. Smith and Kauanui 2008, 247; Kauanui 2008b, 285–86; see also Ramirez 2008, 305). Consequently, "this lack of an intersectional perspective prevents us from ascertaining how colonialism is itself a gendered process" (A. Smith and Kauanui 2008, 247). That is, an intersectional sensibility can help to illuminate the non-metaphorical gendered relationship between the dispossession of land, of bodies, and of knowledges, and turn our attention to the "dangerous intersections" (A. Smith 2005, 1) that constitute the modern/colonial gender system. This system implicates us all in divergent, contradictory, but radically interdependent ways and, if viewed intersectionally, intimates the possibilities for inhabiting our struggle identities in coalitional ways. Moreover, if engaged in a politics of refusal—as opposed to a politics of recognition or representation that inadvertently reproduce settler colonial logics of visibility, knowability, and management—an intersectional sensibility could enable the construction of "mass movements" through the "coalition-building" that "broad-based" efforts to dismantle interlocking systems of power would seem to necessitate (Simpson and Smith 2014, 10; A. Smith 2008, 315). If we grapple with intersectionality as a provisional concept that enables us to live our struggle identities in a radically different way, eschewing the categorial, representational, and political violence in and through which they have been forged to fragment, marginalize, and silence some subjects while exalting and empowering others, can we envision, on the horizon, an intersectional politics of coalition which intimates the decolonial "elsewheres" that all of us—on all sides of colonial divides—urgently need to imagine?

IDENTITIES AND INTERSECTIONALITIES

STRUCTURED ACTION THEORY, LEFT REALISM, POSTMODERN FEMINISM, AND BLACK/MULTIRACIAL FEMINIST CRIMINOLOGY

Claire M. Renzetti

Let me begin with a confession: I struggled with the title for this chapter. For one thing, including all the theories to be discussed makes for an accurate, but not very eloquent title. It certainly does not roll easily off the tongue. More importantly, I do not want to give the impression that this is a "kitchen sink" chapter; that this is the chapter in which one throws in anything and everything that has not yet been covered but needs to be. Such would diminish the signifi cance of each of the theories – an outcome that is opposite to what I intend and also somewhat ironic given that "othering" is a primary concern of these theories. It may also appear at fi rst glance that, apart from the feminist tie, this is a theoretically disparate list. But as I will show, these theories are linked in several ways and together they have made a signifi cant impact on criminology and criminal justice. To begin, then, let us examine the notion of gender as "situated accomplishment" and consider how it has been applied to the study of criminal offending.

MASCULINITIES, FEMININITIES, AND CRIME

As we noted in Chapter 1, *sex* and *gender* are terms typically used interchangeably in everyday conversation, but sociologists distinguish *sex*, a biological category, from *gender*, a socially constructed category. Nevertheless, even in sociological analyses, both sex and gender were – and, unfortunately, often still are – presented as binaries: categories with two mutually exclusive components. An individual is *either* male *or* female (sex), masculine *or* feminine (gender), and their masculinity or femininity derives "naturally" from their biological sex. A radical departure from this framework was introduced in 1987 by Candace West and Don Zimmerman in what has since become "the most cited article ever published in *Gender & Society*," one of the most prestigious academic journals in the fields of sociology and women's studies (Jurik and Siemsen, 2009: 72). Not only did West and Zimmerman attempt to break with the gender binary, they also replaced the traditional conceptualization of gender as a role or attribute of individuals with a more fluid, dynamic conceptualization of gender as accomplishment. Less than ten years later, West and Fenstermaker (1995) expanded the "doing gender approach" to other social categories, such as race and class, in an examination of the interactional aspects of "doing difference."[1] The doing gender/difference approach is also often referred to as *social construction feminism* because it sees gender as being socially created through people's actions and interactions with one another on a daily basis. The build-up of these interactions in the course of everyday life produces not only gendered self-identities, but also gendered social structures that, as Lorber (2009: 245) put it, "congeal" inequality.

To understand this perspective better, let us begin with the observation that social behavior is governed by norms, including gender norms (i.e. rules about masculinity and femininity), and these norms vary by social context or situation, although one consistent outcome is differentiation. In learning these norms, we learn how to "correctly" categorize people – and ourselves (e.g. male *or* female). As we interact, we constantly engage in this categorization, and we also know that others are categorizing us, so we make choices about how we look and act in a given situation based on how we think others might interpret our appearance and behavior. Social constructionists call this process *accountability*. Thus, people "do gender" by appearing and acting in ways that will lead others to identify them in a given situation as "male" or "female." Likewise, one may "do race" to be identified "white" or "Latino" or another race; one may "do sexual orientation" to be identified "gay" or "straight"; and so on. But this is not a process of constructing separate but equal categories, because these categories and the normative traits and behaviors attached to them are also ascribed differential value; some categories are valued more highly than others, and this inequality is reflected and reproduced in social relations and social structures in which people interact everyday – in, for example, families, schools, workplaces. As individuals continuously do gender (or race, or class), then, their "performance" is both constrained by and reproduces these unequal social relations and structures (West and Fenstermaker, 1995).

Before discussing how feminist criminologists have applied social constructionism in their theorizing and research, let us take a closer look at some of the central elements of this perspective. Notice first the importance of agency in social constructionism. From this perspective, individuals do not passively internalize pre-scripted gender roles that subsequently determine their attitudes and behavior; rather, gender is something people must do, or accomplish, in their everyday interactions with others (Connell, 1995). Moreover, how people do gender and what they accomplish varies situationally and is influenced by structural conditions. This means, then, that gender is not static or fixed. Social constructionism allows for multiple varieties of gender, for masculin*ities* and feminin*ities*, that an individual will likely change – and may change dramatically, in fact – as their circumstances change (Miller, 2002). It also allows for the possibility that in some situations individuals may "improvise" their performance of gender, or innovate new ways of doing gender (Messerschmidt, 1997).

But while this element of agency is critical, keep in mind, too, that social constructionists recognize the importance of how structural constraints – for example, in the form of power differences within and across groups – impinge on how gender and other differences can be accomplished. One may be more powerful than others in one context (e.g. a husband exercising power over his wife and children at home), but less powerful than others in a different context (e.g. the same man being subject to the power of his boss at work). "Consequently," as Messerschmidt (1997: 7) argues, "rather than viewing gender, race, and class as discreet 'things' that somehow relate to each other, it is important to visualize them as mutually constituting one another . . ." Furthermore, as Lorber (2009: 245) points out:

> While the social construction perspective allows for changes in gendered practices, change does not come easily, because many of the foundational assumptions of the gendered social order and its ubiquitous processes are legitimated by religion, taught by education, upheld by the mass media, and enforced by systems of social control.

It is James Messerschmidt who has been credited with pioneering the application of social constructionism to criminological theorizing and research through the development of his *structured action theory*. Although Messerschmidt has studied young women's involvement in crime, particularly in the context of street gangs (see Messerschmidt, 1995, 1997, 2002), much of his work focuses on understanding the relationship between masculinities and crime for as he correctly notes, for most criminologists the study of gender and crime means the study of women and crime. But men and boys are gendered too, and although historically they have been viewed as the "normal subjects" of criminological research, "the gendered content of their legitimate and illegitimate behavior has been virtually ignored" (Messerschmidt, 1993: 1; see also Messerschmidt, 1997, 2000).

In examining masculinities in relation to crime, Messerschmidt (1993, 1997) argues that crime is a resource used by men and boys to do gender – more specifically, to accomplish masculinity in a particular setting. Through secondary analyses of others' research as well as his own in-depth interviews with young men, Messerschmidt (2000, 2002) has studied how boys and men ascribe meaning to their behavior and make conscious choices, albeit in the context of structural constraints, about how to behave in a particular situation. He reports, for example, that boys and men living in disadvantaged urban neighborhoods use street crime, such as robbery, not only as a way of getting money or other valuable items, but also as a means for constructing a particular type of masculinity that he calls "hardman" (Messerschmidt, 1993). In another example – an analysis of the 1986 space shuttle *Challenger* disaster – Messerschmidt (1997) explores the construction of corporate masculinities by the white, middle-class managers and engineers involved in the launch decision that resulted in the deaths of all seven *Challenger* astronauts.

Importantly, Messerschmidt (1995, 1997) also discusses how crime may be a resource for some young women to construct particular femininities. He maintains, for instance, that girls in street gangs engage in behaviors, such as fighting and other forms of violence, that some observers might interpret as their attempts to act like boys, but to the girls themselves the behavior has a different meaning. These girls describe themselves as "feminine," but as acting "bad" (see also Jones, 2009). Messerschmidt (1995: 183) labels this femininity "bad-girl femininity," stating that the girls "are doing femininity in terms of activities appropriate to their sex category and in a specific social situation [i.e. the urban street gang]." Elsewhere, Messerschmidt (2002) describes third-wave feminism,[2] including the hip hop and Riot Grrrl subcultures, as constructing a "tough-girl femininity." Messerschmidt (ibid.: 465) makes the significant point that when women and girls are violent they are not just acting like or mimicking men and boys, but rather are "engaging in violence authentically as [women and] girls and as a legitimate aspect of their femininity." Their accomplishment of gender, though, like that of men and boys, is simultaneously shaped by various structural inequalities, such as sexism, racism, social class inequality, and heterosexism.

Structured action theory, as we have noted, advances our understanding of gender and crime in several ways. One important contribution is that it broadens the criminological lens beyond women's victimization. Recall that the feminist theories we discussed in Chapter 3 have been critiqued for overemphasizing women's victimization, subverting their agency and, perhaps inadvertently but nonetheless effectively, reinforcing stereotypes of female passivity and weakness. It follows from such stereotyping that the woman or girl who is aggressive or who "fights back" is anomalous, or worse, pathological, whereas the structured action theorist sees her as doing what everyone must do: accomplishing gender. What is more, in addition to drawing attention to the gendered nature of male criminal offending, structured action theorists do not depict male or female offenders as simply acting out a predetermined "gender role," but rather as actively constructing gender (and race, class and other differences) within the parameters of structural constraints through criminal offending. As Miller (2002: 434) points out, structured action theory "provides a means of bridging the agency/structure divide . . . but does so in a way thoroughly grounded in the contexts of structural inequalities such as those of gender, sexuality, race, class, and age." Criminologists who have conducted research informed by structured action theory have found that crime is not only a means for accomplishing gender in certain contexts, but also that efforts to do gender affect who is victimized. For instance, in their studies of the characteristics of hate crime (e.g. the group nature of the offending, perpetrators' language, their use of alcohol) as well as the characteristics of hate crime perpetrators and victims, Bufkin (1999) and Perry (2001) argue that hate crime is a resource used by some groups of young men to accomplish a particular type of masculinity, specifically, *hegemonic masculinity*: white, Christian, able-bodied, and heterosexual.[3]

Structured action theory, however, has been criticized on a number of grounds.[4] Some critics argue, for example, that the way structured action theory is often applied in criminological analyses is tautological. A tautology is circular reasoning. The concern here is with what critics characterize as structured action theorists' rather myopic view that "whatever groups of boys and girls, or men and women, do is a kind of gender" (Risman, 2009: 81). And as Miller (2002) notes, the tautology problem is related to a second criticism of structured action theory: the tendency to reinforce, rather than challenge, *gender dualism* or what we referred to earlier as the gender binary. For instance, when young straight men engage in gay bashing it is interpreted by structured action theorists as an effort to construct a specific masculine identity, and when young women in a street gang fight with rival gang members, it is interpreted as an effort to construct a specific feminine identity. But to paraphrase Risman (2009), why label behaviors adopted by groups of males or females as alternative masculinities or femininities just because the group itself is made up of biological males and females?[5] For one thing, constructing gender in some situations may not be a primary motivation. Second, as Miller's (2001) research shows, some girls and women strongly identify with boys and men and describe their behavior as masculine, not feminine; that is, they see themselves as "one of the guys." So despite the theoretical conception of multiple masculinities and femininities, these critics maintain that structured action theory often falls short in applying this notion to real-life males and females because of its "selective attention" to gender difference, thereby overlooking instances of "gender crossing," contradictory or contingent gender constructions, gender resistance, and efforts to "undo gender" (Butler, 1990; Jones, 2009; Miller, 2002, Risman, 2009). This concern is extended to studies of differences, such as race and social class, which intersect with gender. Such research shows tremendous variation both across *and within* social groups. For example, there is evidence that some African American gang girls take pride in masculine identities (Miller, 2001), while others embrace feminine identities (Messerschmidt, 2002), and still others are "aggressive for the streets, pretty for the pictures" as part of a strategy to stay safe and survive the very dangerous neighborhoods in which they live their everyday lives (Jones, 2009: 89; see also Miller, 2002, 2008).

It is interesting to note that this latter point actually supports structured action theory in terms of documenting a multitude of masculinities and femininities as well as the agency that social actors exercise in constructing these multiple identities – sometimes highly constrained in their efforts and at other times pushing back hard enough at these constraints to create alternatives and bring about change. But this diversity and both potential and realized social change are precisely what critics do not want structured action theorists to lose sight of. Certainly, it is not easy to think outside the gender binary/dualism box, but it is necessary if we are to understand and appreciate the rich complexity and diversity of people's lived experiences, which for some include criminal offending.

TAKING THE GENDERED NATURE OF CRIME SERIOUSLY: LEFT REALISM

In Chapter 3, we mentioned the emergence of a "new criminology" in the late 1960s and 1970s that was critical of mainstream criminologists for focusing on crimes committed by the powerless (e.g. street crime committed by young men of color in impoverished urban neighborhoods) and ignoring the crimes of the powerful (e.g. white-collar and corporate crime committed by wealthy, white businessmen; human rights violations committed by police or military personnel acting on behalf of governments). In the mid-1980s, though, another form of critical criminology was developed that, while not unconcerned with crimes of the powerful, nevertheless called for more criminological attention to street crime as well as the harsh social control techniques being adopted to address it (e.g. stop and frisk practices, saturation policing, three-strikes-and-you're-out sentencing laws).[6] This perspective, which originated in Great Britain, is known as *left realism*; left realists urged fellow critical criminologists to take crime in the streets, and its effects, seriously (Carlen, 1995).

Left realists acknowledge that many people are seriously harmed by white-collar, corporate, and governmental crime, but at the same time, they argue that many radical and Marxist criminologists have neglected the fact that "ordinary people," especially people who live in impoverished and working-class, high-crime neighborhoods, must cope daily with the severe negative consequences of predatory street crime and thus, rightly, fear it (Currie, 1992; Lea and Young, 1984). Moreover, de-emphasizing the significance of this type of crime relinquishes responsibility for responding to "the crime problem" to right-wing conservatives whose solution is to "crack down on crime," resulting in more people enmeshed in an increasingly draconian criminal justice system (DeKeseredy, 2011b; DeKeseredy and Schwartz, 2010). Such responses, however, may just compound crime's painful effects, since both perpetrators and victims typically live in the same communities and, not infrequently, in the same households.

In developing their theory, left realists originally drew heavily on Marxism as well as on mainstream strain and subcultural theories of crime. For instance, British left realists Lea and Young (1984) maintained that when people who are poor perceive their situation as unfair, they grow discontented and, if they have no legitimate way to address the inequity they are experiencing, they become increasingly frustrated. When unhappy, frustrated people are segregated together in whole communities of disadvantage, they form subcultures that encourage and legitimate criminal behavior.

Left realism has been criticized by criminologists on the political left (e.g. Carlen, 1995; Henry, 1999; Smart, 1990) as well as mainstream criminologists (e.g. Gibbons, 1994). But some critical criminologists see value in the left realist perspective, particularly in accounting for the crimes committed "behind closed doors by patriarchal, abusive men" (DeKeseredy, 2011b: 38). DeKeseredy and Schwartz (2010) distinguish their brand of left realism from other iterations of the theory by foregrounding gender, noting that even recent revisions of left realism have been gender-blind, and by examining how gender intersects with race and social class to shape behavior, including criminal behavior.

DeKeseredy and Schwartz (2010) point out that laissez-faire economic policies in recent years have cost many men their jobs, as corporations move production overseas to countries where labor costs are lower and regulations are weak or nonexistent. Young, working-class men have been especially hard hit by deindustrialization and the restructuring of the economy in countries such as the U.S., Canada, and Great Britain. If they can find work, it is increasingly in low-paying and menial jobs. Yet, these men are steeped in their culture's gendered norms of hegemonic masculinity, including being self-reliant; taking responsibility as the family "breadwinner"; maintaining the "upper hand" over "their" women and children; being unemotional, tough, and aggressive; and steadfastly disdaining even the slightest appearance of femininity, so as not to be ridiculed as "gay" by male peers. If legitimate means (e.g. gainful employment) to live up to the principles of hegemonic masculinity are blocked, then other means, such as violence, may be used to accomplish this type of masculinity. According to DeKeseredy and Schwartz (ibid.: 163):

> Men at the bottom of the socioeconomic ladder flocking together with members of all-male sexist subcultures is not surprising, since they are more likely than their more affluent

counterparts to adhere to an ideology of familial patriarchy ...
Arguably, such subcultures are likely to flourish in the near
future because areas with high levels of poverty and
unemployment are fertile breeding grounds for male-to-male
and male-to-female violence ...

In addition to theorizing how particular social constructions of
masculinity combine with social class constraints to encourage
criminal offending, DeKeseredy and Schwartz (2010) also examine
the role of institutionalized racism, which exacerbates the impact
of many social problems, including unemployment and underemployment, for men of color. Young black, Asian, Latino, and
other minority men experience heightened negative effects of
social and economic disadvantage, which block their ability to
attain the masculine status they value. It is not surprising, then,
that many of these young men support and reinforce one another's
views regarding "respect," the use of drugs and alcohol, and the
objectification and control of women, and engage in crime as a
type of "compensatory masculinity" or as a means of "repairing
'damaged masculinity'" (ibid.: 164).

DeKeseredy and Schwartz's left realism may be considered a
form of feminist left realism. Others (e.g. Carlen, 1995) have also
identified compatibilities between left realism and feminism. Yet,
one of the difficulties with left realism, even of the feminist variety,
is that it does not pay much attention to female offending. Left
realism focuses on how and why socially and economically marginalized men victimize one another as well as their female intimate
partners and women in their communities. But these women share
this disadvantaged status. Can women's lower rates of offending be
explained simply in terms of their adherence to gendered norms of
"emphasized femininity" (Messerschmidt, 1997)? That raises the
tautology problem that we noted earlier with regard to structured
action theory. More empirical research is needed to test the applicability of feminist left realism to women's offending as well as
women's resistance to men's violence. At the same time, while
DeKeseredy and Schwartz (2010: 164) acknowledge that there are
"diverse subcultural ways of doing masculinity" such that there are
many marginalized men who are nonviolent and who treat women
with dignity just as there are many affluent men who abuse women,

neither of these two groups is carefully studied by feminist left realists.[7] DeKeseredy and Schwartz (ibid.: 163) point out, for example, that "there is a large empirical and theoretical literature on the strong correlation between patriarchal male peer support and various types of woman abuse in university/college dating, which involves, for the most part, middle- and upper-class young adults . . ." Is this literature grounded in feminist left realism, or is feminist left realism limited to explaining only the criminal offending of socially and economically disadvantaged men? It is likely that the middle- and upper-class young *female* adults on university campuses, who are disproportionately affected by the offending of their male peers, would argue that this crime, too, should be "taken seriously." This is not to indict DeKeseredy and Schwartz, both of whom are recognized internationally as pro-feminist men and pioneering violence-against-women scholars, but rather to point out that the broader applicability of feminist left realism remains to date largely untested.

Identities and intersectionalities

1 Although the doing gender/doing difference approach is widely used – and, according to its creators (West and Zimmerman, 2009), often misused – today, West and Zimmerman persevered for ten years (through multiple revisions) to get their paper accepted for publication, a fact of which up-and-coming theorists and authors in particular should take note.

2 The label "third-wave feminism" is often applied to the feminism of many young women today to set it apart from the feminism of the 1960s, 1970s, and 1980s, which has been referred to as the "second wave of feminism," distinguishing it from late eighteenth- and early nineteenth-century feminism (i.e. the "first wave") (Renzetti *et al.*, 2012). Third wave feminism is commonly described as rebellious in terms of its celebration of female sexuality, and its emphasis on women's autonomy and agency (Lorber, 2005, 2009). An important element of third-wave feminism is inclusion. Many third-wave feminists have developed a multiracial/multicultural worldview focusing on the consequences of racism, social class inequality, and homophobia in addition to sexism (Baumgardner and Richards, 2000; Renzetti *et al.*, 2012). We discuss this perspective in greater detail later in the chapter.

3 See also Goodey's (1997) analysis of masculinities and fear of crime and Miller's (1998) study of gender and the accomplishment of robbery in the U.S., as well as Brookman *et al.*'s (2007) study of gender and robbery in the UK. Stroud (2012) offers a fascinating analysis of how carrying concealed handguns helps "relatively privileged men" to accomplish hegemonic masculinity "through fantasies of violence and self-defense," especially against racial and ethnic minority men.

4 Here I will highlight only a few of what I consider the most salient criticisms of structured action theory. For a more thorough and nuanced discussion of these criticisms, see the exchange between Miller and Messerschmidt in the November, 2002 issue of *Theoretical Criminology*, which we repeatedly cite in this chapter. See also the symposium on doing gender in the February, 2009 issue of *Gender & Society*; several of the contributions to the symposium are cited in this chapter as well.

5 Once again, the challenge is to recognize that even sex is not a binary category. When we speak of an individual's sex, we may be referring to *chromosomal* sex, *hormonal* sex, *gonadal* sex, or *genital* sex. Although for many people all of these are consistent with the category male or the category female, for some people they are not. For instance, some individuals (approximately 1 in 5,000 to 1 in 15,000 births) are born with a pair of XX sex chromosomes, which makes them chromosomally female, but because of prenatal exposure to androgens (male sex hormones) their external genitals may look more like those of boys than girls. This is a condition known as congenital adrenal hyperplasia. Similarly, some fetuses with male sex chromosomes (XY) are insensitive to androgens – a condition known as androgen insensitivity syndrome – and they are then born with the external genitalia of females. Typically, physicians advise parents of children with these conditions to have their genitals surgically reconstructed or "corrected." But this position has come under increasing criticism because such conditions usually are not threatening to the child's health; as one critic put it, they are only threatening to the child's culture (Kessler, 1996). For further discussion of *intersexuality*, genital ambiguity, and cross-cultural research on multiple genders, see Preves (2003) and Renzetti *et al*. (2012).

6 Stop and frisk refers to the ability of police to stop a person they deem "suspicious" to question them and pat them down (i.e. frisk them) in order to detect weapons. This controversial practice has been challenged as an unconstitutional search, but the U.S. Supreme Court has upheld it as a legitimate way to prevent crime, especially violent crime, and has given police considerable discretion in terms of what they deem "reasonably suspicious." Some people, however, are automatically labeled suspicious because of their membership in a particular group, such as people of color, so they are disproportionately – and unfairly – subjected to this practice. Saturation policing refers to the practice of concentrating large numbers of police officers in small, high-crime areas (known as "hot spots"). The rationale is to have a highly visible and overwhelming police presence in order to deter crime, which, on its face, makes sense. However, the police may be perceived as an "occupying army," particularly in racially segregated and economically disadvantaged neighborhoods. Ironically, some residents of such neighborhoods point out that despite saturation

policing, the police are often quite slow to respond to their calls for help (see, for example, Websdale, 2001). Finally, the three strikes law, adopted in California, was originally intended to reduce the recidivism of violent felons by imposing a life sentence in prison on individuals convicted of a third offense. Most "strike crimes" (i.e. criminal convictions that count in the three-strike tally) are violent felonies, but other, less serious crimes are included as well as are juvenile convictions and out-of-state convictions. The law has resulted in many grossly unfair outcomes (e.g. an individual being sentenced to life in prison for a shoplifting conviction because it was his or her "third strike" while an individual convicted of manslaughter is sentenced to 15 years because it is his or her first conviction). The law has also contributed to the serious – and inhumane – prison overcrowding in California, where one in four inmates is a "striker" (Shouse Law Group, 2012). See also Alexander (2010) for further discussion of these and other, similar practices.

7 As the economic downturn that began in 2007 began to worsen, the media reported an upsurge in cases of domestic violence, both intimate partner violence and child abuse, and attributed the increase to growing depression among men who had recently lost their jobs or who were experiencing severe financial problems. This group included middle-class and wealthy men who had lost positions in high-paying, high-status professions. But while research indicates a strong association between economic hardship and domestic violence, the relationship is complex and, often, economic distress is only one factor that must be considered in conjunction with a host of other risk factors. See Renzetti (2011a) for a further discussion of these issues.

Unit II. The Social Construction of Gender, Systems of Inequalities

Life Doesn't Frighten Me

MAYA ANGELOU

Shadows on the wall
Noises down the hall
Life doesn't frighten me at all.

Bad dogs barking loud
Big ghosts in a cloud
Life doesn't frighten me at all.

Mean old Mother Goose
Lions on the loose
They don't frighten me at all.

Dragons breathing flame
On my counterpane
That doesn't frighten me at all.

I go boo
Make them shoo
I make fun
Way they run
I won't cry
So they fly
I just smile
I just smile
They go wild
Life doesn't frighten me at all.

Tough guys fight
All alone at night
Life doesn't frighten me at all.

Panthers in the park
Strangers in the dark
No, they don't frighten me at all.

That new classroom where
Boys all pull my hair
(Kissy little girls
With their hair in curls)
They don't frighten me at all.

Don't show me frogs and snakes
And listen for my scream,
If I'm afraid at all
It's only in my dreams.

I've got magic charm
That I keep up my sleeve
I can walk the ocean floor
And never have to breathe.

Life doesn't frighten me at all
Not at all
Not at all.

Life doesn't frighten me at all.

Feminism and the Politics of the Common in an Era of Primitive Accumulation

Silvia Federici

Reproduction precedes social production. Touch the women, touch the rock.—Peter Linebaugh, *The Magna Carta Manifesto*

INTRODUCTION: WHY COMMONS?

At least since the Zapatistas, on December 31, 1993, took over the zócalo of San Cristóbal to protest legislation dissolving the ejidal lands of Mexico, the concept of the "commons" has gained popularity among the radical Left, internationally and in the United States, appearing as a ground of convergence among anarchists, Marxists/socialists, ecologists, and eco-feminists.[1]

There are important reasons why this apparently archaic idea has come to the center of political discussion in contemporary social movements. Two in particular stand out. On the one side, there has been the demise of the statist model of revolution that for decades has sapped the efforts of radical movements to build an alternative to capitalism. On the other, the neoliberal attempt to subordinate every form of life and knowledge to the logic of the market has heightened our awareness of the danger of living in a world in which we no longer have access to seas, trees, animals, and our fellow beings except through the cash-nexus. The "new enclosures" have also made visible a world of communal properties and relations that many had believed to be extinct or had not valued until threatened with privatization.[2] The new enclosures ironically demonstrated that not only have commons not vanished, but new forms of social cooperation are constantly being produced, also in areas of life where none previously existed, as, for example, the Internet.

The idea of the common/s, in this context, has offered a logical and historical alternative to both state and private property, the state and the market, enabling us to reject the fiction that they are mutually exclusive and exhaustive of our political possibilities. It has also served an ideological function, as a unifying concept prefiguring the cooperative society that the radical Left is striving to create. Nevertheless, ambiguities as well as significant differences exist in the interpretations of this concept, which we need to clarify, if we want the principle of the commons to translate into a coherent political project.[3]

What, for example, constitutes a common? Examples abound. We have land, water, air commons, digital commons, service commons; our acquired entitlements (e.g., social security pensions) are often described as commons, and so are languages, libraries, and the collective products of past cultures. But are all these "commons" on the same level from the viewpoint of devising an anticapitalist strategy? Are they all compatible? And how can we ensure that they do not project a unity that remains to be constructed?

With these questions in mind, in this essay, I look at the politics of the commons from a feminist perspective, where *feminist* refers to a standpoint shaped by the struggle against sexual discrimination and over reproductive work, which (quoting [Peter] Linebaugh) is the rock on which society is built and by which every model of social organization must be tested.[4] This intervention is necessary, in my view, to better define this politics, expand a debate that so far has remained male-dominated, and clarify under what conditions the principle of the common(s) can become the foundation of an anticapitalist program. Two concerns make these tasks especially important.

GLOBAL COMMONS, WORLD BANK COMMONS

First, since at least the early 1990s, the language of the commons has been appropriated by the World Bank and the United Nations, and put at the service of privatization. Under the guise of protecting biodiversity and conserving "global commons," the bank has turned rain forests into ecological reserves, has expelled the populations that for centuries had drawn their sustenance from them, while making them available to people who do not need them but can pay for them, for instance, through ecotourism.[5] On its side, the United Nations, in the name again of preserving the common heritage of mankind, has revised the international law governing access to the oceans, in ways enabling governments to consolidate the use of seawaters in fewer hands.[6]

The World Bank and the United Nations are not alone in their adaptation of the idea of the commons to market interests. Responding to different motivations, a revalorization of the commons has become trendy among mainstream economists and capitalist planners, witness the growing academic literature on the subject and its cognates: "social capital," "gift economies," "altruism." Witness also the official recognition of this trend through the conferral of the Nobel Prize for Economics in 2009 to the leading voice in this field, the political scientist Elinor Ostrom.[7]

Development planners and policy makers have discovered that, under proper conditions, a collective management of natural resources can be more efficient and less conflictual than privatization, and commons can very well be made to produce for the market.[8] They have also recognized that, carried to the extreme, the commodification of social relations has self-defeating consequences. The extension of the commodity-form to every corner of the social factory, which neoliberalism has promoted, is an ideal limit for capitalist ideologues, but it is a project not only unrealizable but undesirable from the viewpoint of the long-term reproduction of the capitalist system. Capitalist accumulation is structurally dependent on the free appropriation of immense areas of labor and resources that must appear as externalities to the market, like the unpaid domestic work that women have provided, on which employers have relied for the reproduction of the workforce.

Not accidentally, then, long before the Wall Street "meltdown," a variety of economists and social theorists warned that the marketization of all spheres of life is detrimental to the market's well-functioning, for markets too—the argument goes—depend on the existence of nonmonetary relations like confidence, trust, and gift-giving.[9] In brief, capital is learning about the virtues of the "common good." In its July 31, 2008, issue, even the London *Economist*, the organ of capitalist free-market economics for more than 150 years, cautiously joined the chorus. "The economics of the new commons," the journal wrote, "is still in its infancy. It is too soon to be confident about its hypotheses. But it may yet prove a useful way of thinking about problems, such as managing the internet, intellectual property or international pollution, on which policymakers need all the help they can get." We must be very careful, then, not to craft the discourse on the commons in such a way as to allow a crisis-ridden capitalist class to revive itself, posturing, for instance, as the guardian of the planet.

WHAT COMMONS?

A second concern is that, while international institutions have learned to make commons functional to the market, how commons can become the foundation of a noncapitalist economy is a question still unanswered. From Peter Linebaugh's work, especially *The Magna Carta Manifesto* (2008), we have learned that commons have been the thread that has connected the history of the class struggle into our time, and indeed the fight for the commons is all around us. Mainers are fighting to preserve their fisheries and waters, residents of the Appalachian regions are joining to save their mountains threatened by strip mining, and open source and free software movements are opposing the commodification of knowledge and opening new spaces for communications and cooperation. We also have the many invisible, commoning activities and communities that people are creating in North America, which Chris Carlsson has described in his *Nowtopia*.[10] As Carlsson shows, much creativity is invested in the production of "virtual commons" and forms of sociality that thrive under the radar of the money/market economy.

Most important has been the creation of urban gardens, which have spread, in the 1980s and 1990s, across the country, thanks mostly to the initiatives of immigrant communities from Africa, the Caribbean, or the South of the United States. Their significance cannot be overestimated. Urban gardens have opened the way to a "rurbanization" process that is indispensable if we are to regain control over our food production, regenerate our environment, and provide for our subsistence. The gardens are far more than a source of food security. They are centers of sociality, knowledge production, and cultural and intergenerational exchange. As Margarita Fernandez writes of gardens in New York, urban gardens "strengthen community cohesion," as places where people come together not just to work the land but to play cards, hold weddings, and have baby showers or birthday parties.[11] Some have a partnership relation with local schools, whereby they give children after-school environmental education. Not last, gardens are "a medium for the transport and encounter of diverse cultural practices," so that African vegetables and farming practices (for example) mix with those from the Caribbean.[12]

Still, the most significant feature of urban gardens is that they produce for neighborhood consumption, rather than for commercial purposes. This distinguishes them from other reproductive commons that either produce for the market, like the fisheries of the "Lobster Coast" of Maine, or are bought on the market, like the land-trusts that preserve the open spaces.[13] The problem, however, is that urban gardens have remained a spontaneous grassroots initiative, and there have been few attempts by movements in the United States to expand their presence and to make access to land a key terrain of struggle. More generally, how the many proliferating commons being defended, developed, and fought for can be brought together to form a cohesive whole providing a foundation for a new mode of production is a question the Left has not posed.

An exception is the theory proposed by [Antonio] Negri and [Michael] Hardt in *Empire* (2000), *Multitude* (2004), and more recently *Commonwealth* (2009), which argues that a society built on the principle of "the common" is already evolving from the informatization of production. According to this theory, as production becomes predominantly a production of knowledge organized through the Internet, a common space is formed which escapes the problem of defining rules of inclusion or exclusion, because access and use multiply the resources available on the net, rather than subtracting from them, thus signifying the possibility of a society built on abundance—the only remaining hurdle confronting the "multitude" being presumably how to prevent the capitalist "capture" of the wealth produced.

The appeal of this theory is that it does not separate the formation of "the common" from the organization of work and production as already constituted, but sees it immanent in it. Its limit is that it does not question the material basis of the digital technology the Internet relies on, overlooking the fact that computers depend on economic activities—mining, microchip and rare earth production—that, as currently organized, are extremely destructive, socially and ecologically.[14] Moreover, with its emphasis on science, knowledge production, and information, this theory skirts the question of the reproduction of everyday life. This, however, is true of the discourse on the commons as whole, which has generally focused on the formal preconditions for their existence but much less on the possibilities provided by existing commons, and their potential to create forms of reproduction enabling us to resist dependence on wage labor and subordination to capitalist relations.

WOMEN AND THE COMMONS

It is in this context that a feminist perspective on the commons is important. It begins with the realization that, as the primary subjects of reproductive work, historically and in our time, women have depended more than men on access to communal resources, and have been most committed to their defense. As I wrote in *Caliban and the Witch* (2004), in the first phase of capitalist development, women were in the front of the struggle against land enclosures both in England and the "New World," and the staunchest defenders of the communal cultures that European colonization attempted to destroy. In Peru, when the Spanish conquistadores took control of their villages, women fled to the high mountains, where they re-created forms of collective life that have survived to this day. Not surprisingly, the sixteenth and seventeenth centuries saw the most violent attack on women in the history of the world: the persecution of women as witches. Today, in the face of a new process of primitive accumulation, women are the main social force standing in the way of a complete commercialization of nature. Women are the subsistence farmers of the world. In Africa, they produce 80 percent of the food people consume, despite the attempts made by the World Bank and other agencies to convince them to divert their activities to cash-cropping. Refusal to be without access to land has been so strong that, in the towns, many women have taken over plots in public lands, planted corn and cassava in vacant lots, in this process changing the urban landscape of African cities and breaking down the separation between town and country.[15] In India, too, women have restored degraded forests, guarded trees, joined hands to chase away the loggers, and made blockades against mining operations and the construction of dams.[16]

The other side of women's struggle for direct access to means of reproduction has been the formation, across the third world—from Cambodia to Senegal—of credit associations that function as money commons.[17] Differently named, "tontines" (in parts of Africa) are autonomous, self-managed, women-made banking systems, providing cash to individuals or groups that can have no access to banks, working purely on the basis of trust. In this, they are completely different from the microcredit systems promoted by the World Bank, which functions on the basis of shame, arriving to the extreme (e.g., in Niger) of posting in public places the pictures of the women who fail to repay the loans so that some have been driven to suicide.[18]

Women have also led the effort to collectivize reproductive labor both as a means to economize on the cost of reproduction and protect each other from poverty, state violence, and the violence of individual men. An outstanding example are the ola communes (common kitchens) that women in Chile and in Peru set up in the 1980s, when, because of stiff inflation, they could no longer afford to shop alone.[19] Like collective reforestation and land reclamation, these practices are the expression of a world where communal bonds are still strong. It would be a mistake, however, to consider them as something prepolitical, "natural," a product of "tradition." In reality, as Leo Podlashuc notes in "Saving Women: Saving the Commons," these struggles shape a collective identity, constitute a counterpower in the home and the community, and open a process of self-valorization and self-determination from which we have much to learn.

The first lesson to be gained from these struggles is that the "commoning" of the material means of reproduction is the primary mechanism by which a collective interest and mutual bonds are created. It is also the first line of resistance to a life of enslavement, whether in armies, brothels, or sweatshops. For us, in North America, an added lesson is that by pooling our resources, by reclaiming land and waters, and turning them into a common, we could begin to delink our reproduction from the commodity flows that through the world market are responsible for the dispossession of so many people in other parts of the world. We could disentangle our livelihood, not only from the world market but from the war machine and prison system on which the hegemony of the world market depends. Not last we could move beyond the abstract solidarity that often characterizes relations in the movement, which limits our commitment and capacity to endure, and the risks we are willing to take.

Undoubtedly, this is a formidable task that can only be accomplished through a long-term process of consciousness raising, cross-cultural exchange, and coalition building, with all the communities throughout the United States who are vitally interested in the reclamation of the land, starting with the First American Nations. Although this task may seem more difficult now than passing through the eye of a needle, it is also the only condition to broaden the space of our autonomy, cease feeding into the process of capital accumulation, and refuse to accept that our reproduction occurs at the expense of the world's other commoners and commons.

FEMINIST RECONSTRUCTIONS

What this task entails is powerfully expressed by Maria Mies when she points out that the production of commons requires first a profound transformation in our everyday life, in order to recombine what the social division of labor in capitalism has separated. For the distancing of production from reproduction and consumption leads us to ignore the conditions under which what we eat or wear, or work with, have been produced, their social and environmental cost, and the fate of the population on whom the waste we produce is unloaded.[20]

In other words, we need to overcome the state of constant denial and irresponsibility, concerning the consequences of our actions, resulting from the destructive ways in which the social division of labor is organized in capitalism; short of that, the production of our life inevitably becomes a production of death for others. As Mies points out, globalization has worsened this crisis, widening the distances between what is produced and what is consumed, thereby intensifying, despite the appearance of an increased global interconnectedness, our blindness to the blood in the food we eat, the petroleum we use, the clothes we wear, and the computers with which we communicate.[21]

Overcoming this oblivion is where a feminist perspective teaches us to start in our reconstruction of the commons. No common is possible unless we refuse to base our life, our reproduction on the suffering of others, unless we refuse to see ourselves as separate from them. Indeed if "commoning" has any meaning, it must be the production of ourselves as a common subject. This is how we must understand the slogan "no commons without community." But "community" is not intended as a gated reality, a grouping of people joined by exclusive interests separating them from others, as with community formed on the basis of religion or ethnicity. Community as a quality of relations, a principle of cooperation and responsibility: to each other, the earth, the forests, the seas, the animals.

Certainly, the achievement of such community, like collectivizing our everyday work of reproduction, can only be a beginning. It is no substitute for broader antiprivatization campaigns and the reconstitution of our commonwealth. But it is an essential part of the process of our education for collective governance and the recognition of history as a collective project—the main casualty of the neoliberal era of capitalism.

On this account, we must include in our political agenda the communalization/collectivization of housework, reviving that rich feminist tradition that we have in the United States, that stretches from the utopian socialist experiments of the mid-nineteenth century to the attempts that the "materialist feminists" made, from the late nineteenth century to the early twentieth century, to reorganize and socialize domestic work and thereby the home, and the neighborhood, through collective housekeeping—efforts that continued until the 1920s, when the "Red Scare" put an end to them.[22] These practices, and the ability that past feminists have had to look at reproductive labor as an important sphere of human activity, not to be negated but to be revolutionized, must be revisited and revalorized.

One crucial reason for creating collective forms of living is that the reproduction of human beings is the most labor-intensive work on Earth, and to a large extent it is work that is irreducible to mechanization. We cannot mechanize childcare or the care of the ill, or the psychological work necessary to reintegrate our physical and emotional balance. Despite the efforts that futuristic industrialists are making, we cannot robotize "care" except at a terrible cost for the people involved. No one will accept "nursebots" as care givers, especially for children and the ill. Shared responsibility and cooperative work, not given at the cost of the health of the providers, are the only guarantees of proper care. For centuries the reproduction of human beings has been a collective process. It has been the work of extended families and communities, on which people could rely, especially in proletarian neighborhoods, even when they lived alone, so that old age was not accompanied by the desolate loneliness and dependence that so many of our elderly experience. It is only with the advent of capitalism that reproduction has been completely privatized, a process that is now carried to a degree that it destroys our lives. This we need to change if we are to put an end to the steady devaluation and fragmentation of our lives.

The times are propitious for such a start. As the capitalist crisis is destroying the basic element of reproduction for millions of people across the world, including the United States, the reconstruction of our everyday life is a possibility and a necessity. Like strikes, social/economic crises break the discipline of the wage work, forcing on us new forms of sociality. This is what occurred during the Great Depression, which produced a movement of hobo-men who turned the freight trains into their commons seeking freedom in mobility and nomadism.[23] At the intersections of railroad lines, they organized "hobo jungles," prefigurations, with their self-governance rules and solidarity, of the communist world in which many of their residents believed.[24] However, but for a few "box-car Berthas," this was predominantly a masculine world, a fraternity of men, and in the long term it could not be sustained.[25] Once the economic crisis and the war came to an end, the hobo men were domesticated by the two grand engines of labor-power fixation: the family and the house. Mindful of the threat of working-class recomposition in the Depression, American capital excelled in its application of the principle that has characterized the organization of economic life: cooperation at the point of production, separation and atomization at the point of reproduction. The atomized, serialized family house Levittown provided, compounded by its umbilical appendix, the car, not only sedentarized the worker but put an end to the type of autonomous workers' commons the hobo jungles had represented.[26] Today, as millions of Americans' houses and cars have been repossessed, as foreclosures, evictions, and the massive loss of employment are again breaking down the pillars of the capitalist discipline of work, new common grounds are again taking shape, like the tent cities that are sprawling from coast to coast. This time, however, it is women who must build the new commons, so that they do not remain transient spaces or temporary autonomous zones, but become the foundation of new forms of social reproduction.

If the house is the *oikos* on which the economy is built, then it is women, historically the house-workers and house-prisoners, who must take the initiative to reclaim the house as a center of collective life, one traversed by multiple people and forms of cooperation, providing safety without isolation and fixation, allowing for the sharing and circulation of community possessions, and above all providing the foundation for collective forms of reproduction. As already suggested, we can draw inspiration for this project from the programs of the nineteenth century "materialist feminists" who, convinced that the home was an important "spatial component of the economic oppression of women," organized communal kitchens and cooperative households, calling for workers' control of reproduction.[27] These objectives are crucial at present: breaking down the isolation of life in a private home is not only a precondition for meeting our most basic needs and increasing our power with regard to employers and the state. As Massimo de Angelis has reminded us, it is also a protection from ecological disaster. For there can be no doubt about the destructive consequences of the "uneconomic" multiplication of reproductive assets and self-enclosed dwellings, dissipating, in the winter, warmth into the atmosphere, exposing us to unmitigated heat in the summer, which we now call our homes. Most important, we cannot build an alternative society and a strong self-reproducing movement unless we redefine in more cooperative ways our reproduction and put an end to the separation between the personal and the political, political activism and the reproduction of everyday life.

It remains to clarify that assigning women this task of commoning/collectivizing reproduction is not to concede to a naturalistic conception of "femininity." Understandably, many feminists would view this possibility as "a fate worse than death." It is deeply sculpted in our collective consciousness that women have been designated as men's common, a natural source of wealth and services to be as freely appropriated by them as the capitalists have appropriated the wealth of nature. But, quoting Dolores Hayden, the reorganization of reproductive work, and therefore the reorganization of the structure of housing and public space is not a question of identity; it is a labor question and, we can add, a power and safety question.[28] I am reminded here of the experience of the women members of the Landless People's Movement of Brazil (MST), who when their communities won the right to maintain the land which they had occupied, insisted that the new houses should be built to form one compound, so that they could continue to share their housework, wash together, cook together, taking turns with men, as they had done in the course of the struggle, and be ready to run to give each other support if abused by men. Arguing that women should take the lead in the collectivization of reproductive work and housing is not to naturalize housework as a female vocation. It is refusing to obliterate the collective experiences, knowledge, and struggles that women have accumulated concerning reproductive work, whose history has been an essential part of our resistance to capitalism. Reconnecting with this history is today for women and men a crucial step, both for undoing the gendered architecture of our lives and reconstructing our homes and lives as commons.

NOTES

This chapter was previously published as Silvia Federici, "Feminism and the Politics of the Common in an Era of Primitive Accumulation," in *Revolution at Point Zero: Housework, Reproduction, and Feminist Struggle* (Oakland, CA: PM Press, 2012). Reprinted by permission of PM Press (http://www.pmpress.org).

1. The U.K.-based electronic journal the *Commoner* has been a key source on the politics of the commons and its theoretical groundings for over ten years (see http://www.commoner.org.uk).

2. A case in point is the struggle that is taking place in many communities in Maine against Nestle's appropriation of Maine waters to bottle Portland Spring. Nestle's theft has made people aware of the vital importance of these waters and the supporting aquifers and has truly constituted them as a common. See Food and Water Watch, "All Bottled Up: Nestle's Pursuit of Community Water," January 2009, available at https://www.foodandwaterwatch.org/sites/default/files/all_bottled_up_report_jan_2009_.pdf.

3. An excellent site for current debates on the commons is the December 2009 issue of the U.K. movement journal *Turbulence*; see http://www.turbulence.org.

4. Peter Linebaugh, *The Magna Carta Manifesto: Liberties and Commons for All* (Berkeley: University of California Press, 2008).

5. See, on this subject, the important article by Ana Isla "Who Pays for the Kyoto Protocol?" in *Eco-Sufficiency and Global Justice: Women Write Political Ecology*, ed. Ariel Salleh (London: Pluto Press, 2009), 199–217, in which the author describes how the conservation of the biodiversity has provided the World Bank and other international agencies with the pretext for the enclosure of the rain forests, on the ground that they represent "carbon sinks" and "oxygen generators."

6. The United Nations Convention on the Law of the Sea, passed in November 1994, establishes a two-hundred-mile offshore limit, defining an Exclusive Economic Zone, where nations can exploit, manage, and protect resources, from fisheries to natural gas. It also sets regulations for mining in deep sea and for the use of resulting profit.

7. As described by Wikipedia, Ostrom's work focuses on common pool resources and emphasizes "how humans interact with ecosystems to maintain long-term sustainable resource yields." See "Elinor Ostrom," *Wikipedia*, August 19, 2017, available at https://en.wikipedia.org/wiki/Elinor_Ostrom.

8. See, on this topic, Calestous Juma and J. B. Ojwang, eds., *In Land We Trust: Environment, Private Property and Constitutional Change* (London: Zed Books, 1996), an early treatise on the effectiveness of communal property relations in the context of capitalist development and efforts.

9. David Bollier, *Silent Theft: The Private Plunder of Our Common Wealth* (London: Routledge, 2002).

10. Chris Carlsson, *Nowtopia* (Oakland, CA: AK Press, 2008).

11. See Margarita Fernandez, "Cultivating Community, Food and Empowerment," unpublished manuscript, 2003, pp. 23–26. An early, important work on urban gardens is Peter Lamborn Wilson and Bill Weinberg, eds., *Avant Gardening: Ecological Struggle in the City and the World* (New York: Autonomedia, 1999).

12. Fernandez, "Cultivating Community."

13. However the fishing "commons" of Maine are currently threatened with a new privatizing policy, justified in the name of preservation, ironically labeled "catch shares." This is a system, already applied in Canada and Alaska, whereby local governments set a limit to how much fish can be caught and allocate individual shares on the basis of the amount of fishing done in the past. This system has proven to be disastrous for small, independent fishermen who are soon forced to sell their share to the highest bidders. Protest against its implementation is now mounting in the fishing communities of Maine. See "Catch Shares or Share-Croppers?" *Fishermen's Voice* 14, no. 12 (2009), available at http://www.fishermensvoice.com/archives/1209catchsharesorsharecroppers.html.

14. It has been calculated, for example, that just to produce a personal computer, thirty-three thousand liters of waters and fifteen to nineteen tons of material are required. Saral Sarkar, *Eco-Socialism or Eco-Capitalism? A Critical Analysis of Humanity's Fundamental Choices* (London: Zed Books, 1999), 126.

15. Silvia Federici, "Women, Land Struggles, and the Reconstruction of the Commons," *WorkingUSA: The Journal of Labor and Society* 14, no. 1 (2011): 52.

16. Vandana Shiva, *Staying Alive: Women, Ecology and Development* (London: Zed Books, 1989); Vandana Shiva, *Ecology and the Politics of Survival: Conflicts over Natural Resources in India* (New Delhi: Sage, 1991), 102–117, 274.

17. Leo Podlashuc, "Saving Women: Saving the Commons," in Salleh, *Eco-Sufficiency and Global Justice: Women Write Political Ecology*, 268–290.

18. Ousseina Alidou, interview by the author.

19. Jo Fisher, *Out of the Shadows: Women, Resistance and Politics in South America* (New York: Monthly Review Press, 1993); Carol Andreas, *When Women Rebel: The Rise of Popular Feminism in Peru* (Westport, CT: Independent, 1985).

20. Veronica Bennholdt-Thomsen and Maria Mies, *The Subsistence Perspective: Beyond the Globalised Economy* (London: St. Martin's Press, 1999), 141.

21. Ibid.

22. Dolores Hayden, *Redesigning the American Dream: The Future of Housing, Work and Family Life* (New York: Norton, 1986); Dolores Hayden, *The Grand Domestic Revolution: A History of Feminist Designs for American Homes, Neighborhoods and Cities* (Cambridge, MA: MIT Press, 1982).

23. George Caffentzis, "Three Temporal Dimensions of Class Struggle," paper presented at ISA annual meeting, San Diego, CA, March 2006.

24. Nels Anderson, *Men on the Move* (Chicago: University of Chicago Press, 1998); Todd Depastino, *Citizen Hobo* (Chicago: University of Chicago Press, 2003); George Caffentzis, "Three Temporal Dimensions of Class Struggle," in *In Letters of Blood and Fire: Work, Machines, and the Crisis of Capitalism* (Oakland, CA: PM Press, 2013).

25. *Boxcar Bertha* (1972) is Martin Scorsese's adaptation of *Sister of the Road*, the fictionalized autobiography of radical and transient Bertha Thompson.

26. Hayden, *Redesigning the American Dream*.

27. Hayden, *The Grand Domestic Revolution*, 295.

28. Hayden, *Redesigning the American Dream*, 230.

#BlackLivesMatter

Alicia Garza

THE CREATION OF A MOVEMENT

I created #BlackLivesMatter with Patrisse Cullors and Opal Tometi, two of my sisters, as a call to action for Black people after seventeen-year-old Trayvon Martin was posthumously placed on trial for his own murder and the killer, George Zimmerman, was not held accountable for the crime he committed. It was a response to the anti-Black racism that permeates our society and also, unfortunately, our movements.

Black Lives Matter[1] is an ideological and political intervention in a world where Black lives are systematically and intentionally targeted for demise. It is an affirmation of Black folks' contributions to this society, our humanity, and our resilience in the face of deadly oppression.

We were humbled when cultural workers, artists, designers, and techies offered their labor and love to expand #BlackLivesMatter beyond a social media hashtag. Opal, Patrisse, and I created the infrastructure for this movement project—moving the hashtag from social media to the streets. Our team grew through a very successful Black Lives Matter ride, led and designed by Patrisse and Darnell L. Moore, organized to support the movement that is growing in St. Louis, Missouri, after eighteen-year-old Mike Brown was killed at the hands of Ferguson police officer Darren Wilson. We've hosted national conference calls focused on issues of critical importance to Black people working hard for the liberation of our people. We've connected people across the country working to end the various forms of injustice impacting our people. We've created space for the celebration and humanization of Black lives.

THE THEFT OF QUEER BLACK WOMEN'S WORK

As people took the #BlackLivesMatter demand into the streets, mainstream media and corporations also took up the call, and #BlackLivesMatter appeared in an episode of *Law and Order: SVU* in a mash-up containing the Paula Deen racism scandal and the tragedy of the murder of Trayvon Martin.

Suddenly, we began to come across varied adaptations of our work—all lives matter, brown lives matter, migrant lives matter, women's lives matter, and on and on. While imitation is said to be the highest form of flattery, I was surprised when an organization called to ask if they could use "Black Lives Matter" in one of their campaigns. We agreed to it, with the caveat that (a) as a team, we preferred that they not use the meme to celebrate the imprisonment of any individual, and (b) it was important to us that they acknowledge the genesis of #BlackLivesMatter. I was surprised when they did exactly the opposite and then justified their actions by saying they hadn't used the "exact" slogan and, therefore, deemed it okay to take our work, use it as their own, fail to credit where it came from, and then use it to applaud incarceration.

I was surprised when a community institution wrote asking us to provide materials and action steps for an art show they were curating, titled "Our Lives Matter." When questioned about who was involved and why they felt the need to change the very specific call and demand around Black lives to "our lives," I was told the artists decided it needed to be more inclusive of all people of color. I was even more surprised when, in the promotion of their event, one of the artists conducted an interview that completely erased the origins of their work—rooted in the labor and love of queer Black women.

Pause.

When you design an event/campaign/et cetera based on the work of queer Black women, don't invite them to participate in shaping it but ask them to provide materials and ideas for next steps for said event; that is racism in practice. It's also heteropatriarchal. Straight men, unintentionally or intentionally, have taken the work of queer Black women and erased our contributions. Perhaps if we were the charismatic Black men many are rallying around these days, it would have been a different story, but being queer Black women in this society (and apparently within these movements) tends to equal invisibility and nonrelevancy.

We completely expect those who benefit directly and improperly from White supremacy to try to erase our existence. We fight that every day. But when it happens among our allies, we are baffled, we are saddened, and we are enraged. And it's time to have the political conversation about why that's not okay.

We are grateful to our allies who have stepped up to the call that Black lives matter and taken it as an opportunity to not just stand in solidarity with us but investigate the ways in which anti-Black racism is perpetuated in their own communities. We are also grateful to those allies who were willing to engage in critical dialogue with us about this unfortunate and problematic dynamic. And for those who we have not yet had the opportunity to engage with around the adaptations of the Black Lives Matter call, please consider the following points.

BROADENING THE CONVERSATION TO INCLUDE BLACK LIFE

Black Lives Matter is a unique contribution that goes beyond extrajudicial killings of Black people by police and vigilantes. It goes beyond the narrow nationalism that can be prevalent within some Black communities, which merely call on Black people to love Black, live Black, and buy Black, keeping straight cis Black men in the front of the movement while our sisters, queer and trans and disabled folk, take up roles in the background or not at all. Black Lives Matter affirms the lives of Black queer and trans folks, disabled folks, Black undocumented folks, folks with records, women, and all Black lives along the gender spectrum. It centers those that have been marginalized within Black liberation movements. It is a tactic to (re)build the Black liberation movement.

When we say "Black lives matter," we are talking about the ways in which Black people are deprived of our basic human rights and dignity. It is an acknowledgment that Black poverty and genocide is state violence. It is an acknowledgment that one million Black people are locked in cages in this country—one half of all people in prisons or jails—which is an act of state violence. It is an acknowledgment that Black women continue to bear the burden of a relentless assault on our children and our families, and that assault is an act of state violence. Black queer and trans folks bearing a unique burden in a heteropatriarchal society that disposes of us like garbage and simultaneously fetishizes us and profits off us is state violence; the fact that five hundred thousand Black people in the United States are undocumented immigrants and relegated to the shadows is state violence; the fact that Black girls are used as negotiating chips during times of conflict and war is state violence; the fact that Black folks living with disabilities and different abilities bear the burden of state-sponsored Darwinian experiments that attempt to squeeze us into boxes of normality defined by White supremacy is state violence. And the fact is that the lives of Black people—not ALL people—exist within these conditions is consequence of state violence.

When Black people get free, everybody gets free.

#BlackLivesMatter doesn't mean your life isn't important—it means that Black lives, which are seen as without value within White supremacy, are important to your liberation. Given the disproportionate impact state violence has on Black lives, we understand that when Black people in this country get free, the benefits will be wide reaching and transformative for society as a whole. When we are able to end hypercriminalization and hypersexualization of Black people and end the poverty, control, and surveillance of Black people, every single person in this world has a better shot at getting and staying free. When Black people get free, everybody gets free. This is why we call on Black people and our allies to take up the call that Black lives matter. We're not saying Black lives are more important than other lives, or that other lives are not criminalized and oppressed in various ways. We remain in active solidarity with all oppressed people who are fighting for their liberation, and we know that our destinies are intertwined.

And, to keep it real, it is appropriate and necessary to have strategy and action centered around Blackness without other non-Black communities of color, or White folks for that matter, needing to find a place and a way to center themselves within it. It is appropriate and necessary for us to acknowledge the critical role that Black lives and struggles for Black liberation have played in inspiring and anchoring, through practice and theory, social movements for the liberation of all people. The women's movement, the Chicano liberation movement, queer movements, and many more have adopted the strategies, tactics, and theory of the Black liberation movement. And if we are committed to a world where all lives matter, we are called to support the very movement that inspired and activated so many more. That means supporting and acknowledging Black lives.

Progressive movements in the United States have made some unfortunate errors when they push for unity at the expense of really understanding the concrete differences in context, experience, and oppression. In other words, some want unity without struggle. As people who have our minds stayed on freedom, we can learn to fight anti-Black racism by examining the ways in which we participate in it, even unintentionally, instead of the worn-out and sloppy practice of drawing lazy parallels of unity between peoples with vastly different experiences and histories.

When we deploy "All Lives Matter" to correct an intervention specifically created to address anti-Blackness, we lose the ways in which the state apparatus has built a program of genocide and repression mostly on the backs of Black people—beginning with the theft of millions of people for free labor—and then adapted it to control, murder, and profit off other communities of color and immigrant communities. We perpetuate a level of White supremacist domination by reproducing a tired trope that we are all the same, rather than acknowledging that non-Black oppressed people in this country both are affected by racism and domination and simultaneously *benefit* from anti-Black racism.

When you drop "Black" from the equation of whose lives matter, and then fail to acknowledge that it came from somewhere, you further a legacy of erasing Black lives and Black contributions from our movement legacy. And consider whether when dropping the "Black" you are, intentionally or unintentionally, erasing Black folks from the conversation or homogenizing very different experiences. The legacy and prevalence of anti-Black racism and heteropatriarchy is a linchpin holding together this unsustainable economy. And that's not an accidental analogy.

In 2014, heteropatriarchy and anti-Black racism within our movement is real and felt. It's killing us, and it's killing our potential to build power for transformative social change. When you adopt the work of queer women of color, don't name or recognize it, and promote it as if it has no history of its own, such actions are problematic. When I use Assata Shakur's powerful demand in my organizing work, I always begin by sharing where it comes from, sharing about Assata's significance to the Black Liberation Movement, what its political purpose and message is, and why it's important in our context.

THE APPROPRIATION OF BLACK STRUGGLE

When you adopt Black Lives Matter and transform it into something else (if you feel you really need to do that—see the preceding arguments not to), it's appropriate politically to credit the lineage from which your adapted work derived. It's important that we work together to build and acknowledge the legacy of Black contributions to the struggle for human rights. If you adapt Black Lives Matter, use the opportunity to talk about its inception and political framing. Lift up Black lives as an opportunity to connect struggles across race, class, gender, nationality, sexuality, and disability.

And, perhaps more importantly, when Black people cry out in defense of our lives, which are uniquely, systematically, and savagely targeted by the state, we are asking you, our family, to stand with us in affirming Black lives. Not just all lives. Black lives. Please do not change the conversation by talking about how your life matters, too. It does, but we need less watered-down unity and more active solidarities with us, Black people, unwaveringly, in defense of our humanity. Our collective futures depend on it.

NOTE
    1. Black Lives Matter is a chapter-based national organization working for the validity of Black life. They are working to (re)build the Black liberation movement. See the open letter on the movement's website, at http://blacklivesmatter.com/herstory.

Criminological Theory Through the Feminist Lens

Stephanie Scott-Snyder

Theories of Crime

"What we look for most in the female is femininity, and when we find the opposite in her, we must conclude as a rule that there must be some anomaly."

—Cesare Lombroso (as cited in McLaughlin & Muncie, 2013, p. 201)

Experts agree that the gender gap in crime is universal: Women are less likely than men to engage in criminal activity. However, until recently gender-based experiences were largely ignored with regard to their impact on the development of female deviance (Belknap & Holzinger, 1998). Criminologists initially sought to develop a general theory of crime with which to explain all criminal behavior, but this line of thinking had significant shortcomings. This type of one-size-fits-all approach was based on an assessment of male-perpetrated crime and assumed that female offending was the same or similar. Thus, it essentially treated female crime as an offshoot of male crime. In other words, it overlooked the complex psychological, relational, and situational dynamics experienced by women as pertinent to the phenomenon of female offending (Mazerolle, 2008).

Gender figures prominently into discussions about female-perpetrated crime, both as a critical factor against which to assess existing theories about offending and with which to pursue new knowledge and research in an effort to expand the depth of data on gender-specific philosophies. Currently, generalist psychological, sociological, and biological theories of crime exist. While some of these have a masculine focus, others specifically address gender differences. The utility of other models does not differ based on gender, and those models are therefore considered gender neutral. In order to consider the relevance of various perspectives with regard to patterns of female offending, we must challenge our conceptualization of criminal behavior as a masculine activity and view crime committed by women through a feminist lens.

Feminist theory seeks to identify the impact of gender inequality through the application of related philosophies that hold that gender and its associated attitudes and behaviors (i.e., masculinity and femininity) are central to the organization of human interaction, including offending, victimization, and adjudicative processing. These beliefs recognize the marginalization of female offenders as a result of overarching patriarchal structures and compel the reshaping of generalist theories of crime to be inclusive of women (Renzetti, 2009). Following is an examination of several gender-neutral, gender-specific, and feminist models that seek to explain the causes of crime, as well as an analysis of their applicability to female offending.

Sociological Perspectives

Sociological theories of deviance explain crime as a result of societal influence.

Strain Theory

Strain theories are perspectives that view negative emotionality (referred to as "strain") as a key predictor of criminal behavior.

The most prevalent of these models identify the types of strains most likely to result in criminal behavior, explain the relationship between strain and crime, and describe the factors that ultimately lead an individual to use antisocial behavior as a coping mechanism. All such theories acknowledge that only a small portion of strained persons resort to crime (Agnew & Scheuerman, 2015).

According to Merton's classic strain theory (1938), society pressures people to achieve certain financial goals. Individuals lacking the means with which to do so experience a strain (i.e., the uncomfortable disparity between actual achievement and society's expectations). Some of these people respond by committing crimes to ease the negative feelings resulting from the strain.

The classic strain model has been criticized for being classist and androcentric. Many theorists argue that crime can result from the inability to achieve a wide range of aspirations—not just financial success. Additionally, attempts to revise the theory acknowledge that focusing on poverty as an explanation for crime largely ignores the fact that "females constitute the most impoverished group of every Western society, yet females commit by far the least crime" (Faith, 1993).

In response, Robert Agnew developed general strain theory (GST) in 1992, which has since become a principal theory of crime. GST focuses on a wide array of strains, including the inability to accomplish various goals, the loss of assets or possessions, and adverse treatment by others. Strain triggers negative feelings such as frustration, anger, and depression, which, in turn, create the need for the sufferer to ease his or her emotional distress. While there are myriad legitimate and prosocial coping mechanisms available to some individuals, others who lack such resources utilize unhealthy coping strategies, such as engaging in criminal or delinquent behavior. In this way, crime is used to reduce or escape the negative impact of strain. For example, someone who is chronically unemployed may steal or sell drugs to get money, physically aggress against a boss who fired him or her, or abuse drugs as a way of self-medicating. Research supports the idea that the strains identified by GST increase the likelihood of crime (Agnew & Scheuerman, 2015).

Multiple studies propose that general strain theory helps to explain gender disparities in crime. According to Baron (2004), anger is a significant predictor of a vast array of criminal behaviors, ranging from violence to property crimes. Although strain triggers anger in both males and females, females are more likely to experience concurrent negative emotions such as guilt, disappointment, fear, worthlessness, and depression (Broidy, 2001; Ngo & Paternoster, 2013). Depression appears to be more closely related to strains in females than in males; however, males experiencing depression (as a result of strain) are more likely to offend than are their female counterparts (Ostrowsky & Messner, 2005). Additionally, the depression caused by strain in girls predicts suicidal thoughts, regular alcohol use, running away, and violent offenses, but is related to suicidal ideation alone among boys (Kaufman, 2009).

The sources of strain also appear to vary by gender. Girls report more psychological, physical, and sexual abuse and experience more strain surrounding close relationships, while boys experience more stress about external achievement (i.e., material success). Walker and Bright (2009) add that there is a correlation between the strain caused by disrespect and subsequent humiliation and the respondent's use of aggression to regain stature (i.e., "masculinity"). They believe that this accounts for the contradiction between individuals with apparent low self-esteem who exhibit high levels of aggression. Although the researchers do not specify gender differences in this assertion, this perspective is useful for the examination of the connection between humiliation, anger, and violence in females (Belknap, 2015).

Differential Association Theory

Unlike GST, differential association theory (DAT) views deviance from a learning standpoint. DAT proposes that criminal behavior is learned via social interaction. In other words, would-be offenders learn (and replicate) the values, attitudes, methods, and motivations relating to criminal activity. Although DAT itself does not specifically address female offending, the feminist perspective recognizes DAT as positively contributing to the examination of gender differences in delinquency. For example, the social and familial constraints (curfew, expectations to stay close to home, and overall less freedom) imposed on girls, in combination with the fact that girls are more likely to be disciplined for minor infractions and sexual experimentation, may account for the fact they commit relatively fewer crimes as compared with boys. In other words, the gender gap in crime may be explained (at least in part) by the differential opportunities to learn criminal behavior. This significant difference in socialization is thought to result in different (i.e., gendered) behaviors (Hoffman-Bustamante, 1973). It follows, then, that the increase in girls' delinquency rates in recent years may be a result of the increased freedoms experienced by females. According to Cressey (1964), greater equality between the sexes is likely to lower gender distinctions in crime.

Social Control Theory

Social control theory (SCT) stipulates that people engage in criminal behavior when their bond to society has weakened and therefore social constraints have diminished. SCT, developed by Travis Hirschi (1969) and originally called social bond theory (SBT), identifies four categories of social bonds that impose restrictions on people's behaviors: attachment, commitment, involvement, and belief. The theory specifies that an individual's likelihood to offend is related to his or her ties to one of the following: conventional people such as parents, conventional institutions and/or behaviors in his or her employment or recreation, and societal rules (norms) (Belknap, 2015).

Gottfredson and Hirschi (1990) shifted the emphasis from social control to self-control in *A General Theory of Crime*, thus advancing the notion that self-control interacts with criminal opportunity to account for delinquency. That is, people with access to opportunities for offending *and* low self-control are more likely to commit crimes. While the general theory of crime (GTC) suggests that gender disparities result from how the aforementioned characteristics are related to self-control (and social control), it has been widely critiqued for ignoring violence against women, research on gender divisions within families, the role of power/control as it relates to crime, and how social and self-control might interact (Taylor, 2001).

Building on SCT, power control theory (PCT) is one of the few models to explicitly incorporate gender: "A key premise . . . is that positions of power in the workplace are translated into power relations in the household and that the latter, in turn, influence the gender-determined control of adolescents, their preferences for risk-taking, and the patterning of gender and delinquency" (Hagan, Simpson, & Gillis, 1987, p. 812). To further support this hypothesis, research reveals that greater gender differences in delinquency are more prevalent in patriarchal homes (i.e., where the mother assumes a lower status than the father), than in egalitarian homes (i.e., where both parents are equal or the mother is the only parental figure) (Hagan, Gillis, & Simpson, 1985). Therefore, in a home where sexism is not woven into the parents' relationship, there should theoretically be a lower instance of gender differences in the children's behaviors. These findings submit that the power constellation in the parents' relationship specifically influences daughters' potential for engaging in delinquent behavior (Belknap, 2015).

Biological Theories

Biological theories assert that there is a direct correlation between biological risk factors and criminal behavior. In fact, some early researchers believed that a link existed between physique and personality. Caesar Lombroso, often regarded as the father of criminology, held that criminality was an inborn trait and that offenders could be identified based solely on their physical appearance (Bartol & Bartol, 2008).

Twins, Adoption, and Criminal Behavior

Twin studies have been conducted to determine the heritability of criminality. Presumably, if biology is the key determinant of personality and behavior, identical twins should be carbon copies of one another because they share the same genes. Research reveals that identical twins *do* share more personality and cognitive traits than do fraternal twins. However, identical twins with varying environmental experiences (e.g., different prenatal/chorionic environments [Rhee & Waldman, 2002], separate homes, varying peer groups, etc.) go on to engage in different behaviors and to have different criminal outcomes, suggesting that environment can "turn on" or "turn off" the genetic influences at different developmental stages. Studies indicate that some combinations of genes do appear to put certain children at risk for engaging in antisocial behavior, but the interaction of that biological risk with the environment is what plays a critical role in whether said criminal behavior will come to pass. Overall, the research supports the heritability of nonviolent crime, but does not favor the same genetic emphasis for violent offending (Bartol & Bartol, 2008).

The influence of biology as compared with environment has also been examined through the use of adoption studies. A review of Danish records specifically focused on the relationship between the criminality of sons and that of their fathers, both biological and adoptive, thus excluding mothers and daughters from the discussion. The researchers found that when the biological father had a criminal history and the adoptive father had none, 22% of adopted sons later went on to have a criminal record. In cases where the biological father had no arrest record, but the adoptive father did, 11.5% of adopted sons engaged in criminal behavior. However, when both the biological and adoptive fathers were offenders, the adopted son's risk of pursuing criminal activity greatly increased. Thus, the researchers determined that although environmental factors do play a role in the development of criminal behavior, genetics do appear to exert an undeniably strong influence (Hutchings & Mednick, 1975).

A more comprehensive and inclusive study involving more than 14,000 European adoptees evaluated the criminal records of biological and adoptive parents and revealed a significant relationship between the criminality of both male and female adoptees and their biological parents. Specifically, if either biological parent had been convicted of a crime, the child exhibited a higher risk of engaging in criminal activity; this risk was especially strong for male adoptees who were chronic offenders. Perhaps unexpectedly, there was no indication that the type of crime committed by the biological parent had any impact on the nature of the offense committed by their biological child. Furthermore, there was no evidence that the children had any knowledge of their parents' offense histories (Mednick, Gabrielli, & Hutchings, 1984, 1987). As a result, Gabrielli and Mednick (1983) stated, "It is reasonable . . . to conclude that some people inherit biological characteristics which permit them to be antisocial more readily than others" (p. 63).

In Utero Experiences/Birth Complications

In addition to genetic markers, certain in utero experiences, including exposure to toxic substances such as opiates and methadone, can put children at risk for behavioral problems later in life. Additionally, fetal exposure to alcohol can cause serious complications. Lead poisoning before and after birth (from hand-to-mouth behavior) is also associated with the development of conduct problems. Although lead paint is not common in many homes today, this continues to be an issue in lower-income areas (Dodge & Pettit, 2003).

Additionally, birth complications, especially when combined with psychosocial risks (e.g., maternal rejection, marital discord, an absentee father, parental mental illness) can lead to antisocial behavior (Raine, Brennan, & Mednick, 1997). However, pregnancy and/or birth complications alone do not to trigger violence or criminality (Bartol & Bartol, 2008). Neurological dysfunction resulting from deficient brain development, on the other hand, is correlated with serious and violent offending (Ishikawa & Raine, 2004). This is especially true if the dysfunction affects the frontal lobe of the brain, which is responsible for the executive functions of organized thought, planning, and self-regulation.

Trait Theory

Trait theorists posit that people's personality traits are inborn and remain constant across time, place, and situation. According to Eysenck (1977, 1996; Eysenck & Gudjonsson, 1989), criminal behavior is the result of an interaction between environment and the characteristics of an individual's nervous system. Therefore, to understand an offender's specific behavior, one must examine his or her neurophysiological composition *and* his or her unique socialization history. Eysenck proposed that various combinations of neurobiological, environmental, and personality elements result in different types of crime (Eysenck & Eysenck, 1970) and that criminal behavior cannot be understood in terms of either heredity *or* environment alone (Eysenck, 1973).

Although Eysenck (1996) did not believe that people are born criminal, his theory places significant weight on a genetic predisposition toward antisocial behavior, as he opined that some individuals are born with nervous system characteristics that predispose them to engage in criminal activity: "It is not crime itself or criminality that is innate; it is certain peculiarities of the central and autonomic nervous system that react with the environment, with upbringing, and many other environment factors to increase the probability that a given person would act in a certain antisocial manner" (Eysenck & Gudjonsson, 1989, p. 7).

According to Eysenck, there are four higher-order factors of personality: general intelligence, extraversion, neuroticism, and psychoticism, all of which describe temperament. Extraversion and neuroticism are the core concepts of the theory. The extraversion dimension reflects the basic functions of the central nervous system (CNS) and is a continuum representing an intensifying need for stimulation. At one end of the spectrum are extroverts who have a high need for excitement and stimulation-seeking and at the other end are introverts who do not have such needs. Eysenck (1967) believed that people differed along this axis due to genetic variations in their CNS and cortical arousal. Because extraverts get bored more easily, consistently seek stimulation, and have a more intense need for excitement, they are more likely to engage in behavior that is against the law. They require greater levels of excitement/stimulation to feel aroused and thus satisfied (Bartol & Bartol, 2008).

Another core concept is neuroticism or emotionality, which reflects the biological predisposition to respond physiologically to stressful events. A person high on this scale has intense reactions and is likely to be moody, sensitive, and anxious even in low-stress environments. The neuroticism–stable axis deals with innate differences in the autonomic nervous system. Neurotics have an overactive sympathetic nervous system, so they engage the "fight-or-flight" response rapidly; they become emotional quickly and maintain that state for more considerable periods of time than do their stable counterparts. In contrast, stables have an underactive sympathetic nervous system and an overactive parasympathetic nervous system (Bartol & Bartol, 2008).

Psychoticism is the final dimension developed by Eysenck and is most similar to primary psychopathy. It is characterized by cruelty, callousness, lack of emotionality, an attraction to the unusual, disregard for danger, and a dislike of other people. Psychotics are typically hostile and mean-spirited; they enjoy lying and "getting one over" on others. While no neurophysiological mechanism has been identified to explain the development of this trait, it is believed that high levels of testosterone, in combination with low levels of the enzyme monoamine oxidase, along with minimal serotonin, may play a role (Bartol & Bartol, 2008).

Feminist Theories

Feminist theories of crime are a group of related ideas that view the social construct of gender as not only a central organizing feature of social life, but also of both victimization and offending. At the root of these philosophies is the idea that women must not be treated as a homogeneous group. Rather, it is critical to acknowledge each individual's unique set of circumstances (e.g., social strata, privilege, race, culture, victimization history, age, sexuality, etc.) and how these elements shape each woman's experience with criminality (Renzetti, Goodstein, & Miller, 2006). Moreover, feminist theories maintain that because of the patriarchal and sexist nature of the world in which we live, females of all ages have been marginalized not only in society, but also as research subjects; therefore, the feminist literature is in its infancy. This in and of itself creates a plethora of issues, including relatively few female offenders having been used as research subjects (i.e., small sample sizes or case study research design), and thus the inability to generalize from the findings to the larger population of female offenders. In other words, the lack of attention that has been paid to studying female-perpetrated crime has resulted in limitations when attempting to extrapolate larger meaning from the current data.

Masculinization and Opportunity Theories

In its inception, masculinization theory was a groundbreaking feminist viewpoint developed by Freda Adler (1975) in her book *Sisters in Crime*. She hypothesized that women's participation in liberation movements changed their roles in the family and in the workplace as they slowly transformed from submissive and passive to independent, assertive, and aggressive members of society. As a result, widespread changes in socialization began to occur and women underwent a "masculinization" process. In other words, as women fought for the same rights as men, they started to develop personality characteristics and means of interacting that were previously perceived as masculine.

According to Adler, this masculinization process was highlighted by criminal behavior in the 1970s. At the time, although men committed the majority of criminal acts, the female crime rate in the United States was rising faster. Not only were women engaging in more criminal activity, but the nature of their crimes was also becoming more violent—women were committing traditionally male crimes. As women became more progressive in their thinking and approach to the social and professional world with which they interacted, they began to integrate "masculine" characteristics into their personalities: aggressiveness, pushiness, stubbornness, etc., and they began to use crime as a means with which to achieve their goals. As a result of masculinization, women's rates of property and violent offenses increased (Small, 2000).

While masculinization theory perhaps offers a viable explanation for the pattern and trends of female offending in first-world nations, it falls short in that it is not inclusive of developing countries where women have far fewer rights than their male counterparts. It has been criticized by feminist scholars because it is based on a male-centric viewpoint (Islam, Banarjee, & Khatun, 2014).

Somewhat similar to masculinization theory is opportunity theory. Coined by Rita Simon (1976), this perspective asserts that males are more criminally active because they have greater access to social and professional opportunities than do women. Therefore, it stands to reason that if women's opportunities were to increase, so would their criminal behavior—or at least certain types of it. For instance, if women had more opportunities to become employed, they would also have more opportunities to engage in employment-related offenses (e.g., embezzlement, fraud, etc.). However, where this theory differs from masculinization theory is that it holds that one can logically assume that as women become financially independent, their rates of violent crime would decline, as most such offenses are committed against spouses:

> As women feel more liberated physically, emotionally, and legally, and are less subjected to male power, their frustrations and anger decrease . . . [which results] in a decline in their desire to kill the usual objects of their anger of frustration: their husbands, lovers, and other men upon whom they are dependent, but insecure. (Simon, 1975, p. 40)

Overall, opportunity theory predicts that as women's opportunities increase, so will their propensity to commit white-collar crimes (e.g., larceny/theft, fraud, forgery, etc.), but their violent crime will decrease. As with masculinization theory, opportunity theory has been criticized for its inability to be applied in the global context.

Marginalization and Crime

Viewing female offending from the perspective of the marginalization of women has garnered significant support. Proponents of economic marginalization acknowledge that simply because women have more access to education or to the labor force does not necessarily mean improved financial status (and stability) for the vast array of women (Chesney-Lind, 1997). There is *still* a pay differential between men and women hired into the same position, with the *average* woman's salary being only 78% of her male colleague's (O'Brien, 2015). According to the economic marginalization perspective, female-perpetrated crime is strongly associated with unemployment, underemployment, inadequate welfare support, and an increase in the number of single female households with multiple children (Small, 2000). These conditions predispose women to commit crimes due to financial necessity—and these factors continue to be an issue today.

However, the marginalization of women is not restricted to the area of economics. From a young age, girls are bombarded with the message that they are peripheral objects in a man's world: not as good as men, not equal to men, and frighteningly vulnerable. Victimization of females of all ages (e.g., trafficking, molestation, sexual torture, domestic abuse, etc.) at the hands of males is widespread. As it relates to crime and deviance, this social marginalization and exploitation of females predisposes them to not only engage in criminal activity, but also to turn to drugs in order to self-medicate as a result of the (often unresolved) trauma (Chesney-Lind & Sheldon, 2014).

The Relationship Between Victimization and Offending. Girls are abused more frequently than boys (Laidler & Hunt, 2001) and have typically endured abuse in at least one sphere (physical, sexual, emotional) prior to the commission of their first offense (Lake, 1993). In a survey of justice-involved girls in California, 92% of respondents reported a history of abuse (Langton & Piquero, 2007).

Research underscores the concept that childhood abuse is a precursor to violence for some females, with one in four violent girls having endured sexual abuse as opposed to one in 10 nonviolent girls (Laub & Sampson, 1993). Why, then, do some female victims of abuse develop deviant and violent behavioral patterns while others do not? While abuse and exposure to trauma as well as other stressors are irrefutably connected with subsequent conduct problems (Lauritsen, 1993), some theorists suggest that dysfunction in violent female offenders' coping mechanisms may intensify the adverse effects of childhood trauma and victimization (Li, 1999). That is, violent female offenders have not only been victimized at higher rates than their nonviolent counterparts, but they also tend to lack adequate coping skills with which to manage various stressors, including past trauma (Loeber, 1996).

Cycle of Violence. The cycle of violence theory builds on the notion that victimization and offending are correlated, and it is perhaps one of the most useful perspectives regarding the development of delinquency in girls and women. According to Widom (1998), a history of childhood victimization "increases the likelihood of delinquency, adult criminality and violent criminal behaviour" (p. 226). Her theory stipulates that childhood maltreatment is a substantial risk factor for subsequent offending. This is critical to viewing criminal behavior through the feminist lens because of the fact that females are abused at much higher rates than males. Therefore, it assists us in understanding one of the unique pathways to crime for women.

Widom's (1998) research indicates that individuals who have endured physical or sexual abuse or neglect as children are nearly twice as likely to be arrested for violent offenses than are same-aged individuals (of the same race and from the same neighborhood) who have not been abused. In fact, people who have experienced childhood sexual abuse in tandem with either physical abuse or neglect are at the greatest risk for running away (considered a juvenile status offense), and victims of child sexual abuse are much more likely to be arrested for prostitution than nonvictimized persons (Belknap, 2015).

Widom's (1998) research implies that maltreated children engage in criminal behavior at an earlier age, are convicted more often, are more likely to reoffend, and are at a greater risk to become habitual offenders than are children who are not abused. Widom (1998) concludes that "childhood victimization significantly increases a person's risk of arrest as follows: by 59% as a juvenile, by 27% as an adult, and by 29% for a violent crime" (p. 226).

Perhaps one of the most comprehensive theories about the development of deviant behavior is Beth Richie's (1996) pathways to crime (for battered women). Through a host of interviews, Richie developed a theory of gender entrapment in order to understand the relationship between intimate partner violence, the cultural concept of gender identity, and female offending. Through her work, Richie was able to identify six pathways to crime: three for African American battered women, two pertaining to African American and Caucasian battered women, and one specific to African American and Caucasian battered women in addition to African American nonbattered women (see Table 2.1 on the next page).

Conclusion

As part of an effort to develop a general theory of crime, criminologists initially conceptualized female offending as an offshoot of male-perpetrated crime. However, this hypothesis was vastly flawed, and subsequently a multitude of theoretical perspectives emerged (e.g., psychological, sociological, biological, developmental), each offering explanations about the etiology of antisocial behavior. While many of these theories were sound and could be applied to female offending, they were initially articulated from a masculine perspective.

It was not until the establishment of feminist theories of criminal behavior that gender was truly recognized as a central feature underlying female offending. Feminist theories explored how the unique nature and impact of gendered experiences, such as the marginalization and victimization of women, can and do shape the types of crimes committed by women.

When analyzing the cases in this book or in society at large, it is common to find that several theories are relevant to the same offender. Individuals who engage in serious criminal behavior often present with numerous risk factors that fall into multiple domains.

TABLE 2.1 Women's Pathways to Crime

Pathways Correlated with African American Battered Women	
Women held hostage	This trajectory involves women whose batterers use violence to isolate them and/or hold them hostage. These women are often charged for the deaths of their own children, when caused by the abuser.
Association and projection	This pathway represents those women who violently aggress against men *other* than their batterer. Their crimes are symbolic revenge, and their victims serve as a proxy for their abusers.
Poverty	As economic abuse and hardship are intertwined with domestic violence, women in this category often commit property or other financially motivated offenses (e.g., robbery, theft, forgery, receiving stolen property, burglary, etc.).
Pathways Correlated with *Both* African American and Caucasian Battered Women	
Sexual exploitation	These women are often arrested for prostitution-related offenses after having been forced or coerced to engage in illegal sex work by their abusers.
Fighting back	This pathway involves battered women who commit criminal acts such as arson or assault during an attack; they view their behavior as self-defense.
Pathway Correlated with African American and Caucasian Battered Women *and* Nonbattered African American Women	
Addiction	This pathway takes various shapes. For African American women who are battered, drug use typically follows an abusive episode and is a way for them to emotionally reconnect with the abuser. For African American women who are not abused, drug use is more voluntary. For Caucasian battered women, selling drugs may be a way to achieve financial independence and ultimately the ability to leave the batterer.

Source: Adapted from Richie (1996).

When those offenders are women, those precipitating risks often coincide with gendered events, thus overlapping feminist theories. That is not to say that a biological risk (e.g., exposure to drugs in utero) condemns someone to a future of crime. However, when that risk is combined with a developmental risk, such as insecure attachment, and a gendered risk, such as sexual violence, those multidimensional pressures work together to increase the likelihood of offending.

La Prieta

Gloria Anzaldua

Anzaldúa began working on "La Prieta" in 1979 and hurried to finish it in time for the publication of *This Bridge Called My Back* in 1981. This essay, or autohistoria, includes important autobiographical information about Anzaldúa: her early menstruation and her subsequent sense of alienation from family and friends, her mugging in 1974, and her hysterectomy and near-death experience in 1980. Like the piece that follows, with its blurring of conventional gender roles and critique of heterosexuality, "La Prieta" also points to Anzaldúa's formative role in queer theory, her challenge to conventional views of reality, and an early version of her spiritual activism.

La Prieta

When I was born, Mamagrande Locha inspected my buttocks looking for the dark blotch, the sign of indio, or worse, of mulatto blood. My grandmother (Spanish, part German, the hint of royalty lying just beneath the surface of her fair skin, blue eyes, and the coils of her once blond hair) would brag that her family was one of the first to settle in the range country of south Texas.

Too bad mi'jita* was morena, *muy prieta*, so dark and different from her own fair-skinned children. But she loved mi'jita anyway. What I lacked in whiteness, I had in smartness. But it was too bad I was dark like an Indian.

"Don't go out in the sun," my mother would tell me when I wanted to play outside. "If you get any darker, they'll mistake you for an Indian. And don't get dirt on your clothes. You don't want people to say you're a dirty Mexican." It never dawned on her that, though sixth-generation American, we were still Mexican and that all Mexicans are part Indian. I passed my adolescence combatting her incessant orders to bathe my body, scrub the floors and cupboards, clean the windows and the walls.

And as we'd get into the back of the "patrón's" truck that would take us to the fields, she'd ask, "Where's your gorra (sunbonnet)?" La gorra—rim held firm by slats of cardboard, neck flounce flowing over my shoulders—made me feel like a horse with blinders, a member of the French Foreign Legion, or a nun bowed down by her wimple. One day in the middle of the cotton field, I threw the gorra away and donned a sombrero. Though it didn't keep out the Texas 110 degree sun as well as the bonnet, I could now see in all directions, feel the breeze, dry the sweat on my neck.

When I began writing this essay, nearly two years ago, the wind I was

---

* Shortened form of "mi hijita."

accustomed to suddenly turned into a hurricane. It opened the door to the old images that haunt me, the old ghosts and all the old wounds. Each image a sword that cuts through me, each word a test. Terrified, I shelved the rough draft of this essay for a year.

I was terrified because in this writing I must be hard on people of color who are the oppressed victims. I am still afraid because I will have to call us on a lot of shit like our own racism, our fear of women and sexuality. One of my biggest fears is that of betraying myself, of consuming myself with self-castigation, of not being able to unseat the guilt that has ridden on my back for years.

> These my two hands
> quick to slap my face
> before others could slap it[1]

But above all, I am terrified of making my mother the villain in my life rather than showing how she has been a victim. Will I be betraying her in this essay for her early disloyalty to me?

With terror as my companion, I dip into my life and begin work on myself. Where did it begin, the pain, the images that haunt me?

Images That Haunt Me

When I was three months old tiny pink spots began appearing on my diaper. "She's a throwback to the Eskimo," the doctor told my mother. "Eskimo girl children get their periods early." At seven I had budding breasts. My mother would wrap them in tight cotton girdles so the kids at school would not think them strange beside their own flat brown mole nipples. My mother would pin onto my panties a folded piece of rag. "Keep your legs shut, Prieta." This, the deep dark secret between us, her punishment for having fucked before the wedding ceremony, my punishment for being born. And when she got mad at me she would yell, "He batallado más contigo que con todos los demás y no lo agradeces!" (I've taken more care with you than I have with all the others and you're not even grateful.) My sister started suspecting our secret—that there was something "wrong" with me. How much can you hide from a sister you've slept with in the same bed since infancy?[†]

[†] Anzaldúa refers here to a hormonal imbalance which caused her to menstruate from infancy, threw her into adolescence in early childhood, and triggered horrendously painful periods each month. See her *Interviews/Entrevistas* for more on this topic.

What my mother wanted in return for having birthed me and for nurturing me was that I submit to her without rebellion. Was this a survival skill she was trying to teach me? She objected not so much to my disobedience but to my questioning her right to demand obedience from me. Mixed with this power struggle was her guilt at having borne a child who was marked "con la seña," thinking she had made me a victim of her sin. In her eyes and in the eyes of others I saw myself reflected as "strange," "abnormal," "QUEER." I saw no other reflection. Helpless to change that image, I retreated into books and solitude and kept away from others.

The whole time growing up I felt that I was not of this earth. An alien from another planet—I'd been dropped on my mother's lap. But for what purpose? One day when I was about seven or eight, my father dropped on my lap a 25¢ pocket western, the only type of book he could pick up at a drugstore. The act of reading forever changed me. In the westerns I read, the house servants, the villains, and the cantineras (prostitutes) were all Mexicans. But I knew that the first cowboys (vaqueros) were Mexicans, that in Texas we outnumbered the Anglos, that my grandmother's ranch lands had been ripped off by the greedy Anglo. Yet in the pages of these books, the Mexican and Indian were vermin. The racism I would later recognize in my school teachers and never be able to ignore again I found in that first western I read.

My father dying, his aorta bursting while he was driving, the truck turning over, his body thrown out, the truck falling on his face. Blood on the pavement. His death occurred just as I entered puberty. It irrevocably shattered the myth that there existed a male figure to look after me. How could my strong, good, beautiful, god-like father be killed? How stupid and careless of god. What if chance and circumstance and accident ruled? I lost my father, god, and my innocence all in one bloody blow.

Every 24 days, raging fevers cooked my brain. Full flowing periods accompanied cramps, tonsillitis, and 105° fevers. Every month a trip to the doctors. "It's all in your head," they would say. "When you get older and get married and have children the pain will stop." A monotonous litany from the men in white all through my teens.

The bloodshed on the highway had robbed my adolescence from me like the blood on my diaper had robbed childhood from me. And into my hands unknowingly I took the transformation of my own being.

> Nobody's going to save you.
> No one's going to cut you down

cut the thorns around you.
No one's going to storm
the castle walls nor
kiss awake your birth,
climb down your hair,
nor mount you
onto the white steed.

There is no one who
will feed the yearning.
Face it. You will have
to do, do it yourself.[2]

My father dead, my mother and I turned to each other. Hadn't we grown
together? We were like sisters—she was 16 when she gave birth to me.

Though she loved me she would only show it covertly—in the tone of her
voice, in a look. Not so with my brothers—there it was visible for all the
world to see. They were male and surrogate husbands, legitimate receivers
of her power. Her allegiance was and is to her male children, not to the
female.

Seeing my mother turn to my brothers for protection, for guidance—a
mock act. She and I both knew she wouldn't be getting any from them.
Like most men they didn't have it to give, instead needed to get it from
women. I resented the fact that it was OK for my brothers to touch and
kiss and flirt with her, but not for my sister and me. Resenting the fact that
physical intimacy between women was taboo, dirty.

Yet she could not discount me. "Machona-india ladina" (masculine-wild
Indian), she would call me because I did not act like a nice little Chicanita
is supposed to act: later, in the same breath she would praise and blame
me, often for the same thing—being a tomboy and wearing boots, being
unafraid of snakes or knives, showing my contempt for women's roles,
leaving home to go to college, not settling down and getting married,
being a politica, siding with the Farmworkers. Yet while she would try to
correct my more aggressive moods, my mother was secretly proud of my
"waywardness." (Something she will never admit.) Proud that I'd worked
myself through school. Secretly proud of my paintings, of my writing,
though all the while complaining because I made no money out of it.

Vergüenza (Shame)

. . . being afraid that my friends would see my momma, would know that she was loud—her voice penetrated every corner. Always when we came into a room everyone looked up. I didn't want my friends to hear her brag about her children. I was afraid she would blurt out some secret, would criticize me in public. She always embarrassed me by telling everyone that I liked to lie in bed reading and wouldn't help her with the housework.

. . . eating at school out of sacks, hiding our "lonches"‡ papas con chorizo behind cupped hands and bowed heads, gobbling them up before the other kids could see. Guilt lay folded in the tortilla. The Anglo kids laughing—calling us "tortilleros," the Mexican kids taking up the word and using it as a club with which to hit each other. My brothers, sister, and I started bringing white bread sandwiches to school. After a while we stopped taking our lunch altogether.

There is no beauty in poverty, in my mother being able to give only one of her children lunch money. (We all agreed it should go to Nune, he was growing fast and was always hungry.) It was not very romantic for my sister and me to wear the dresses and panties my mother made us out of flour sacks because she couldn't afford store-bought ones like the other mothers.

> Well, I'm not ashamed of you anymore, Momma.
>
> My heart, once bent and cracked, once
> ashamed of your China ways.
> Ma, hear me now, tell me your story
> again and again.
> —NELLIE WONG, "From a Heart of Rice Straw,"
> *Dreams of Harrison Railroad Park*

It was not my mother's fault that we were poor, and yet so much of my pain and shame has been with our both betraying each other. But my mother has always been there for me in spite of our differences and emotional gulfs. She has never stopped fighting; she is a survivor. Even now I can hear her arguing with my father over how to raise us, insisting that all decisions be made by both of them. I can hear her crying over the body of

‡ For the English word "lunches."

my dead father. She was 28, had had little schooling, was unskilled, yet her strength was greater than most men's, raising us single-handed.

After my father died, I worked in the fields every weekend and every summer, even when I was a student in college. (We only migrated once when I was seven, journeyed in the back of my father's red truck with two other families to the cotton fields of west Texas. When I missed a few weeks of school, my father decided this should not happen again.)

. . . the planes swooping down on us, the fifty or a hundred of us falling onto the ground, the cloud of insecticide lacerating our eyes, clogging our nostrils. Nor did the corporate farm owners care that there were no toilets in the wide open fields, no bushes to hide behind.

Over the years, the confines of farm and ranch life began to chafe. The traditional role of la mujer was a saddle I did not want to wear. The concepts "passive" and "dutiful" raked my skin like spurs, and "marriage" and "children" set me to bucking faster than rattlesnakes or coyotes. I took to wearing boots and men's jeans and walking about with my head full of visions, hungry for more words and more words. Slowly I unbowed my head, refused my estate, and began to challenge the way things were. But it's taken over thirty years to unlearn the belief instilled in me that white is better than brown—something that some people of color never will unlearn. And it is only now that the hatred of myself, which I spent the greater part of my adolescence cultivating, is turning to love.

La Muerte, the Frozen Snow Queen

I dig a grave, bury my first love, a German Shepherd. Bury the second, third, and fourth dog. The last one retching in the backyard, going into convulsions from insecticide poisoning. I buried him beside the others, five mounds in a row crowned with crosses I'd fashioned from twigs.

No more pets, no more loves—I court death now.

. . . Two years ago on a fine November day in Yosemite Park, I fall on the floor with cramps, severe chills and shaking that go into spasms and near convulsions, then fevers so high my eyes feel like eggs frying. Twelve hours of this. I tell everyone, "It's nothing, don't worry, I'm alright." The first four gynecologists advise a hysterectomy. The fifth, a woman, says wait.

. . . Last March my fibroids conspired with an intestinal tract infection and spawned watermelons in my uterus. The doctor played with his knife. La Chingada ripped open, raped with the white man's wand. My soul in one corner of the hospital ceiling, getting thinner and thinner, telling me to clean up my shit, to release the fears and garbage from the past that are hanging me up. So I take La Muerte's scythe and cut away my arrogance and pride, the emotional depressions I indulge in, the head trips I do on myself and other people. With her scythe I cut the umbilical cord shackling me to the past and to friends and attitudes that drag me down. Strip away—all the way to the bone. Make myself utterly vulnerable.

. . . I can't sleep nights. The mugger said he would come and get me. There was a break in the county jail and I *just know* he is broken out and is coming to get me because I picked up a big rock and chased him, because I got help and caught him. How *dare* he drag me over rocks and twigs, the skin on my knees peeling, how *dare* he lay his hands on my throat, how *dare* he try to choke me to death, how *dare* he try to push me off the bridge to splatter my blood and bones on the rocks twenty feet below. His breath on my face, our eyes only inches apart, our bodies rolling on the ground in an embrace so intimate we could have been mistaken for lovers.

That night terror found me curled up in my bed. I couldn't stop trembling. For months terror came to me at night and never left me. And even now, seven years later, when I'm out in the street after dark and I hear running footsteps behind me, terror finds me again and again.

No more pets, no more loves.

. . . one of my lovers saying I was frigid when he couldn't bring me to orgasm.

. . . bringing home my Peruvian boyfriend and my mother saying she did not want her "Prieta" to have a "mojado" (wetback) for a lover.

. . . my mother and brothers calling me puta when I told them I had lost my virginity and that I'd done it on purpose. My mother and brothers calling me jota (queer) when I told them my friends were gay men and lesbians.

. . . Randy saying, "It's time you stopped being a nun, an ice queen afraid of living." But I did not want to be a snow queen regal with icy smiles and fingernails that ripped her prey ruthlessly. And yet, I knew my being distant, remote, a mountain sleeping under the snow, is what attracted him.

> A woman lies buried under me,
> interred for centuries, presumed dead.
>
> A woman lies buried under me.
> I hear her soft whisper

the rasp of her parchment skin
fighting the folds of her shroud.
Her eyes are pierced by needles
her eyelids, two fluttering moths.[3]

I am always surprised by the image that my white and non-Chicano friends have of me, surprised at how much they *do not* know me, at how I do not allow them to know me. They have substituted the negative picture the white culture has painted of my race with a highly romanticized, idealized image. "You're strong," my friends said, "a mountain of strength."

Though the power may be real, the mythic qualities attached to it keep others from dealing with me as a person and rob me of being able to act out my other selves. Having this "power" doesn't exempt me from being prey in the streets nor does it make my scrambling to survive, to feed myself, easier. To cope with hurt and control my fears, I grew a thick skin. Oh, the many names of power—pride, arrogance, control. I am not the frozen snow queen but a flesh and blood woman with perhaps too loving a heart, one easily hurt.

I'm not invincible, I tell you. My skin's as fragile as a baby's. I'm brittle bones and human, I tell you. I'm a broken arm.

You're a razor's edge, you tell me. Shock them shitless. Be the holocaust. Be the black Kali. Spit in their eye and never cry. Oh broken angel, throw away your cast, mend your wing. Be not a rock but a razor's edge and burn with falling. —Journal Entry, Summer Solstice, 1978.

Who Are My People

I am a wind-swayed bridge, a crossroads inhabited by whirlwinds. Gloria, the facilitator, Gloria, the mediator, straddling the walls between abysses. "Your allegiance is to La Raza, the Chicano movement," say the members of my race. "Your allegiance is to the Third World," say my Black and Asian friends. "Your allegiance is to your gender, to women," say the feminists. Then there's my allegiance to the Gay movement, to the socialist revolution, to the New Age, to magic and the occult. And there's my affinity to literature, to the world of the artist. What am I? *A third world lesbian feminist with Marxist and mystic leanings.* They would chop me up into little fragments and tag each piece with a label.

You say my name is ambivalence? Think of me as Shiva, a many-armed and -legged body with one foot on brown soil, one on white, one in straight society, one in the gay world, the man's world, the women's, one limb in the literary world, another in the working class, the socialist, and the occult worlds. A sort of spider woman hanging by one thin strand of web.

Who, me, confused? Ambivalent? Not so. Only your labels split me.

Years ago, a roommate of mine fighting for gay rights told MAYO, a Chicano organization, that she and the president were gay. They were ostracized. When they left, MAYO fell apart. They, too, being forced to choose between the priorities of race, sexual preference, or gender.

In the streets of this gay mecca, San Francisco, a Black man at a bus stop yells "Hey Faggots, come suck my cock." Randy yells back "You goddamn nigger, I worked in the Civil Rights movement ten years so you could call me names." Guilt gagging in his throat with the word, nigger. . . . a white woman waiting for the J-Church streetcar sees Randy and David kissing and says "You should be ashamed of yourselves. Two grown men—disgusting."

. . . Randy and David running into the house. The hair on the back of my neck rises, something in their voices triggers fear in me. Three Latino men in a car had chased them as they were walking home from work. "Gay boys, faggots," they yelled, throwing a beer bottle. Getting out of their car, knife blades reflect the full moon. . . . Randy and David hitting each other in the hall. Thuds on the wall—the heavy animal sounds.

. . . Randy pounding on my door, one corner of his mouth bleeding, his glasses broken, blind without them, he crying "I'm going to kill him, I'm going to kill the son of a bitch."

The violence against us, the violence within us, aroused like a rabid dog. Adrenaline-filled bodies, we bring home the anger and the violence we meet on the street and turn it against each other. We sic the rabid dog on each other and on ourselves. The black moods of alienation descend, the bridges we've extended out to each other crumble. We put the walls back up between us.

Once again it's faggot-hunting and queer-baiting time in the city. "And on your first anniversary of loving each other," I say to Randy, "and they had to be Latinos," feeling guilt when I look at David. Who is my brother's keeper, I wonder—knowing I have to be, we all have to be. We are all responsible. But who exactly are my people?

I identify as a woman. Whatever insults women insults me.

I identify as gay. Whoever insults gays insults me.

I identify as feminist. Whoever slurs feminism slurs me.

That which is insulted I take as part of me, but there is something too simple about this kind of thinking. Part of the dialectic is missing. What about what I do not identify as?

I have been terrified of writing this essay because I will have to own up to the fact that I do not exclude whites from the list of people I love; two of them happen to be gay males. For the politically correct stance we let color, class, and gender separate us from those who would be kindred spirits. So the walls grow higher, the gulfs between us wider, the silences more profound. There is an enormous contradiction in being a bridge.

Dance To the Beat of Radical Colored Chic

This task—to be a bridge, to be a fucking crossroads for goddess' sake.

During my stint in the Feminist Writers' Guild many white members would ask me why Third World women do not come to FWG meetings and readings. I should have answered, "Because their skins are not as thick as mine, because their fear of encountering racism is greater than mine. They don't enjoy being put down, ignored, not engaged in equal dialogue, being tokens. And, neither do I." Oh, I know, women of color are hot right now and hip. Our afro-rhythms and latin salsas, the beat of our drums is in. White women flock to our parties, dance to the beat of radical colored chic. They come to our readings, take up our cause. I have no objections to this. What I mind is the pseudo-liberal ones who suffer from the white women's burden. Like the monkey in the Sufi story, who upon seeing a fish in the water rushes to rescue it from drowning by carrying it up into the branches of a tree. She takes a missionary role. She attempts to talk for us—what a presumption! This act is a rape of our tongue, and our acquiescence is a complicity to that rape. We women of color have to stop being modern medusas—throats cut, silenced into a mere hissing.

Where Do We Hang The Blame?

The pull between what is and what should be.

Does the root of the sickness lie within ourselves or within our patriarchal institutions? Did our institutions birth and propagate themselves and are we merely their pawns? Do ideas originate in human minds or do they exist in a "no-osphere," a limbo space where ideas originate without our help? Where do we hang the blame for the sickness we see around us—

around our own heads or around the throat of "capitalism," "socialism," "men," "white culture"?

If we do not create these institutions, we certainly perpetuate them through our inadvertent support. What lessons do we learn from the mugger?

Certainly racism is not just a white phenomenon. Whites are the top dogs and they shit on the rest of us every day of our lives. But casting stones is not the solution. Do we hand the oppressor/thug the rocks he throws at us? How often do we people of color place our necks on the chopping block? What are the ways we hold out our wrists to be shackled? Do we gag our own mouths with our "dios lo manda" resignation? How many times before the cock crows do we deny ourselves, shake off our dreams, and trample them into the sand? How many times do we fail to help one another up from the bottom of the stairs? How many times have we let someone else carry our crosses? How still do we stand to be crucified?

It is difficult for me to break free of the Chicano cultural bias into which I was born and raised, and the cultural bias of the Anglo culture that I was brainwashed into adopting. It is easier to repeat the racial patterns and attitudes, especially those of fear and prejudice, that we have inherited than to resist them.

Like a favorite old shoe that no longer fits, we do not let go of our comfortable old selves so that the new self can be worn. We fear our power, fear our feminine selves, fear the strong woman within, especially the black Kali aspect, dark and awesome. Thus we pay homage not to the power inside us but to the power outside us, masculine power, external power.

I see Third World peoples and women not as oppressors but as accomplices to oppression by unwittingly passing on to our children and our friends the oppressor's ideologies. I cannot discount the role I play as accomplice, that we all play as accomplices, for we are not screaming loud enough in protest.

The disease of powerlessness thrives in my body, not just out there in society. And just as the use of gloves, masks, and disinfectants fails to kill this disease, government grants, equal rights opportunity programs, welfare, and food stamps fail to uproot racism, sexism, and homophobia. And tokenism is not the answer. Sharing the pie is not going to work. I had a bite of it once and it almost poisoned me. With mutations of the virus such as these, one cannot isolate the virus and treat it. The whole organism is poisoned.

I stand behind whatever threatens our oppression. I stand behind whatever breaks us out of our bonds, short of killing and maiming. I stand with whatever and whoever breaks us out of our limited views and awakens our atrophied potentials.

How to turn away from the hellish journey that the disease has put me through, the alchemical nights of the soul. Torn limb from limb, knifed, mugged, beaten. My tongue (Spanish) ripped from my mouth, left voiceless. My name stolen from me. My bowels fucked with a surgeon's knife, uterus and ovaries pitched into the trash. Castrated. Set apart from my own kind, isolated. My life-blood sucked out of me by my role as woman nurturer—the last form of cannibalism.

El Mundo Zurdo (the Left-handed World)[4]

The pull between what is and what should be. I believe that by changing ourselves we change the world, that traveling El Mundo Zurdo path is the path of a two-way movement—a going deep into the self and an expanding out into the world, a simultaneous recreation of the self and a reconstruction of society. And yet, I am confused as to how to accomplish this.

I can't discount the fact of the thousands that go to bed hungry every night. The thousands that do numbing shitwork eight hours a day each day of their lives. The thousands that get beaten and killed every day. The millions of women who have been burned at the stake, the millions who have been raped. Where is the justice to this?

I can't reconcile the sight of a battered child with the belief that we choose what happens to us, that we create our own world. I cannot resolve this in myself. I don't know. I can only speculate, try to integrate the experiences that I've had or have been witness to and try to make some sense of why we do violence to each other. In short, I'm trying to create a religion not out there somewhere, but in my gut. I am trying to make peace between what has happened to me, what the world is, and what it should be.

"Growing up I felt that I was an alien from another planet dropped on my mother's lap. But for what purpose?"

The mixture of bloods and affinities, rather than confusing or unbalancing me, has forced me to achieve a kind of equilibrium. Both cultures deny me a place in *their* universe. Between them and among others, I build my own universe, El Mundo Zurdo. I belong to myself and not to any one people.

I walk the tightrope with ease and grace. I span abysses. Blindfolded in the blue air. The sword between my thighs, the blade warm with my flesh. I walk the rope—an acrobat in equipoise, expert at the Balancing Act.

The rational, the patriarchal, and the heterosexual have held sway and legal tender for too long. Third World women, lesbians, feminists, and feminist-oriented men of all colors are banding and bonding together to right that balance. Only *together* can we be a force. I see us as a network of kindred spirits, a kind of family.

We are the queer groups, the people that don't belong anywhere, not in the dominant world nor completely within our own respective cultures. Combined we cover so many oppressions. But the overwhelming oppression is the collective fact that we do not fit, and because we do not fit *we are a threat*. Not all of us have the same oppressions, but we empathize and identify with each other's oppressions. We do not have the same ideology, nor do we derive similar solutions. Some of us are leftists, some of us practitioners of magic. Some of us are both. But these different affinities are not opposed to each other. In El Mundo Zurdo I with my own affinities and my people with theirs can live together and transform the planet.

Notes

1. From my poem, "The Woman Who Lived Forever." All subsequent unacknowledged poems will be from my own writings. [This poem has not been published but can be found in manuscript form in Anzaldúa's archives in the Nettie Lee Benson Latin American Collection, University of Texas, Austin.]

2. From "Letting Go." [A later version of this poem appears in *Borderlands / La Frontera*, 186–88.]

3. From "A Woman Lies Buried Under Me." [This poem has not been published but can be found in manuscript form in Anzaldúa's archives in the Nettie Lee Benson Latin American Collection.]

4. This section consists of notes "Toward a Construction of El Mundo Zurdo," an essay in progress. [This essay has not been published but can be found in Anzaldúa's archives in the Nettie Lee Benson Latin American Collection.]

Unit III. Intimacy and Sexuality: Bodies and Beauty

Postfeminist Sexual Culture
Rosalind Gill

Over the last decade, "porno chic," the "pornification" of society, and the "sexualization of culture" have become major topics of concern in news media, in policy arenas, and in academic study. The notions of "pornification" and "sexualization" capture the growing sense of Western societies as saturated by sexual representations and discourses, and in which pornography has become increasingly influential, permeating mainstream media and contemporary culture. Porn stars have emerged as best-selling authors and celebrities; a "porno chic" aesthetic can be seen in fashion, music videos, and advertising; and practices once associated with the sex industry—for example lap dancing and pole dancing—have become newly respectable, promoted as a regular feature of corporate entertainment or recreational activity. This shift speaks to something more than the idea that "sex has become the big story" (Plummer 1995: 4). As Feona Attwood has noted, it denotes a range of things:

> a contemporary preoccupation with sexual values, practices and identities; the public shift to more permissive sexual attitudes; the proliferation of sexual texts; the emergence of new forms of sexual experience; the apparent breakdown of rules, categories and regulations designed to keep the obscene at bay; [and the] fondness for the scandals, controversies and panics around sex.
>
> (Attwood 2006: 77)

This chapter gives an overview of some of the key feminist perspectives on sexualization, to highlight areas of debate and indicate directions for future research. It is worth noting that debates about the sexualization of culture constitute a complicated and contested terrain, one suffused with strong feelings, and frequently polarized. Too often the field seems distorted by the long shadows of earlier debates. Regarding the "sex wars" or "porn wars" of the early 1980s, Drucilla Cornell (2000) has argued that every feminist was made to take a position or was forcibly allocated one. Unlike academic domains that do not attract such passion, academic writing about sexualization is characterized by heightened emotion and a distinctively "performative" quality in which scholars rhetorically conjure "harm," claim authority, express "concern," present themselves in a favorable light, defend against particular readings of their argument, etc. My own—no less rhetorical but perennially uncomfortable—position here, as someone who is neither anti-sex nor anti-porn, is not sanguine or celebratory about the modes of sexism (and racism, classism, and heteronormativity) at work in contemporary "sexualized" culture. Sex positive but anti-sexism, I remain suspicious about the rhetorical/performative work—and the epistemic violence—done by such labels; I have consistently advocated complicating polarized positions in the emerging "sexualization wars."

The sexualization of culture?

Anxieties and concerns about sexualization have come to the fore in recent years across several spheres. They can be seen in influential reports from think tanks (e.g. Rush and La Nauze 2006; APA 2007; Fawcett Society 2009), government reports (e.g. Byron 2008; Buckingham *et al.* 2010; Papadopoulos 2010; Bailey 2011); activist campaigns (for example to change the licensing laws for lap dancing clubs), as well as a variety of well-publicized popular books (e.g. Levy 2005; Durham 2009; Levin and Kilbourne 2009). The titles of reports, books, and feature articles signal some of the contours of the anxieties—particularly those concerning children—e.g. "so sexy, so soon" or "too much, too young." Concerns have centered on the direct sexualization of children in, for example, the resurgence of the child beauty pageant, as well as on the persistent interpellation of children in sexual terms, often evidenced by the marketing to younger and younger girls of "sexualized" clothing, such as padded bras and G-string knickers. More broadly, anxieties are expressed about the increasing volume and intensity of "sexualized" material in the media, which leads, it is argued, to a raft of harms for girls and women, including poor attainment at school, depression, low self-esteem, and eating disorders (APA 2007).

Media coverage of these discussions of "sexualization" has been extensive, but the media occupy a contradictory position. They are best thought of in multiple terms as a key site of sexualization, of concerns about sexualization, and, furthermore, of *concerns about concerns* about sexualization. At least in the UK, newspapers are replete with "sexualized" representations (pictures of semi-naked women, "sexy" stories, adverts for telephone sex lines, etc.); they have also been a central location for critical discussions of "sexualization"—with certain newspapers taking the role of "moral guardians," with repeated articles about the dangers of sexualized culture. These are frequently accompanied by multiple pictures of the offending content—as seen in the *Daily Mail*'s outraged coverage of the TV talent show *The X Factor*: the newspaper reproduced several stills from the program's allegedly shocking and inappropriate dance routines—including some which had apparently not even been aired. Newspapers also produce a different kind of article, which I call the "sexualization fatigue think piece." Here journalists adopt a superior, world-weary tone of boredom about the banality of the sexualization debates, and/or worry about the harm of moral panics; they suggest that the elevated public concern about sexualization either distracts from more important issues (e.g. poverty) or lends legitimacy to increased surveillance of the individual or regulation of the media. We should be wary, then, of examining the media only as a site of sexualization—and be aware of its complicated, multiple positionings.

Feminist perspectives on "sexualization"

Different and diverse feminist positions engage with the sexualization of culture. Some contemporary radical feminist arguments are reminiscent of the second-wave anti-pornography perspectives of Andrea Dworkin (1981) and Catherine MacKinnon (e.g. Dworkin and MacKinnon 1988). Sheila Jeffreys's (2009) *The Industrial Vagina* is an impassioned polemic against the "global sex trade" that connects the mainstreaming of pornography to military prostitution, sex tourism, and the trafficking of women and children. Gail Dines (2010) connects the "gonzo" porn that dominates the internet to the wider hypersexualized culture (see also Tankard Reist 2009).

Other—contrasting—third-wave positions build from the sex-positive feminism of the same period (Califia 1994; Juffer 1998; Johnson 2002; Jenkins and Church Gibson 2003) to offer more optimistic views of sexualization grounded in understandings of women not as victims but instead as producers and consumers of "sexual" material—in ways that break significantly with constructions of women as passive and asexual (Lumby 1997; Smith 2007; Attwood 2009). "A whole series of signifiers are linked to promote a new, liberated, contemporary sexuality for women; sex is stylish, a source of physical pleasure, a means of creating identity, a form of body work, self-expression, a quest for individual fulfilment" (Attwood 2006: 86).

A further distinctive feminist perspective explores contemporary sexualization as a postfeminist and neoliberal phenomenon linked to consumerism and discourses of celebrity, choice, and empowerment (Coleman 2008; Gill 2008; Munford 2009; Whitehead and Kurz 2009; Ringrose and Eriksson Barajas 2011). Some see in contemporary sexualized culture not a more feminist sexual future but a turning backwards (Whelehan 2000), a "retro sexism" (Williamson 2003) in which objectifying representations of women are wrapped up in a feisty discourse of fake empowerment (Levy 2005).

None of this latter work sits comfortably in the old "anti-porn" versus "sex positive" binary. Much of it is explicitly pro-sex, but its target of critique is the way in which sexualization, power, and commerce intersect—often at the expense of the possibilities of exploring, experimenting, and celebrating diverse sexualities.

Looking at media portrayals of women, my own work (Gill 2008, 2009a; Harvey and Gill 2011a, 2011b) has charted a shift from "objectification" to "sexual subjectification." Women are no longer depicted as passive sex objects, but hailed as confident, freely choosing, seemingly empowered sexual subjects. I examine the exclusions of this change—only some women (young, slim, attractive) are accorded sexual subjecthood—and the shift in subjectivity it invites/requires. Developing the Foucaultian notion of "technologies of selfhood," I see contemporary sexualized, consumerist, and neoliberal societies as calling forth a new postfeminist feminine subject who is incited to be compulsorily sexy and always "up for it." Given a corresponding shift in the sexual representation of men's bodies in the media, I have also examined how young men respond to the increasingly idealized and eroticized representation of the male body (Gill *et al.* 2000; Gill 2011; see also Evans *et al.* 2010).

These divergent feminist approaches have generated a wide range of debates and points of contestation. Three important areas of tension relate to media influence and audience agency, power and difference, and what can be "done" about sexualization, with media literacy offered as a kind of panacea.

Media influence: beyond victims and agents

Many of the debates about sexualization hinge, in different ways, on an understanding of the effects of a putatively "sexualized" culture, and individuals' capacities to resist, refuse, or resignify its meanings—notions often treated in shorthand as instances of "agency" or "empowerment." Underlying these debates are profoundly different understandings of the media and its influence. On one side is the dominant, US tradition, with its roots in psychology, which sees (sexualized) media as negatively affecting individuals' attitudes, beliefs, and behaviors. Media emerge here as homogeneous, monolithic, and all powerful: *The Media*, rather than a diversity of different media, platforms, genres, and productions, with—presumably—different kinds of representations of girls and young women, and, moreover, in which girls are increasingly involved as active producers, not merely consumers. Such a view can be seen in the APA's Task Force on the Sexualization of Girls (APA 2007); its report on time spent "with the media" made no distinctions between different kinds of media and how they are used, e.g. watching a documentary versus reading a magazine versus playing an online game versus updating a Facebook profile.

At its heart is the notion of media audiences as passive dupes who unquestioningly and uncritically absorb media messages "hypodermically" injected into them. Influence is characterized almost exclusively in terms of "mimicry" and "imitation." For example, Sharon Lamb and Zoë Peterson (2012) ask, "Why do girls imitate sexualized media and how conscious is this imitation?" They speculate on the meanings and pleasures of imitation but do not question the idea that this *is* the fundamental psychological process at issue in girls' engagement with the media. Moreover, when discussed in relation to the media, young women emerge as isolated, atomized, passive individuals, rather than engaged social actors embedded in family, friendship, school, and many other networks. Individuals often are treated as tabulae rasae (who, without the media, presumably would freely go on to develop a "healthy" sexuality). A particularly problematic idea of childhood innocence is frequently mobilized in debates about children and sexualization (e.g. Buckingham 2000; Egan and Hawkes 2008)

A contrasting tradition of research is found in some audience media and cultural studies scholarship (e.g. Radway 1984; Ang 1985; Hermes 1995; Gauntlett and Hill 1999). This research often starts agnostic about the putative intensification of sexualization; it sees the media more positively as offering "tools to think with" (Bragg and Buckingham 2009) rather than as agents of harm. Framed partly as a response to the psychological tradition, this work critiques media effects and presents audiences as active, knowledgeable, sophisticated, and critical users or consumers of media (Buckingham and Bragg 2004; Smith 2007; Jackson and Vares 2011).

David Buckingham and Sara Bragg champion the view that children are not naïve or incompetent consumers but use a range of critical skills and perspectives when interpreting sexual content. Moreover, children's responses to sexual imagery display "a well-developed understanding of how such images are constructed and manipulated," and children and young people are "literate" and "highly critical" consumers (Buckingham and Bragg 2004: 238). This sees children as actively deciding how far to engage with sexualized culture.

Such research is important in exploring the diverse meanings people give to engagements with media and in according proper respect to audiences, particularly children and young people. At times, however, this research can offer overly optimistic readings—seeing autonomy and choice and resistance everywhere. Bragg and Buckingham present young people as "autonomous, calculating and self-regulating entities in control of their own quest for knowledge in relation to sex and sexual material" (2009: 136) and able to make their own decisions, judgments, and choices. These apparently extend even to the "choice" of whether to be a child: "the media are creating new ways of being a child—not corrupting but confronting young people with choices about whether to remain a child or whether and when to enter the 'adult' world of sexual media" (2009: 136). Here, then, "child" becomes simply another discursive identity category, which subjects can choose or choose not to inhabit—as if that choice were fully within their control.

Perhaps reacting against the negative focus on "harms," this research emphasizes both the "pleasures" of sexualized culture and how problematic meanings may be resisted. For example, Holland and Attwood argue that women participating in pole dancing classes "resisted" the idea of objectification and "reworked" traditional indicators of femininity "into experiences of sexual agency and power" (2009: 177).

The difference between this and more "critical" readings may come down to an attitude or affective disposition, a tendency to read optimistically or pessimistically. But it also raises theoretical and methodological concerns, notably the tendency to take at face value interviewees' statements rather than seeing them as themselves performative. Moreover, with important exceptions (e.g. Ang 1985; Walkerdine 1997a, 1997b), the tradition relies on the assumption that respondents are "transparent to themselves"—i.e. able to excavate and lay bare their feelings and influences, as if they were entirely rational unitary subjects. Such a perspective is no more able than is the "effects" tradition to understand the complicated terrain of desire, intimacy, and sexuality. We need new psychosocial perspectives that move beyond the idea of both dupes/victims and autonomous agents, and we need more sophisticated formulations of the complex relationship between media and individuals, between culture and subjectivity.

Power and difference: thinking intersectionally about sexualization

Although notions of agency and empowerment animate debates about "sexualization," the literature rarely considers power. Curiously, empowerment is treated as an individualized phenomenon which, although clearly connected to gender and age, is not related analytically to issues of power, inequality, or oppression. Why is sexualization so infrequently connected to sexism or to racism, to class inequality or homophobia? These questions relate to my concerns about the utility of the notion of "sexualization." While they appear to speak to something apparently new and real, the notions of "sexualization" or "pornification" or "raunch" (McNair 2002; Levy 2005) are rife with problems. The terms are too general. They are difficult to operationalize and therefore to use analytically. They tend to homogenize, ignoring differences and obscuring the fact that different people are "sexualized" in different ways and with different meanings. Sexualization does not operate outside of processes of gendering, racialization, and classing, and works within a visual economy that remains profoundly ageist, (dis)ablist, and heteronormative (Gill 2009b). Furthermore, the terms seem to pull us back into a moral domain, rather than one of politics or ethics—they pull towards judgments about "explicitness" and "exposure" rather than questions about equality or justice. Might it not be more productive to talk about sexism rather than sexualization? For all their force in animating and inspiring a new generation of feminists (Banyard 2010), I worry too that these terms reinstate the terms of the "sex wars" of the 1980s, with their familiar polarizations and discomfiting alliances between pro-censorship feminists and right-wing religious organizations (Cornell 2000).

This is worsened by the profoundly classed, racialized, and heteronormative framing of the debates themselves, whose privileged object of anxiety and "concern" has been the white, Western, middle-class, girl-child, sometimes figured as a "typical 13-year-old girl"—able-bodied, Anglo-American, presumed heterosexual (APA 2007; Lamb and Peterson 2012). This figure is repeatedly mobilized in academic, policy, and media reports and comes to constitute or define who is "at risk" (Harris 2004: 13). She becomes discursively overdetermined to such an extent that her specificity is rendered invisible: She is always already (pre)figured, she shapes what becomes thinkable about "sexualization." What if we changed her gender or ethnicity, or thought of her as a lesbian or as living with a disability? This would open new ways of thinking—sexual experiences might not be framed so strongly in terms of risk and danger.

More broadly, we urgently need an intersectional approach to the complex nexus of sex, media, and power. Avtar Brah and Ann Phoenix explain that intersectionality signifies:

> The complex, irreducible, varied and variable effects which ensue when multiple axes of differentiation—economic, political, cultural, psychic, subjective and experiential—intersect in historically specific contexts. The concept emphasizes that different dimensions of social life cannot be separated out into discrete and pure strands.
>
> (Brah and Phoenix 2004: 76)

This, then, is a call to think about "sexualization" and sexual empowerment *with* sexism, racism, ageism, classism, homophobia, (dis)ablism, and also to think transnationally (Imre *et al.* 2009). Besides *integrating* sexism with other axes of power and difference, it is also a matter of facing up to the complex dynamics and complicities in play in the current moment—precisely those complicities that repeatedly locate white, middle-class, heterosexual North American girls as the privileged subjects of the debate.

Responding to "sexualization": beyond "media literacy"

How should we respond to "sexualization"? What should we say about the growing status of "media literacy" as an apparent panacea? The notion of media literacy as a Good Thing is fast taking on the status of common sense. There is a European Charter for media literacy. UNESCO pledges that "empowerment of young people through information and media literacy is an important prerequisite for fostering equitable access to information and knowledge, and building inclusive knowledge societies" (UNESCO 2006, quoted in Lunt and Livingstone 2012). Who could object to young people (indeed all people) getting the tools to deconstruct and critique media messages so they have a healthy skepticism? What's not to like?

One problem with media literacy is the implicit understanding of subjectivity on which it rests. The project of critique, dissection, comparison, and deconstruction relies on a model of the subject as unified and rational; it operates largely as a cognitive process. The idea seems to be that if someone is media literate—if they can discourse critically on an image's or text's aims and techniques—they will somehow be inoculated or protected against its otherwise harmful effects. It relies upon the idea of subjectivity as coherent, rather than split or contradictory, with the assumption that affect follows knowledge in rather a neat and obedient manner. I question this contention.

My research with Sue Jackson and Tiina Vares (e.g. Jackson *et al.* 2013; Vares *et al.* 2011) challenges the easy celebration of media literacy. The "tween" girls we studied show varying degrees of media literacy, with some of them extremely critical consumers of media, even from the age of ten. They are familiar with the language of critique and take pleasure in "unpacking" media images to reveal their artifice. In particular the girls enjoyed displaying their awareness that media images are constructed, with many exchanges about techniques such as airbrushing, the use of Photoshop, or the difference between magazines' "before and after" shots, in which "*everything* had changed," not just the area of the body that "should" have done.

Some girls discussed their anger about "anorexic models," girls in magazines with "perfect skin," and, more broadly, the gap between media images of girls and young women and those in the real world. They were contemptuous of the idea that celebrity endorsements would persuade them to buy any particular product. Indeed, in many senses the girls seemed archetypal media literate subjects—knowing, critical appraisers of adverts, magazines, and a whole variety of other genres. Yet despite this—despite an extraordinarily sophisticated vocabulary of critique—they said media representations still got to them, still had an ability to hurt them, still—as they repeatedly told us—made them "feel bad" or "feel sad" and/or made them long to look a particular way or to own a particular product. In other words, the girls' ability to produce subtle and sometimes angry decodings of media content did not seem to displace alternative, powerful responses to what they saw, read, and heard. The girls did not seem to feel "better" or more "empowered" by dint of their knowledge of media practices. They might enjoy showing off this knowledge but it did not negate or change other, often painful, feelings. In some cases, having the knowledge made them feel even more trapped—by the sense that they understood how it all worked: They saw through the "fake-ness" (as they put it), yet still felt they had to live up to the particular images of beauty they were fed.

Another objection is found in a critique of the way that media literacy forces the work of deconstructing media back on to individuals. This is part of a wider shift in power and governance towards greater self-governmentality, in which individuals are constituted as self-governing subjects. In relation to media regulation it can be seen at a policy level (at least in the UK): with a move away from state regulation and an increasing focus on media literate individuals self-regulating in relation to media content (Arthurs 2004). Media literacy thus becomes an *individual obligation*; we are made responsible for our own engagements with media—both what we use and how we engage. To champion media literacy, then, is to endorse this shift in power, and to make individuals responsible for the work of thinking critically and deconstructing media content. But it also, surely, espouses a kind of defeatism, for it suggests that media cannot be changed. All that can be changed is how we engage with them. Thus young people are asked to come equipped with tools to deconstruct sexism; young women are exhorted to become better at dissecting media's "sexualized" images and critiquing harmful images.

Why have we (feminists) become so quietist? When did engaging with sexist media seem to call out for an ever more sophisticated and literate media user, rather than a campaign to stamp out sexism? Have we given up on changing the world, to focus only on tweaking our critical orientations to it? As well as being part of a wider shift in the operation of power, I take this issue to be deeply gendered, part of the "postfeminist problem" in which gender inequality is no longer taken very seriously in Northern/Western developed societies, is not felt to be a "real" problem or form of oppression (see Gill 2007). Quite rightly, we do not respond to racism in the media with calls to educate young black people to better deconstruct racist images. On the contrary, we work to eradicate racism; we speak of its institutional nature, as a structural feature endemic to many organizations, including media (Downing and Husband 2005; Rattansi 2007). Yet issues pertaining to gender, sexuality, and sexualization show little evidence of such a robust response. Instead, calls for media literacy education imply that an informed populace of "critical" young women is the best that can be hoped for. Perhaps ironically, this focus can itself seem sexist, not only because it treats gender oppression as trivial, but also because it emphasizes the requirement for girls and young women to work on the self, to perfect the ways they engage with media, to become ever more responsible neoliberal subjects. Might it not be time to get angry again, to try to change the world? Media literacy as a kind of catch-all solution to "sexualization" needs to be interrogated.

Conclusion

The term "sexualization" speaks to a variety of phenomena, perceived changes in culture, and significant shifts in representational practices over the last two decades, e.g. the increased visibility of eroticized depictions of the male body in public space and the "postfeminist" return to displaying a sexualized female body in the media. However, as an analytical category it has limited usefulness. It polarizes debate and accentuates division. It pushes moralistic rather than political responses to representational culture. It flattens and homogenizes significant differences in the way bodies are figured and materialized in the media. I am repeatedly struck by the "lifted out" quality of debates about sexualization—removed from the messy, complicated, power-suffused sites of everyday life (e.g. schools) and anchored only in a number of endlessly recirculated hyperreal (in Baudrillard's terms) examples, such as child beauty pageants or the sale of items of "inappropriate" clothing. The tools and vocabularies supplied by "sexualization" do not now offer us leverage to think, act, and intervene. We must go beyond both the "effects" and the "critical readers" paradigms, to develop more nuanced, psychosocial engagements that push past the familiar figures of the cultural dope or the autonomous, freely choosing agent. We need to think further about power and difference. And in moving from scholarship to activism or policy response, we need to question whether "media literacy" is the best way to respond to a media and a wider culture that remain characterized by stark inequality and injustice.

References

American Psychological Association (APA) (2007) *Report of the APA Task Force on the Sexualization of Girls*, Washington, DC: APA.

Ang, I. (1985) *Watching Dallas: Soap Opera and the Melodramatic Imagination*, London: Methuen.

Arthurs, J. (2004) *Television and Sexuality: Regulation and the Politics of Taste*, Maidenhead: Open University Press.

Attwood, F. (2006) "Sexed Up: Theorizing the Sexualization of Culture," *Sexualities* 9(1): 77–94.

——(2009) *Mainstreaming Sex: The Sexualization of Western Culture*, London and New York: I. B. Tauris.

Bailey, R. (2011) *Letting Children Be Children: The Report of an Independent Review of the Commercialisation and Sexualisation of Children*, London: Department of Education

Banyard, K. (2010) *The Equality Illusion: The Truth about Women and Men Today*, London: Faber & Faber.

Bragg, S. and D. Buckingham (2002) *Young People and Sexual Content on Television*, London: Broadcasting Standards Commission.

——(2009) "Too Much Too Young? Young People, Sexual Media and Learning," in F. Attwood (ed.) *Mainstreaming Sex: The Sexualization of Western Culture*, London: I. B. Tauris.

Brah, Avtar and Ann Phoenix (2004) "Ain't I a Woman? Revisiting Intersectionality," *Journal of International Women's Studies* 5(3) (May): 75–86.

Buckingham, D. (2000) *After the Death of Childhood: Growing up in the Age of Electronic Media*, Cambridge: Polity.

Buckingham, D. and S. Bragg (2004) *Young People, Sex and the Media*, Basingstoke: Palgrave Macmillan.

Buckingham, David, Rebekah Willett, Sara Bragg, and Rachel Russell (2010) *Sexualised Goods Aimed at Children: A Report to the Scottish Parliament Equal Opportunities Committee*, Edinburgh: Scottish Parliament Equal Opportunities Committee.

Byron, T. (2008) *Safer Children in a Digital World: The Report of the Byron Review*, London: Department for Children, Schools and Families, and the Department for Culture, Media and Sport.

Califia, P. (1994) *Public Sex*, Pittsburgh: Cleiss Press.

Church Gibson, P. (ed.) (1993) *More Dirty Looks: Gender, and Power*, London: BFI.

Coleman, R. (2008) "The Becoming of Bodies: Girls, Media Effects and Body Image," *Feminist Media Studies* 8(2): 163–80.

Cornell, D. (2000) *Feminism and Pornography*, Oxford: Oxford University Press.

Dines, G. (2010) *Pornland: How Porn Has Hijacked Our Sexuality*, Boston: Beacon Press

Downing, J. and C. Husband (2005) *Representing Race: Racisms, Ethnicity and the Media*, London: Sage.

Durham, M. G. (2009) *The Lolita Effect: The Media Sexualization of Young Girls and What We Can Do about It*, London and New York: Duckworth Overlook.

Dworkin, A. (1981) *Pornography: Men Possessing Women*, New York: Plume/Penguin Publishing.

Dworkin, A. and C. MacKinnon (1988) *Pornography and Civil Rights: A New Day for Women's Equality*, Minneapolis: Organizing Against Pornography.

Egan, D. and G. Hawkes (2008) "Girls, Sexuality and the Strange Carnalities of Advertisements," *Australian Feminist Studies* 23: 307–22.

Evans, A., S. Riley, and A. Shankar (2010) "Technologies of Sexiness: Theorizing Women's Engagement in the Sexualization of Culture," *Feminism & Psychology* 20: 1–18. doi: 10.1177/0959353509351854.

Fawcett Society (2009) *Corporate Sexism: The Sex Industry's Infiltration of the Modern Workplace*, London: Fawcett.

Gauntlett, D. and A. Hill (1999) *TV Living: Television, Culture and Everyday Life*, London: Routledge.

Gill, R. (2007) *Gender and the Media*, Cambridge: Polity.

——(2008) "Empowerment/Sexism: Figuring Female Sexual Agency in Contemporary Advertising," *Feminism & Psychology* 18(1): 35–60.

——(2009a) "Supersexualize Me! Advertising, (Post)feminism and 'the Midriffs'," in F. B. Attwood (ed.) *Mainstreaming Sex: The Sexualization of Culture*, London and New York: I. B. Tauris.

——(2009b) "Beyond the 'Sexualization of Culture' Thesis: An Intersectional Analysis of 'Sixpacks', 'Midriffs' and 'Hot Lesbians' in Advertising," *Sexualities* 12: 137–60.

——(2011) "Bend It Like Beckham? The Challenges of Reading Gender in Visual Culture," in P. Reavey (ed.) *Visual Psychologies*, London and New York: Routledge.

——(2012) "Media, Empowerment and the 'Sexualization of Culture' Debates," *Sex Roles* 66: 736–45.

Gill, R., K. Henwood, and C. Maclean (2000) "The Tyranny of the 'Sixpack?': Understanding Men's Responses to Representations of the Male Body in Popular Culture," in C. Squire (ed.) *Culture in Psychology*, London: Routledge.

Harris, Anita (2004) *Future Girl: Young Women in the 21st Century*, London and New York: Routledge.

Harvey, L. and R. Gill (2011a) "Spicing It Up: Sexual Entrepreneurs and *The Sex Inspectors*," in R. Gill and C. Scharff (eds.) *New Femininities: Postfeminism, Neoliberalism and Subjectivity*, Basingstoke: Palgrave Macmillan.

——(2011b) "*The Sex Inspectors*: Self-help, Makeover and Mediated Sex," in K. Ross (ed.) *Handbook on Gender, Sexualities and Media*, Oxford: Blackwell.

Hermes, J. (1995) *Reading Women's Magazines: An Analysis of Everyday Media Use*, Cambridge: Polity.

Holland, S. and F. Attwood (2009) "Keeping Fit in 6 Inch Heels: The Mainstreaming of Pole Dancing," in F. Attwood (ed.) *Mainstreaming Sex: The Sexualization of Western Culture*, London: I. B. Tauris.

Imre, A., K. Mariniak, and A. O'Healy (2009) "Transcultural Mediations and Transnational Politics of Difference," *Feminist Media Studies* 9: 385–90. Doi: 10.1080/14680770903232961.

Jackson, S. and T. Vares (2011) "Media 'Sluts': 'Tween' Girls' Negotiations of Postfeminist Sexual Subjectivities in Popular Culture," in R. Gill and C. Scharff (eds.) *New Femininities: Postfeminism, Neoliberalism and Subjectivity*, Basingstoke: Palgrave Macmillan.

Jackson, S., T. Vares, and R. Gill (2013) "'The Whole Playboy Mansion Image': Girls Fashioning and Fashioned Selves within a Postfeminist Culture," *Feminism & Psychology* 23: 143–62.

Jeffreys, S. (2009) *The Industrial Vagina: The Political Economy of the Global Sex Trade*, London: Routledge.

Jenkins, H. and P. C. Gibson (2003) *More Dirty Looks: Gender, Pornography & Power*, London: BFI.

Johnson, M. L. (2002) *Jane Sexes It Up: True Confessions of Feminist Desire*, New York: Four Walls Eight Windows.

Juffer, J. (1998) *At Home with Pornography*, New York: New York University Press.

Lamb, S. and Z. Peterson (2012) "Adolescent Girls' Sexual Empowerment: Two Feminists Explore the Concept," *Sex Roles* 66 (11/12): 703–12.

Levin, D. E. and J. Kilbourne (2009) *So Sexy So Soon: The New Sexualized Childhood and What Parents Can Do to Protect Their Kids*, New York: Ballantine Books.

Levy, A. (2005) *Female Chauvinist Pigs: Women and the Rise of Raunch Culture*, New York: Free Press.

Lumby, C. (1997) *Bad Girls: Media, Sex and Feminism in the 90s*, London: Allen & Unwin.

Lunt, P. and S. Livingstone (2012) *Media Regulation*. London: Sage.

McNair, B. (2002) *Striptease Culture: Sex, Media and the Democratization of Desire*, London: Routledge.

Munford, R. (2009) "BUST-ing the Third Wave: Barbies, Blow Jobs and Girlie Feminism," in F. Attwood (ed.) *Mainstreaming Sex: The Sexualization of Western Culture*, London: I. B. Tauris.

Papadopoulos, L. (2010) *Sexualization of Young People Review*, London: UK Home Office. http://www.homeoffice.gov.uk/documents/Sexualization-young-people.

Plummer, K. (1995) *Telling Sexual Stories: Power, Change and Social Worlds*, London: Routledge.

Radway, Janice (1984) *Reading the Romance*, Chapel Hill, NC: The University of North Carolina Press.

Rattansi, A. (2007) *Racism: A Very Short Introduction*, Oxford: Oxford University Press.

Ringrose, J. and K. Eriksson Barajas (2011) "Gendered Risks and Opportunities? Exploring Teen Girls' Digitised Sexual Identity in Postfeminist Media Contexts," *International Journal of Media and Cultural Politics* 7(2): 121–38.

Rush, E. and A. La Nauze (2006) *Corporate Paedophilia: Sexualization of Children in Australia*, Canberra: The Australia Institute.

Smith, C. (2007) *One for the Girls: The Pleasures and Practices of Reading Women's Porn*, Bristol: Intellect Books.

Tankard Reist, M. (ed.) (2009) *Getting Real: Challenging the Sexualization of Girls*, Melbourne: Spinifex.

Vares, T., S. Jackson, and R. Gill (2011) "Preteen Girls Read 'Tween' Popular Culture: Diversity, Complexity and Contradiction," *International Journal of Media & Cultural Politics* 7: 139–54. Doi: 10.1386/macp.7.2.139_1.

Walkerdine, V. (1997a) *Daddy's Girl: Young Girls and Popular Culture*, Basingstoke: Macmillan.

——(1997b) "Video Replay: Families, Films and Fantasy," in V. Burgin, J. Donald, and C. Kaplan (eds.) *Formations of Fantasy*, London: Methuen.

Whelehan, I. (2000) *Overloaded Popular Culture and the Future of Feminism*, London: Women's Press.

Whitehead, K. and T. Kurz (2009) "Empowerment and the Pole," *Feminism & Psychology* 19(2): 224–44.

Williamson, J. (2003) "Sexism with an Alibi," *Guardian*, May 31.

Gender, Race, Ethnicity, Class, and Sexuality in Rural America

Carolyn Sachs

The media and popular stereotypes portray rural places in the United States as white, patriarchal, working class, and heterosexual havens where racism, sexism, homophobia, and ethnocentrism abound. The issues of gender, race, ethnicity, and class infuse all aspects of life and work in rural America. While a number of rural sociologists address these structures and identities in detail, a deeper understanding of these issues and the complex relations between them has not permeated the broader study of rural places.

Looking toward globalization proves useful. Global changes including heightened global restructuring, neoliberalism, and the pull back from state welfare impact gender, race, ethnicity, sexuality, and class issues in rural America. In addition, global efforts by the United Nations (UN) and a number of nongovernmental organizations to push for human rights, especially women's rights, rights of indigenous people, rights for gays, lesbians, and transgender people, and rights of minorities impact the lives of rural people in the United States.

I begin by offering several critiques of our understandings of rural people in the United States. First, much of the scholarship on gender, race, ethnicity, and class in rural America stops short of interrogating global issues and intersections of these issues. Second, despite decades of work on issues of gender, race, ethnicity, and class, much of this scholarship remains at the margins of academic understanding of rural places and rural life. Our understandings of gender, race, ethnicity, and class have not been adequately integrated into the broader understanding of rural life. Third, scholarship has not effectively investigated the intersections of these different identities and structures. Black feminist scholars and critical race scholars have called for attention to intersectionality— the complex relationships among between gender, race, ethnicity, sexuality, and class—in efforts to understand social life. With a few exceptions, studies of intersectionality in rural spaces remain elusive.

In this chapter, I first look at gender through focusing on global drivers of shifts in women's and men's employment in rural areas, women's movement into agriculture, a focus on reproductive labor, and theoretical shifts toward intersectionality. Second, I discuss race and ethnicity in two sections on crossing borders, focusing on Latinos in the United States and staying behind which focuses primarily on blacks in the South. Third, in the section on moving past heteronormativity, I argue for greater attention to sexuality. Next, I discuss how class issues in rural areas have often been studied through demographic and spatial analysis of pockets of poverty, but less attention has focused on the way differences across rural spaces impacts gender, race, ethnicity, and class issues. Then, I briefly mention two other global drivers impacting these issues: climate change and global human rights initiatives. Finally, I provide suggestions for future work.

Enter the Global Feminization of Work: From Bad Jobs to Worse

Restructuring of employment opportunities in the rural United States involves the precipitous decline in manufacturing employment, natural resource related jobs in forestry and fisheries, the demise of agricultural employment, and the increase in service-related jobs. As these shifts alter the gender, racial, and ethnic composition of the rural workforce, rural places and families also change.

Perhaps most striking is the change in work patterns of men and women in rural areas. With the shift to service-sector employment, rural women have been both pushed and pulled into the work force (Smith 2011). The decline in jobs for rural men in manufacturing and natural resources pushed women into the workforce in order to increase income in their households (Falk and Lobao 2003). In fact, as Jensen and Jensen (2011) show in their detailed analyses of data from the Current Population Survey, rural men have been more disadvantaged from structural shifts in the economy than either urban men or rural women. Rural men's situations in the labor market have worsened over time in contrast to rural women, whose employment situations have improved markedly. The trend toward the feminization of employment in the United States is mirrored in many regions of the world as a key component of neoliberal globalization. The feminization of employment involves both the increasing proportion of women in the workforce and the deterioration of labor conditions for both men and women (Peterson 2005). Women's formal employment has increased worldwide, while men's employment is declining—this does not necessarily translate into empowerment for women, but rather deteriorating working conditions for men. As Peterson (2005, 509) writes: "In short, as more jobs become casual, irregular, flexible and precarious, more women—and feminised men—are doing them."

Even though rural women's employment has increased, they often work in unfavorable circumstances of low pay, unpredictable hours, and temporary employment. Women's employment in the rural United States is best understood in the broader context of globalization and neoliberalism. As Patricia Fernández-Kelly (2007) suggests in comparing women workers in factories in the United States with those in other parts of the world, most women's search for jobs is driven by their concern to maintain living standards for themselves and their families rather than to achieve emancipation. As she states, "despite their comparative prosperity—U.S. women bear a striking resemblance to their counterparts in China, Nicaragua, and Mexico. Despite such commonalities, national background and race continue to fragment gender and class consciousness" (Fernández-Kelly 2007, 520).

Into the Fields: Shifting Gender Relations in Agriculture

Shifts in the global restructuring in agriculture, natural resource extraction, and manufacturing have differential impacts by gender, race, ethnicity, and class. Much of the scholarship on rural women in the United States has focused on women in agriculture, especially women farmers. Recently scholars have focused on the increase in women farmers, especially on sustainable and organic farms (Trauger et al. 2009; Hall and Mogyorody 2007), but with limited analysis of the impact of global agricultural restructuring on gender issues in farming in the United States. Global and regional trade agreements that cut subsidies and supports for traditional commodities often result in shifts in gender relations on farms. Global and national policies that favor large-scale corporate agriculture have led to the decline in the number of medium-sized farms and the heavy reliance of small- and medium-sized farms on off-farm employment. In some instances, men leave farms or seek employment off the farm, opening up space for women to move into farming or in some places resulting in the feminization of agriculture. Studies in Europe have emphasized how policies that have shifted to support multifunctional agriculture, such as tourism, have shifted gender relations on farms, undermined patriarchal power, and created more equitable and empowering opportunities for women (Brandth and Haugen 2010). At the same time, these shifts have resulted in redefinitions of masculinity on farms. Limited attention has been directed at how these global shifts impact gender relations or women on farms in North America. Shifts in the global agrifood system created by various trade agreements, loan repayment policies, and corporate agriculture have impacted women in agriculture in multiple ways (Sachs and Alston 2010). The global South has responded through production and processing of non-traditional crops such as vegetables, fruits, and flowers, which rely heavily on women's labor. Women are valued laborers because they can be paid less and are willing to work in more-flexible and less-stable work arrangements. The global and the local are highly linked in terms of women's employment opportunities; "the comparative advantage of agrifood industries in global markets rests on the comparative disadvantage of rural women in national labor markets" (Preibisch and Grez 2010, 291). While women are often the preferred workers in corporate agricultural production in developing countries, single migrant male workers who are most often from Mexico are often the preferred hired agricultural laborers in the United States and Canada (Preibisch and Grez 2010.) Rural sociologists have rarely studied the complex intersections of gender, race, and ethnicity in corporate agriculture in North America.

Beyond the Market: What about Reproduction?

While neoliberal globalization clearly alters the employment landscape in rural areas, the impact of these shifts extends beyond formal employment. As Peterson (2005, 27) notes, these shifts "reduce the emotional, cultural and material resources necessary for the wellbeing of most women and families." Women in most regions of the globe, and especially those who lack resources, are spending increasing amounts of time on reproductive labor, including feeding their families, providing health care, taking care of children and the elderly, and providing emotional support. The legacy of structural adjustment programs that have reduced government services have left the provision of many of these services to the unpaid work of women. While there is some evidence that rural men are taking up reproductive work, few studies have compared shifting gender divisions of labor in households between rural and urban areas. Also, the decline and lack in government services also means declining employment for women in rural areas, especially in so-called good jobs such as social work and teaching.

Shifts in women's and men's work patterns result in changes in household relationships as well. In her ethnographic study of a sawmill closure in a small logging and mill town in rural California, Sherman (2011) reveals the multiple ways that gender roles shift in response to men's job loss. Some men respond by adhering to rigid masculine identities and struggle to maintain traditional gender roles. This struggle often has devastating consequences including substance abuse and domestic violence. However, she also found a surprising amount of resilience and adoption of flexible masculine roles that emphasized more active fathering roles.

In many rural communities, reliance on government programs and services is often low due to limited availability of services or lack of adequate transportation. With the neoliberal push for the decline of government services and social supports, rural programs are often the first to go. For example, fewer programs exist to support rural women who are victims of sexual assaults. In addition, women are often reluctant to report sexual assaults due to lack of anonymity, physical isolation, and distrust of public agencies. People with HIV/AIDS in rural areas are also less likely to seek and obtain adequate treatment due to lack of appropriate health care providers, stigma attached to the disease, and transportation issues (Preston and D'Augelli 2012; Heckman et al. 1998).

Clearly, global shifts in employment opportunities have altered gender relations. In some cases, a re-inscription of traditional gender roles results in problematic family and household dynamics. In other cases, what Brandth and Haugen (2010) refer to as the detraditionalization of gender roles in rural areas offers possibilities for new and more equitable relations between rural men and women. Exactly when, where, and how these different dynamics play out deserves further study.

Moving beyond Western Feminism to Intersectionality

Critiques of feminist scholarship from third world women and US women of color have moved scholarship from focusing on women to the intersections of gender, race, ethnicity, citizenship, and sexual identity to studying intersectionality. Crenshaw (1991) coins the concept of intersectionality to describe how black women's experiences are shaped by both racism and sexism and cannot be understood by looking at race or gender experiences separately. Mohanty's (1988) classic critique of Western feminist writings about women in developing countries reveals that through portraying women in developing countries as unilaterally poor, uneducated, and disempowered, women in developed countries then seem to be agentic, empowered, and positioned to save the women in developing countries. This move of describing the "other" as universally disempowered and undifferentiated must be avoided in rural scholarship on gender, sexuality, race, and class. These theoretical pushes to move beyond simple analysis of gender, nation, class, ethnicity, and race can provide direction for future work in rural sociology.

Crossing Borders: Latinos in the Rural United States

Another major shift in rural areas is the increased employment of Latino/as, especially Mexicans, in the rural United States. More than ten years after the implementation of NAFTA, economic prosperity in Mexico continues to plummet and Mexicans have responded by crossing the border in pursuit of livelihoods (Patel 2009). As NAFTA policies support agribusinesses and larger scale industries on both sides of the border, Mexicans have lost out and are migrating when possible (Pechlaner and Otero 2010) Recently, immigrants from Mexico have begun to move outside of their traditional destinations in California and the Southwest to new destination rural communities (Nelson, Oberg, and Nelson 2010). Migrants to rural areas differ compared to migrants to urban areas, and one study found that the characteristics of migrants coming to rural areas after the passage of NAFTA shifted. These more recent migrants are more likely to be single, less educated, less fluent in English, have less work experience, and are more likely to come from small towns and rural places in Mexico (Farmer and Moon 2009).

aThese new destination rural communities often have meat-processing plants, other agricultural processing facilities, or tourist- and service-related jobs. An increasing number of largely Latino/a farmworkers are settling in rural communities. This influx of Latino immigrants to rural communities in the United States has raised concerns about the impact of new immigrants on rural populations (Jensen 2006; Kandel and Cromartie 2004; Lichter and Johnson 2007). The most recent studies show that the influx of large numbers of Latino/as have surprisingly little impact on the economic well-being of local populations (Crowley and Lichter 2009). Most studies focus on local communities and longer-term populations rather than on the immigrants' well-being. One exception is Pfeffer and Parra's (2009) study of rural immigrants in New York, where they find that new immigrants' networks and social ties are instrumental in helping them find jobs. In another study, Schmalzbauer (2011) looked at the well-being of immigrants and the gender dynamics in households. She found that immigrant women who transgressed their traditional gender roles and assumed jobs in the formal economy tried to protect men's masculinity by performing a particular gender script. The rise of anti-immigration movements in states and local communities has made life exceedingly difficult for immigrants, especially those without documentation.

Staying Behind: Racism Reigns

The long history of disfranchisement, discrimination, and violence against rural blacks in the United States is clearly tied to global trade in commodities and people from the time of the Atlantic slave trade. While some changes have occurred, the political economy of the plantation South has left a legacy of black rural poverty steeped in racism (Tickamyer and Duncan 1990). In discussing the persistent problems in the Black Belt region, R. Wimberly (2010, 178) notes that despite civil rights, technological shifts and globalization "race, region, and rurality still combine to restrict both children and adults from enjoying the many social advantages and opportunities held by U.S. residents of other regions." With globalization, blacks in rural America have provided free and cheap labor to fuel global trade for centuries.

Black land ownership continues to decline (Gilbert, Sharp, and Felin 2002). For blacks in the rural South, land represents more than economic security, but also a level of independence and personal security. Rural blacks have deep emotional attachments to the land (Falk 2004; Dyer and Bailey 2008). However, they continue to lose access to this land.

Native Americans continue to live in dire economic circumstances. Nearly 60 percent of Native Americans who live outside of metropolitan areas live in poor counties. Those who live on reservations experience extreme poverty and unemployment. Economic development largely eluded them until the 1987 legislation that legalized gaming operations on tribal land (Gonzales 2003). Controversy exists surrounding the impact of gaming on tribal land, but certainly many tribes experience increased income, better infrastructure, and improved social services. However, more research is needed in terms of the short- and long-term impact of gaming on social and cultural issues on reservations.

Possible benefits of globalization seem to have passed by many of these communities, but some places are more deeply impacted. For example, climate change as the result of the incessant use of fossil fuel will likely have major impacts on indigenous people in the Arctic region (Cuomo, Eisner, and Hinkel 2008). There is now unsubstantiated evidence that further changes associated with global warming will have a profound impact on and generate additional risks for Arctic communities.

While class and race intersect with rural poverty in the Deep South, some other pockets of rural poverty remain predominantly white. Persistent poverty and class inequality in Appalachia has long been understood through the political economic structures of the region and referred to as internal colonialism. Clearly, Appalachian poverty and class inequality reflects the dominance and control of outside corporate interests. The abundance of coal that is primarily owned and controlled by outside interests has brought anything but prosperity to the region. Shifts from deep mining to shift mining to mountaintop removal have brought about increasing degradation of the landscape and water systems in Appalachia in conjunction with the decline in the number of jobs available in the coalfields. Recent discoveries of natural gas in Marcellus Shale in the mid-Appalachian region and the availability of hydraulic fracturing technologies have resulted in local people selling mineral rights. Although these new natural gas developments promise jobs and employment possibilities, they are also characterized by outside ownership of mineral rights and severe environmental threats to water systems.

Moving past Heteronormativity

Much of the literature on rural places assumes a heteronormativity in terms of identities, households, and communities. In the mid- to late-1990s, some scholars began to interrogate rural sexualities with a focus on gay and lesbian identities in rural places. The early scholarships on rural gays and lesbians emphasized their marginality in rural places. In fact, in her article, "Get Thee to a Big City," Kath Weston (1995) neatly sums up early academic thinking on rural gays and lesbians. Rural places were viewed as overwhelming heterosexual, homophobic, and downright dangerous for rural gays and lesbians. Even more recent work argues that rural communities constitute spaces of highly conventional sexualities (Little and Leyshon 2003). Life for rural gay men in particular is extremely difficult as they face social stigma related to homosexuality and the lack of anonymity in rural places (Preston and D'Augelli 2012). But there is emerging scholarship on rural sexuality that challenges the assumption that rural places are unilaterally inhospitable to gays and lesbians. Gray (2009) argues that the urban LGBT emphasis on visibility and coming out occludes the presence of queer people in rural areas. She argues that rural queer practices are invisible to those observing through an urban or academic lens. Exactly how life is for rural gay men clearly varies by location.

Across Different Spaces: Pockets of Poverty and More

All rural places in the United States are not the same (Falk and Lobao 2003). How gender, race, ethnicity, and class impact rural people's lives in these various types of rural spaces deserves further attention. Feminist scholars insist on the importance of situated knowledges—of taking care not to universalize about views from nowhere. Cindy Katz (2001) creatively weaves together how to understand globalization works in particular locations without romanticizing the local. Her motivation is to find new political responses that "transcend both place and identity and foster a more effective cultural politics to counter the empirical, patriarchal, and racist integument of globalization" (Katz 2001, 1,216).

In looking at class issues in rural spaces, many scholars have studied the concentration of poverty in particular rural countries, especially in the South, the Appalachian region, and the Texas borderland. Shortage of jobs and limited upward mobility for workers is nothing new for rural people, especially in certain locations (Tickamyer and Duncan 1990). Licthter et al.'s (2012) recent analysis found that rural pockets of poverty might be drying up with the exception of high levels of concentrated poverty among minorities. In fact, approximately one-half of rural blacks and one-third of rural Hispanics live in poor counties, and the concentration of rural minority children is more extreme, with over 80 percent living in poor counties.

Impoverishment, lack of access to land, high unemployment, and inequality between and within places does not bode well for rural blacks living in the Black Belt south. From R. Wimberly's (2010) perspective, changing the course of poverty in the Black Belt region is the major challenge facing rural sociologists. D. Wimberly (2010, 116) argues that government cutbacks promoted by neoliberal globalizations have replaced possible solutions for the Black Belt, including "minimum wages, unemployment compensation, labor rights protection, Social Security disability benefits, antidiscrimination enforcement; progressive taxation, adequately-paid government jobs (often replaces with privatized services): government-supported medical care; and government-provided income, food, and housing support for the poor."

Considering Other Global Drivers: Climate Change and Human Rights

Two other trends related to globalization with differential impacts by gender, race, ethnicity, and class are worth mentioning. First, climate change and the resultant warming, increases in drought and desertification, and more violent and unpredictable storms and weather will have different impacts. Indigenous people, people living in substandard housing, and poor women have been and will continue to be more affected by climate change. The recent movement for climate justice often focused on inequalities at the nation-state level, but women and indigenous people are increasingly pushing for attention to their rights.

At the global level, the UN and other organizations have been pushing for human rights for women, lesbian, gay, and transgender people; minorities; and indigenous people. Emphases on social and political rights have resulted in major shifts in social and cultural arenas but have been less successful in providing economic justice. How these international movements impact changing gender, race, ethnicity, and sexuality issues in rural places remains a question to be explored.

For the Future

While much research has been conducted on gender, race, ethnicity, sexuality, and class in rural America, many issues call for further investigation. Here, I suggest five areas of research that will enhance our understanding and possibilities for change in rural places.

1.   As globalization continues to impact rural America, a deeper infusion of scholarship inclusive of questions of gender, race, ethnicity, and sexuality will enrich our understanding of rural life in the United States. Despite strong scholarship in these areas, some of these concerns remain marginal and not fully integrated into the broader scholarship of rural America. More scholarship focusing on these groups is particularly absent in certain areas such as community and natural resource sociology. While several excellent detailed community and ethnographic studies have tackled issues of gender, race, or ethnicity, much more work is called for in different types of communities. More quantitative studies can also contribute to our understandings of how gender, race, and ethnicity relate to community concerns across a wider range of rural places.

2.   Rural scholars can address the issues discussed above through a deeper engagement with feminist scholarship and critical race theory in their calls for intersectional analysis. Many studies focus on race, gender, or ethnicity in rural places, but only a few studies seriously interrogate how these multiple identities impact the livelihoods and well-being of rural people. Efforts to understand these complicated identities open up a vast realm of new scholarship.

3.   As global attention increasingly turns to issues of climate change, a growing number of groups are insisting on climate justices. As in the environmental justice movement, people of color in the United States have often been most affected by environmental problems. People of color, indigenous people, and poor women are often most impacted by natural disasters, as witnessed in the events related to Hurricane Katrina. African Americans, women, and the elderly experienced the most loss and had fewer resources to adapt to the devastation from the flooding. People who live in marginal

environments will be most impacted by climate change and many of these are people of color.

4.   Very limited scholarship exists on rural sexualities especially focused on lesbians, gays, bisexuals, and transgender people's lives in rural communities. Heteronormativity prevails in our understanding of rural places and metronormativity prevails in our understanding of the LGBT community. New scholarship on rural sexualities raises difficult questions. Some studies suggest that gays and lesbians experience extreme prejudice, stigma, and violence in rural places, while others suggest that urban biases misrepresent the difficulties encountered by rural sexual minorities. Clearly, these issues vary in different types of rural places, but the door is wide open for more research.

5.   Gender, race, ethnic, class, and sexuality injustices are always being challenged. Many of these movements now cross national borders and have now gone global through efforts to resist impacts of globalization by women, people of color, and sexual minorities. The Occupy Wall Street movement that protests against social and economic inequality is largely an urban social movement. But global protests are not limited to urban people. Most notably, a growing worldwide movement led by *La via Campesina* is mobilizing indigenous people, small farmers, and women to push for social and economic justice related to climate justice, sustainability, and biodiversity. Studies of agency and resistance, as well as collaborations of rural sociologists with practitioners and community organizers, will help lead the way to social justice in rural America.

References

Brandth, Berit, and Marit Haugen. 2010. "Doing Farm Tourism: The Intertwining Practices of Gender and Work." *Signs (Chicago, Ill.)* 35 (2): 425–46. http://dx.doi.org/10.1086/605480.

Chakroborti, Neil, and John Garland. 2012. *Rural Racism*. London: Routledge.

Crenshaw, Kimberly. 1991. "Mapping the Margins: Intersectionality, Identity Politics, and Violence against Women of Color." *Stanford Law Review* 43 (6): 1241–99. http://dx.doi.org/10.2307/1229039.

Crowley, Martha, and Daniel T. Lichter. 2009. "Social Disorganization in New Latino Destinations." *Rural Sociology* 74 (4): 573–604. http://dx.doi.org/10.1526/003601109789864026.

Cuomo, Chris, Wendy Eisner, and Kenneth Hinkel. 2008. "Indigenous Knowledge, Environmental Change, and Subsistence on Alaska's North Slope." *S&F Online* 8 (1). http://sfonline.barnard.edu/ice/cuomo_eisner_hinkel_01.htm.

Dyer, Janice, and Conner Bailey. 2008. "A Place to Call Home: Cultural Understandings of Heir Property among Rural African Americans." *Rural Sociology* 73 (3): 317–38. http://dx.doi.org/10.1526/003601108785766598.

Falk, William. 2004. *Rooted in Place: Family and Belonging in a Southern Black Community.* New Brunswick, NJ: Rutgers University Press.

Falk, William, and Linda Lobao. 2003. "Who Benefits from Economic Restructuring? Lessons from the Past, Challenges for the Future." In *Challenges for Rural America in the Twenty-First Century*, ed. David Brown and Louis Swanson, 152–65. University Park: Penn State University Press.

Farmer, Frank, and Zola Moon. 2009. "An Empirical Examination of Characteristics of Mexican Migrants to Metropolitan and Nonmetropolitan Areas of the United States." *Rural Sociology* 74 (2): 220–40. http://dx.doi.org/10.1111/j.1549-0831.2009.tb00390.x.

Fernández-Kelly, Patricia. 2007. "The Global Assembly Line in the New Millennium: A Review Essay." *Signs (Chicago, Ill.)* 32 (2): 509–21. http://dx.doi.org/10.1086/508226.

Gilbert, J., G. Sharp, and M.S. Felin. 2002. "The Loss and Persistence of Black-Owned Farms and Farmland: A Review of the Research Literature and Its Implications." *Southern Rural Sociology* 18: 1–30.

Gonzales, Angela. 2003. "Gaming and Displacement: Winners and Losers in American Indian Casino Development." *International Social Science Journal* 55 (175): 123–33. http://dx.doi.org/10.1111/1468-2451.5501012.

Gray, Mary L. 2009. *Out in the Country: Youth, Media, and Queer Visibility in Rural America.* New York: New York University Press.

Hall, Alan, and Veronika Mogyorody. 2007. "Organic Farming, Gender, and the Labor Process." *Rural Sociology* 72 (2): 289–316. http://dx.doi.org/10.1526/003601107781170035.

Heckman, T.G., A.M. Somlai, J. Peters, J. Walker, L. Otto-Salaj, C.A. Galdabini, and J.A. Kelly. June 1998. "Barriers to Care among Persons Living with HIV/AIDS in Urban and Rural Areas." *AIDS Care* 10 (3): 365–75. http://dx.doi.org/10.1080/713612410. Medline:9828979.

Jensen, Leif. 2006. "New Immigrant Settlements in Rural America: Problems, Prospects and Policies." Carsey Institute Report 1(3). Durham: University of New Hampshire.

Jensen, Leif, and Eric Jensen. 2011. "Employment Hardship among Rural Men." In *Economic Restructuring and Family Well-Being in Rural America*, ed. Kristin Smith and Ann Tickamyer, 40–59. University Park: Penn State University Press.

Kandel, W., and J. Cromartie. 2004. *New Patterns of Hispanic Settlement in Rural America.* Rural Development Research Report 99. Washington, DC: Economic Research Service, USDA.

Katz, Cindy. 2001. "On the Grounds of Globalization: A Topography for Feminist Political Engagement." *Signs* (Chicago, Ill.) 26 (4): 1213–34. http://dx.doi.org/10.1086/495653. Medline:17615660.

Lichter, Daniel, and Kenneth Johnson. 2007. "The Changing Spatial Concentration of America's Rural Poor Population." *Rural Sociology* 72 (3): 331–58. http://dx.doi.org/10.1526/003601107781799290.

Lichter, Daniel, Domenico Parisi, and Michael C. Taquino. 2012. "The Geography of Exclusion: Race, Segregation, and Concentrated Poverty." *Social Problems* 59: 364–88.

Little, Jo, and Michael Leyshon. 2003. "Embodied Rural Geographies: Developing Research Agendas." *Progress in Human Geography* 27 (3): 257–72. http://dx.doi.org/10.1191/03091 32503ph427oa.

Mohanty, Chandra. 1988. "Under Western Eyes: Feminist Scholarship and Colonial Discourses." *Feminist Review* 30 (Autumn): 61–88.

Nelson, Peter B., Alexander Oberg, and Lise Nelson. 2010. "Rural Gentrification and Linked Migration in the United States." *Journal of Rural Studies* 26 (4): 343–52. http://dx.doi.org/10.1016/j.jrurstud.2010.06.003.

Patel, Raj. 2009. *Stuffed and Starved: Markets, Power and the Hidden Battle for the World's Food System.* London: Portobello.

Pechlaner, G., and G. Otero. 2010. "The Neoliberal Food Regime: Neoregulation and the New Division of Labor in North America." *Rural Sociology* 75 (2): 179–208. http://dx.doi.org/10.1111/j.1549-0831.2009.00006.x.

Peterson, V. Spike. 2005. "How (the Meaning of) Gender Matters in Political Economy." *New Political Economy* 10 (4): 499–521. http://dx.doi.org/10.1080/13563460500344468.

Pfeffer, Max J., and Pliar A. Parra. 2009. "Strong Ties, Weak Ties, and Human Capital: Latino Immigrant Employment outside the Enclave." *Rural Sociology* 74 (2): 241–69. http://dx.doi.org/10.1111/j.1549-0831.2009.tb00391.x.

Preibisch, Kerry, and Evelyn Encalada Grez. 2010. "The Other Side of el Otro Lado: Mexican Migrant Women and Labor Flexibility in Canadian Agriculture." *Signs (Chicago, Ill.)* 35 (2): 289–316. http://dx.doi.org/10.1086/605483.

Preston, Deborah, and Anthony D'Augelli. 2012. *The Challenges of Being a Rural Gay Man: Coping with Stigma.* New York: Routledge.

Sachs, Carolyn, and Margaret Alston. 2010. "Global Shifts, Sedimentations, and Imaginaries: An Introduction to the Special Issue on Women and Agriculture." *Signs* (Chicago, Ill.) 35 (2): 277–87. http://dx.doi.org/10.1086/605618.

Schmalzbauer, Leah. 2011. "'Doing Gender,' Ensuring Survival: Mexican Migration and Economic Crisis in the Rural Mountain West." *Rural Sociology* 76 (4): 441–60. http://dx.doi.org/10.1111/j.1549-0831.2011.00058.x.

Sherman, Jennifer. 2011. "Men Without Sawmills: Job Loss and Gender Identity in Rural America." In *Economic Restructuring and Family Well-Being in Rural America*, ed. Kristin Smith and Ann Tickamyer, 82–102. University Park: Penn State University Press.

Smith, Kristin. 2011. "Changing Roles: Women and Work in Rural America." In *Economic Restructuring and Family Well-Being in Rural America*, ed. Kristin Smith and Ann Tickamyer, 60–81. University Park: Penn State University Press.

Tickamyer, Ann, and Cynthia Duncan. 1990. "Poverty and Opportunity Structure in Rural America." *Annual Review of Sociology* 16 (1): 67–86. http://dx.doi.org/10.1146/annurev.so.16.080190.000435.

Trauger, A., C. Sachs, M. Barbercheck, K. Brasier, and N.E. Kiernan. 2009. "'Our Market is Our Community': Women Farmers and Civic Agriculture in Pennsylvania, USA." *Agriculture, Food and Human Values* 26 (1): 43–55.

Weston, Kath. 1995. "Get Thee to a Big City: Sexual Imaginary and the Great Gay Migration." *GLQ: A Journal of Lesbian and Gay Studies* 2 (3): 253–77.

Wimberly, Dale. 2010. "Quality of Life Trends in the Southern Black Belt, 1980–2005: A Research Note." *Journal of Rural Social Sciences* 25 (1): 103–18.

Wimberly, Ronald. 2010. "It's Our Most Rural Region; It's the Poorest, It's the Black Belt South, and It Needs Our Attention." *Journal of Rural Social Sciences* 25 (2): 175–82.

Queering Romance, Sexuality, Gender Identity, and Motherhood

Roberta Seelinger Trites

QUEERING ORIENTATION AND GENDER IDENTITY

Perhaps the most blatant ways that feminist fictions for the young question traditional Western binaries occurs in those novels that interrogate sexuality, orientation, and gender identity. These books refuse multiple binaries, such as binaries of cis/trans identity or straight/gay identity. At their best, these books show teenagers celebrating their sexuality. As the narrator says in Beth Goobie's *Hello, Groin*: "No matter how much you tell yourself that your body is just a subplot in your life, it isn't. It's the *main* plot"; later, the narrator adds, "we live in our whole body. . . . Our entire body is our mind. . . . We think and feel and hope with our groin, just as much as with our brain and heart" (57, italics added, 252, 256).

Kokkola observes that GLBTQ novels frequently reinforce binaristic thinking about orientation, particularly when they rely on a "butch-femme division" that "reinforces the normative boundaries 'queer' attempts to destroy" (113). Kokkola perceives lesbian novels as themselves having many parallels with adolescent sexuality, particularly in the way that lesbianism and adolescent sexuality are delegitimized by a variety of cultural attitudes (102–3). Relying on the work of Barbara Creed, Kokkola demonstrates that lesbianism and adolescent sexuality fall prey to the following skepticisms: "adolescents like lesbians are questioned as to whether what they do really counts as sex" (102); sexual acts of lesbians and adolescents are "disparaged rather than outlawed" (102); like adolescent sexuality, lesbianism is often portrayed as an immature phase; heteronormativity defines both lesbian and adolescent sexual practices; adolescent and lesbian sexuality are both labeled as "insatiable" (103); and lesbian and adolescent desire are both portrayed as "narcissistic and in need of taming" and in terms of "loneliness" (103). Kokkola firmly establishes that critics of YA literature need to understand these parallels as a way to resist them. Her argument that age-based norms define adolescent sexuality in YA novels will resonate with anyone who recognizes that adult sexual behavior is depicted as stable in adolescent literature, while adolescent sexuality is portrayed as unstable.

Kokkola also traces how lesbian novels must ultimately grapple—as most LGBTQ novels do—with homophobia. Gay sexuality is a "problem" to be solved, and it is invariably "solved" against a homophobic nemesis (98).[4] To Kokkola's outstanding work, I would also like to invite an increased awareness of the material dimensions of lesbianism in at least one novel, Emily M. Danforth's *The Miseducation of Cameron Post* (2012)—a novel in which lesbianism is most assuredly defined against a homophobia that remains regrettably stable, but a novel in which materiality is also clearly linked to *becoming*. For example, Danforth's description of Cameron's first kiss emphasizes the material, the physicality, of the act. She and a friend, both twelve-year-olds, are playing in a barn made excruciatingly hot by a summer heat wave. Cameron does a handstand, which leaves her shirt bunched around her neck, so after she rights herself, her friend asks Cameron to show her the tan line from her swimsuit again. The friend traces the white strip of skin with her finger and says, "It looks like a bra strap" (8). Cameron feels goose-bumps, and they discuss whether they need to wear bras when they start junior high in the fall. Cameron stuffs straw down her friend's shirt—who then finishes drinking her root beer and dares Cameron to kiss her: "There's nothing to know about a kiss like that before you do it. It was all action and reaction, the way her lips were salty and she tasted like root beer. The way I felt sort of dizzy the whole time" (10). The scene emphasizes the heat, the straw, the barn, the root beer, the girls' clothing, and the sensation of their tongues touching each other. The two girls kiss again, making clear that their desire for one another entails more than a mere dare. Later, they discuss whether they would "get in trouble if anyone found out," and they cite how they know the codes of heteronormativity: through television, the movies and "the world. . . . Anything else was something weird" (11). The materiality of their physical expression of desire is defined, shaped, and limited, by the discursive. Cameron's coming-out to herself, her *becoming*, is thus linked to her memories of "the feel of her mouth that day in the hayloft, the taste of her gum and the root beer we'd been drinking. The day she dared me to kiss her. And the very next day my parents' car had veered through the guardrail" (45). Cameron's parents die in the automobile wreck, and she blames herself for their deaths, linking her own sense of sexuality with death in very material ways.[5]

In the first half of the novel, Cameron never quite shakes the sense of shame with which she connects her orientation and her parents' death. Nevertheless, every stage of her coming-out story—that is, every stage of her *becoming* an out lesbian first to herself, then to her friends, and then to a disapproving community—is implicated in the material. When she explores her sexuality with an out lesbian she meets through swim team, she describes:

> our ever-expanding make-out repertoire—hands up each other's shirts while hidden within the blue tunnel slide on the playground next to Malta's pool; Lindsey's tongue in my mouth behind the Snack Shack not five minutes after I won the Scobey meet; . . . pressed together, our swimsuit tops pulled down and the straps dangling from our waists like slack suspenders while we were supposed to be drying off and staying warm in Lindsey's dad's camper during a thunderstorm. (98–99)

Both the materiality of their bodies and the materiality of the locations where they touch each other affects these girls' sense of their shared sexuality.

When Cameron falls in love, it is with Coley, and their sexual expressions of their feelings are also rooted in the material, although Cameron knows she is relying on discourse to describe the experience. She says of their first kiss: "I'm not going to make it out to be something that it wasn't: It was perfect" (182). She then shifts the narration to focus on the material: "Coley's soft lips against the bite of the liquor and sugary Coke still on our tongues. She did more than just not stop me. She kissed me back. She pulled in with her arms, her ankles latching behind my thighs, and we stayed like that until

I could feel my boots sinking so far into the rain-softened clay-thick mud beneath me" (182–83). When they have enough privacy to engage in genital sex, Cameron again focuses on the material: the taste of what they have been drinking, the size and shape of their clothing as they disrobe each other, the contrast of their hot bodies to the cool sheets, the scent of Coley's lotion, the way specific parts of Coley's body feel under Cameron's fingertips and tongue. They acknowledge each other's size and are startled that they both experience each other as "so small" (224). Cameron describes the intimacy of the position they are in when Coley orgasms, acknowledging how "her whole body tensed and her breaths came in ragged jumps and her thighs pressed together against my head. . . . But I didn't know what to do in the aftermath, where to put my body, what to say" (225). Ultimately, Cameron feels awkward and uncertain about both her own materiality and her own discourse—but she has found Coley's *jouissance* pleasurable.

Coley's brother interrupts them before Cameron orgasms, and he forces Coley to admit to their mother what the girls have been doing. Coley relies on discourse to exonerate herself, depicting Cameron in terms of "the pursuer" who has "attempted corruption" of Coley because of Cameron's "sick infatuation" (248). Cameron's aunt decides to send her to a Christian camp dedicated to convincing teenagers that being gay is sinful so they can "break free from the bonds of sexual sin and confusion by welcoming Jesus Christ into their lives" (252). Thus begins Cameron Post's "miseducation." Camp Promise is predicated on the type of religious belief that argues "sin" can be controlled both by cognitive self-discipline and the discourse one uses to think about one's self and that sin. The camp subscribes to the type of "sinful body" argument that Elizabeth Grosz cites as accruing to early Christianity via Plato's thinking, as I have discussed in Chapter 4 (Grosz 5). The camp privileges discourse over embodiment—and Cameron Post directly critiques this type of thinking. At the camp, she makes two friends who smoke marijuana with her and who aren't particularly chatty: "We were good with smoking and not talking. All of us did so much talking at Promise, even those of us who didn't really say anything in all that talking" (310). Talk-therapy constitutes the camp's allegedly therapeutic approach, and Cameron accuses the counselors of making it up as they go, saying "You guys don't even know what you're doing here, do you? You're just like making it up as you go along . . . and you're gonna pretend like you have answers that you don't even have and it's completely fucking fake" (382)—and she rightly labels their methods "pseudoscientific" (421). Using her own words, she labels the counselor's therapy "emotional abuse" (400);

after one boy tries to castrate himself and pours bleach on his wounds to cleanse himself from his allegedly impure gay thoughts, a state investigator comes to interview the residents of the camp. Cameron tells him: "the whole fucking purpose of this place is to make us hate ourselves so that we change. We're supposed to *hate* who we are, despise it" (400, italics in the original). Cameron means that they are supposed to learn the right type of discourse so that they can hate their material bodies and their physical urges.

The text underscores the relationship between Cameron's actions and her emotions in two material ways: through the geography of Montana and through her compulsive decorating of her childhood dollhouse. Throughout the text, she frequently describes Montana's weather—its harsh, dry, landscape-browning summers, its sudden thunderstorms, its vast skies. She claims that Montana has two seasons, "winter and road construction" as a way of showing how a "saying like that encapsulates just how present the natural world is in Montana, and how aware of it you are—the sky, the land, the weather, all of it" (403). Her parents have drowned in Quake Lake, a lake that was created during a massive earthquake when Cameron's mother was twelve; she had been camping in the area flooded by the earthquake the day before. Her best friend's brother has drowned in that deluge, just as Cameron's parents will eventually die in the same body of water when Cameron herself is twelve. Montana's geography is a material presence throughout the novel that is greater than any other force—even the force of young Cameron's sexuality.

Before he died, Cameron's father has built her an elaborate dollhouse. After her parents' deaths, Cameron turns into a scavenger who collects things (and sometimes steals them) to decorate the interior of the dollhouse. Her ill-trained therapist at Camp Promise connects these artifacts to her parents' deaths and tells her that "these material fragments" are "trophies of your sins"; "you collect these items, and then you display them as a way of attempting, I think, to control your guilt and discomfort regarding both these relationships and your behavior" (433). The counselor later admonishes Cameron: "You've so convinced yourself that God was punishing you for your [lesbian] sins . . . that you're blind to any other assessment, and because of that your parents are no longer people to you; they're simply figures that were manipulated by God for his great plan to teach you a lesson. . . . Your parents did not die for your sins. They didn't need to: Jesus already did" (452). With the two close friends she has made at the camp, Cameron then runs away, rejecting her counselor's fundamentalist interpretation of her sexuality and her grief about her parents' death. In a scene perhaps more imbued than it needs to be with symbolic imagery, Cameron swims in Quake Lake, lighting a candle and talking to her parents' spirits and indicating that she thinks they would have liked getting to know her as she is. "Maybe while you were alive I hadn't even *become* me yet. Maybe I still haven't *become* me. I don't know how you tell for sure when you finally have," she tells her parents, immersed in the baptismal lake water, holding a burning candle, looking at the skeletons of trees that grew on the land before the earthquake triggered the mountain to fall and create Quake Lake (468, italics added). The geography and Cameron's materiality have merged, and she has begun to heal—not because she somehow wants to overcome her lesbianism but precisely because her *becoming* entails accepting her orientation.

The novel illustrates aptly what Kokkola demonstrates about the lesbian ghost, a trope of lesbian literature first identified by Terry Castle. "Adolescent desires, especially queer desires, can be rendered invisible—*ghosted*—by a viewpoint that literally cannot see them" (Kokkola 122). As a trope, the ghost problematizes the relationship between the material and the non-material: it is an otherworldly manifestation that presents itself in the physical world but is not exactly material. And ghosts recur frequently in Cameron's metaphorical language. When twelve-year-old Cameron has a sleepover with the girl who shares her first kiss, they are in bed, and that girl's father knocks on the door; it will be his unpleasant task to drive Cameron back to her grandmother's house to learn that her parents have died. The girls have heard the phone ring late at night; they hear her father approaching the door: "there was empty time between the end of those steps and the heavy rap of his knuckles: ghost time" (24). Their sexuality has been ghosted; it is invisible to the grieving adults around them. After her parents die, while Cameron visits the video store from which she rents as many lesbian-erotic DVDs as she can, she walks "toward the store, hoping my cap would keep me invisible—I felt like a ghost anyway" (34). Cameron enjoys the kitchen of her aunt's church because "I liked being a ghost in this place, unseen" (111). But after Cameron has been outted as a lesbian, it's not so much that she is invisible as that other people try to be invisible around her: her grandmother "ghosted around the house" until Cameron is sent to Camp Promise (261). Her good friend Adam at the camp tells her "I'm the ghost of my former gay self" (310), and the other friend Cameron runs away with, Jane, tells her that the skeletal trees sticking out of Quake Lake look like "the ghosts of trees" (457). Cameron thinks "the wind fluttering" through those trees sounds like "cheesy scary movie ghost whisper that somehow wasn't cheesy at all" (458). Cameron then asks Adam about "that Lakota giant—the one who was supposed to be like visible to man forever ago, but isn't now, and lives on a mountain surrounded by water" (458); Adam teases Cameron, "Why, did you see him?" (459). This is the whole point of the ghost-imagery in *The Miseducation of Cameron Post*: its goal is to make the lesbian visible, no longer a ghost either to herself or to other people.

The Miseducation of Cameron Post contains many standard tropes of LGBTQ stories that Kokkola identifies: Cameron's coming-out is the focus of the story; that coming out is predicated against homophobia that is allowed to remain stable and culturally entrenched; Cameron and her most beloved lover create a butch-femme binary; Cameron is warned by an experienced lesbian that her bisexual lover will eventually betray her to embrace heteronormativity, and Cameron's lesbianism is ghosted. Despite relying on these tropes, *The Miseducation of Cameron Post* does not shy away from the materiality of lesbian sexuality, nor does it reduce lesbianism only to discursive terms. Lesbian *becoming*, like lesbian desire, is discursively inflected in this novel but it is also a material phenomenon rooted in the physicality of young women's bodies.

Beth Goobie's *Hello, Groin* (2006) follows many of the same tropes, complete with homophobia left intact, at least one butch-femme binary, and a focus on coming out. *Hello, Groin*, however, problematizes sexuality, wresting it away from the gay/straight binary that troubles many YA coming-out novels. Dylan's love interest is her best-friend Jocelyn, who is dating Dikker—a boy of whom Dylan disapproves perhaps because she is jealous of him and because he makes Jocelyn feel bad about herself. When Dylan suggests they break up, Jocelyn gets angry and says, "For some reason known only to His very divine self, God dumped us *normal* people with a shitload of hormones and you just got a sprinkling, which you take care of with the occasional mastie" (8, italics added). Jocelyn's use of the word "normal" here is very telling: by the end of the novel, she proves to be happily self-actualized and bisexual. It is textually significant that she self-identifies as "normal," even though it takes Dylan a melodramatically long time to accept her own orientation and to recognize what most readers know by the time the two girls kiss: that Jocelyn is bisexual.

Dylan, of course, only has eyes for Jocelyn—and the opening chapter is a poignantly drawn scene that blends fantasy and realism, sleeping and dreaming, the material and the discursive. Dylan is bicycling Jocelyn to school, with Jocelyn clinging tightly to her from behind. The two girls enter a mysterious "white haze that. . . . glowed a brilliant white and was so tall it touched the underside of the bridge and over-rode the nearest bank by at least a hundred feet" (1–2). When Dylan asks Jocelyn what it is, she answers, "the river's dreaming" (1), and the girls walk into the bubbly cloud. "The whole thing was a little like walking through a trance, thinking in soft colors, sweet scents and vague secret murmurings" (3). Jocelyn strips naked, begins to unbutton Dylan's shirt, but instead grabs her by the hand and spins her in circles, "while everything we couldn't seem to say whirled white and sweet around us" (4). The bubbly mist has been caused by a spill upriver from a soap factory, but the girls have experienced a moment of sexual joy enveloped in images of purity. The text is discursively positioning their sexualities as clean, not dirty.

Not everyone in their community agrees, of course. Dylan's work is censored after she constructs a school project of a "girl and a guy" and "the parts of their bodies . . . each have a different book title" (93). The school's administration objects when she places Joyce Carol Oates's *Foxfire* over the girl's groin because Dylan likes the way the book depicts female sexuality:

> Of course it's about sex. . . . Everything we do in life is sex, isn't it? . . . I mean, it all comes from the same place inside you, doesn't it? And that place is either a place of following rules and doing what you're told, or figuring things out for yourself. . . . Because isn't that the way you really learn—about sex, love, justice, reality, anything? I mean, how can you figure out the universal meaning of something if you don't work out the personal meaning for yourself first? (Goobie 60–61)

Dylan's thinking here is fairly binaristic in terms of inside/outside and breaking or following rules, but this is the intellectual starting place from which she begins to honestly interrogate her orientation.

Dylan grows angry as she realizes how much conventional thinking dominates the discourse about teenage sexuality:

> It's like everyone thinks that what goes on between a teenager's legs is dirty. . . . I mean, whether you're having sex with someone or not. That part of your body is automatically indecent *because* you're a teenager. . . . Anyway, why does that part of your body have to be treated like a wild animal that should be caged and controlled? Why can't it be about decency and honor and what's true and good. . . . and wise? (138–39, italics in the original)

When Dylan finally kisses Jocelyn, she asks if they can't spend some time "just *being* like this" before they explore their sexuality further (238, italics in the original). Dylan's ontological request privileges both the material nature of sexual intimacy and the ontological legitimacy of being lesbian.

Dylan does not have the insight to recognize that she is decoupling binaries, but she acknowledges that "we live in our whole body, right? Our whole body is our heart and mind, maybe even our soul. So I think our heart and soul and mind live in our groin, just like anywhere else. And we need to make that part of us be about truth and respect and love, just like our heart" (252). Dylan understands that her *becoming* is integral to her sexuality—a sexuality that her culture may view as queer but that the text itself normalizes, as it also does Jocelyn's bisexuality. *Hello, Groin* celebrates female sexuality across a spectrum of sexualities, while it also depicts strong girls who advocate for themselves and others. Although orientation is only one aspect of identity politics, *Hello, Groin* enacts feminism in depicting female sexuality as a source of empowerment.

Advances in feminism in twenty-first century YA literature owe much to the contributions of gay YA novels to feminist discourse. Indeed, this chapter's reliance on queer theory indicates how many significant contributions gay men have made to destabilizing gender binaries, fighting homophobia, creating a culture of inclusion, and validating the relationship between one's orientation and one's gender identity. For example, Russel, the narrator of *The Geography Club* (2003), is a gay teenager who is afraid to come out in his homophobic high school. He and a group of friends form a gay-lesbian support group that they deceptively call the "Geography Club" to throw off their judgmental peers. Russel's new boyfriend, Kevin, is part of the group, as is his best friend, Min, and her girlfriend, Terese. Russel's narration sometimes reads like the reports of an anthropologist who is observing high school culture in a detached manner, but he also adds notes of critique to his commentary, as when he describes his disgust for how misogynistic the heteronormative athletes are when they talk about girls and sex: "Now that I had some idea what real intimacy was, it just made the guys sound like idiots, and cruel idiots at that" (181). His critique of these boys' behavior establishes the book's feminist ideology. Moreover, the book is as respectful of lesbian sexuality as it is gay sexuality, and the book features several strong female characters, including Min and her partner and a straight girl, Belinda, who joins the Geography Club because her mother's alcoholism has led her to need the emotional support the group offers. These girls are independent, articulate, strong, and decisive—and their characters are well-rounded, unique, and distinct from one another. Indeed, Min proves to be the most ethical and emotionally strong member of the Geography Club because of her insistence that the group has responsibility for the school's social pariah, Brian Bund. The group eventually "comes out" as the Gay-Straight-Bisexual Alliance—but their ability to call themselves what they really are can only happen because of Min's, Russel's and Brian's shared sense of ethics.

Although gender identity and orientation are not the same, the depiction of trans identity in adolescent literature is usually tied to sexuality. Trans characters question not only their gender identity and affiliation, but they must sometimes defend their orientation. In other words, when characters accept the gender they were assigned at birth, whether "Assigned Female at Birth" (AFAB) or "Assigned Male at Birth" (AMAB), they will, during adolescence, likely explore their orientation along the spectrum that includes heterosexuality, bisexuality, pansexuality, and gay or lesbian sexuality. But for trans characters—that is, those who do not experience themselves as the gender they were assigned at birth—issues of sexual orientation become both more complex and more heteronormative.

Don Latham writes about transgender issues in Louise Erdrich's *The Birchbark House* and its sequels. Latham employs the term "gender variant" to describe the two AFAB characters in the series who queer gender norms: Old Tallow and Two Strike ("Manly-Hearted" 131). Old Tallow is an independent and androgynous older woman who loves her dogs more than anyone; she helps Omakayas, the protagonist, and her family. Two Strike is Omakayas's rebellious cousin who ultimately alienates Omakayas by being so competitive—and Two Strike's gender-bending negatively affects her ability to marry. According to Latham, Old Tallow and Two Strike complicate the performance of gender roles in that Old Tallow embraces both the maternal role of nurturing and the patriarchal role of hunter, while Two Strike "represents a rejection of the feminine and an embracing of the masculine" ("Manly-Hearted" 135). For Latham, it is the social roles that these people perform that establish them as gender variants: it is their physical activities, more than discourse, that define these characters as trans characters ("Manly-Hearted" 133). Latham concludes that these novels "explore both limitations of and liberation from narrowly defined gender roles," providing an important contrast to the protagonist's more traditional assumption of feminine roles ("Manly-Hearted" 148–49). Latham's insistence on paying attention to the material (in the form of dress and work) provides a useful way for thinking about gender variation.

Latham's work relies on Butler's theories about performance and on Michelle Abate's work on tomboyism in *Tomboys: A Literary and Cultural History*. Abate, too, invokes Butler, arguing that "the tomboyish character highlights the performative nature of masculinity and femininity" (*Tomboys* 10). Abate's history of the emergence of the tomboy is also sensitive to materiality: Abate tracks how the hoyden figure of the mid-nineteenth century emerged into the tomboy in response to "changes in the nation's social, political and even economic climate"; by the 1920s, for example, "women were voting, engaging in such formerly masculine activities as smoking and drinking, and even asserting their right to participate in the 'male' world of work"—all of which are phenomena linked to materiality (*Tomboys* x).[6] Abate notes, however, that tomboyism was also linked in some eras with "proto-lesbianism," particularly during the Cold War era (*Tomboys* xi, 170). Abate establishes the tomboy as "a powerful concept and a pervasive cultural phenomenon" (*Tomboys* xxiii) that is particularly important for the powerful "gender-bending" that tomboys perform (*Tomboys* xxiv). Finally, it must be noted that Abate directly emphasizes the materiality of the tomboy:

> Tomboyism is also a distinct bodily identity. Together with being linked to corporeal traits like short hair, it is also predicated on such bodily acts as tree-climbing. Contemplating how the body-based realms of gender and race mutually construct and even reinforce each other, my discussion frequently pivots around questions of embodiment and disembodiment. (*Tomboys* xxviii)

Embodied actions and physical activity, as much as discursive phenomena, permit gender-bending to occur.

Mallan observes that stories that queer gender tend to work against a "backdrop of heteronormativity, with the result that the narratives deal with what could be regarded as an uncomfortable subject by providing a liberal account of empowerment and equality, and by emphasizing the difficulties that protagonists from relatively privileged and established social groups endure" (*Gender* 129). She reads Ellen Wittlinger's *Parrotfish* (2007) as a story about a trans male who tries to disrupt gender binaries by finding a "middle" space in between the two genders; Mallan points out that when the protagonist renames himself, he finds a gender-neutral name that incorporates "gray" as a morpheme: "Grady" (*Gender* 131). Grady problematizes the idea of performing gender when he questions why people have to "act" like girls or boys and can't just act "like themselves," but Mallan also notes he cannot escape thinking about identity as a stable construct: "His suggestion that people should act like themselves has implications for queer subjectivity as it dismisses gender categories, but at the same time (and somewhat contradictorily) it insists on a stable subject ('themselves')" (*Gender* 132). Like Latham and Abate, Mallan also observes that gender depends on discourse, performance, *and* the material: Grady must physically bind his breasts, and his performance as a male is disrupted when his period starts unexpectedly at school; he also defines himself in terms of activities that occur in the material world because he is someone who enjoys "guy stuff": carpentry and working on cars (Mallan, *Gender* 133). A drag show at school allows Grady to problematize masculinity and femininity as constructs, but he falls inadvertently into another gendered binary that Mallan identifies: gender performance as "inauthentic" or "authentic" (*Gender* 136). Mallan observes that this binary "reinforces an ontology (as an account of what gender *is*) that aligns with the dominant discourse of gender binary and its norms" (*Gender* 136). Even when authors attempt to destabilize gender binaries by creating trans characters, they sometimes still reinscribe the performativity and materiality of gender in binaristic terms.

Another novel that reinforces this observation of Mallan's—and her observation that trans characters often reinscribe middle-class values—is the trans female at the heart of Julie Anne Peters's *Luna* (2004). Luna/Liam lives in a world with rigid gender binaries: her parents fight about gender roles, and Luna sometimes hates her sister, Regan, (who narrates the novel) for identifying with the gender she was assigned at birth. Luna's sister sometimes thinks Luna/Liam experiences a massive Cartesian split: "as if his body wasn't connected to his brain" (18). Even while trying to problematize gender binaries, the book reinscribes them, as when Luna's sister thinks of Luna as "off both [gender] scales" or "between scales"; "he really was off the scale. Boy by day, girl by night. Except he was a girl all the time, inside. It was hardwired into his brain, he said, the way intelligence or memory is. His body didn't reflect his inner image. His body betrayed him" (50–51). But gender is also performative in this novel: Luna has to "play" to people's "expectations. Dress the part. Act the role" (51). Luna's *becoming* initially revolves around material performance—wearing fingernail polish and wigs and feminine clothes—but when she decides to transition, her *becoming* involves changes that are permanent, material, and visceral, including having her Adam's apple surgically altered and having sex reassignment surgery. Nevertheless, the novel shares the same reinscription of stable identity that Mallan identifies in *Parrotfish* when Grady asks, "Why couldn't people just be accepted for who they were?" (Wittlinger 51). Kimberley Reynolds acknowledges the "highly unreal dimension to this book" and assesses it as "more about the problems of living a transgender existence than an exegesis of current thinking about gender" (*Radical* 129). Although Reynolds initially argues that the book is "encouraging [readers] to move beyond the binaries of male/female, masculine/feminine into more nuanced ways of understanding sexual difference and orientations" (*Radical* 129), she also perceives that the book ultimately betrays contemporary understandings of gender that are based in queer theory: "it ignores 'the neithers, the boths, the incoherencies' (Rabinowitz 20) that queer theory has worked so hard to bring to our attention" (Reynolds, *Radical* 129–30).

It seems useful then to ask how the book is feminist. In the fact that Luna feels more emotionally and psychologically empowered as a female than a male, the novel demonstrates a young woman identifying what she wants and pursuing the goals, despite the costs.[7] Moreover, the cis female narrator gains respect for her own gender identity as she recognizes that being female is positive and life-affirming. Luna's sister, Regan, also shares an equal relationship with her boyfriend, despite a series of initial miscommunications. Most important, Regan comes to realize that she's wrong to blame her mother for ignoring Luna's transexuality. Once Regan realizes that their mother has known all along that Liam rejected the gender he was assigned at birth, the girl is angry that their mother has not done more to help Luna and guide her father to accept Luna as a daughter. When Regan has this epiphany, she is unsure whether their mother has been secretly supporting Luna or enabling Liam to commit suicide, and she begins to think of her mother as a "monster," but Luna won't allow that (228). "Yes, Mom's always known. She just hasn't known how to cope with it," Luna says, after which Regan can allow herself to question: "Had I jumped to the wrong conclusion about her? I hoped so. God, I hoped so" (241). Although the book is simplistic about everything from social class to gender binaries, at the very least, it demonstrates the complexity of the mother/daughter relationship when that relationship includes a trans daughter.

Mallan and Reynolds both demonstrate that trans novels are not perhaps the best vehicles for advancing queer theory; they are not always the most successful feminist novels, either. Nevertheless, the entire field of adolescent literature has become more sophisticated and inclusive because of the ways that feminism and queer theory have insisted that cultural attention needs to be given to issues of both gender *and* gender identity. Novels about trans teenagers are participating in a complex cultural conversation about the instability of gender, even when the characters themselves appear to accept gender binaries too easily. And while these particular trans novels focus more on gender identity and orientation than they do on sexuality, sexual desire is an inherent part of both plots. Luna, for example, insists that she is not gay, even though she is attracted to cis males: "I'm not gay. . . . It's not the same. I'm a girl" (94). As Liam, Luna experiences homophobia—his father and a school mate both accuse him of being gay, while Grady in *Parrotfish* first calls himself a "tomboy," then a "lesbian," and is homophobically accused of being a closeted lesbian by his physician because the man can't recognize that Grady is trans (Wittlinger 9, 54). Grady distinguishes gender identity from orientation, and claims that the phase in which s/he "came out" as a lesbian was "just a pit stop on the queer and confused highway" (Wittlinger 18). But Grady is as heterosexual as Luna is, which ultimately reinforces heteronormative sexuality in both novels.

Issues of sexuality seem even more complex for characters who are intersex. Take, for example, I. W. Gregario's *None of the Above*, in which Krissy Latimer, the homecoming queen of her high school, dates a popular and kind-hearted football player. Because they are both athletes, they frequently run together in what becomes a metaphor for how synchronized they are emotionally: "Over hundreds of runs, Sam and I had established a rhythm, a pace that we no longer had to think about, as if we were running to the same internal song" (11). Fully in control of her own sexuality, Krissy decides that they will have sex the night of homecoming; she's had a birth control shot months earlier, and Sam wears a condom, to ensure that she's physically safe. But the experience does not go as she has anticipated. Even though she is sexually excited and trusts Sam, she experiences pain even more unusual than that which usually accompanies the rupturing of a hymen:

> Sam untangled himself to get a condom, and when he turned back the feel of him on top of me was headier than any champagne.
> And then, oh my God. Pain.
> It felt like someone had taken an electric drill to my insides. I gritted my teeth and tried to power past it, but it was too much. Sam shifted, trying to go deeper, and I whimpered. (19)

The young couple decides to wait for another time—and that time is even more painful and leaves Krissy with lacerations that alarm her enough that she makes an appointment to see a gynecologist.

The gynecologist conducts a sonogram and determines that Krissy has no uterus—which explains why she's never gotten her period—and that she actually has two gonads that have never descended, which is why she has no pubic hair (although she does have normal breasts). A urologist confirms the diagnosis: Krissy has androgen insensitivity syndrome (AIS), sometimes also referred to as a "disorder of sex development" (DSD)—a term that the author rejects in the afterword because of the pejorative term "disorder" (332). Krissy is intersex.

It should be noted that the author of *None of the Above* is herself a urologist and that the novel sometimes reads like the type of self-help book that earns "problem novels" a bad name. Gregario provides extensive textual commentary about the nature of AIS, and she critiques the use of the term "hermaphrodite" and all of the many forms of discrimination that intersex people experience. She provides a thorough bibliography, including information about online support groups for people with AIS. She also occasionally pokes fun of conventions in YA publishing: after Sam breaks up with her because he cannot accept that Krissy is intersex, he begins to date "the head of the football boosters club. The only thing that would've been more cliché was if she were a cheerleader" (277). Following another standard trope of YA literature, Krissy's mother is dead (which is part of why she has not heretofore received adequate gynecological care), and the way Sam breaks up with Krissy is also clichéd. He falls into predictably violent homophobia:

> "Get away from me," he said, without even looking up. . . ."I've got nothing to say to you, you homo. . . ." I grabbed at his arm again. . . . He rounded on me. I could feel the muscles in his arm spasm.
> "Sam, please [. . .]," I begged. "Let me explain."
> "What the fuck is there to explain? . . . I thought I loved you, you fucking man-whore. And you've been lying to me. I have nothing to say to you. Ever. Again." (114, bracketed ellipses in the original)

More interesting by far than the text's reliance on clichés is the process of *becoming* by which Krissy accepts that she is female because she self-identifies as female. First, she is terrified of the word "hermaphrodite" and grieves that she is "something in between" being "a man or a woman" (54);

she believes that she is "a car that came off the assembly line all messed up. I was a lemon" (58), but her urologist won't let her accept this line of thinking. Krissy asks that doctor, "Am I trans, then? Like a man trapped in a woman's body?" (59), and the doctor answers honestly, "I know it's really confusing, but chromosomal sex, gender identity, and sexual orientation are all separate concepts" (59). The text acknowledges the materiality of hormone-producing sexual organs. Unfortunately, Krissy continues to think of herself as a "freak" for a while (60), even though she can acknowledge: "Nothing about me had changed, either. Yet everything was different" (64). Krissy friends' use of words like "mannish" or "girly" begins to disturb her as she grows to understand how complex gender identity is, and she realizes, "My life had been one big puzzle, except I never knew it" (70)—but she cries with relief when she realizes that because she has no cervix, she will never die of cervical cancer, as her mother has. Fearing a related cancer of the sex organs, however, she elects to have her testicles removed. After the surgery, "I had hoped, expected even, to suddenly feel like I was a girl again. But all I felt like was an empty jar" (147). As long as Krissy still defines gender in black and white terms, her body feels "empty" to her.

By the time Krissy reaches out to talk to her ex-boyfriend again, she has begun to show signs of accepting herself as she is. Sam tells her, "I. Don't. Date. Men.," so Krissy points out that he's seen her naked—so he should know better: "I am *not* a man. . . . You've seen me [. . .] *all of me*. How can you not accept that?" (171, bracketed ellipses in the original). Her assertion of her identity matters more to herself than to him. Although he cannot accept her as she is, Krissy is beginning to acknowledge that she is not male. For example, after she picks up a guy in a bar, she worries "*What if he finds out that you're a boy?*" (184, italics in the original), but internally, she shouts back at herself: "*I'm a girl*" (184, italics in the original). She finds out something about the vulnerability of her own femininity when that character tries to molest her: he grows violent and tries to grab beneath her skirt to find her "dick"; she again thinks "*I'm a girl*" (312). She does not experience full catharsis, however, until a childhood friend named Darren rescues her from this violence, like a fairy-tale knight in shining armor, and she realizes she is in love with Darren:

> All the anxiety and guilt and self-loathing that I'd been holding in for weeks came out in the catharsis Dr. LaForte had been hoping for since I started therapy. But it wasn't fear that pushed all my emotions past the tipping point; it was the realization that I was kind of in love

with Darren Kowalski for making me laugh minutes after I'd survived a potential hate crime. I cried like a baby, and as embarrassing as it was to have a meltdown with the object of my affection sitting there patting me awkwardly on the arm to get me to stop, the release was so liberating that I didn't care. (320)

Krissy has accepted herself as a girl, as heterosexual, and as intersex—although it's a bit unfortunate she has to be "saved" by a heteronormative cis male.

In other words, too much of Krissy's story is binaristic. Her self-definition is greatly influenced either by men (such as Sam, Darren, and her father) or by the series of all-female doctors she has (gynecologist, urologist, psychiatrist). On the other hand, the book does acknowledge that gender identity exists on a spectrum, as does orientation. Darren's father is gay, and so Darren sounds wise when he tells her, "If there's one thing I learned from my dad leaving my mom, it's that love isn't a choice. You fall for the person, not their chromosomes" (324). Darren's effort to make loving someone be about personality rather than biology complicates that contentious issue by touching on dualistic thinking about "nature" and "culture." Is a chromosome an indisputable effect of science/nature? This book implies an answer of "no": gender identity is self-defined; it is influenced by multiple factors, including chromosomes, hormones, familial nurturance, self-perception and self-definition during childhood and adolescence, and cultural attitudes. If *None of the Above* falls into too many heteronormative romance conventions, at least Krissy is a strong, loving, and self-defined girl who deserves to be loved by someone equally strong, loving, and self-defined. Moreover, she has moved from thinking about herself as always-already female, to thinking about herself pejoratively as a "hermaphrodite," to thinking about herself as a "man" to accepting herself as intersex in positive terms that allow her to self-define as a girl. The text could not be more clear in its efforts to empower individuals to determine and self-define their own gender identity.

Where YA novels still often fail to be progressive, however, is in their depiction of female masturbation. Katy Stein points out that the inclusion of masturbation as a topic in YA literature is itself a twenty-first century phenomenon, since the depiction of female masturbation in twentieth-century novels was "practically nonexistent" (416); nevertheless, she relies on Foucault's theorizations about sexuality in *History of Sexuality* when she asserts: "Despite the argument that young adult literature is saturated with transgressive content, depictions of female teen masturbation … [remain] situated within traditional, adult-centered values intended to continue and ultimately control teenage sexuality" (415); Stein analyzes how various novels that depict female masturbation do so to validate the masculine presence in heterosexuality and to institutionalize anxiety-ridden discourses about female masturbation. Stein identifies a spectrum of textual attitudes towards female masturbation: in Meg Cabot's *Ready or Not* (2005) and Phyllis Reynolds Naylor's *Dangerously Alice* (2006), female masturbation is a "last resort" for sexually frustrated girls (415); in Judy Blume's *Deenie* (1973) and Ibi Kaslik's *Skinny* (2004), masturbation is "deviant" (417); and even transgressive novels like Beth Goobie's *Hello, Groin*, which attempts to normalize masturbation as an individualized issue of teen sexuality, still inadvertently depict masturbation in problematic ways. "In seeking to define, regulate, and normalize sexuality, these institutions thus encourage its overall repression, positioning the teens to seek approval, answers, and forgiveness from the agencies of power for their emerging sexual desires" (Stein 426).

4. See also Thomas Crisp (333–48) and Corrine M. Wickens (148–64).

5. For more on the relationship between sexuality and death, see Trites (*Disturbing* 122–23) and Kathryn James' excellent *Death, Gender, and Sexuality*.

6. Crucial to Abate's work is her important observation about how racialized the tomboy character was: the tomboy's first manifestation was invested in racial purity: "From their inception, tomboys demonstrated how unruly female behavior that was formerly seen as socially 'bad' could be racially good" (xii). Abate finds it paradoxical that "this code of conduct that was intended to strengthen white women, and by extension, the white race was consistently yoked with various forms of nonwhiteness" (xii). She observes that "both syllables of the term 'tomboy' evoke common racial pejoratives" (xii).

7. Luna's tripping off to an apparently happy ending, made easy by the availability of money and one supportive trans sponsor evokes Michelle Abate's comments about Carlton Mellick's reappropriation of such terms as "fag" and "faggiest." Abate writes: "While these lines may be meant to encourage and even empower, they ring hollow. Contrary to Mellick's remarks, combating heterosexism, ending homophobia, and allowing non-gender normative individuals to gain acceptance requires a great deal more than merely thinking 'really happy thoughts'" ("Faggiest" 410). Luna, too, seems to be thinking "really happy thoughts," which I'm sure every reader of this book wishes were enough to make life end happily ever after for all trans teenagers.

BY MOLLY M. GINTY

Is 'Female Viagra' Feminist?

A new drug divides the women's health movement

IT'S BEEN CALLED THE FIRST "Viagra for women" and hailed as a health breakthrough. But Addyi (generic name fliban-serin) is sparking ire just as it claims to spark desire. Is this drug a boon for feminism because it finally gives women what men have enjoyed since 1998: prescription medication that can effectively boost sagging libidos? Or are the drug's pluses (an average increase of 0.5 to 1 "sexually satisfying events per month") not really worth its potential side effects of nausea, dizziness and fainting?

Since the FDA approved Addyi in August 2015, feminist debate on these *questions has raged. Heightening the* controversy is the fact that feminist organizations, with funding from the drug's maker, Sprout Pharmaceuticals, played an active role in getting the drug approved. Fourteen groups, including NOW, the National Association of Clinical Nurse Specialists, and the American Sexual Health Association, formed a coalition called "Even the Score" that lobbied the FDA as part of a larger goal of "level[ing] the playing field when it comes to the treatment of women's sexual dysfunction."

Does Addyi work? And is it a worthy feminist cause? Seeking answers, *In These Times* spoke with Sally Greenberg, executive director of the National Consumers League and a member of the Even the Score Coalition, and Diana Zuckerman, president of the National Center for Health Research and a critic of both Addyi and Even the *Score. Joining the conversation were* two women's health experts who have

Female Viagra: a tough pill for some to swallow.

not taken public sides in the controversy: Monica Raye Simpson, executive director of SisterSong Women of Color Reproductive Health Collective, and Susan F. Wood, director of George Washington University's Jacobs Institute of Women's Health and the FDA's former assistant commissioner for women's health.

Sally, can you tell us why you're a fan of this drug?

SALLY: We can argue whether there are four or 26 treatments for male sexual dysfunction. But the fact is that there are really zero pharmacological options for women with sexual dysfunction. *A number of organizations believe a* treatment like this is long overdue. The

new treatment is approved for a very specific condition: Hypoactive Sexual Desire Disorder (HSDD), which has been recognized in medical literature since 1977 and is characterized by the total disappearance or significant reduction of sex drive and distress about the condition. This is the most common category of women's sexual dysfunction, an issue that made the FDA's list of the top 20 unmet health needs. We think flibanserin is a breakthrough treatment and hope this opens the door so women can have the same treatment options as men.

What do others think about HSDD and how to treat it?

MONICA: HSDD is impacting the lives

of many women. Forty percent of women have sexual problems, including a lack of sexual desire, inability to orgasm, and pain or discomfort. We want to create opportunities for women to engage in conversation with their healthcare providers about things that might make their sexual lives better. Maybe that's not a drug. Maybe it's what's happening in women's lives. We're living in a very stressful environment—especially in communities of color—and that definitely impacts women's sexual drive. People are not exercising. We do not have adequate access to healthcare. When thinking about this disorder, we should ask, "How do we create better environments that will also help people connect with each other?"

DIANA: Men have drugs for one type of sexual problem, and that is erectile dysfunction. That's a physiological problem that's quite specific. Women also have treatments for a physiological problem related to sexual enjoyment: vaginal dryness. There is no drug for men or women for loss of libido, which can be an emotional and psychological issue as well as a physiological problem.

How well has flibanserin been shown to work, and what are the risks?

SALLY: For women in the clinical trials, the number of sexually satisfying events per month went from 2.5 to 5 per month. *[Editors' note: The average increase of 0.5 to 1 cited by the FDA included placebo controls].* That meant flibanserin met the measures set by the FDA, which created an advisory committee that voted 18 to 6 to approve flibanserin.

DIANA: There were two ways that the sexual benefit was measured in the studies. The first was a daily diary, the other was a monthly estimate. As a researcher, I think it's ridiculous to ask women to measure their sexually satisfying experiences based on their memory of the past month. I can remember my daily experiences over the last week, but couldn't accurately remember them over the exact time-frame of one month. The daily diary found no significant improvement compared to placebo, but the monthly measure found a small improvement: an average of less than one additional satisfying sexual experience per month. That small benefit might be worthwhile for a drug without risks, but that is not true of Addyi.

SALLY: I think there may have been some unconscious gender bias when the FDA rejected the drug the first two times. Drugs that treat male sexual dysfunction have far more dire side effects—stroke, heart attack, four-hour erection, etc.—and we allow men to decide with their healthcare practitioners about whether they're going to take on those risks. Millions of men have access to those drugs, and women should have the same rights to decide to take on the risks.

There has been a lot of inaccurate information about this drug, including that it has life-threatening side effects. Its risks are nausea, dizziness and fatigue. It has a black-box warning not to be taken with alcohol. Eleven thousand women were involved in clinical trials, and 58 percent of them said they were social drinkers and had no problem using alcohol in small quantities with this drug.

DIANA: You don't die of nausea, but who wants to live with it? Other risks include passing out and difficulty sleeping—which could result in women nodding off while driving.

The day after the FDA approved the drug, its parent company, Sprout Pharmaceuticals, sold for $1 billion. Was this drug rushed through because profit was at stake?

SUSAN: I don't think the FDA rushed it through that way. Individual reviewers objected quite definitively to the approval, but the more senior-level reviewers made the decision to approve it, in part because of patient demand. I think that the public relations advocacy campaign, which was financed by Sprout, had an effect on both the advisory committee and the senior reviewers at the FDA.

DIANA: That's what money will buy. You have a room full of patient advocates who were brought there—whether their way was paid or they were encouraged by this very highly publicized campaign. The advisory committee members are human; they're very heavily influenced by people in the room, who were cheering and booing. So they compromised on the science, I believe, in order to please the patients, some of whom were not even eligible to take this drug, since it is approved only for women who are pre-menopausal, not drinking alcohol at all, and so on.

What does the way all of this has gone down mean for feminism?

SUSAN: Feminism is a big tent, and we all work together on some things and disagree on others, and that's not necessarily unhealthy. The unhealthy aspects included the company's strategy of "divide and conquer."

MONICA: This is where feminism really shows its disconnect from the most marginalized communities. For men, Viagra was huge. For women, I don't know if this is. I just think there are so many questions.

DIANA: To me, the focus on this debate is very unfortunate given all the very real health issues facing women. For example, there are a hundred contraceptives on the market in the United States, and some are much safer than others. Women are dying unnecessarily as a result of the ones that aren't as safe. We are having a hell of a time trying to get anybody to pay attention. It is just not a sexy issue, and certain companies have a vested interest in making sure no one is talking about it.

SALLY: I view this drug as a breakthrough for women. Men have had many treatment options for sexual health for decades—women have had few, if any. The FDA listened to women suffering from a condition, HSDD, that undermines their relationships, their health and their self-esteem, and approved a treatment.

Feminism and Sexuality

Philip N. Cohen

There are different kinds of feminist theory, which use different social and institutional points of entry into the problem of gender inequality. Naturally, there are lots of ways to categorize feminisms, but for my purposes it is useful to divide them according to the place of labor and economics versus sexuality in their conceptual schemes. For some feminists, drawing from the Marxist tradition, gender inequality flows from the division of labor. As a result, their emphasis is on the nature and organization of work and on the place of gender in that system. Others, drawing from the writing of radical feminists, see gender inequality as based primarily in the realm of sex and sexuality.[1]

Families are centers of both work and sexuality. There is a gender division of labor within families—one that has weakened substantially but remains strong. And there is a further division of labor between families and the market economy, which has implications for gender because of the different gender dynamics in those two arenas. To oversimplify: one arena, the family, is more regulated by tradition and informal interactions, while the other, the market, falls under the rule of law and more impersonal economic forces.[2]

I addressed work-related aspects of gender inequality most closely in chapter 6. Here I turn toward sexuality, which also appears both inside and outside of families—and at the border between families and the wider world (as when sex leads to marriage or children). The concepts are not so clearly separated, of course. For example, are the gender questions around motherhood and reproduction really about work or sexuality? And what about politics—which arena requires most attention? Consider this collection of essays an introductory shove toward these issues—which I hope will stimulate your own discussions about gender, sexuality, and families.

1. NOT YOUR FEMINIST GRANDMOTHER'S PATRIARCHY

It would be wrong to look at Donald Trump's election and say, "See, nothing changes!" Leading up to November 2016, it appeared from election polling that Hillary Clinton would win because of a strong lead among women, while Donald Trump would lose despite drawing the majority of male votes.[3] And that would not have been new. In the 2012 election, women were the majority of voters, and the majority of them voted for Obama; the weaker sex clearly was men. The same thing happened 1996, when men couldn't stop the reelection of Bill Clinton.[4] In the end, Hillary Clinton did win the majority of female votes (although enough White women came out for Trump to push him over the top in the swing states needed to win the Electoral College). Nevertheless, if women contribute substantially to the election of the most powerful man in the world, this fact tests our ability to think systematically about power and inequality. How is it possible to see the unprecedented transformation in women's relative status and still claim men's continued dominance? A common approach is to list data points and have more of them on the side you prefer. For example, you could say, "Women are closing the earnings gap and increasing their presence in leadership positions, and men are doing more housework; but on the other hand, a lot of women are raped and Donald Trump won the election." That's three facts to two in favor of progress, so your overall interpretation is communicated implicitly. But describing a complex situation does not require vague or opaque prose. We can be specific and accurate while also making concrete general statements at a higher level of abstraction.

For giving critical responses to generalizations about women's relative progress, I have been described as part of a "feminist academic establishment" that is "uneasy when women make progress" and "prefers to use statistics that are least favorable to signs of women's progress."[5] Hana Rosin, whose record of misstating facts in the service of inaccurate conclusions I documented extensively (see chapter 6), described me as someone who likes to engage in "data wars" over the details of gender inequality.[6] But an attention to data is necessary for gaining perspective on the big picture—it would be wrong to simply point to Trump and drop the mic.

In our academic research on gender inequality, my colleagues and I study variation and change. That means figuring out why women's employment increased so rapidly, why some labor markets have smaller gender gaps than others, why some workplaces are less segregated than others, why couples in some countries share housework more than those in other countries, why women in some ethnic groups have relatively high employment rates, and so on.[7] These patterns of variation and change help us understand gender in our system of inequality. Systemic patterns don't just happen. People (in the aggregate) have to get up in the morning and do inequality every day. To understand how it works and why it doesn't, we need to see how and why it varies—for example, why and to what extent some people resist equality while others dedicate their lives to perpetuating it. Someone who studies inequality but doesn't care about change and variation is not a social scientist.

Patriarchy

"It's easy to find references to patriarchs, patriarchy or patriarchal attitudes in reporting on other countries," writes economist Nancy Folbre. "Yet these terms seem largely absent from discussions of current economic and political debates in the United States. Perhaps they are no longer applicable. Or perhaps we mistakenly assume their irrelevance."[8]

The United States, like every society in the world, remains a patriarchy: all societies today are ruled by men. That is not just because every country (except Rwanda and Bolivia) has a majority-male national parliament, and it is the case despite the handful of countries with women heads of state (including, now, the United Kingdom).[9] It is a systemic characteristic that combines dynamics at the level of the family, the economy, the culture, and the political arena. Top political and economic leaders are the low-hanging fruit of patriarchy statistics. But they probably are in the end the most important—the telling pattern is that the higher you look, the more male it gets. If a society really had a stable, female-dominated power structure for an extended period of time, even I would eventually question whether it was really still a patriarchy. Female heads of state are important, but they are not a female power structure.

In my own area of research things are messier because families and workplaces differ so much and power is usually jointly held. But I'm confident in describing American families as mostly patriarchal. Maybe the most basic indicator is the apparently quaint custom of wives assuming their husbands' names, which is one literal definition of *patriarchal*. This hasn't generated much feminist controversy lately. But to an anthropologist from another planet, this *patrilineality* would be a major signal that American families are male dominated. Among US-born married women, only 6 percent had a surname that differed from their husband's in 2004 (it was not until the 1970s that married women could even function legally using their "maiden" names).[10] Only half of respondents think it should be required for a woman to take her husband's name, but 68 percent of women and 78 percent of men think it's "generally better." Among younger women it is more common for women to keep their names, which is one indicator of the direction of change.[11] But there is no end to the tradition in sight. In fact, progress may have slowed. A (small) study that compared attitudes among college students between 1990 and 2006 found no change in the percentage of women who planned to keep their birth names upon marriage, around 8 percent.[12]

Of course, the proportion of people getting married has fallen, and the number of children born to unmarried parents has risen. Single parenthood—and the fact that this usually means single motherhood—reflects both women's growing independence and the burdens of care that fall on them.[13] At the elite end of the social scale, the growing single-mother-by-choice movement looks like evidence of women's growing dominance in the family—well-off women choosing to go it alone and run their families from a position of strength. But at the lower end single parenthood is more complicated. There is an element of women's improving position relative to men, as in "I'm already poor, I don't need a poor man to help with that." But single motherhood also reflects, and creates, the heavy burden of child rearing that mothers bear. What researchers called the "feminization of poverty" a few decades ago—as single-mother families increased their representation among the poor population—doesn't go in the win column for feminism. That's why I don't share Liza Mundy and Hana Rosin's view that single mothers should be called "breadwinners," using the term formerly applied to men who held dominant positions in families that included subordinate wives.

Differences That Matter

The social critic Barbara Ehrenreich—in a 1976 essay she might or might not like to be reminded of—urged feminists to acknowledge distinctions that matter rather than to tar everything with the simplistic brush of "patriarchy." In China, one of the world's most entrenched patriarchal systems, women undeniably made tremendous progress over the twentieth century, but the revolution was far from complete. Ehrenreich wrote: "There is a difference between a society in which sexism is expressed in the form of female infanticide and a society in which sexism takes the form of unequal representation on the Central Committee. And the difference is worth dying for."[14]

China presents an extreme case. Its extremely harsh patriarchy was fundamentally transformed—into a different sort of patriarchy. By the late 1970s female infanticide (as well as the brutal practice of footbinding) had indeed been all but eradicated—tremendous improvements for women, saving millions of lives.[15] With the advent of the one-child policy in the 1980s, however, female infanticide gave way to sex-selective abortion (and female representation on the ruling committees dropped), representing an important transformation.[16] It's important to acknowledge the continued male dominance of Chinese society but also to pay attention to, and learn from, the pattern of and prospects for change.

Like Ehrenreich, I think we need to look at the variations to understand the systemic features of our society. Men losing out to women in national elections is an important one. Given the choice between two male-dominated parties with wide differences on social policy in 2008 and 2012 (and almost in 2016), women voters (along with Blacks, Latinos, and the poor) bested men and got their way. I wouldn't minimize that, or ignore the scale and direction of change. The American patriarchy has weakened.

I expect some readers will go right to their favorite statistics or personal experiences in order to challenge my description of our society as patriarchal. In that tit-for-tat, men (like Trump) leading the vast majority of the most powerful institutions, and American family names usually following the male line, become just another couple of data points. But they shouldn't be, because some facts are more important than others.

FEMINISM AND SEXUALITY

1. For a different way of categorizing feminisms, and a more thorough introduction, I recommend Lorber's (2011) edited collection.

2. I describe the institutional arenas concept to structure my textbook (Cohen 2014b).

3. Presidential Gender Watch (n.d.).

4. In the same vein, the majority of Whites voted against Obama in 2008. These results are based on exit polls. See CNN.com (1996, 2008); NBC News (2012).

5. Mundy (2012b).

6. Rosin (2012b).

7. Cohen and Bianchi (1999); Cohen and Huffman (2003); Huffman, Cohen, and Pearlman (2010); Geist and Cohen (2011); Read and Cohen (2007).

8. Folbre (2012).

9. Inter-Parliamentary Union (2016).

10. Gooding and Kreider (2010).

11. Powell et al. (2012).

12. Scheuble, Johnson, and Johnson (2011).

13. Folbre (2010).

14. Ehrenreich (1976).

15. Coale and Banister (1996); Mackie (1996).

16. Hvistendahl (2011).

Unit IV. Gender, Immigration, Racism and Sexism

Yemayá

Gloria Anzaldua

Throughout much of her adult life, Anzaldúa felt particularly close to Yemayá, the Yoruban orisha (goddess) associated with the oceans and other waters. Anzaldúa's house in Santa Cruz was located about one block from the Pacific Ocean. Almost every day Anzaldúa took a long walk along the ocean, on West Cliff Drive. This previously unpublished poem, last revised in January 2001, reflects Anzaldúa's intimate relationship with the ocean Yemayá.

Yemayá

I come to you, Yemayá,
ocean mother, sister of the fishes.
I stop at the edge of your lip
where you exhale your breath on the beach—
into a million tiny geysers.
With your white froth I anoint my brow and cheeks,
wait for your white-veined breasts to wash through me.

Yemayá, your tongues lick me,
your green mouths nibble my feet.
With your brine I inhale the beginnings of life.
Your silver tongues hiss then retreat
leaving hieroglyphs and silence on the sand.

Take me with you, Yemayá.
Let me ride your flaking tortoise shell,
dance with your serpents and your seals.
Let me roar down the marble cliffs of your shoulders
varooming into waterfalls—
chipping into a million emeralds!

Beached at the edge of your lilac skirt,
you lay driftwood, a feather, a shell at my feet.
Your silver tongues hiss then retreat.
I wipe the salt spray from my face.
Yemayá, ocean mother,
I take you home in a bottle.
Tonight I will sleep on your rolling breasts.
Esta noche sueño contigo.

"WHERE ARE YOU FROM?": "NO, WHAT I MEAN IS, WHERE ARE YOU REALLY FROM?"

Roksana Badruddoja

Notions of "Home"

I found myself stepping off a New York City PATH train to an unusually chilly weekday afternoon in September 2004. I buttoned my salmon and cream tweed-style jacket and walked toward the address I had written down in my daily planner. I approached a doorway to an almost hidden apartment building; I rang the doorbell, and Sunita buzzed me in. Sunita shares haunting words with me: "I always get asked, 'Where are you from?' And, if I don't give the *right* answer, then I get, 'No, what I mean is, where are you *really* from?'"

As a second-generation Bangladeshi-American woman, born to and raised by immigrant parents in the United States, I conceptualized this chapter from a personal self project (see Spivak 1988; hooks 1990; Puar 1994a), one that stemmed from not being able to coherently articulate the answer to the question, "Where are you from?" I have come to realize that I am not the only one to struggle to answer the question of home satisfactorily. Mohanty (1993) offers a personal story about a flight she was taking back to the United States after participating in a conference in the Netherlands: "On a TWA flight … the professional white man sitting next me asks: a) which school do I go to? And b) when do I plan to go home?—all in the same breath …" (351). The "Other" narrative is legitimized and enforced by the question "Where are you from? … Where are you *really* from?" Visweswaran (1993) shares,

Certainly the question, "Where are you from?" is never an innocent one. Yet not all subjects have equal difficulty in replying. To pose a question of origin is subtly to pose a question of return, to challenge not only temporally, but geographically, one's place in the present ... it is a question which provokes a sudden failure of confidence, the fear of never replying adequately. (301)

Puar (1994a) argues that the reason we struggle is that it is the question that is problematic, not the answer. The question becomes exclusionary and racist: The purpose is to remind us that we neither belong here nor fit in.

"Monolithic" or "linear notions of home" refer to the naturalized, apparently self-evident qualities that are attached to the idea of "home" (see Gillis 1997). Most multicultural models assume assimilation as the benchmark and often link "home" to a single spatial location. The context of the question "Where are you from?" is embedded in the construction of home as a "situated, fixed, safe sphere, with ties to place."

Mohanty (1993), in extending her story about her TWA flight, says,

I have been asked the "home" question (when are you going home) periodically for fifteen years now. Leaving aside the subtly racist implications of the question (go home—you don't belong here), I am still not satisfied with my response. What is home? ... I am convinced that this question—how one understands and defines home—is a profoundly political one. (352)

As a trained sociologist and a professor of women's and gender studies with an interest in post-colonial studies, I am particularly concerned about thinking through diverse languages, images, myths, and rituals through which home is represented and constituted. I insist that non-linear notions of home have an existence independent of actual living arrangements (Gillis 1997). Here "home" is a mental construct that is no less real than the household itself. It is constituted through a set of cultural practices.

Grappling with the psychological impact of encountering the question "Where are you from?" (see Puar 1994a, 21), I begin to think through U.S. racialization projects and the notion of "home" in this chapter. I use it as a basis to think about my life along with the lives of the women who participated in this year-long feminist ethnographic research.

In this chapter, I review the ethnographic data to show that that "home" cannot be written as "one fixed place nor as a safe place, and movement is not only mobility but it also about displacement" (Puar 1994a, 76). More specifically, my research participants suggest that we should begin to understand "home" by becoming aware of home as ideologically constructed, not only across space but also through time.

"Where Are You *Really* From?"

Unanimously, my research participants are often asked where they are from. The tacit assumption behind the question of home is one of foreignness. Consider Kalpana Vrudhula's poem, cited in Visweswaran (1993), "Do not belong to this or that, but I am here":

Are you from India?
No, my parents are.
Oh, How exciting! You know I saw the movie Gandhi, I
thought it was great ... Have you been?
Oh, yes, of course!
(I've only gone once, I was already 23)

The guy I work with is from India. You must know him? His name, uh ... let me think, oh yes, Patel? (306)

In her poem, Vrudhula conveys the ignorance with which most Americans view South Asia (Vrudhula specifically makes references to India). Vrudhula expresses the ways in which second-generation South Asians handle the presumption that they are really not from here, and Vrudhula's lack of response to the question of home reflects the nature of the question, a denial that Vrudhula and other South Asian-Americans are from here, there, and everywhere.

Juhi explains that she is often asked where she is from simply because people find it difficult to categorize her phenotypic characteristics within available racial and ethnic structures, thus rendering Juhi as exotic:

[I remember being] at a St. Patrick's Day party with my friends. They were all white, [and] this one guy says, "My friend and I have been staring at you for the past half hour wondering what you are." I wanted to punch the guy, so I said, "What do you think I am?" He literally guessed fifteen different things ...

Juhi connects the question of home to an insinuation that she is not *really* from here and does not have a stake in maintaining American nation-state borders, and, therefore, is not *truly* American:

The thing I don't get is I am American. I am just as American as you are because I was born in this country. Maybe my parents weren't born in this country but I grew up here. Maybe some of [my experiences] were different but I've had a lot of the same experiences like you. I went to the same type of school and college, and I work in the same type of job.

Then the question of home, first, is prompted by the ambiguous ways in which race is defined in the United States. Second, the question of home is embedded in the genealogy of U.S. and "western" colonization (situated in a discourse that ties home to a single space). How long has one *really* been here in the context of family and lineage?

Rupa, another woman who participated in my fieldwork, shares with me a story about identity and changing notions of home:

> *I have a girlfriend who just went back to Taiwan within the past week, and she wrote me this story over the e-mail about how she was sitting in a Chinese language class and the teacher asked her in Chinese, "Where did you come from?" She did not know how to answer so the teacher thought she was stupid. "Does that mean am I from Taiwan, or am I from Chicago, or am I from New York?"*

Puar (1994b), Grewal (1994), and Foucault (1990; 1994; 1995) provide a wonderful backdrop in which to situate Rupa's words. Puar writes,

> *Immigration is not a one-time movement; it is a complex shifting of localities of physical and emotional states, which begins way before and extends far beyond the actual event. As children of immigrants, we are denied these realities by western society, yet constantly reminded of them. The actuality and validity of our displaced, "outsider" identities is hence negated. Why else should this question be asked?* (22)

Grewal contends that hegemonic discourses of this nation use racist images of minority groups as a formative structure of citizenship (70). Racist images are absorbed into economics, racialized structures of the nation-state, U.S. imperial history and militarism, and the globalization of capital and labor. And Foucault rejects the idea of knowledge, truth, and language as neutral, arguing that knowledge is always connected to power: (Modern) discourses that formalize knowledge regulate and control our experiences.

The women I interviewed are more than aware that as South Asians in America, they are positioned—by whites and nonwhites—within essentialist categories that operate and support hierarchies of privilege, domination, power, and control. There is indeed a denial that my research participants have multiple alliances and multiple homes that may even be contradictory.

At times, Rupa works within a bifurcated boundary—South Asian and American—by explaining her parents' immigration from Bangladesh to America and her location in the assimilation model as an "ABCD," or someone who is U.S.-born. But most of the time, she redraws the boundary by simply stating that she is from upstate New York. Rupa says,

> *I might take the time of giving them the complicated answer, "I was born and raised here, and my parents are from blah blah." But mostly I'll say "Logan Square," and that is it …*

Similarly, Jhumpa expresses, "When someone asks me where I am from … it really makes me antsy because I know what they are trying to get at. But I will just be like, 'oh, I am from L.A.'" In an effort to both work within and redraw the fictive and constructed boundaries between South Asian and American, Laila, another one of my participants, asks for clarification before answering the question of home,

> *I always ask an explanation question, "Do you mean where my family is from or where I grew up?" I don't know if they want to know if I am from Virginia or if they want to know my ethnicity or if they want to know if I was born in this country.*

Unlike Vrudhula's experiences, my research participants also describe being questioned by South Asians immigrants. Priyanka talks to me about one of her train rides into Manhattan:

> *One morning an Indian man got on, and he sat down right next to me. He finally decided to say something. First, he asked me if I was Indian, which is the standard first question … He [then] asked me if I spoke Hindi … After all that, he asked me, "So, how long have you been in this country?"*

Auditi shares her answer to "Where are you from?" while traveling in India: "If I am traveling in India … invariably the question is, 'Where are you from?' I say that 'I am American,' and they say, 'No, you're not American.'" Priyanka and Auditi's challenged self-notions underscore the women's "foreignness." South Asians also jettison my research participants as "Americans" on several levels. While citizenship privileges provide the women with a certain amount of invincibility, their privilege is not just about freedom, but it also includes "Otherness."

But my informants voice that they find desi voyeurs to be less oppressive than non-desi voyeurs. Jhumpa says,

> *I feel like it is more innocent in a way. I feel really guarded when white people ask me that question. I don't get as guarded when people of color, especially South Asians, ask me that question. They want to know as much as I want to know, because if I do meet someone else that is Bengali I am like really, I am Bengali too, and there is a connection there.*

Rupa says, "White men [bother me the most, but] if somebody is really nice and it is an elder, I will ask them what they mean …" Indira expresses, "I was asked that a lot in college by South Asians or even when I went to India because I don't look Bengali enough. And Juhi says, "Sometimes they won't necessarily assume that I am a South

Asian, but they'll approach me in a way that I am because I am in a situation where I would meet other South Asians, so it doesn't bother me as much." Jhumpa, Rupa, Indira, and Juhi show that in matters of racial and ethnic identity, the person doing the identifying is consequential. Bashi (1998) writes:

> It makes a difference who is doing the categorical defining, and who is policing the boundaries of these definitions. It comes down to a question of power: who holds it, where the power-holders see themselves and others in the existing hierarchy, where they think they should be in the racial hierarchy ... and how they use their power to realize those norms. (965)

Ethnicity, thus, is a matter of structure and power—which ethnicities are available for sorting, and who gets to do the sorting (see Nagel 2003, 42). Such are the monolithic, unmarked, and normative understandings of what an "American" nationalist self and an imagined "true" South Asian is.

Mobile Diasporas

Clearly, the configuration of home is staged as a "situated, fixed, safe sphere, with ties to place" (Puar 1994a. 75), but my informants show that "home" must be written as ideologically constructed, not only across space but also through time. That is, home is constituted through a set of cultural practices. Ronica voices the floating and transnational nature of home, swiftly challenging the linear teleology that often accompanies the discussion of home:

> I feel pretty strongly that if I try to create my identity here [U.S.], ignoring South Asia and my relationship to South Asia, it would totally make me feel like I was missing out, and it would make feel like I didn't have a real place in the world.

In the sense of transnational, I feel real committed to going back to South Asia as often as I can and doing things there by giving back to a community that my family benefited from ... When I go to India it is very much about sharing the privilege that I have [from being an American].

Ronica comments on how post-1965 migration from South Asia, unlike migration in the 1800s, carried citizenship rights for many. The discourse of citizenship (and class privilege) has profound effects on the notion of home for immigrants, their children, and subsequent generations: (American) citizenship produces transnational mobile bodies that travel freely transatlantically (from West to East to West). Puar (1994b) reflects, "I clutched on to [my passport] as proof of my right to movement, seeing the American eagle on its front as a sign of democracy, the freedom to move—the façade of citizenship" (87). Ronica is a "shifting and multiply positioned" subject (with particular privileges of class and nation), resulting in a notion of diaspora that no longer uses a "linear teleology." Rupa also accentuates the complexities involved in defining her sense of home within a linear teleology:

Right after the [Bush–Gore] elections, I wrote this really depressing poem ... One of the things I wrote was, how do I call this my land when it is practically an accident that I am even here? My dad could have gotten residency in Canada or in the U.K., but I ended up here. What are my ties here really? What does it mean to be Bengali or Muslim, growing up in this little shit town in [the East Coast]? Bangladesh, what does it mean that I call it "back home"?

Rupa shows that "home" cannot be written as "one fixed place nor as a safe place, and movement is not only mobility but it [is] also about displacement" (Puar 1994a, 76). Rupa suggests dissatisfaction with fixed and immobile conceptualizations of "home."

But Rupa also underscores that a shifting and multiply positioned notion of diaspora "functions as a threat to certain homes while becoming the construct of home for certain Others": It is neither a "natural" space, nor is it nation-friendly (see Puar 1994a, 76–77). Rupa vocalizes the physical and sexual imagery that accompanies what it means to be both an American woman and a Bangladeshi woman; standards that she is far from:

> *Yeah, I was born here [the U.S.], but I don't have that draw; that pull it is not the same. I currently embody everything that the majority of, at least eligible, voters hate. I am queer, Muslim, and brown. Of course I come back to my senses ... The last time I went to Bangladesh, I remember on Eid, I was decked out ... in a sari and my cousin put her wedding jewelry all over me ... We took rickshaws to another khala's [maternal aunt] house ... and on the way all the men in the street were coming up to the rickshaw and leering in my face, [asking], "Cheley na mey?" [Boy or girl?] and they were mean ... So I am "Othered" in that way.*

Like Polanyi's (1944) "double movement," Rupa's traveling is about privilege, but it is certainly not about freedom.[45] Diasporic subjects like Rupa engage with struggles in "both homes."

Tina breaks down monolithic and linear notions of "home" by questioning the notion of "authentic" cultural expression. Tina describes her trepidation with joining Indian students' groups and associations in college: "They [foreign students from India] came here to do their undergraduate or graduate work. ... They thought of us as fake Indians, not authentic ..." The call of authenticity posits Tina in opposition to *Fresh-Off-the-Boat* or *FOB*, "suggesting it is the 'real' immigrant who can address the 'mother country' as home and exist as its cultural authority in the West" (Puar 1994a, 100). Rekha realized during a trip to India that she is not an "authentic Indian." She uses the example of her training in *kathak*, a North Indian form of classical dancing, to articulate her inauthenticity. Rekha shares with me that her trip to India allowed her to discern that her interest in kathak had little to do with devotion to the art of dancing. Rather, dance practices and performances were about socializing and participating in her Bengali-American community in the Midwest:

> *When I went to India, I saw what a real Indian was like—what it meant to be Indian in India. Here [America], I am going around doing this Indian dance and I look Indian … It [dancing] was about the social network I had myself entrenched in, which was going to parties and functions. That seemed to me almost fabricated and, most importantly, I felt like I couldn't truly represent what that [Kathak] really was … I am not one of those people in India. I couldn't ever truly represent that.*

The women construct notions of what it means be a *real* "South Asian" and what it means to be an "American," and cultivate experiences of "discovering" an "authentic self" that are problematic (see Puar 1994a, 84).

Tina's travels to Calcutta are captured by the legacy of the white traveler on vacation—luxury, leisure, and privilege: "People take us for granted. They think that dollars grow on trees. Every time we go back, it is assumed that we are going to treat them just because we are from the U.S." Noopur observes, "My [family in India] make comments that we have everything. … Outside of America, [life] is made out to look like we snap our fingers and five hundred dollars falls into my lap." Ronica reflects:

> *When I am in Calcutta … It is so embarrassing to be totally singled out and treated like you are a prima donna … What's embarrassing about that is knowing that I haven't done*

anything to receive that privilege or to receive that recognition
[except] be born in another country.

Mohanty (1993) writes, "Notions of home and community are located within a deeply political space, where racialization and gender and class relations and histories become the prism through which [to understand], however partially, what it could mean to be South Asian in North America ... [and] the meanings attached to home and community in India" (353). My informants' herstories are class-, race-, and gender-specific negotiations of the transnational experience of crafting a South Asian-American identity.

Bhabha (1994) provides an impressive context in which to embed my participants' experiences:

> *The problematic enunciation of cultural difference becomes,*
> *in the discourse of relativism, the perspectival problem of*
> *temporal and spatial distance. The threatened "loss" of*
> *meaningfulness in cross-cultural interpretation, which is*
> *as much a problem of the structure of the signifier as it is a*
> *question of cultural codes (the experience of other cultures),*
> *then becomes a hermeneutic project for the restoration of*
> *cultural "essence" of authenticity.* (179)

The "authentic" therefore seems to be an amorphous and constantly shifting figure, "depending on geopolitical locations and categories, constructing the mutually exclusive either/or nature of the paradigmatic figure" (Puar 1994a, 84). Mankekar (1994) speaks wonderfully to the women's struggles in defining "home" by foregrounding the ability of diasporic subjects to engage with struggles in "both our 'homes'" (351). She uses the notion of cultural bifocality to acknowledge the engagements, connections, and continuities between "discontinuous spaces." An emphasis on continuities and connections makes room for diasporic stories that are not about loss or starting anew. In this light, the recreation of the aspects of home can be seen as products of considerable effort and agency on the part of the women; the project of "home" can be seen as reassertions of their identity—an act of choice in the face of particular constraints—rather than passive conformity with tradition.

The women involved in my fieldwork articulate their identities within a constellation of intersecting loyalties that are multiple, contradictory, shifting, and overlapping. My research participants' oral histories suggest that while citizenship privileges provide the women with invincibility like the "white liberal traveling subject," they have come to realize that South Asia and America are "home and "not-home." My research participants produce a complex process of identity within U.S. Orientalism, multiculturalism, and racism, at times affirming binary formulations such as "South Asian" and "American" while also redrawing the boundaries between South Asia and America (see Naber 2006).

Globalization and Women's Labor

Hester Eisenstein

In the burgeoning literature on globalization, only a limited number of studies focus on the centrality of women's labor. Yet this process has drawn millions of women, particularly women of color, into a new female proletariat.[1] As Delia Aguilar notes:

> To speak of globalization without center-staging women of color would be a grave mistake. In the era of globalized economics where a race to the bottom is crucial for superprofits, it is primarily the labor power of "Global South" women ... that is the cheapest of all. From the maquiladoras in Mexico ... to assembly plants and export processing zones [EPZs] in Central America, the Caribbean, and the Pacific Rim, to subcontractors and garment sweatshops in global cities and in nations of the periphery, it is women's labor that allows and guarantees maximum profitability for the corporate elite, a tiny minority of the world's inhabitants. (Aguilar 2004a, 16–17)

Globalization as the word is generally used refers to a complex series of events stretching over a time span of some four decades beginning in the early 1970s. It involves a range of actors, from government and corporate leaders and major investors to central bankers and heads of international financial institutions.[2] In this account I will emphasize those parts of the process that seem most relevant to my argument: the ways in which the managers of the global economy are making use, not just of women's labor, but also of feminist ideology.

For global managers and their cheering section in the corporate media, globalization is a process of integrating countries into the world market by dismantling the mechanisms, from tariff policy to capital flows, that gave countries control over international investment. The collapse of communism in the former Soviet Union and its allies after 1989 facilitated this process enormously. Using "free-trade" agreements such as the North American Free Trade Agreement (NAFTA) and structural adjustment programs (SAPs), the globalizers have transformed local economies across the world, allegedly "reforming" and modernizing them to get rid of archaic entities such as state-owned enterprises. To the globalizers this is an unmitigated good, and they have been assiduous in promoting this process as beneficent.

But from a more critical perspective, globalization has been a process of impoverishment and disfranchisement for many hundreds of millions of people. The macroeconomic changes adopted by Global South countries under the pressure of debt have in effect abrogated their economic sovereignty, opening their economies, with very few restrictions, to international corporations seeking a cheap and docile labor force and a high return on their investments (I will explain this process in detail in Chapter 5).[3]

In the developed world, meanwhile, the "social compact" extracted by labor unions and Left political parties from governments in the postwar era is under severe attack, symbolized by the attempt of President George W. Bush to demolish social security (thankfully unsuccessful) and to partially privatize the provision of Medicare (partially successful).[4] Highly paid manufacturing jobs have been cut dramatically, and a low-wage service economy has been constructed. The tax structure has been skewed to benefit the rich and the very rich, and a process of increasing inequalities has affected the United States along with the rest of the world. With the decline of unions, a "flexible" workforce of part-time, contract employees has emerged, producing an economy where some one-quarter of workers are earning poverty wages. All of these changes make up the process of globalization.

GLOBALIZATION DEFINED

What exactly does globalization mean? The word itself was introduced into the management literature in the early 1980s, and was rapidly taken up by the business and mainstream press.[5] The originator of the term was a much-acclaimed business writer, Theodore Levitt, who in 1983 pointed to the need for multinational corporations to make changes, both in their manufacturing techniques and in their sales strategies, calibrated to local social behaviors and cultural preferences, in order to be able to sell their products worldwide. Keep an eye on those social behaviors! This is the entering wedge for the uses being made of women, as workers and consumers, and the uses being made of feminist ideology, in the newly globalized world order.[6]

To grasp the process, it is useful to draw an analogy to the growth of the United States in the nineteenth century. One basis of the enormous wealth that was accumulated was the creation of a single market across the entire continent, so that goods could be shipped freely from state to state (see Tabb 2001). In the twenty-first century, the aspiration of the globalizers is similarly to create a single market out of the entire world. This means the destruction of all barriers to the free flow of capital, from tariffs to capital controls, so that nation-states in effect become like the states within the U.S. federal system: open for business without impediment.

New York Times columnist and writer Thomas Friedman is one of the major celebrants of globalization. According to Friedman, the relatively closed national economies of the pre-1970s cold war system controlled their own monetary and fiscal policies. But in the newly globalized economy, the main decisionmakers are no longer the political leaders of nation-states, but the Electronic Herd. Members of the Herd include institutional investors such as pension funds, corporations investing their profits, and, in recent years, "hedge funds" investing pools of capital around the world and betting on the rise and fall of commodities, companies, and national currencies. In this new era, the Electronic Herd roams freely across the globe. With the new diversity of financial instruments, everything can be bundled into tradable items, from mortgages to overseas bonds. The elimination of capital controls fosters a series of stampedes, with investors seeking the highest returns rushing in and out of national economies (Friedman 2000).

The removal of governmental regulations and other barriers to world investment was extremely profitable in periods of rapid economic growth. But this transformation also concealed major dangers should the world economy encounter a downturn. This was dramatically evident from 2007–2008, when a worldwide credit crisis ensued, linked to the issuance of housing mortgages in the United States to people who could ill afford them. The resulting foreclosures sent waves of panic throughout the world financial markets.[7] Particularly after the dramatic bankruptcy of Lehman Brothers, and the "rescues" orchestrated by the U.S. government of Bear Stearns, AIG Insurance, Fannie Mae (the Federal National Mortgage Association), and Freddie Mac (the Federal Home Mortgage Corporation), governments all over the world stepped in with multibillion-dollar bailouts of their own troubled financial institutions.

But to return to the optimistic narrative of Thomas Friedman: he calls the giant multinational corporations (MNCs)—companies such as Ford, Intel, Compaq, (the late)Enron, and Toyota—the Longhorn cattle, carrying out foreign direct investment, building factories, utilities, energy plants, and other long-term projects all across the globe. In the preglobalized era, when countries still maintained tariff walls, MNCs built factories abroad to jump over those walls and sell directly in foreign markets. But now, to compete in the global market, they can divide up their production chain geographically, producing and assembling their goods in the cheapest possible places.

Countries compete for the entry of MNCs because they need foreign capital, international standards and technologies, foreign partnerships, and market information. Governments now must heed the market, as political power no longer stems from holding office (Friedman 2000, 101ff.). Just as states in the United States compete with one another for corporate investment, with tax breaks and cheap land and utilities, so now all nations must compete for the favor of the Longhorns and the Electronic Herd.

This competitive vision is evident on the back pages of *The Economist,* where endless charts array the countries of the world according to their economic indicators, from gross domestic product (GDP) to trade balances to foreign reserves.[8] The overriding goal for each country is to attract investment, and to do this each must conform to the dictates of international economic orthodoxy, which means having to cut taxes, reduce public spending, privatize government enterprises, and eliminate capital controls, so that investors are no longer prevented from bringing their profits home.

The mainstream press celebrates this competition, and cheers on countries seen as conforming to the demands of the international investors. Thus, the former Soviet republic of Kazakhstan, and its capital Almaty, with skyscrapers sprouting in its newly created downtown, is featured in the *New York Times.* Dennis Price, general director of Bogatyr Access Komyr, the biggest Kazakh coal mining company, lets us know that "his" country is "well on the road to having one of the 50 most competitive economies in the world" (Greenberg 2006).

The "modernization" of women is considered an important indicator of a country's progress in the international economy. Thus, we learn from the editor of the Kazakh edition of *Cosmopolitan* magazine that "women are getting married later, they have their own apartments. Attitudes about sex are changing very fast" (Greenberg 2006). A similar phenomenon is taking place in India, where advertising campaigns have widely disseminated the image of a "modern" woman. In these ads "there is a sense of inevitability ... that India and Indian women have emerged out of decades of state control and finally have the opportunity to express themselves. There is a sense of having been 'behind' other countries for decades and having finally 'caught up.' The new liberal Indian women have finally joined a global league of modern female consumers" (Oza 2006, 25). I will return to this theme of women as an emblem of modernity in Chapter 2.

The Long Boom

The background to the current era of globalization is the worldwide economic boom that preceded it. The period from the end of World War II in 1945 to the mid-1970s is often called the Golden Age, or the Long Boom—the longest period of sustained economic growth in the history of the United States. Powered by the giant economy of the United States, most countries also experienced unprecedented economic growth, and some—such as Japan and South Korea—became powerful economic actors in their own right.

At home, the U.S. economy went into high gear. Consumer spending, pent up during the war years, sparked growth in cars and household appliances. Housing spending soared, meeting the needs of millions of returning soldiers and their families. Many (mostly white) families moved to the new suburbs like Levittown in Long Island, supported by the creation of Fannie Mae, which offered low-cost mortgages. Substantial public investments by the federal government included the G.I. Bill, which paid for college education for veterans; the national interstate highway system; schools; and utilities. Meanwhile, high levels of military spending resumed with the outbreak of the Korean "conflict" (1950–1953) and then the war in Vietnam (1965–1973) (Tanzer 1995).

Working families provided a ready market for consumer goods. Suburbanization meant the growth of shopping centers and drive-through restaurants, plus the automobile. "No single product—with its extensive linkages to other economic sectors, including highway construction and petroleum refining—has ever so dominated the imagination of the population, or the base of a national economy, as did the car. Perhaps one in six Americans owed his or her job to the car" (Bluestone and Harrison 1982, 114).

On the world stage, the United States emerged from World War II with more than half of all the usable productive capacity in the world, serving as banker to former allies and enemies alike. U.S. domination was cemented by the Bretton Woods Agreement of 1944, which effectively made the U.S. dollar the principal reserve currency. Under this agreement, the currencies of most other countries had fixed exchange rates pegged to the dollar. To participate in international trade, countries were required to acquire dollars, since they could not use their own currencies to pay for goods and services from abroad. The agreement also established the World Bank and the International Monetary Fund (IMF), the international financial institutions (IFIs) located in Washington, DC, that were designed to help rebuild countries after the devastation of World War II, and to regulate currency exchanges, so as to prevent a recurrence of the trade rivalries that had triggered the Great Depression of the 1930s.[9]

As the United States expanded with military bases and international security agreements, U.S. corporations with the necessary size and experience went with it. These companies made massive investments abroad in new plant and equipment, producing for foreign markets and later for the U.S. market. Direct investment by private U.S. capital abroad grew rapidly. The plants, mines, distribution centers, and offices of multinational corporations began to establish a global-scale production system. By 1978, one-third of overall profits for the 100 biggest corporations and banks came from overseas operations (Bluestone and Harrison 1982, 113).

Competing with the West were the Communist powers of the Soviet Union (after 1917) and of China (after 1949). Between the capitalist West and the Communist East were the countries of the Third World. The concept of a Third World

(*Tiers Monde*) was introduced by the French journalist Albert Sauvy in 1952. The First World was the West—the United States and its capitalist allies. The Second World was the Communist bloc of the USSR and Eastern Europe, Communist China, and North Korea, which "rejected market capitalism for socialist planning" (Prasad 2007, 11). Finally, the "ignored, exploited, scorned Third World" (Sauvy quoted in Prasad 2007, 10–11) was made up of the newly independent countries that, like the Third Estate of the French Revolution, sought to establish their own economic and political sovereignty.[10] The concept of an independent Third World was embodied in an important international conference at Bandung, Indonesia, in 1955, where leaders including Jawaharlal Nehru of India, Sukarno of Indonesia, and Gamal Abdel Nasser of Egypt founded the Non-Aligned Movement. Although divided ideologically, these nations all sought to make their own decisions about the path to development and modernity.

The ideological rivalries of the cold war gave Third World countries considerable room for maneuver, as the United States and the USSR competed to provide development assistance. Despite its free-market rhetoric, the United States supported state-led development for its allies: Japan, Taiwan, and South Korea. Even though there was great diversity among the developing countries in Asia, Africa, and Latin America, most pursued a common development strategy, which involved a significant role for the state in encouraging industrialization and economic growth. This was clearly the case for the Communist countries of the Soviet Union and China, whose revolutions had taken them out of the orbit of the capitalist system. But for other countries of the Third World, although still within the capitalist orbit, many governments sought to maintain sovereignty over their own economic development. Thus, in Latin America, Argentina and Brazil pursued a policy of "import substitution." Keeping tariff walls high, they encouraged local industry to grow, while seeking funds to build their infrastructure from such First World institutions as the World Bank.

The End of the Long Boom and the Restructuring of the World Economy

Much has been written about the transformation of the international economy since the end of the Long Boom, when, in the early 1970s, economic growth began to slow down worldwide. The challenge to U.S. economic hegemony had been building since the 1960s. The United States was threatened by the economic recovery of Europe and Japan, faced with a strengthened challenge from Third World nationalism abroad (symbolized by the Organization of Petroleum-Exporting Countries [OPEC] price revolution of 1973), and encountering rebellious social movements at home, from Black Power to the women's movement. Weakened by the prolonged war in Vietnam, the United States was losing its competitive advantage. High profit rates began to fall, and no major technological innovations had emerged to match the stimulus to growth represented by the cars, highway, and housing investments of the 1950s (Tanzer 1995).

In response to what both government and corporations perceived as a crisis of profitability, the 1970s saw the inauguration of a radical restructuring of the U.S. and world economy: the deindustrialization of the United States and the rise of the service economy, the ideological shift to neoliberalism, and the intensification of the U.S. role as an imperial power on the world stage. Initially, corporations moved some of their industrial production overseas to areas of cheap labor. Subsequently, they were able to use computerized technology to create just-in-time methods that lowered costs by eliminating big inventories. And reduced transport costs allowed them to streamline delivery by sea and by air.

In Third World countries, governments were induced or forced to open their borders to the free flow of foreign investment. This led them to restructure their economies to focus on currency-earning export industries such as electronics and textiles, drawing on the cheaper labor of women.

In developed economies, a struggle began to limit the role of the welfare state and to replace progressive taxation with tax cuts for the richest families. With globalization came an increasing gap between rich and poor, both within countries and among countries across the globe. Growth rates stagnated, but profits soared (see Amott 1993, 24–48; Pollin 2003, 17–18; Tabb 2001).

The Ideological Shift from Keynesianism to Neoliberalism

The structural changes produced by the search for higher profitability, described in greater detail in what follows, were accompanied by a sea change in political and economic ideology, usually characterized as a shift from Keynesianism to neo-liberalism: an all-out assault on the consensus symbolized by the New Deal.[11]

The Golden Age from 1945 to the mid-1970s had seen a kind of truce between capital and labor, with government accepting a major role in the preservation of high employment, and corporations grudgingly accepting a role for unions in collective bargaining over wages and conditions. The consensus was that government would intervene in the economy to stimulate growth and to preserve a minimal safety net for workers excluded from the workforce.[12]

Broadly, then, *Keynesianism* refers to the use of government monetary and fiscal policy to stimulate demand, to "prime the pump." That government had a major role to play in directing the market was widely accepted across the political spectrum in the United States, from the Eisenhower years through the presidency of Richard Nixon. It was agreed that smoothing out periods of recession and providing programs to sustain consumption through the elements of a "social wage" were normal functions of government. Hence, this period witnessed the introduction of health insurance programs such as Medicare and Medicaid; job creation programs such as the Comprehensive Employment and

Training Act; and community development programs directed toward inner-city enclaves such as those programs introduced after the urban uprisings of the 1960s. Even direct income support in the form of a guaranteed payment to all families was being considered by the Nixon administration in 1971 (see Fortunato 2007, 47). As Nixon is widely quoted as saying, "We are all Keynesians now."[13]

The shift to neoliberalism meant a turn toward deregulation of the economy. Neoliberalism preached a minimal role for government, but as many scholars have argued, what it really meant was that governments now became the engines of globalization. As the power of trade unions weakened, governments enhanced their capacities for control and repression, expanding incarceration and police powers, while whittling away the economic safety net.

Both a philosophy of limited government and a set of prescriptions for economic growth, neoliberalism was born in Chicago: "Starting from a tiny embryo at the University of Chicago with the philosopher-economist Friedrich von Hayek and followers like economist Milton Friedman at its nucleus, the neoliberals and their funders created a huge international network of foundations, institutes, research centers, publications, scholars, writers and public relations experts to develop, package, and push their doctrine" (George 2002, 4). As Alan Nasser points out, what is conventionally termed *neoliberalism* was really a return to the pre–New Deal consensus of permitting the business cycle to proceed untrammeled by government intervention. The ascendancy of this set of ideas is linked to the regimes of Margaret Thatcher in England (1979–1990) and Ronald Reagan in the United States (1981–1989), and received renewed vigor under the administration of George W. Bush. Its political effectiveness can be dated from the successful passage of Proposition 13 in California in 1978, which set limits on the growth of property taxes, and the firing of the striking Professional Air Traffic Controllers by President Reagan in 1981 (Amott 1993, 34; Nasser 2003).

The elements of the neoliberal offensive, driven by an increasingly effective coalition of right-wing and right-leaning politicians, were many. They included attacks on labor and the right to organize; delegitimization of the welfare state and the concept of progressive taxation; devaluing of the role of government in stimulating economic growth and full employment; privatizing or contracting out of public functions and organizations; and deregulation to remove the constraints on corporations imposed by government policies in such areas as environmental regulation, affirmative action, banking, utilities, and the media.

This process began with the New York City fiscal crisis of the 1970s. New York's municipal bankruptcy became the occasion for a counterattack on "bloated" unions and "out-of-control" welfare spending. Placing New York City in receivership under the control of the banks, the leadership of the city enforced what was in effect the first structural adjustment program (see Tabb 1982, 11; it was in the New York City fiscal crisis that "the liberal 1960s turned into the neoconservative 1970s." On structural adjustment, see "Counterrevolution in the Third World" later in this chapter).

The fiscal crisis of New York, Tabb notes, began the turn from "redistributive liberalism" to "neoconservative privatization" (Tabb 1982, 12). This ideological offensive represented a rollback of the social gains of the 1960s and early 1970s. Think tanks such as the Manhattan Institute and writers such as Charles Murray (1984) began to push this new ideology, which placed "personal responsibility" and an attack on dependency at the center of its worldview. The targets included not only the New Deal under Franklin D. Roosevelt, and the social programs of the 1960s in the United States, but also the "Evil Empire" of the Soviet Union. With the fall of the USSR in 1989–1991, the new ideologues expressed triumphalism over the end of the cold war, demonizing the remaining countries, Cuba for one, that made state economic planning and the elimination of poverty, disease, and illiteracy their main goals.

The rhetoric of neoliberalism condemned welfare and the welfare state as undermining individualized liberty and self-determination. As Nancy Fraser and Linda Gordon (2003) note, the ideological sleight of hand here was to conflate personal dependency (a feature of human life from birth as a helpless infant to old age) with dependency on the state, and to elevate autonomy and independence as the principal (and only) human virtues. The language was genderized: the expression, dripping with contempt, the *nanny state,* still used on a regular basis by the British weekly *The Economist* and even on occasion by the *New York Times,* evokes the idea that those who depend on the state for their sustenance are weak, that is, female, whereas those who successfully navigate the rough waters of the market are strong and virile, aka male (see Sawer 1996 for this point; see also Folbre 2001, 83–108, for a history and defense of the nanny state).

Deindustrialization and the New International Division of Labor

The U.S. economy had already begun a process of deindustrialization, or the growth of the rust belt. From the 1960s onward, manufacturers began replacing the postwar domestic strategy of moving industries such as textiles from the unionized North to the nonunion South with a new international strategy. They began to move some elements of production overseas, taking advantage of cheaper labor, anti-union policies, and the establishment of free-trade export-processing zones. The traditional U.S. industrial base was hollowed out, as great industrial cities such as Buffalo, Pittsburgh, and Cleveland lost their manufacturing base (see Freeman 2000, 24–30; Froebel, Heinrich, and Kreye 1980; Mies 1998, 112–120).

Scholars dubbed this change a "new international division of labor" (see Fernandez-Kelly 1989; Froebel et al. 1980; Mies 1998). What was the old international division of labor? From the rise of colonialism, colonized countries had provided raw materials to the governing powers such as the Netherlands and Great Britain, which turned those materials into manufactured goods to sell back to their colonies. Colonialism involved a brutal restructuring of indigenous economies, including the transport of peoples for slavery and indentured servitude from continent to continent, accompanied by the deliberate destruction of long-standing local industries, most famously the ancient and legendary indigenous muslin of Bengal, to provide a market for products from the colonial powers (see Kabeer 2000, 54–56; McMichael 2004).[14] In this period, core or developed countries sold two-thirds of their manufactured exports to the periphery and absorbed four-fifths of their primary production (Dicken 1998, 21).

In the postindependence era from the late 1950s on, the countries emerging from colonial rule in Asia, Africa, and Latin America sought to achieve economic independence through a process of industrialization. But the United States and the other industrial giants steadily tried to preserve the old colonial pattern. As the late Harry Magdoff noted, the goal of U.S. foreign policy after 1945 was to "make the world safe for mineral development." This meant integrating developing countries into world capitalist markets so that they never took a path toward self-reliance. They were to depend on exports of raw materials, adapting their industrial structure toward specialized exports at a price acceptable to the buyer. Thus, in Latin America, despite industrialization and the stimulus of two world wars, agriculture and minerals still made up 90 percent of exports (Magdoff 1969, 198).

In the new era of intensified international economic competition, this pattern was gradually replaced by a new industrial strategy of placing some elements of production in the former colonies to take advantage of the cheaper labor force. This was particularly widespread in the case of the electronics, toys, footwear, and textiles industries, where female labor was preferred. From Taiwan to Malaysia and Indonesia, from Mexico and the Caribbean to South America, women's "nimble [and cheap] fingers" made them the workforce of choice for these labor-intensive industries, which increased the profits of the multinational corporations, while they also brought in much-needed foreign currency to local governments (see Wichterich 2000, 1–33).

The growth of export-processing zones continues to this day, relying primarily on a young, cheap, fairly uneducated female labor force that is subject to extreme exploitation. EPZs grew from 79 in 25 countries in 1975 to more than 3,000 in 116 nations in 2002. Employment in the zones was estimated in 2004 at just under 42 million.[15] With labor organizing suppressed, and environmental regulations virtually nonexistent, these workers "endure unhealthy and unsafe working conditions," earning salaries that are inadequate to support them or their families. There is high turnover in these jobs, sometimes due to disabilities caused by the work, and sometimes due to the employers' preference for younger women: the average Mexican worker, for example, spends about three years in maquiladora employment (Cravey 1998, 6–7).

Simultaneously, other areas of production were retained within the continental United States through the use of automation and immigrant labor, primarily female, to reduce costs (see Fernandez-Kelly 1989). Despite this, a second wave of outsourcing took place, particularly in the white-collar service sector, from call centers in India to airline ticket centers in the Caribbean (see, for example, Glater 2004). Here, too, female labor was crucial, and companies went out of their way to make the work attractive to local women (see Freeman 2000 on "pink-collar" data entry processing in Barbados, for example).

Thus, one key element of globalization was the dispersion of manufacturing, and subsequently services, to cheap labor areas of the world, most notably China, via the establishment of a global assembly line. In some categories of production, the profitability of these areas is assured by the use of a low-paid female labor force. Here is the first use of women's labor as part of globalization. (For more on EPZs, see Chapter 5.)

The Growth of the Service Sector

Another major feature of globalization was the growth of the service sector. The traditional way of defining services was as a residual category, for things neither "dug out of the ground" nor manufactured (Dicken 1998, 388). Even though this definition is still essentially valid, modern service activities are a range of "lubricating" activities, that is, areas that "service" the entire range of production, as well as areas that represent human services in their own right. Service inputs are needed at every stage of production, from planning (feasibility studies) to actual production (quality control, accounting, and training) to "downstream" (advertising, repairs, maintenance, i.e., "service" itself!). But in addition, the service sector includes transportation and public utilities; wholesale and retail trade; finance, insurance, and real estate (FIRE); government; health; education; and business and personal services. This sector accounts for the largest share of GDP in all but the least-developed market economies (Dicken 1998, 387). (For a definition of GDP, see note 8 for this chapter.)

The expansion of the service sector was a worldwide phenomenon: "The field of services has been internationalized in response to the spread of multinational or transnational corporations (TNCs). As manufacturing TNCs have proliferated globally, so, too, have the major banks, advertising agencies, legal firms, property companies, insurance companies, freight corporations, travel and hotel chains, car rental firms and credit card enterprises" (Dicken 1998, 392). The growth of the service sector was well under way in the United States after World War II. But the process accelerated starting in the 1970s. From 1970 to 2000, service sector jobs more than doubled, from 49 million to 102 million, while employment in goods-producing industries increased by only 15 percent (from 26 million to 30 million).[16]

With the growth of the service sector came a rapid increase in women's employment. In the United States from 1970 to 2000, of the 57 million new jobs created, about 60 percent of these went to women. This trend was already visible by the mid-1980s. The shift reflected "both the increase in women's labor force participation and the disproportionate increase in service industries and in occupations where significant numbers of women [were] employed"(Kuhn and Bluestone 1987, 9). As economist Heidi Hartmann notes: "The process of drawing women into the service sector was an interactive process. The service sector grows because the availability of cheap female labor provides the supply and because the use of women in the labor market rather than at home also provides the demand for replacement services (fast food replacing home cooking, for example)…. And the shift toward the commercialization of personal services is required by women's increased labor force participation" (Hartmann 1987, 55). As a result, the percentage of the adult U.S. female population employed outside the home rose from 35 percent in 1960 to over 60 percent today (Mather 2007).

Despite the attempts after World War II to return women to domesticity, married women increasingly stayed in paid employment from 1940 onward. In 1940, the labor force participation rate among married women was only 15.6 percent, whereas today it is well over 60 percent. (See Chapter 2 for further discussion.) For employers, this was crucial, since, particularly with the growth of the service sector, married women constituted a major untapped pool of labor. As we will see, the powerful taboo against married women in the workforce was overcome by a combination of the economic need for a dual-worker household and the ideology of 1970s feminism.

The Explosion of the Financial Sector

Underlying the rapid growth of the service sector was the enormous expansion of the financial sector. Increasingly, investors sought profits not through the process of manufacturing, but through finance. As the editors of *Monthly Review* note, the "enormous financial expansion of the system" has become "a primary means of utilizing economic surplus." Kevin Phillips argues that "in the last few decades, the United States economy has been transformed through what I call financialization. The processes of money management, securities management, corporate reorganization, securitization of assets, derivatives trading and other forms of securities packaging are steadily replacing the act of making, growing and transporting things" (cited in "Crises" 2002, 53). In Table 1.1, a comparison of goods-producing industries with those of finance, insurance, and real estate (FIRE), as a percent of GDP, shows the dramatic change. "In the absence of sufficient profit opportunities for the goods-producing industries, capital sought other means to make profits. That is where the explosion of debt came on stage" ("Crises" 2002, 53–54).

Table 1.1

	1947	1977	2000
Private goods-producing industries	41.9	32.9	22.5
Finance, insurance, and real estate	9.7	13.9	19.6

The 1970s and 1980s were marked by intensive growth in financial investment and speculative transactions. The explosion in financial services is linked to another feature of globalization, namely, the deregulation of financial markets. Before the 1960s, countries exerted careful control over financial markets and institutions, so as to manage their economies and try to avoid periodic crises. But from the mid-1960s onward, these controls were dismantled.

Bank lending across national borders in the 1960s was only about 1 percent of the GDP of market economies. By the mid-1980s, it had reached 20 percent of much higher levels of GDP. Richard Barnet describes the global financial network as a maze of transactions, "a chain of gambling casinos ... [through which] trillions of dollars flow through the world's foreign exchange markets each day, of which no more than 10 percent is linked to trade in goods and services" (quoted in Tanzer 1995, 6). One measure of this growth of finance is that in 2006 the Bank of International Settlements, the Basel-based bank for central banks, calculated that the value of the total amount of financial "derivatives" outstanding was $415 trillion, or eight times the total value of world GDP for the year (Weiss 2007, 3).

The increase in the size of the service sector reflected a major shift in where investors were putting their money. From the end of World War II through the 1970s, goods production (mining, construction, and manufacturing) accounted for about 32 percent of all new private (nonresidential) investment, whereas in the 1980s and 1990s its share was only 18 percent. In contrast, in the FIRE sector, the share of investment flows jumped from 16 percent in the first period to 30 percent in the second period.

Increased employment in this financial sector was required to handle the massive volumes of information being transferred in this industry. "Access to large pools of appropriate (often female) labor was a key requirement" (Dicken 1998, 418). Thus, the explosion in financial transactions directly impacted the employment of women. Again, the figures tell the story. In the 1960s and 1970s, the share of FIRE in GDP remained virtually constant, at between 13 and 14 percent. However, the percentage of employees in FIRE who were women increased sharply, from 46 percent in 1960 to 58 percent in 1980. Then, in the 1980s and 1990s, while the percentage of employees in FIRE who were women leveled off, the total FIRE sector grew rapidly, reaching 20 percent of GDP by 2000.[17] The two factors together, the increasing feminization of the FIRE sector and the increasing growth of the FIRE sector itself, were a major source of increased employment for women.

Suppression of Labor Unions and Shift to a Low-Wage Contingent Workforce

A closely linked development was the suppression of labor unions. In the business press, unions were blamed for the inflationary pressures that in reality stemmed largely from the combination of prosecuting the war in Vietnam and pursuing Lyndon Johnson's War on Poverty. The firing of the striking air traffic controllers under Reagan in 1981, as noted earlier, is often cited as a symbolic turning point. Unions were perceived by management as a drag on profitability, and the Reagan years inaugurated a period of severe attacks on labor organizing that has continued to the present day. (See further discussion of the continuing attacks on labor unions in Chapter 4.)

In addition, new models of employment were being developed that were to replace the traditional expectations of permanent well-paid employment with a workforce heavily based on contingent, low-wage labor. The pioneer in this area was the fast-food industry, where the ideal employee was young and replaceable, and where training was minimal, as was the expectation of promotion into management. These patterns were reproduced in "big box" retailing, with Wal-Mart the leading example. But low-wage jobs spread across the entire economy. More than 30 million workers, a majority female and a large percentage of them minority and immigrant, worked in areas ranging from poultry and fish processing, retail store work, hotels, janitors, and call-center workers, to child care workers (see Shulman 2005, 6–7).

A similar, if less visible, transformation took place in university hiring. Out of 1.1 million faculty members in the United States in 2003, only 28 percent were tenured and full-time and 12 percent were tenure track (that is, presumably on the way to receiving tenure); the remaining 60 percent of faculty members were part-time or non–tenure track (see Jacobe 2006, 46). At the City University of New York, where I teach, the majority of all classes are taught by adjunct professors with no job security, earning about $3,000 per semester for a three-credit course (Rajendra and Hogness 2008, 4). Inevitably, low-paid, part-time jobs such as adjuncting or working at Wal-Mart are largely women's jobs. (For more on this topic, see Chapter 4.)

Counterrevolution in the Third World

Meanwhile, for Third World countries, there were also drastic changes. The big jump in oil prices in 1973, under a revitalized OPEC, with the accompanying influx of petrodollars into First World banking institutions, had created conditions where banks and investors lent freely to the developing states of Latin America, Asia, and Africa.[18] But the decision of U.S. policymakers to dramatically increase interest rates as a weapon against inflation—the so-called Volcker shock of 1979–1982—sharply increased the cost of borrowing.[19]

> Two other shocks compounded the impact of U.S. policy on the Third World. The 1979–1980 oil price increase raised import costs for all the oil-poor LDCs [least-developed countries] while the recession in the West reduced demand for developing country exports. These three factors—interest rate increases, oil price hikes, and recession in the … [developed countries]—increased the need for foreign money even as it became less available. The debtors hung on by using new loans for the oil bill and for interest payments on previously borrowed money. In the last half of 1981 Latin America borrowed a billion dollars a week, mostly to pay off existing debt. (Frieden 2006, 374)

In the summer of 1982, Mexico declared bankruptcy, and this triggered an abrupt halt in private lending to the developing world: "The flow of funds shifted abruptly from southward to northward. In 1981 twenty billion more dollars had flowed into Latin America than flowed out; in 1983, as lending ended and governments scrambled to pay their debts, a net twenty billion dollars flowed out of Latin America" (Frieden 2006, 374). A debt crisis "of 1930s proportions" was the result (Frieden 2006, 374). This created an opening for the use of SAPs and a counterattack against state-led development in the Third World.

Creditors forced Third World countries to approach the International Monetary Fund "to plan a program of macroeconomic stabilization and economic adjustment," with targets for inflation, government spending, budget deficits, and other so-called conditionalities. Other investors regarded an agreement with the IMF as a "seal of approval," and would agree to resume their lending (Frieden 2006, 375). Thus, the debt crisis of the 1980s recapitulated the municipal crisis of New York City in the 1970s, but on a global scale. Just as major financial institutions were able to restructure the New York economy, so international banks could use the crisis to reshape the priorities of Third World governments.

The new neoliberal doctrine was first tried out under the dictatorship of Augusto Pinochet in Chile (1973–1990). It was subsequently imposed by the international financial institutions, particularly the Bretton Woods institutions (the International Monetary Fund and the World Bank), which used the debt crisis of the 1980s to restructure the economies of those countries that had come under their sway.[20] The new functions of the IFIs constituted, in effect, a counterrevolution against Third World countries, as SAPs, with their requirements of privatizing, cutting public spending, and reorienting economies toward acquiring foreign currency to repay their debt, effectively ended the era of state-led development.

Through the imposition of conditionalities, the IFIs virtually forced indebted governments to accede to a radical series of changes. In the name of what neoliberal economists termed *macroeconomic stabilization* and *structural reform,* governments were induced to devalue their currencies, cut public expenditures, end food and fuel subsidies to "realign" domestic prices to the world market, liberalize trade, privatize state enterprises, and regularize titles to land, often resulting in the forfeiture by peasant farmers of their customary land rights to large landlords (Chossudovsky 2003, 35–64).

A third international financial institution, the World Trade Organization (WTO), established in 1995, and based in Geneva, Switzerland, reinforced these policies with a set of rules about "free trade" that gave preference to the interests of corporations over national governments. The WTO, through its secret dispute mechanism, sought to ensure that national legislation on issues such as labor, health, and the environment did not interfere with "competitiveness" in the world marketplace. Establishing a series of protocols on agriculture, trade-related investment, intellectual property rights, and services, the WTO required member states to override national or even state and local regulations that barred the door to "free" (that is corporate) access to local markets (McMichael 2004, 172ff.).[21] These policies opened the door to the dramatic expansion of overseas operations by multinational corporations.[22]

Collectively, these draconian requirements were referred to in the mainstream economic press as the Washington Consensus.[23] The fall of the Soviet Union and of its satellite Eastern European regimes after 1989–1991 gave this set of policies new outlets, as formerly state-run enterprises were privatized, and national economies were forced to abandon state-led development. As Fred Rosen comments, with the sweeping adoption of the Washington Consensus, "the imperfect egalitarian instincts of Keynesian economics and social democratic policies were swept into the dustbin of ideas, left there to commingle with other antiquities like alchemy and astrology" (Rosen 2003).

We should note that the Washington Consensus, applied with such rigor to developing economies, was never required of the developed countries.

> Let's be clear right away that neoliberal theory is one thing and neoliberal practice is another thing entirely. Most members of the Organization for Economic Co-operation and Development (OECD)—including the U.S. federal government—have seen state intervention and state public expenditures increase during the last thirty years.... Even in the United States, President Reagan's neoliberalism did not translate into a decline of the federal public sector. Instead, federal public expenditures increased under his mandate, from 21.6 to 23 percent of GNP [gross national product], as a consequence of a

spectacular growth in military expenditures from 4.9 to 6.1 percent of GNP. (Navarro 2007, 21)[24]

In addition to the United States, some other countries were able to retain their state-led development policies and experienced rapid economic growth: the Tigers of Taiwan, Singapore, Hong Kong, and South Korea, and the newly industrializing countries such as Malaysia, not to mention China. But others in South Asia, Latin America, and sub-Saharan Africa, under the impact of SAPs over the period since the 1980s, suffered low growth and devastating increases in poverty, malnourishment, and disease. Widespread criticism of the impact of SAPs during the 1990s led the World Bank to modify its policies, acknowledging the burdens on "highly indebted" countries and placing a new emphasis on the need for "poverty reduction" (see Petchesky 2003, 142–151). Although this shift was a response to the intensified poverty produced by SAPs, particularly in Africa, governments were still required to follow the basic macroeconomic policies that had produced the intensified poverty in the first place: "The privatization of essential services, like water and electricity and the deterioration or privatization of public services, such as health and education, have never been in the interests of the poor. For instance, the imposition of user fees on health care or education has led to a sharp drop of hospital attendance and school enrolment from poor or low-income families and increased the gender gap, since girls and women are the main victims of those policies" (Dembele 2003). In extreme cases, SAPs helped to produce "failed states," where the fundamental elements of governance no longer functioned, and "ethnic" violence and civil war were the norm (see Federici 2000; for more on SAPs, see Chapter 5).

From the point of view of the U.S. elite, this ensemble of changes has been necessary to maintain the dominance of the United States, both as the premier economy in the world and as its overwhelmingly preeminent military power. Corporate globalization, then, has a military as well as an economic component. In a revealing policy document produced by the Office of Force Transformation in the Pentagon, Thomas Barnett and Henry Gaffney Jr. describe the world as divided into two parts: the globalizing countries and the countries in the "gap":

> As globalization deepens and spreads, two groups of states are essentially pitted against one another: countries seeking to align themselves internally to the emerging global rule (e.g., advanced Western democracies, Vladimir Putin's Russia, Asia's emerging economies) and countries that either refuse such internal realignment or cannot achieve it due to political/cultural rigidity or continuing abject poverty (most of Central Asia, the Middle East, Africa, and Central America). We dub the former countries the Functioning Core of globalization and the latter countries the Non-Integrating Gap. (Barnett and Gaffney 2003, 2)

In this analysis, the gap is where terrorism comes from, and it is the duty of the U.S. military to keep these new barbarians at bay. The authors argue that the United States pays in kind for its enormous balance-of-payments deficit by providing "security" to the rest of the world. Thus, the war on terror fits readily into a strategy of corporate globalization. At this writing, these policies have come together in the occupation of Iraq and the proposed privatization of much of its economy (see Klein 2004).

THE NET EFFECT OF THE CHANGES

What has been the net effect of the changes of the last four decades? In countries enjoying a massive influx of foreign investment, such as China, India, and South Africa, an increasing number of people have joined the middle class, and elites in particular are profiting, as individuals and as a class (see Oza 2006, for example, on India). But the enrichment of middle and upper classes is matched by the impoverishment of working and poor people. The effects of globalization include a decline in public health across the globe; an increase in desperate migration, from agricultural areas to the cities, and from poor countries to rich ones; and a growth of urban slums, not, as in the nineteenth century, because of industrialization, but rather because of its absence. As formal economy jobs shrink, the informal economy grows apace (see Beneria 2003; Davis 2006).[25]

The claims by globalizers of economic progress are belied by the statistics. Vincent Navarro argues that "neoliberal policies have been remarkably unsuccessful at achieving their declared aims: economic efficiency and social well-being." When we compare rates of economic growth in 1960–1980 with 1980–2000 for developing countries (excluding China), for annual economic growth the figures are 5.5 percent versus 2.6 percent. For annual economic growth per capita, they are 3.2 percent versus 0.7 percent.[26] In addition, "Mark Weisbrot, Dean Baker, and David Rosnick have documented that the improvement in quality-of-life and well-being indicators (infant mortality, rate of school enrollment, life expectancy, and others) increased faster during 1960–1980 than 1980–2000" (Navarro 2007, 23).

Even though developed countries also experienced lower growth in the neoliberal period, their much higher starting point means that income inequalities between the developing and developed countries have increased dramatically. In addition, inequalities have grown within countries. "If we consider these two types of inequalities together—that is, within countries and across countries, as Branco Milanovic has documented, the top 1 percent of the world population receives 57 percent of the world income, and the income difference between those at the top and those at the bottom has increased from 78 to 144 times" (Navarro 2007, 24).

Similarly, in the United States, Mark Weisbrot argues that the major impact of globalization for people is a "dramatically worse" income distribution:

> The central issue for Americans facing the global economy is income distribution. Whether it's international trade or investment, or immigration, the main impact on most Americans' lives has been on the distribution of income. And that distribution has gotten dramatically worse over the last 30 years: the rich have gotten a lot richer, the poor have languished, and the middle class has shrunk. From 1972 to 2001, the bottom 20 percent of wage and salary earners got only 1.6 percent of the increase in this income over the three decades. The majority got less than 11 percent. But the richest one percent received 18.4 percent of the increased income—vastly more than went to the majority of Americans. (Weisbrot 2006, 1)

All of the policies brought in under the aegis of neoliberal ideologies, including deregulation, reduction of public expenditure, and privatization of services, have benefited the richest part of the population at the expense of the poor and the working class (Navarro 2007, 25). In fact, we have witnessed the creation of a global class divide, where the elites from transnational corporations—those whom Jeff Faux has called "the Party of Davos"—feel solidarity with one another across national borders, while the poor of all nations are essentially abandoned to their fate (see Faux 2006; Davos is the town in Switzerland where the World Economic Forum usually meets). Thus, even though globalization is described as a process of improving people's lives across the world, in fact we have been witnessing a globalization of poverty (see Chossudovsky 2003; Davis 2006).

It is important to counter the glossy tales in the mainstream press about the benefits of globalization with the lived realities of the current system. These include the brutal deaths among those who seek to migrate illegally from the poor to the rich countries, and the daily dehumanizing life of the poor, living in favelas under the regime of drug lords and complicitous police forces (not to mention the urban planners and administrators who maintain the boundaries).

The same situation prevails in the inner cities of the United States, where racially isolated dead zones provide the revolving population for ever-growing numbers of prisons. As policymakers convince the public that poverty, homelessness, and the other corrosive effects of neoliberal capitalism are no longer the responsibility of government, there is increasing acceptance by the middle class of a permanent zone of hell to which the "underclass" is consigned, without hope of redemption. It is the job of the police to maintain this zone as separate as possible from the lives of the middle class. This is the meaning of debates over the level of crime and whether or not future mayors will keep the crime rate down (see Schwarz 2001; Stevens 2001).

The New Enclosures

Many writers see the modern process of globalization as a renewal of the enclosure movement that occurred during the early phase of agricultural capitalism in Great Britain. Karl Marx interpreted the enclosure movement of the early modern period in England as a necessary precondition for the rise of industrial capitalism. "Improving" landlords eliminated the rights and privileges of peasant tenants—their access to the commons, their claim on particular pieces of farmland over the harvest cycle—using law and force to repeal the last vestiges of feudalism and turn agriculture into a market-driven process of production. The thousands of peasants thus driven off the land became vagabonds who were first housed in poorhouses and then served as the reserve army of labor as industrialization took off (Wood 1999).

In the same way, contemporary globalization has as its goal the integration of all remaining parts of the world into one market economy. George Caffentzis, Iain Boal, Silvia Federici, and others have introduced the idea that the contemporary capitalist project of globalization is a continuation of the English enclosure movement. This is a global elimination of the commons, a new enclosure movement, whose goal is to bring the still traditional areas of the world into the global marketplace (Boal 2007; Federici 2001).[27] David Harvey (2003) names this process "accumulation by dispossession." Older cultures are to be transformed, and their traditions of collective and tribal connections eliminated, so that self-sufficient, subsistence economies are replaced with societies made up of individuals and consumers.

If we accept this interpretation of globalization, we are witnessing a renewed phenomenon of "enclosure" in country after country across the globe. The pattern of privatization, a key feature of neoliberalism, has been extended from public health, education, and housing to water, with devastating effects. For example, in South Africa communities that cannot afford the fees imposed by private water companies have experienced serious outbreaks of cholera from people drinking unsanitary water.[28]

The process of industrialization in England was accompanied by intense displacement and disruption as a traditional rural way of life was broken up to make way for the factory system of the industrial era. A similar process is under way now, with many Third World countries experiencing what we might call a process of partial industrialization—the establishment of export enclaves (always subject to removal to even lower wage countries)—while their agricultural system is subject to a process of conversion to agribusiness.

In China, the massive migration of peasants from agricultural land, as they are uprooted by developers and drawn into factory work, has displaced 150 million peasants, who live in shantytowns under conditions of extreme exploitation (Kwong 2006). Some estimate that this is the largest internal migration in world history: "An estimated 20 million children have been left behind to fend for themselves, and rural authorities have noted a marked increase in robbery, petty crime, suicide and rape involving these unsupervised children. In cases where only the husbands depart for the cities the wives are left to care for children and in-laws and to till the family farm. Many are so overburdened that they choose to end their lives, most commonly by swallowing pesticides. China has the highest rate of female suicide in the world, and its rural rate is three times that of the cities" (Kwong 2006, 20). In India, competition from agribusiness, and from cheap agricultural imports, has begun to devastate farmers, who for some years now have been committing suicide in very large numbers (Pollin 2003, 138–142).

I have often tried to evoke the enormity of the change from feudalism to an industrialized society with my undergraduates at Queens College. Imagine, I tell them, that you are a family of serfs living under the feudal system. The bad news is that you have to stay there, and so do your children, for the foreseeable future. The good news is that you will probably not starve to death. When I present them with the idea that, in contrast, unless they have inherited wealth they will all have to sell their labor, women and men alike, for most of their lives, they are totally blasé. This is not news to them, nor does it appear horrific. When I suggest to them that their view of themselves as a commodity is the product of a long historical development, going back centuries, they usually roll their eyes in disbelief (although one or two people in each class appear to grasp how momentous a change this is in human subjectivity). In other words, most of my students, like most Americans, have internalized the requirement of competing in the marketplace for their subsistence as the most normal of situations, barely worthy of comment.

But this acceptance of the harsh requirements of the market, which my students share with most people in the industrialized world, is by no means a fait accompli in the places to which globalized capital is now spreading. Resistance to neoliberalism is showing signs of growth. The antiglobalization movement was gaining traction in the years before September 11, 2001, with its challenges to the international financial institutions in campaigns such as "Fifty Years Is Enough!" and its documentation of the increasing immiseration and growing inequalities around the world, both within countries and from country to country. Particularly in Latin America, strong, organized social movements, in some cases with a major presence of indigenous actors, have rolled back privatization—as in the famous case of the water system in Cochabamba, Bolivia—and have brought to power antineoliberal leaders such as Hugo Chávez in Venezuela, Evo Morales in Bolivia, and other left-leaning politicians (Danaher 1994; Grandin 2006).

Women have been major actors in the resistance to globalization. Some of the most well-known are intellectuals and activists such as the novelist and essayist Arundhati Roy and the ecological scientist Vandana Shiva, both of India, and 2004 Nobel Prize winner Wangaria Muta Maathai of Kenya, founder of the women's Green Belt movement, which has planted millions of trees in her home country and elsewhere in Africa. But masses of indigenous, peasant, and working-class women have also been in the forefront of many of these struggles. In India, women have been major participants in the Save the Narmada anti–big dams movement, and have led the Chipko movement (the original "tree huggers") that protects crucial forests against logging in Uttar Pradesh and elsewhere. Recently in Nigeria, women have become major actors in the struggle against the environmental and social impact of the operations of the big oil companies in the Niger Delta of that country. Most famous, perhaps, is the activism of the highly visible indigenous women of Chiapas, Mexico, in the Zapatista movement, whose uprising in 1994 in response to NAFTA was widely considered to be the beginning of the visible antiglobalization movement. Similarly, in the developed world, women have been leaders in movements to contest the destruction of the union movement, to resist the dumping of toxic waste, and to fight for public education, housing, and the rights of immigrants (see Ezeilo 2007; Maathai 2006; Marcos 2005; Naples 1998; Rowbotham and Linkogle 1994b; Roy 1999; Shiva 1989, 67ff.).

In response to the claims of the worldwide social justice movement, leaders of the G-8 and other members of the international elite have been forced to give at least lip service to the idea of ending poverty and debt.[29] (See Chapter 5 for further discussion of this point.) Former President Bill Clinton is enjoying a new career as an advocate of worldwide AIDS prevention and treatment, in collaboration with Bill and Melinda Gates. Given the widespread political and cultural resistance to globalization, it is an ever more urgent task for the elites of Davos to promote the virtues of neoliberal capitalism to the people being subjected to it. It is in this context, I want to argue, that the "freedom" experienced by women in the developed world becomes a selling point across the globe.

1. Cf. Fernandez-Kelly 2007, 509: as of 1978, "women were becoming the new face of the international proletariat." For an introduction to the literature on globalization, see Sklair 2002. For an overview of women, work, and globalization, see Beneria 2003; Rai 2002; and Visvanathan et al. 1997.

2. In this book I am accepting the use of the term *globalization* since it has become so widely used, although many writers on the Left consider *neoimperialism* a better expression.

3. "Macroeconomic" refers to the performance of an economy as a whole (as opposed to the "microeconomics" of individual firms, industries, or markets). Macroeconomic policies, including levels of taxation, interest rates, and money supply, can be used to influence employment, inflation, and economic growth. In this book I use the term *Third World* or *Global South* to designate those

countries still struggling with the aftereffects of colonialism. The mainstream press uses the term *emerging markets* to refer to countries that are seen as promising targets of international investment.

4. For details of the struggle over attempts to privatize Medicaid, see www.ncpssm.org.

5. See Levitt 1993. "The underlying concept may be traced back to McLuhan's (1960) notion of the 'global village' but was explicitly introduced into the management literature in Levitt's (1983) paper on the globalization of markets" (Dicken 1998, 15n1). Cf. Feder 2006: "His concept that business was becoming globalized, which Mr. Levitt defined as the changes in technologies and social behaviors that allow multinational companies like Coca-Cola and McDonald's to sell the same products worldwide, first appeared in a 1983 *Harvard Business Review* article 'The Globalization of Markets.'"

6. See, for example, Byron 2007 on how Procter & Gamble is targeting 1 billion very poor women in developing countries by packaging shampoo and other products into tiny single-use packets that they can afford.

7. The mortgages were bundled into tradable securities owned by banks, hedge funds, and other investment institutions. The disputed value of some of these "toxic" mortgages led to mutual distrust and an unwillingness to grant credit.

8. GDP is the sum of all goods and services produced annually within a country. It is used to compare the total value of one country's economy against another. Feminist economists have pointed to the inadequacy of these figures, which exclude all of the unpaid work performed by women in households and the work of women in the "informal" sector, such as street vending. GDP figures are also tilted against environmental policies: a forest that is cut down counts, but not a forest left standing. On this point, see Folbre 2001, 68–71.

9. A third international financial institution was established in 1948: the General Agreement on Trade and Tariffs (GATT), which was designed to reduce tariff rates on trade in manufactured goods. GATT was succeeded by the World Trade Organization in 1995 (McMichael 2004, 168–172).

10. The First Estate was the clergy; and the Second Estate, the nobility. The Third Estate comprised the remainder of the entire population, led by the bourgeoisie, whose claims for political representation were a starting point of the revolutionary process.

11. Keynesianism is named for the influential British economist John Maynard Keynes, who argued in the 1930s that government spending was necessary to counter the underconsumption that was helping to prolong the Great Depression. The term *neoliberalism* is confusing to most Americans as it sounds like liberalism, that is, the left of the political spectrum as opposed to conservatism on the right. But it refers to a return to a free-market ideology, labeled *liberalism* in the context of English politics.

12. Of course, the "consensus" in the United States was hard fought, and labor historians are now emphasizing the intensity of labor conflict during the years from 1945 to the mid-1970s (see, for example, Lichtenstein 2002).

13. "In fact, it was economist Milton Friedman, who said . . . 'In one sense, we are all Keynesians now; in another, nobody is any longer a Keynesian.' (*Time* magazine, February 4, 1966). What Nixon said in 1971 was 'I am now a Keynesian in economics' (*New York Times,* January 4, 1971)" (Bartlett 2008).

14. "Dhaka muslin was in demand in the court of the Mughal emperor and among the aristocracy of Europe as the finest textile in the world and description of its delicacy and beauty abound in the historical literature" (Kabeer 2000, 55). As the British textile industry mechanized, the British first limited the sale of Bengal cloth at home with prohibitive tariffs, and eventually the competition from British textiles ended the production of both local cotton and muslin. Dhaka was reduced to a ghost town, and the governor-general of the East India Company told London in 1835 that "the misery hardly finds a parallel in the history of commerce. The bones of the cotton

weavers are bleaching the plains of India" (cited in Kabeer 2000, 56). This is also the quote made famous by Karl Marx in *Capital I* (1909, Chapter 15, Section 5, 471).

15. See Perman et al. 2004, 4.

16. U.S. Census Bureau 2002, 416, Table 653: "Employment by Industry, 1970–1994," and 385, Table 591: "Employment by Industry, 1980–2001."

17. White House 2002. Calculated from Table B-12: "Gross Domestic Product by Industry, 1959–2000."

18. Petrodollars are the dollars received by the members of OPEC from Western countries in exchange for their oil, which are then deposited in Western banks.

19. This shock was named for Paul Volcker, chair of the Federal Reserve Board under Presidents Jimmy Carter and Ronald Reagan, from 1979 to 1987.

20. These were called the Bretton Woods institutions after the name of the town in New Hampshire where representatives of the British and U.S. treasuries designed the founding bodies of the postwar economic order: the World Bank and the International Monetary Fund.

21. The WTO succeeded the GATT agreement signed in 1944 in Havana, Cuba, and implemented in 1947; this was an international treaty that sought to assure free trade among member nations. Regular international negotiations on the terms of free trade have continued and have become the site of renewed contestations between the developing and the rich countries (McMichael 2004, 194–195). In 2008, the "Doha" round of WTO negotiations launched in 2001 ended in failure as the newly intensified demands by developing countries for protections against imports were rejected by the United States (see Loyn 2008).

22. Just to take the case of agribusiness: "Three agribusiness firms headquartered in the United States operate meat-packing operations across the world, raising cattle, pigs, and poultry on feedstuffs supplied by their own grain marketing subsidiaries elsewhere in the world. Cargill, headquartered in Minnesota, is the largest grain trader in the world, operating in 70 countries with more than 800 offices or plants and more than 70,000 employees. It has established a joint venture with Nippon Meat Packers of Japan called Sun Valley Thailand, from which it exports U.S. corn-fed poultry products to the Japanese market. ConAgra, headquartered in Nebraska, owns 56 companies and operates in 26 countries with 58,000 employees. It processes feed and animal protein products in the United States, Canada, Australia, Europe, the Far East, and Latin America. Tyson Foods, headquartered in Arkansas, runs a joint venture with the Japanese agribusiness firm C. Itoh, which produces poultry in Mexico for both local consumption and export to Japan" (McMichael 2004, 104–105).

23. The *Washington Consensus* is "a term coined in 1990 by John Williamson of the Institute for International Economics, a think tank in that city" ("Wanted: A New Regional Agenda" 2003, 2). Of course, the term refers not to Washington, DC, the city, as disingenuously suggested by *The Economist,* but to Washington, the seat of U.S. economic and military power.

24. The OECD comprises thirty member countries in Europe plus the United States, Japan, and South Korea, all considered developed economies. Reagan's expansion of public spending was paid for by an increase in the deficit and an increase in taxes for the majority (while he dramatically reduced taxes for the 20 percent of the population with the highest incomes) (Navarro 2007, 21).

25. The informal economy refers to forms of income that are not usually part of the official economy: they are not taxed or regulated, but are off the books, including everything from street vendors and sex workers to drug traffickers.

26. For China, the figures are 4.5 percent versus 9.8 percent and 2.5 percent versus 8.4 percent, reflecting the impact of continued state-led development.

27. "George Caffentzis, the philosopher of money, and his colleagues in the Midnight Oil Collective were the first, in the early 1980s, to develop the idea that the neoliberal project is, in its essence, a form of 'new enclosures,' taking the tactics of the English enclosures to a planetary level and creating this time a fully globalized proletariat" (Boal 2007, 3).

28. "Five of South Africa's nine provinces have now reported cases of cholera. The country's department of health announced on Friday that there have been 64 deaths and nearly 18,000 infections since the outbreak began last August.... Critics have accused the government of exacerbating the problem by introducing charges for access to clean water—a move that has prompted some people to save money by getting their water from contaminated sources" ("Cholera in South Africa Spreads" 2001).

29. The G-8 was originally the Group of 7—the United States, the United Kingdom, France, West Germany, Japan, Italy, and Canada. Founded in 1975, it holds annual meetings in which finance ministers set economic policy for the world economy. Russia was admitted in 1996, hence the G-8.

Unit V. Family Systems, and Reproductive Rights: The Politics of Women's Work Inside and Outside the Home

Letter to My Friend

June Jordan

As YOU ARE heading for the door, I touch your shoulder. "I'm sorry about Danny," I say.

I am. I am choked with horror.

Your schoolmate from 7th through 12th grades, Daniel Pearl was kidnapped and murdered in Pakistan, just a month ago. You had read about this in the papers and, at first, you had not recognized your Danny. He had always been "one of the nice boys; a nice Jewish boy," but then, evidently, he had grown into a remarkably handsome guy with a beautiful French wife, responsibilities as chief of the Wall Street Journal's South East Asia Bureau, and an invincible, activist wish to cross boundaries: To talk and to listen to people entirely different from himself, people as different as a Pakistani Islamist and a father who is the son of a Holocaust survivor.

According to the taped killing of Danny, he was forced to "admit" that he was a Jew, that his mother was a Jew, that his father was a Jew, that his grandfather was a Jew. Your own mother found this particular coercion "humiliating." But why? You and I had wondered, awkwardly, about this. And then you'd said, "because his whole life was internationalist, and he was always expanding his embrace, his witness, and because he was so fearlessly open, and willing, and expecting to do good. . . "

Or, as *The New York Times* reported, Danny's wife remembers one of their last conversations in which she'd asked him if they were going "to settle," and he'd said, "No, We're going to change the world."

Danny's widow, Mariane, is 7 months pregnant, and she had spoken at The Memorial Service with humbling composure. In fact, as you reported to me, the entire ceremony was humbling, and strange, because not one relative, or friend, rose to express anger or to call out for vengeance. Instead, a "Daniel Pearl Foundation To Promote Cross-cultural Understanding" had been announced, as well as the setting up of a special fund to support Danny's wife and child.

What was anyone feeling, really?

What did you feel?

You had e-mailed me from Los Angeles, on Sunday, letting me know you were going to the Memorial Service and that, afterwards, you'd undertake the long, long drive up to the Bay Area. You needed that long trip with only yourself speeding through that vast and neutral landscape. Once you arrived, I had watched your face and your hands, looking for signs of any emotion. But I saw nothing. At last I asked, "Don't you have any feelings about this?"

And you had answered me, at once: "I'm furious! And I wanted somebody to deal with this fact: Danny was killed because he was a Jew! And why would anybody hate Jews? Why would anybody hate Danny? And what can we/what should we—as a community/a community of Jews—what should we do?"

There is that question.

And Danny is dead.

And you have always been delicate and small, but this afternoon, to me, you seemed so small: There should be more of you. In every sense, there should be more of you. I am outside your community. And I want to figure out a way to stand beside you, and a way to stand together. And I don't know how exactly I can do that, so, for now, I am sending you this letter:

In the very few hours since you left my house, the newswires report that Israeli soldiers shot 24 year old Issa Faraj as he played with his children inside the West Bank Dheishe Refugee Camp; Israeli tanks fired on journalists holed up in a hotel at the edge of al-Amari refugee camp, and more than a hundred Israeli tanks and troops invaded the Palestinian town of Ramallah, killing 38 Palestinians.

The thing is that I can't even undertake to write to you / to reach out to you, my friend, without the unholy carnage of Israel-Palestine exploding in my face.

Who was Issa Faraj?

I want to ask about your trip home, and what you're thinking about— And these gratuitous snippets of terrible news push me away into another place where other words pound into my head: What about context! Why are there refugee camps, in the first place?

It is as though political disaster overwhelms what needs to be as personal, as specific, as the chicken soup you brought to me.

This ongoing tanks and Apache helicopters versus stones and suicide bombers' purgatory poisons the process of thought, itself: thoughts spoken, or not.

And even though all violence is not the same—in its consequences or its capacities, all violence is horrifying.

Is there some way to assert this principle of equality-in-death that will not diminish any of the dead?

Is there some way to assert this principle of equality-among-the-living that will not demean, or diminish, any of the lives under attack?

I think there are reasons for hope: Israeli and American Jews insisting on a principled commitment to one, equality-driven standard for the judgment of every policy, every action.

- 300 Israeli Reservists refusing to further serve in the I.D.P. because they do not view Israel's military occupation as a defensibly defensive exercise of power
- Israel's Women In Black which, for more than 14 years, has persisted, and flourished, into a global movement against all violence, against the occupation, and against the privileging of one people above another
- Bereaved Israeli and Palestinian parents who, recently, attempted to comfort each other, as they gathered outside the United Nations, and stood, together, next to 1,000 coffins draped by their respective flags
- "Jewish Voices Against Israel's Occupation of Palestinian Territories" which (more than 600 Jewish Americans) placed an ad in the 3/17/02

Sunday NY Times, declaring, "The Settlements Must Go. The Occupation Must End. There Can Be No Peace Without Justice."

These brave public declarations arise from an idea of equality that no difference, no conflict, can, morally, be allowed to obscure.

This bravery lets me believe that perhaps what we euphemize as "The Middle East" will not, forever, remain an abominable abyss.

These courageous affirmations bring me back to your schoolmate, Danny Pearl, and the humility his activist life continues to elicit.

And I am encouraged to challenge the racist, lopsided postures of our government.

In this crisis, for example, it is not okay to use my tax dollars to perpetuate the dispossession, humiliation, and wretched impoverishment, of an entire people.

That is not okay with me.

That is not okay with more and more of us—we who have been sidelined and silenced by the White House, and inside our own homes, and face-to-face with our fears that we will be called anti-Semitic if we speak up.

Can we stand face to face, and tell the truth to each other?

If you and I can talk again, and then, again—if I can say out loud these things that wring my soul—

If you can trust me, still, enough to tell me more about the jeopardy of anti-Semitism that you, at last, believe, now that your Danny, now that, of all men, Daniel Pearl is dead from hatred that will not yield even to his nobility of work and purpose—

If I can trust you, still, to hear my grief for Danny, and to share my grief for Issa Faraj—

If we refuse double standards churning to deform friends into enemies—
Oh!

How I wish Issa Faraj could continue playing with his children!

How I wish Daniel Pearl could hold his first-born in his arms!

My heart is sick from all demonic machinations neither one of us would ever advocate or condone.

Your Danny is dead.

And how can we honor his heroic wish: "to change the world"?

I have no simple answers.

But perhaps our willingness to listen and to say all that we know, and feel—all that we dare—perhaps that will help us to build something better than we can even, now, imagine.

March 26, 2002
Berkeley

Motherhood
Between Mammy and a Hard Place

Tamara Winfrey Harris

At the 2012 Democratic National Convention, First Lady Michelle Obama announced that her most important role in the White House is "mom-in-chief."[1]

Some white feminists weren't having it.

What was up with this Ivy League–trained, corporate legal powerhouse making like a political wifebot? As writer Libby Copeland lamented on *Slate* magazine's *Double X* blog, "Why are presidential candidates' wives all the same?"[2]

Except Michelle LaVaughn Robinson Obama, from the South Side of Chicago, ain't Laura Bush. Or even Hillary Clinton. Michelle Obama is a black woman. And her ability to prioritize motherhood—much less be the symbol of motherhood for a nation—is revolutionary.

Black women are not the inheritors of the cult of true womanhood's picture of wifely domesticity. For them, the fight has not been to prove that they can be something other than mothers as much as it has been to have the myriad ways they mother recognized and cherished in a society whose family values rarely include them and those they love.

It has always been accepted that black women can care for other people's children. In slavery, many of them did the dirty work of homemaking—the cooking, cleaning, and mommying for masters and mistresses. Later, black domestics helped make it possible for middle-class white women to enter a workforce of which black women (and poor women of all races) were already an exploited part. In 2014, the number of "black women pushing white babies around" on the Upper West Side of New York City prompted a photography exhibition by Ellen Jacobs called *Substitutes*.[3] But modern black mothers exist between this comfortable evocation of Mammy and a hard place.

Moments in Alright

Noreen Raines became a self-proclaimed "science nerd" after receiving a microscope for Christmas when she was eight years old. In 2005, Raines, the mother of four, launched Big Thinkers to inspire lifelong science learning in the state of Georgia, through interactive stage shows, in-school programming, birthday parties, summer camps, and workshops.[4]

Attack of the Single Black Mother

More than 70 percent of black births happen outside marriage.[5] From Tea Party candidates to black clergy, folks will tell you that statistic is a sin and a shame. For a society that is mistrustful of sexually active, unmarried women and wedded to the superiority of male-led households, those numbers demonstrate unchecked aberrance and are used to confirm stereotypes about black women's femininity and sexuality. This statistic is positioned as the reason for every social ill plaguing the black community and, once again, very likely the fault of black women.

Conservative columnist George Will said on ABC's *This Week* that single mothers present a bigger threat to African Americans than the loss of voting rights. Jimi Izrael, frequent contributor to NPR, wrote in his book *The Denzel Principle* that high rates of black divorce and single-parent families "really reflects less on black men and more on black women and their inability to make good choices."[6]

Dr. Sarah J. Jackson says that black women's sexuality and motherhood have been part of public discourse since slavery, when our reproduction was an integral part of the economy, like the livestock that kept the agricultural engine going.[7] People were as inclined to talk about black women birthing babies as they were cows bearing calves. And, like those cows, black women were viewed as uncivilized and unintentional breeders. The institution of slavery required a voluntary blindness to the idea of black family. "If you're treating a group of people like animals, you have to believe that they're not capable of making the same emotional bonds with their children that you are. Otherwise, you might feel bad about selling their children off down the river," Jackson says.

Here again, the Moynihan Report and its support for the stereotypes of the Matriarch, Sapphire, and Jezebel play a role in ensuring that the public discussion of black motherhood is relentlessly negative.

"If the male isn't the primary breadwinner of the family, then the children of that family are forever deviant. It's right there on the page," says Jackson.

Ronald Reagan, in his 1976 presidential campaign, abetted this idea with his bogeywoman, the "welfare queen."[8] His frequently repeated anecdote about the Cadillac-driving Chicago woman who swindled government programs out of hundreds of thousands of dollars by using disguises, fake names and addresses, and possibly a stolen baby,[9] cemented the idea that black female reproduction is unreasonable, tied to lasciviousness, and reflects a desire to leech off the state rather than to be a loving parent and contributor to the future of society.

As with marriage, the structure of family is undeniably changing all over—most American women under thirty, regardless of race, will give birth outside marriage;[10] across the Atlantic, in Iceland, 66 percent of children are born to unmarried women; and heterosexual marriage rates are falling and divorce rates rising in the United States and abroad.[11] But black women and their families are still seen as dysfunctional, and uncommonly so.

Opponents of single motherhood say they have black children's best interests in mind and point to decades of research that indicates that children do best when they're raised in healthy two-parent families. But, according to the Center for Law and Social Policy,[12] research results related to the offspring of single-parent households are often oversimplified and exaggerated. Most children in single-parent families grow up just fine, and it is still unclear how much of the disadvantages to children are caused by poverty or family structure or whether marriage itself makes the difference or the type of people who commonly marry.

Demonizing single black motherhood does not improve the lives of children. On the contrary, the idea that 70 percent of black boys and girls are congenitally damaged stigmatizes them.

"It's messed up that we have to figure out how to keep our kids from being negatively impacted by generations of misinformation about the way that our households are run," says Stacia Brown,[13] thirty-five. "I don't want my child to feel that the way we live is something that we have to defend to the world."

Stacia herself was raised by a single mother. And she learned from her mother to protect her own daughter from the stain of so-called illegitimacy.

"We didn't use stigmatized language around our family structure when I was growing up," she says.

And when a young Stacia was confronted with condemning language about her family, it felt foreign. "I thought, 'We're happy here.' It didn't feel like, 'Oh my gosh, I don't have a dad and my life is definitely really bad because of this.' I mean, I do have a daddy, he just lived in another state. I have a lot of things that felt like bigger barriers to my long-term success than fatherlessness or whatever."

Stacia, who co-parents with her child's father, says, "We need to, in our households, set our standard for how we're going to feel about ourselves. When your kids hear you say, 'I don't want to be a statistic,' they feel like their household is. . . . There's something wrong with it. You're bringing that into your house.

"Even if somebody at school dogs them about it, when they come home, you've got to be able to say, 'Nah, we're not accepting that.'"

The negative focus on single black motherhood is also not

about helping black communities. If it were, those who rail against unmarried mothers would spend at least equal time calling for affordable family planning and reproductive health care, universal access to good child care, improved urban school systems, a higher minimum wage, and college education that doesn't break the banks of average people. And they would admit that the welfare-queen image is a distortion and a distraction.

Heidi Renée Lewis, thirty-three, says condemnation of single-parent families also unduly shames mothers trying to do their best. She tells a story about attending a neighborhood outing with her oldest son and his father while she was pregnant with their second child.

"Our kids are only nineteen months apart. This one woman that I grew up with said to my cousin, 'Oh my God! I can't believe Heidi is having another baby. Didn't she just have a baby?' My cousin said, 'Well at least they're both by the same man!'"

Heidi's cousin had three children with two fathers. "She was kicking herself in the face to defend me," she says.

"I grew up with more examples of nontraditional than traditional. Women on welfare, struggling. All the women I knew on welfare worked, just like most people on welfare work. There was still this 'don't be like them' narrative. Why would I want to be like people who weren't being affirmed? People hate to feel ashamed."

Heidi's parents were married when she was born. They grew up together and were high school sweethearts. When they married, her father built a house for his young wife, across the street from his in-laws in a small Ohio town. But it was the eve of the 1980s crack epidemic, and Heidi's father became addicted. Her parents divorced.

Heidi always wanted to get married, in part to prove that she could do what her parents could not. A child of the '80s, she was partly influenced by popular culture—"[Whether the families were] piss poor like Roseanne and Dan or upper middle class like Clair and Cliff, we were being indoctrinated with that traditional family model"—but she was also guided by her beloved grandmother's conservatism. "My grandfather, even though he was a minister, was more forgiving than my grandmother. My grandmother was not for the shit like out-of-wedlock babies! Oh my God, no!

"What I really think I wanted was to have kids and for my kids to not have the family trouble that I had. They would not have to go through divorce, and they would not have to have a drug-addicted parent, and they would not have to have parents who married other people and made life uncomfortable that way."

In graduate school and unmarried (though in a committed relationship), Heidi became pregnant.

"I was devastated . . . not devastated, but I was scared. . . . I'll tell you how respectability crept its way back in. . . . I was like, 'Well, I'm not married, but at least I have a bachelor's degree! . . . I finished school, and I'm halfway through a masters. Damn! Can I get a break for that?'"

Though she and her husband have been together for eleven years, they married only five years ago . . . or was it six?

"I can't even remember. What is this, 2014? I think we got technically married in 2009? I don't know. Yeah, 2009. You know what? Our wedding anniversary is the same as the day we first got together. We didn't change the day cause we felt like we wanted to honor the whole eleven years. Who gives a shit that it's not on the official paper?"

If America were having an honest conversation about black motherhood, the screeds about the scourge of baby mamas would also note that birth rates among African American women are lower than ever before in recorded history and that part of the explanation for the high percentage of out-of-wedlock black babies lies with the fact that fewer black women are marrying and many of those women are deciding not to have children. Married black women are also having fewer children.[14]

No. The conversation about black single motherhood in America is driven by gender- and race-biased moral panic and is primarily a means to exonerate systemic inequality for America's problems, while leveraging age-old stereotypes to scapegoat black women and their children. The reduction of black motherhood to concerns about indiscriminate fucking, emasculating black men, draining the public teat, and releasing frightening, no-daddy-having offspring onto beleaguered American streets stains every black mothering experience, no matter how much individual realities differ.

Despite their decades-long marriage, Michelle Obama was derisively called then-candidate Barack Obama's "baby mama" in a Fox News graphic.[15] Yvette Perry, a married mother of twins, found her swollen fingers uncomfortable in her wedding rings after giving birth. But she wore the rings anyway to avoid being stereotyped as a single black mother. It didn't help. "A new graduate student in my program, who had seen me at a couple of welcome/orientation activities with my babies, kept going on about how much respect she had for me. It took me a while to figure out that she assumed I was a single mother."[16]

When life experiences collide with stereotypes, drawing a distinction can be even tougher, the burden heavier.

Thirty-four-year-old Brandee Mimitzraiem[17] is not the woman people imagine when they hear about single black mothers. She is working on her PhD in theology and philosophy and is a member of the clergy in the AME Church. She gave birth to two sons, becoming a single mother by choice after realizing at twenty-six that marriage would never be for her.

"I do see myself reflected a lot in the stereotype and it bothers me," she says. "You know, I've had to go on food stamps. My babies are on Medicaid right now, because I cannot afford insurance for the three of us.

"People say, 'You're getting a PhD. It's not the same. You're not like them.'" But I am, and my kids go to school with 'them.' I take those issues of class very seriously. I'm not going to look down on somebody else because they don't have the same education as me. I don't have a baby daddy, but at the same time, I'm a black single mom, whose kids are on Medicaid. And I get talked about horribly for actually raising my kids, too."

All black mothers are forced to expend energy (as if being a parent isn't hard enough) trying to outrun the idea that they are bad mothers who birth and then neglect bad kids with uninvolved, bad daddies.

Now, *that* is a sin and a shame.

Moments in Alright

Tanya Fields wants fellow mothers and children in her Bronx neighborhood to have access to locally sourced and nutritious food. She started the BLK Projek to create economic development opportunities for underserved women and is working to develop a women-led cooperative food business and urban farm using undeveloped land.[18]

The Purposeful Mother

Most single black mothers are not postgraduate, degree-holding pastors, but neither are they the pariahs of the public imagination. The negative perception of black mothers flattens the experiences of single mothers and ignores single mothers by choice, single mothers whose partners are involved in their children's lives, unmarried mothers who live and parent with their partners, lesbian mothers, and married mothers in traditional families. It also obscures the fact that most black mothers, no matter their family structure, attempt to thoughtfully and successfully raise their children.

"Black parenting is never theorized as something that has intentionality," says Heidi Renée Lewis. "It's like we're just . . . popping out babies."

But many single mothers take care to create strong support systems before their children enter the word—something that Brandee points out is important for traditional families, too. "Raising kids without a village is impossible. Period. If you're only dependent upon what's in your house to raise your children, your children are failing and you're failing as a parent."

Because black mothers are positioned as "other," it is easy for people to miss the elements of universality in parenting experiences—the worrying, the work, and the joy.

Stacia says the things that keep her up at night have less to do with single mothering than mothering full stop. Her four-year-old suffers from hearing loss and has experienced some developmental delays. Stacia and her co-parent worry about how to best advocate for her. For four years, Stacia parented long distance with her child's father, who this year moved closer to be a bigger presence in his daughter's life, challenging the assumption that unless they are married, fathers always remain uninvolved.

The push and pull of co-parenting is not much different from what married parents do, Stacia says, pointing out that the burden of child care is rarely shared equally even between married parents. There are negotiations over finances and quality time, whether one parent will stay home, how child care will work, and who will fetch the children from school.

The commonalities of parenting are also apparent when black mothers express their love for their children.

Brandee marvels at "how the world amazes them and the things that come out of their mouths." Stacia loves little girl hugs and affection and the new way being a mother makes her see the world, but also the mystery of conceiving and nurturing another human being.

Heidi says, "I get to teach my kids things. I get to make an impact on the world. I get to teach them values that I learned and also teach them things differently."

Brandi Summers becomes emotional while speaking about her baby daughter: "I didn't know I had the capacity to love anything as much as I love her. I couldn't draw or write how much I love her."[19]

It is clear that black mothers are no different from other mothers in terms of their devotion and concern for their children. What is unique is how they are obligated to, from an early age, teach their children how to navigate their minority status and the racism that accompanies it.

"Being black has demanded that I parent my children regarding race, gender, socioeconomic problems, and issues even when I wasn't ready, in the mood, whatever," says Heidi. "I did not ask to have to tell my daughter why she was the only brown girl in ballet. The world demanded that I do that, because she is just the kind of kid who picks up on that kind of shit.

"With the Trayvon Martin verdict, I had to tell my son that if you're in a situation where somebody is about to do something to you, don't just scream. Scream your address or your middle name or something to let somebody know who the hell you are.... I will never forget that fucking debate over who was screaming: George Zimmerman or Trayvon Martin? I said, 'Well, I got an answer for that! Scream some shit that nobody but you knows. Scream, 'Help me! This man is attacking me and my middle name is Aaron Patrick!'

"Why do I have to do that? Because I'm raising black children in the United States of America in the twenty-first century."

· ·

Moments in Alright

"My daughter sometimes slept under my desk when I worked nights," says DeShong Perry-Smitherman, who became a mother at sixteen. DeShong went on to become an Emmy Award–winning news producer. And with her business partner, Ericka Gibson, she cofounded A Girl's Gift, Inc., a program designed to teach girls leadership and entrepreneurial skills.[20]

· ·

Brandi says she has a lot of fears about "raising a black girl in this world. My race still becomes very, very clear even in the fact that I'm a mom. I stopped noticing when I'm alone, like it's just me in a room full of white people, but if I'm with my daughter and we're in a room full of white people and white kids, I just notice it right away. I want her to be with some kids of color or I'm wondering what these parents are teaching their children about black kids. I'm paranoid about all that. How is she going to see the world?"

But black mothers find little support in addressing problems of race or the routine challenges (and joys) of parenting because the way people think about black parenting is so limited.

Ain't I a Mommy?

In a 2008 *Bitch* magazine article, titled "Ain't I a Mommy,"[21] Deesha Philyaw lamented the exclusion of black mothers from the "mommy memoir" boom. As a married, black, stay-at-home mom, Philyaw found her experience virtually missing from parenting literature. Also, the stay-at-home mom versus working mom argument that the media seemed obligated to rehash ad nauseam was presented only through the eyes of upper-middle-class white women, ignoring that throughout the history of black women in America, most of them have had no choice but to work.

"I really needed to see myself in those pages. In other memoirs, I saw college-educated, stay-at-home moms who felt equal parts gratitude, mental fatigue, and boredom, but I didn't see any women who were black like me." Philyaw wrote.

Michelle Hughes, a single mother through adoption, says it is nearly impossible to find books about black parents adopting black children.[22]

"The only support you get is with other single black-adoptive moms," she says. "I'm an organizer. If I don't have what I need, I put it together. I founded an African American adoption room because I couldn't find one on Facebook."

Stacia launched a blog called Beyond Baby Mamas "to talk about some of the feelings that I was having and the experiences and stigma and all that stuff like that, but then also some of the unique triumphs of being a co-parent or solo parent."

Many black mothers find themselves having to create their own support systems online and elsewhere because the belief that all black mothers are single and that single mothers are dysfunctional messes leaves the real needs of African American mothers unaddressed.

It is within this social context, with its poisoned view of black motherhood, that our African American First Lady of the United States exists. Feminists eager to see Michelle Obama strike a blow against stereotyped roles for women can be assured that she is doing just that. Far from commonplace, her presence as a mother in the White House defies conventions about black women as mothers, wives, and caretakers for their families.

I imagine that a woman as accomplished as the FLOTUS has the strength to make her needs known and that if she has, for now, chosen motherhood, that it is the role she wants. That choice alone is a privilege not afforded most women in our modern economy, much less black ones.

The push back against the role Michelle Obama has chosen for herself is illustrative of the way black mothers' desires and experiences are ignored in favor of the stories others would prefer to tell about them. It is no more noble to demand that a black woman flex her Harvard law degree instead of her role as a wife and mother than it is to insist that her family is illegitimate unless she is wearing a wedding ring—they are both part of a sad history of acts against black female agency and a case of public interference in our private choices.

Those who have long wished to brand Michelle Obama a dangerous radical may have it right—just not in the way they think. The First Lady's most incendiary act of bomb throwing was when she stood on stage, the descendant of slaves, in front of millions, at an arena in what was once the Old South, and said unapologetically: "At the end of the day, my most important title is still 'mom-in-chief.' My daughters are still the heart of my heart and the center of my world."

Forget what you've heard. That proclamation was not business as usual. Many black women, who struggle each day to have the glorious complexity of their motherhood noticed and valued, saw it for what it was—an act of rebellion.

And one not unlike the private resistance black mothers across America enact daily, just by being.

"I didn't create the struggle. I didn't ask for these myths about the welfare queen and the mammy and the junk," Heidi says. "We're just trying to do as black mothers the best we can with what we've been given, trying to be as radical as we can in a world that doesn't allow for radical anything to thrive.

"This is what I was born into, so I'm navigating that and trying to be true to whoever it is that I am, within that context, in the best way possible."

Motherhood: Between Mammy and a Hard Place

1. Lisa Belkin, "Michelle Obama: What Does She Mean by 'Mom In Chief'?" *Huffington Post*, September 5, 2012, http://www.huffington-post.com/lisa-belkin/obama-mom-in-chief_b_1858440.html.

2. Libby Copeland, "Why Are Presidential Candidates' Wives All the Same?" *Slate*, September 7, 2012, http://www.slate.com/articles/double_x/doublex/2012/09/first_wives_club_why_are_presidential_candidates_spouses_all_the_same_.html.

3. Sadie Whitelocks, "Black Women Pushing White Babies: Photo Series Exposes the Racial Divides in the World of a NY Nanny," *Daily Mail*, January 15, 2014, http://www.dailymail.co.uk/femail/article-2540015/Black-women-pushing-white-babies-Candid-photo-series-exposes-deep-racial-divide-New-York-nannies-young-wards.html.

4. Big Thinkers Science Exploration, "Founder," http://www.big-thinkers.com/index.php?option=com_content&view=article&id=162&Itemid=159.

5. Jesse Washington, "Blacks Struggle with 72 Percent Unwed Mother Rate," NBCNews.com, November 7, 2010, http://www.nbcnews.com/id/39993685/ns/health-womens_health/t/blacks-struggle-percent-unwed-mothers-rate/#.VBeBF_ldWa9.

6. Evan McMurry, "George Will: Single Moms 'Biggest Impediment' to Black Progress," Mediaite, August 25, 2013, http://www.mediaite.com/tv/george-will-single-moms-biggest-impediment-to-black-progress/; Jimi Izrael, *The Denzel Principle: Why Black Women Can't Find Good Black Men* (New York: St. Martin's, 2010), 21.

7. Sarah Jackson, interview by the author, November 2, 2012.

8. Ian Haney-Lopez, "The Racism at the Heart of the Reagan Presidency," *Salon*, January 11, 2014, http://www.salon.com/2014/01/11/the_racism_at_the_heart_of_the_reagan_presidency/.

9. Gene Demby, "The Truth Behind the Lies of the Original 'Welfare Queen,'" NPR, December 20, 2013, http://www.npr.org/blogs/codeswitch/2013/12/20/255819681/the-truth-behind-the-lies-of-the-original-welfare-queen.

10. Jason DeParle and Sabrina Tavernise, "For Women Under 30, Most Births Occur Outside Marriage," *New York Times*, February 17, 2012, http://www.nytimes.com/2012/02/18/us/for-women-under-30-most-births-occur-outside-marriage.html?pagewanted=all&_r=0.

11. Gardiner Harris, "Out-of-Wedlock Birthrates Are Soaring, U.S. Reports," *New York Times*, May 13, 2009, http://www.nytimes.com/2009/05/13/health/13mothers.html.

12. Mary Parke, *Are Married Parents Really Better for Children?* (Washington, DC: Center for Law and Social Policy, 2003), http://www.clasp.org/resources-and-publications/states/0086.pdf.

13. Stacia Brown, interview by the author, June 28, 2014.

14. Ta-Nehisi Coates, "Understanding Out-of-Wedlock Births in Black America," *The Atlantic*, June 21, 2013, http://www.theatlantic.com/sexes/archive/2013/06/understanding-out-of-wedlock-births-in-black-america/277084/.

15. Jim Rutenberg, "Fox Forced to Address Michelle Obama Headline," *New York Times*, June 12, 2008, http://thecaucus.blogs.nytimes.com/2008/06/12/fox-apologizes-for-michelle-obama-headline/?_php=true&_type=blogs&_r=0.

16. Yvette Perry, interview by the author, June 24, 2014.

17. Brandee Mimitzraiem, interview by the author, July 29, 2014.

18. "Meet the Eco Warriors: Tanya Fields," The Next Eco Warriors, http://www.nextecowarriors.com/tanya-fields/.

19. Brandi Summers, interview by the author, July 11, 2014.

20. DeShong Perry-Smitherman, interview by the author, Indianapolis, December 15, 2014.

21. Deesha Philyaw, "Ain't I a Mommy," *Bitch*, Summer 2008, 46.

22. Michelle Hughes, interview by the author, July 25, 2014.

CARING, DISABILITY STUDIES, AND NARRATIVE STRUCTURE

Roberta Seelinger Trites

In insisting on the intra-activity of the enacted and the represented, Karen Barad advances a philosophy that rejects the linguistic turn and its epis-temological emphasis on the primacy of language. Barad's theories, along with the work of such material feminists as Nancy Tuana, Stacy Alaimo, and Susan Hekman, invite us to collapse the Saussurean dichotomy between signifier and signified, which is the very distinction from which much post-structural thinking emerged. Similarly, the concepts of *self* and *other* create another false binary that material feminists, especially ecofeminists, reject because they recognize how interrelated phenomena are. Just as the human subject cannot be defined without the context of the environment, human subjects are not formed solely in opposition to one another in a permanent state of othering. As Barad writes: "Existence is not an individual affair. Individuals do not preexist their interactions; rather, individuals emerge through and as part of their entangled intra-relating" (ix).

Alice Curry demonstrates how ecofeminism and feminist ethics of care are interrelated aspects of material feminism: "Analyses of systemic im-balances of power and privilege at the macrolevel delimit the potential for acknowledgement of gendered power-plays at a smaller scale—within the family, household and the body—and the crucial ways in which such microlevel systems of gender difference impact the formal sphere" (74).[1] Feminist ethics of care acknowledges the importance of multiplicity; feminist ethics of care also recognizes how individuals are shaped by forces that include (and are not limited to) the environment, the material, and interacting with other people. Feminist ethics of care argues, in particular, that identity formation occurs within a matrix of human interactions, in-cluding the necessary role of being the "cared-for," as Nel Noddings defines one crucial element in the relationship of care in her book *Caring*; the other crucial element is the "one-caring" (4). She asserts that "human caring and the memory of caring and being cared for . . . form the foundation of ethical response" (1). For Noddings, the word *care* connotes both nurturance and the idea of taking on a burden (9), and all care involves a certain level of what she calls "engrossment" (17). She distinguishes what she refers to as "natural caring," something akin to instinctual care, from "ethical caring," which is the learned art of caring when we don't necessarily want to but know we must: "Ethical caring, the relation in which we do meet the other morally, will be described as arising out of natural caring—that relation in which we respond as one-caring out of love or natural inclination" (4–5). She regards caring as a foundation of human social structures: "Taking *relations* as ontologically basic simply means that we recognize human encounter and affective response as a basic fact of human existence" (Noddings 4, italics in the original).

Both the "one-caring" and the "cared-for" participate in "contribut[ing] to the relation; my caring must be somehow completed in the other if the relation is to be described as caring" (Noddings 4). Although Noddings uses the term "feminine," she makes the point several times that men and women both participate in non-competitive models of caring that she labels as "feminine" (xvi, 2, 8). She also underscores that empathy requires understanding the material condition of the "cared-for": "When my caring is directed to living things, I must consider their natures, ways of life, needs, and desires. And, although I can never accomplish it entirely, I try to apprehend the reality of the other. . . . To be touched, to have aroused in me something that will disturb my own ethical reality, I must see the other's reality as a possibility for my own" (Noddings 14). In other words, empathy is required in an ethics of care, and that empathy is based, in part, on our perception of the cared-for's physical and cognitive world: "Apprehending the other's reality, feeling what he feels as nearly as possible, is the essential part of caring from the view of the one-caring" (Noddings 16).

In *Feminist Morality*, the feminist ethicist Virginia Held also addresses how several aspects of feminist ethics of care are based in the material:

> A feminist view of culture includes, though it may not be limited to, an understanding of the material forms of the production and development of culture, and of the material lives of those who make culture and are shaped by it. A feminist view of culture recognizes the expensiveness of the equipment and the vastness of the economic resources needed to exert influence through the media in contemporary society. It includes recognition of the embodied reality of human life, as women strive to assure the security of our persons and as mothers struggle to earn enough to feed and safeguard the fragile bodies of children. But it includes, as well,

awareness of the everyday symbolism of such nonhierarchical activities as women together doing what needs to be done in caring cooperatively for children or publishing a newsletter. And it understands the cultural change involved in women and men working together as genuine equals in jobs of equal standing—and feeling comfortable doing so. (3)

While Held acknowledges both the importance of men and women working together and the importance of cooperation (rather than competition), she also acknowledges the materiality of the adult body, of cultural production, of media, of security and safety, and of children as embodied beings.

Mary Jeanette Moran demonstrates an ethics of care in which female characters in children's and YA novels can "unite the personal satisfaction of intellectual achievement with the communal goal of caring for others," while still avoiding "the expectation that they must sacrifice themselves in the service of their relationships" ("Use" 23). Moran acknowledges, however, the potential essentialism that an ethics based on caring can hold, writing:

> Although many scholars have found that caring ethics enhance various strands of feminist moral thinking and political action, even those who embrace this idea tend to recognize the essentializing potential of revaluing care as an ethical practice—the same potential that inheres in any attempt to reclaim a quality that has been associated with an oppressed group. . . . To constitute a truly feminist approach to morality, ethics of care must consciously deconstruct such essentialist assumptions while also challenging the idea that caring acts are less morally and intellectually advanced than those based on rationality. ("Use" 23)

Moran observes that those who dismiss ethics of care as sexist are missing the point ("Mother" 182–87). Feminist ethics recognizes that ethical decisions require both the analytics of "separation" and the emotionality of "connection": "once we have moved away from a paradigm that values separation above all else, care emerges as a legitimate goal of ethical decisions in addition to, or perhaps even instead of justice" (Moran, "Mother" 183).

Moran bases her theory in part on Virginia Held's premise that "caring should not replace thought" (Held 79), insisting that social justice will be furthered "the more we can conceive of an ethic of care as the product of choice, the farther we move away from a system that expects women—and women only—to have the capacity to care for others and to enact that care no matter what the cost to themselves" (Moran, "Use" 24). Moran then analyzes the Judy Bolton series to show that non-reciprocal relationships are destructive, that the "one-caring" must also engage in self-care, and that intellectual activity—such as writing, in Judy's case—is the basis of a healthy ethics of care.

In subsequent articles, Moran relies on Madeleine L'Engle's novels to demonstrate how feminist ethics of care can also provide a model for the "relational self" ("Making" 76) and for a rethinking of maternal ethics of care ("Mother" 194–95). Moran refers to ethics of care as a "less oppositional dynamic" than those ethical models that posit the individual as an "independent, autonomous subject" ("Making" 76). She traces how the feminist ethics of care adopts a model by which "the relational self acknowledges its debt to others as well as its responsibility to them—a much less oppositional dynamic" than theories that define the self in opposition to the other ("Making" 76). As an example, Moran shows how Meg Murray and her brothers "defeat evil by recognizing the relational nature of themselves and other people" ("Making" 76); Meg, Charles Wallace, and their twin brothers, Sandy and Dennys, must recognize and accept difference in order to "resist othering those who seem different" and in order to "find ways to connect across that difference" ("Making" 79). Moreover, although Meg's pregnancy in *A Swiftly Tilting Planet* could have proven to be a "restrictive" or inhibiting force, Moran demonstrates that it is actually Charles Wallace "who must relinquish his sense of autonomous self-hood as he inhabits the bodies of people from various time periods," while it is a pregnant Meg who saves him ("Mother" 195). Moran argues that L'Engle depicts characters who "empathize with others . . . to disrupt the antagonistic self-other dynamic" ("Making" 87).[2]

It is the *relationality* of feminist ethics of care that leads me to consider it as a form of material feminism because relationships require a physical component—an element of human interaction that Noddings's emphasis on the physical aspects of caring as a primary parent-child relationship makes clear. Thus, analyzing the rhetoric of connectedness (as opposed to the rhetoric of competition and/or separation) and the rhetoric of caring can help us understand more about feminist agendas in twenty-first century preadolescent and adolescent literature. As Moran writes, "the development of care ethics constitutes feminist philosophy's most distinctive and significant contribution to the field" ("Mother" 182).

In this chapter, I will thus rely on Moran's theories about ethics of care in children's and adolescent literature to analyze rhetorics of caring and cooperation as they occur both in feminist intersections with Disability Studies and in feminist intersections with narrative theory and reader response theory. As enacted in the twenty-first century study of children's and adolescent literature, Disability Studies, feminist narrative theory, and feminist reader response theory all tend to emphasize material aspects of caring, relationality, and cooperation. To demonstrate how interactions between feminist ethics of care and Disability Studies work, I will analyze *Cinder* (2012), a novel by Marissa Meyer that problematizes disability in feminist terms. Narrative layering also helps authors interrogate levels of care, so the remaining novels I have selected for analysis in this chapter include embedded narratives—stories within the story—that help the protagonist grow in her ethics of care. Thus, to explore how feminist narrative theories of children's and adolescent literature are imbued with ethics of care, I will provide readings of Jennifer Donnelly's *Revolution* (2010) and Kate DiCamillo's *Flora & Ulysses* (2013). And in the final section, to interrogate feminist reader response theory in the YA novel as a function of ethics of care, I will investigate Linda Sue Park's *Project Mulberry* (2005). What all of the theorists and all of the novels I have included in this chapter share is a valuation of caring and relationality.

DISABILITY STUDIES AND THE ETHICS OF CARING

Disability theorist Rosemarie Garland-Thompson asserts that one defining principle of feminist disability studies "is to augment the terms and confront the limits of how we understand human diversity, the materiality of the body, multiculturalism, and the social formations that interpret bodily differences," and she rightly insists that "integrating disability as a category of analysis and a system of representation deepens, expands, and challenges feminist theory" (15). Central to her argument is the implication that discrimination against the disabled requires that certain rhetorical structures remain in place. Garland-Thompson effectively establishes the connection between feminist ethics of care and feminist disability studies: both involve a belief system that privileges understanding, acceptance, and valuing other people. She also specifically cites feminist disability analysis as a type of material feminism in the way it can "illuminate . . . the investigation of the body: its materiality, its politics, its lived experiences, and its relation to subjectivity and identity" (22).

One theorist of English Education, Patricia A. Dunn, also makes clear the connection between Disability Studies and ethics of caring as a form of material feminism in *Disabling Characters: Representations of Disability in Young Adult Literature* when she writes: "Many barriers contributing to disability are material or attitudinal; either way, they are built. They are constructed. And whatever is constructed can be named, mitigated or removed" (1). Dunn's concern here is with both rhetorical and physical structures. With this succinct analysis, Dunn demonstrates the intersection of the linguistic turn and the material turn: as she notes, "barriers" are constructs that come in two forms: the "attitudinal" and the "material." Dunn argues in favor of a consciousness that recognizes the power of both the discursive and the material as constructs with which people with disabilities engage. She argues that "one of the main features of a disability rights perspective is that it turns the spotlight of critique on society" (19). Dunn's work thus invites us to critique rhetorics that stigmatize disability in YA literature.

Dunn analyzes Harriet McBryde Johnson's *Accidents of Nature* (2006), which focuses on Jean, a protagonist who has cerebral palsy, and on the caustic friend she meets at a summer camp, Sara, whose primary form of mobility comes from maneuvering a wheelchair. At first, Jean is uncertain how to respond to Sara's anger and cutting wit, but she begins to understand that at the heart of Sara's rebelliousness is an anger that "norms," as Sara calls them, perceive themselves as better than the campers (whom Sara defiantly refers to as "crips"). As Dunn sees it, the novel critiques ableist attitudes, including the following: "that 'just trying harder' will 'fix' anything, that people with disabilities are sexless beings, and that walking is the ultimate goal" (Dunn 20). Jean begins to question independence as a value, recognizing instead that being in a wheelchair may be the most efficient mode for her own mobility. Dunn believes that Jean has learned to value "interdependence" more than independence—and that is why I believe that the heart of Dunn's argument resides in an ethics of care, an ethics that insists that both the temporarily able-bodied (as Dunn refers to herself) and people with disabilities work together "to imagine—and help build—a different world view"—one that is more inclusive, accommodating, and ethical (Dunn 12).

Garland-Thompson argues that the "ability/disability system" has four facets: "first, it is a system for interpreting and disciplining bodily variations; second, it is a relationship between bodies and their environments; third, it is a set of practices that produce both the able-bodied and the disabled; fourth, it is a way of describing the inherent instability of the embodied self" (17)—and she cites Haraway, among others, to note that "current feminist work theorizes figures of hybridity and excess such as monsters, grotesques, and cyborgs to suggest their transgressive potential for a feminist politics" (Garland-Thompson 21).

Marissa Meyer's *Cinder* is a cyborg novel that interrogates disability in almost exactly these four terms.[3] Cinder lives in New Beijing, a city in a dystopic future, where "humans" are a distinct class with higher social status than hybrid-human "cyborgs," who, in turn, have higher status than completely mechanized androids. The "ability/disability" system set in place in this novel allows the human residents of New Beijing to "interpret" themselves against cyborgs—and when necessary—to discipline them. The system helps all three types of sentient beings establish themselves within an environment; humans and cyborgs and androids know who they are by defining themselves in opposition to others. Most important, Meyer uses the unstable body of the cyborg Cinder to demonstrate Garland-Thompson's concept of the "inherent instability of the embodied self" and to critique the social practice of defining ability in opposition to disability.

Cinder's multiplicity as a cyborg first became necessary because she was disfigured and partially dismembered in a horrific fire when she was a very young child. Although Gooderham argues that fantasy is a "metaphorical mode" by which we can explore complex social issues via fantastic worlds (173), Cinder is no metaphor for a teenager with a disability. She is a human being who has been physically disabled by this fire: she has a robotic hand and an artificial leg to replace those she lost in the fire; the foot on that leg does not always function properly. Cinder later discovers that her brain has been rewired, and she has four metal ribs and metal vertebrae. Medically, she is "36.28 not human" (82). All of her cyborg parts were designed to replace body parts lost in the fire—although the text makes clear that her reproductive organs are intact and fully functioning (116). (In other words, she is a disabled teenager who will be able to be both sexually active and to procreate.) Meyer here is connecting disability and ability; Cinder's cyborg abilities, including the wiring in her brain, are part of what give her almost super-human powers as a mechanic and as a technician: "Most of her customers couldn't fathom how a teenage girl could be the best mechanic in the city, and she never broadcast the reason for her talent. The fewer people who knew she was cyborg, the better" (10). Cinder hides her cyborg status because she regards it as a stigmatizing disability. When she looks in a mirror, she thinks, about herself: "Her mechanical parts were the only disturbing thing in Cinder's reflection" (190). Readers are meant to empathize with Cinder, and they quickly understand the book's message: that any society that would discriminate against cyborgs is in the wrong. Meyer uses the trope of the cyborg to communicate about the wrongness of discriminating against difference and/or disability. As Flanagan observes, although Cinder is "disabled," the novel is "indicative of the posthuman body's propensity for renewal and rejuvenation" (*Technology* 64).

Cinder's multiplicity becomes even more complicated when she learns that she actually belongs to another human race that has populated the moon for centuries: the Lunars. The news astounds her, and she uses technological rhetorics—especially rhetorics involving mechanics, mathematics, and discourse itself—to explain how her brain processes this information. For example, when the doctor tells her she is Lunar, "the word washed over Cinder as if he were speaking a different *language*. The *machine* in her brain kept ticking, ticking, like it was working through an impossible *equation*" (175, italics added). Lunars have special abilities that allow them to manipulate other people's "bioelectricity"; that is, Lunars have the ability to brainwash and manipulate people through mind control. The Lunars view as inferior any Lunar who is born cognitively incapable of submitting to bioelectricity; they call such Lunars "shells"—and shells are either killed at birth or segregated from others, isolated in orphanages where they serve as fodder for the government's biopolitical experimentations. In other words, shells are the Lunar equivalent of cyborgs: they are the disabled bodies against which "normal" people define themselves. When Cinder first learns she is a Lunar, she believes that she is a shell, but it turns out that her bioelectrical powers were disabled by the doctors who performed the surgeries that transformed her into a cyborg because they wanted her to live on Earth undetected as a Lunar. Cinder is thus not only a cyborg and a Lunar, but she is also an illegal alien—one with a great potential for mind control. She is horrified by the knowledge of how multiply-othered she is: "To be cyborg *and* Lunar? One was enough to make her a mutant, an outcast, but to be *both*? She shuddered" (178, italics in the original). Her self-perception shifts radically as she realizes that "everything she knew about herself, her childhood, her parents, was wrong. A made-up history. A made-up girl" (179). Cinder's body is, indeed, a hybrid "made-up" of both human tissue and technology.[4]

Cinder and her adopted family fear a Lunar plague that has begun to infect the Earth. Although she is actually a foster child in this family, the relationships are clearly those inspired by Cinderella motifs of stepmother and stepdaughter. The plague Cinder and her foster family face evokes all the dystopic fears common to an ecofeminist novel: this plague has the potential to annihilate much of the world's population, and it is being used as a biopolitical weapon by the Lunars against the Earthens. Cinder was adopted at the age of eleven by a man who died soon after from this plague, and early in the novel, one of her two foster sisters, Peony, dies of it, too. One of Meyer's most significant rewritings of the Cinderella tale-type is to depict Cinder in a loving and caring relationship with this sister, Peony. In her anger at Peony's death, Cinder's foster mother sells her cyborg foster daughter to the government for plague research—and the researchers discover that Cinder is immune to the plague. The chief researcher, Dr. Erland, immediately begins to suspect that she is immune not only because she is Lunar, but also because she might also be the moon's lost Princess Selene, who is believed to have been burned to death years earlier by her evil aunt, who now rules the moon as Queen Levana.

Cinder's relationship with Levana and with her foster mother provide the clichéd woman vs. woman competition of the ancient Cinderella tale. Meyer, however, focuses more on the ethics of care in this novel than she does on female competition. She depicts female vs. female competition as problematic. Cinder, for example, cares deeply for her stepsister Peony and tries to bring her a cure for the plague. When Peony dies in her arms, Cinder gives the antidote to a young boy she knows, caring for him despite the way his mother has discriminated against Cinder for being a cyborg. Cinder also serves as the "one-caring" for her feminized android, Iko, after the wicked stepmother dismantles her. Cinder finds a way to salvage the computer chip on which Iko's personality is stored and eventually restores her to life, albeit in an altered embodiment. Most of all, Cinder takes on the role of one-caring for the emperor's son, Prince Kai, on whom she has a crush, just like most of the girls (and Iko!) in New Beijing—and also because this is, after all, a dystopic YA novel, apparently it *must* include a heteronormative love story. Kai brings his personal android, Nainsi, to Cinder; Cinder is able to both repair the feminized android and make sure Kai knows that Queen Levana will kill him if he carries through on the marriage Levana has proposed with Kai as a diplomatic alliance. Cinder is one-caring for many.

Kai only considers accepting Levana's marriage proposal because of his emerging sense as the newly-crowned emperor: he must be the one-caring for the entire population of his empire. His father has only recently died of the plague, and Kai will do anything that it takes to rescue his people, including marrying Levana so that she will give him the Lunar antidote to this biopolitical crisis. Cinder tells Kai that she perceives him as a caring leader: "You're going to be one of those emperors that everyone loves and admires. . . . I mean it. Look how much you *care*, how hard you're trying," and she points out to him the relationality of his role: "It's not like you're alone. You have advisors and province reps and secretaries and treasurers"

(228, italics added). Kai reciprocates Cinder's feelings, and it is very clear that he wishes to build a relationship with her. He asks her to the festival ball several times and tells her he does not want to marry Levana because he "might have actual feelings for someone"—Cinder herself (295). He gifts her with a pair of elegant gloves, in case she chooses to join him at the ball, despite her rejections of his many offers to join him there.

Cinder's ability to perceive herself as one-caring for Kai is wrapped up in both issues of intra-activity and her perception of herself as racialized as a Lunar and disabled as a cyborg. At times she perceives her cyborg body parts as loathsome, but at others, she can recognize that their meaning has shifted for her because they have empowered her so greatly. Cinder's *becoming* shifts throughout the novel through the process of her own identity leading her to desire to merge with a new identity. For example, Cinder has first learned she is "36.28% cyborg" when she sees a holograph of her own body; her observation of that image shifts her perception of herself, demonstrating that the intra-action of matter and meaning are processual, ongoing, and affect agency. She thinks to herself, ". . . her chest. Her heart. Her brain. Her nervous system. What *hadn't* been tampered with?" (117). She thinks these thoughts only moments before Prince Kai sees the same holographic image—and then Cinder thinks about what she believes he is perceiving as he "recoil[s] from the image" (126). He is seeing "a girl. A machine. A freak" (126). Her sense of who she is shifts even more greatly when she realizes that she is Lunar, knowledge that she also believes she must protect Kai from. "He thought she was a mere mechanic, and he was, perhaps, willing to cross *that* social divide. But to be both cyborg and Lunar? To be hated and despised by every culture in the galaxy? He would understand in a moment why he needed to forget her" (292). Cinder believes that she must protect Kai from the knowledge that she is multiply-othered, thinking at one point, for example, "She hadn't considered that being noticed by the queen could put Kai in jeopardy too" (223).

After Cinder learns Levana will kill Prince Kai once they have married, Cinder delivers that news to Kai during the ball at great personal risk to herself. As Cinder reclaims her bioelectric powers of mind control at the ball, she thinks of it as her "awakening gift" (354) and is grateful that she can neither blush nor cry, so she thinks her "hateful cyborg body was good for one thing," at least, when she confronts Queen Levana (355). Cinder tells Levana she is not a shell, and against all odds, Cinder is able to overpower Queen Levana's highly potent bioelectricity. "Fire exploded in her spine, racing along her nerves and wires, slithering down the metal braces in her

241

limbs. . . . It felt as if her body were trying to dispel all her cyborg parts—explosions and sparks and smoke tearing at her flesh" (363). But instead of expelling her mechanical enhancements, her body grows so overheated that she melts the gloves Kai has given her to wear to the ball. "She felt different. Strong. Powerful. On fire" (364). Her desire to defeat Levana has shifted her *becoming*. Moreover, she is defined in this moment of *becoming* by her embodiment—including her embodied cognition.

When Cinder then flees from Queen Levana's mind control and runs down the steps of the palace, her entire cyber-foot (rather than just her slipper) falls off. She is revealed to the prince for what she is: a Lunar, a cyborg, a human hybrid, and she stands in the mud on only one foot, disabled. She assumes he can never love her now that he knows these things about her, and she believes it would be even worse for him if he knew she were both "cyborg and Lunar" (292). Because of his own limitations, Kai cannot yet accept all of Cinder's differences. Valuing his role as one-caring for a nation more than his role of one-caring for *her*, Kai allows Queen Levana to capture Cinder and keep her as a prisoner. As Flanagan observes, this narrative "rewrite[s] the humanist [ending] of its [pretext]" in that the novel closes "with a form of narrative closure that defies the liberal humanist traditions" that demand stories about young women end in heteronormative marriage (*Technology* 65). The sequels, however, reveal that Kai is able to overcome his prejudices and become one-caring to both Cinder and his nation, just as Cinder will continue as one-caring for him and become one-caring for her nation: the moon. She never does stop caring for Kai, however, despite how her shifting perceptions of her body's *mattering* affect her *becoming* throughout the series. Ultimately, Cinder's life is changed by the intra-activity of matter and meaning, especially in the ways that she comes to value being a cyborg and Lunar, but despite all of the changes she undergoes, she never abandons her feminist ethics of care. By the end of the series, Cinder forsakes competitive models of female vs. female competition and advocates a cooperative ethics of care, based in relationality and respect for difference. Her perspective is the ethical stance that advocates for disability rights, especially given that by the end of the series she has helped those who stand in for the disabled in this novel—the cyborgs and the mutants—to gain equal rights on both Earth and Luna. Androids are, unfortunately exempted from this attention to equal rights, presumably because they are entirely mechanized.

Any number of feminist theorists in children's and adolescent literature have engaged with feminist issues of narrative structure. Not least among them are Lissa Paul in "Enigma Variations"; Holly Blackford in *The Myth of Persephone in Girls' Fantasy Literature*; Kerry Mallan in *Secrets, Lies, and Children's Fiction*; and Sara K. Day in *Reading Like a Girl*, all of whose theoretical models intersect in some way with the ethics of care. What unites the work of these critics with Mary Moran's and Patricia Dunn's work on adolescent literature then is these narrative theorists' underlying use of the rhetoric of care; that is, these feminists who explore children's and adolescent literature all make arguments that in some way foreground caring and relationality.

For example, as early as 1987, with her essay "Enigma Variations: What Feminist Theory Knows about Children's Literature," Lissa Paul published an influential essay about caring and the interrelationships between feminism and children's literature. In that essay, Paul explores three specific forms of entrapment children, especially girls, experience: physical, linguistic, and economic entrapment. She then writes about the literary strategies by which child characters (especially girls) escape entrapment: through a combination of deceit and trickeries and through imaginative energies that help them envision a way to transcend their situation. Significantly, Paul praises Margaret Mahy's *The Changeover* (1984) for the way the novel enacts a specifically feminist quest: the novel is about one girl's effort to rescue a family member from entrapment. Relying on Annis Pratt and archetypal theory, Paul identifies an important narrative pattern in children's literature. She says of the protagonist of *The Changeover*, her "quest is personal and domestic, she fights for someone she loves. She uses the tricksterish tactics of the weak and powerless. . . . The values in Mahy's book are connected with individual humanity rather than public glory" (198). Although Paul does not connect her own work to feminist ethics of care, the link is clearly there in Paul's privileging the importance of personal interrelationships and cooperative models of sharing power. Thus, as early as 1987, Paul began encouraging the entire field of children's and adolescent literature to value as feminist those fictions that demonstrate relational selves interconnecting in the roles of one-caring and cared-for.

Holly Blackford's *The Myth of Persephone in Girls' Fantasy Literature* also traces a significant narrative structure that has played a pivotal role in fantasy novels with female protagonists since at least the Victorian age.

Blackford observes that many Victorians were influenced by the myth of Persephone and Demeter; these Victorians shifted traditional attention from the role of the grieving mother to the role of the daughter separating from her mother (1). Although the ethics of care are not the specific object of Blackford's concern, the myth is nevertheless imbued with issues about the dynamics between Demeter, as the one-caring, and Persephone as the cared-for. Persephone's separation from her mother allows her to individuate and to become in turn the one-caring for Hades during the seasons of the year she spends in the Underworld. The myth, moreover, illustrates the distinction Noddings makes between "natural care"—or care that comes from the primacy of the parent-child relationship—and "ethical care," the care we learn to give others outside of that relationship—and sometimes, even when we do not necessarily wish to be the one-caring. Noddings identifies Demeter as the prototypical "one-caring" who demonstrates what natural caring is (40–41), while Persephone demonstrates the cared-for becoming the one-caring as an act of ethical caring in the way she takes care of Hades six months of a year, despite having been kidnapped and not originally wishing to be married to him.

In Blackford's analysis of the narrative structures influenced by this mythology, the pattern is a "perpetuation of a very old fertility ritual. Girls go to the underworlds so they can partially return and fuel the perpetuation of more Demeters" (4). The girl is initially tempted by some sort of toy—in Persephone's case, a narcissus—and in children's literature, the variants often include a "pair of Hades figures, one a mysterious adult and one a brooding though irresistible boy" (5). Blackford cites Barrie's *Peter Pan* (1911), Burnett's *Secret Garden* (1911), and Rowling's *Harry Potter and the Chamber of Secrets* (1998) as fantasy stories that follow this pattern. Sometimes, the girl must also face a "Black Demeter": a mother figure who is infuriated by her daughter's absence, as Mrs. Darling and Mrs. Weasley are (4). "These texts dwell on the psychological conditions of Persephone figures who invariably reach for 'the lovely toy' or narcissus because they are developmentally ready to do so, unfortunately without the slightest understanding of consequences. Chasms open to reveal dark lords who threaten to subsume the girls: the ancient paradox of Persephone's plight" (4). It should be noted that it is only through a compromise by which Persephone can balance her duties as one-caring and one cared-for that order and balance are restored to the seasons.

Lissa Paul praises the protagonist of *The Changeover* for becoming, in effect, both the one-caring to her little brother and Demeter to that boy's Persephone. Her little brother has been abducted by a Hades-like incubus who is sucking his soul; the protagonist must save her brother from this underworld. The narrative crisis in Jennifer Donnelly's intricately-plotted *Revolution* is also triggered by a little brother: Andi is consumed with grief because her younger brother, Truman, died when a crazed man grabbed him on the streets of New York and stepped in front of a speeding delivery van; Truman and the man are both killed. Two years later, Andi is slipping deeper and deeper into a grief-induced depression, and so is her mother. Both of them are mentally ill, and neither one is fully capable of filling the role of one-caring for the other, although Andi does manage to keep her mother fed. (This novel lends itself easily to a story about disability rights for those with mental illness. Andi and her mother are making their world work, despite their differences from societal norms.)

The novel unfolds on three different levels. The first level of narration is set in modern-day New York. Andi's memories of Truman make him the brooding boy who sets Andi on her quest to regain faith in the meaning of life; Andi's father is the Byronic dark figure who whisks her to another world where she does not want to be when he insists that his daughter will accompany him to Paris during Christmas break because he does not like how poorly she is doing in school He simultaneously has Andi's mother committed to a psychiatric hospital during their absence, so Andi is relieved of her duties as one-caring, albeit against her will (and her mother's). Hades has thus stolen Persephone and banished Demeter from his world.

Andi wears around her neck a small key that her brother gave their father long ago. Andi's father is a geneticist who told his family when the children were younger that he was looking for "the key to the universe. To life" (28). While he is still quite young, Truman finds an ornate and elegant antique key to give his father, earnestly believing that since his father now has the key, their father will spend more time with them and less time at the lab. After Andi's father wins the Nobel Prize and is even more absent from home, Truman steals the key back from him—and so after his death, Andi wears it on a ribbon around her neck as a way of remembering her sweet brother.

During the Christmas break two years after Truman's death, Andi is resentful about being dragged to Paris to work on her senior project. The project involves her studying a specific chord progression created by an eighteenth-century French musician, Malherbeau, whom Andi believes has influenced contemporary musicians from Leonard Bernstein to John Lee Hooker and from Miles Davis to Radiohead. Andi and her father are staying at the home of a historian who has summoned her father to Paris to examine the genetics of a heart believed to be that of the late Dauphin, who would have grown to become Louis XVII had he survived the French Revolution. Among the historian's collection of French Revolutionary artifacts is an elegant antique guitar, which Andi—a disciplined and trained guitarist—plays beautifully. But her brother's key serves as the "toy" that helps her open the story into the second plot level—one which also involves the dynamics of ethical caring.

Truman's key helps Andi open a false bottom in the antique guitar case, where she finds the diary of Alexandrine (or Alexe), a teenaged performer who eventually serves as a paid companion to the Dauphin, Louis-Charles. Andi reads Alexe's diary and learns that this girl, too, has great love for what becomes a little-brother figure to her, the young Dauphin. He is the brooding boy who draws Alexe into the role of Persephone in a secretive underworld of caring for the young prince once his parents are imprisoned. His uncle, the Duc d'Orléans, serves as the Byronic hero who pulls Alexe deeper into the conspiracy: he pays Alexe to be a spy because he wishes himself to become king. Orléans's heart is black, just like his eyes, which are compared to "midnight" multiple times (175, 180, 218, 317, 343). He beats Alexe almost senseless at one point for not following his orders, but she nevertheless continues to care for Louis-Charles as best she can. The mother for whom Alexe grieves, however, is not her own mother, but Marie-Antoinette, who plays the role of Demeter in this second level of the narrative. After Louis-Charles has been separated from his mother and imprisoned, Alexe tries to say good-bye to the queen: "But she did not hear me. She heard only him, her child, crying for days on end from his new room, on the floor beneath hers. She would not speak. She would not eat. She would only stare at the wall and rock" (327). Marie-Antoinette gives Alexe one of the King's ornate guitars—the same one Andi eventually plays—and begs Alexe to play for her son: "Play for him. Keep his poor heart merry. Then she sank to the floor, wrapped her arms around her knees, and keened" (327). Marie-Antoinette's ethics of care define who she is within this novel: her self-care suffers because she cannot serve as one-caring for her son, Louis-Charles.

Alexe knows that Louis-Charles loves not only music, but he also loves fireworks. She conspires to buy fireworks that will go off outside of his window in the fortress where he is held so that he will know someone loves him and is thinking of him. She is aware that her activities are illegal. The final entry in her journal describes how a guard has attacked her, fatally wounding her. Alexe runs down to the catacombs, where she writes her last journal entry and hides the diary in the guitar case's secret panel. The historian who is friends with Andi's father had bought the guitar years earlier, amazed that the guitar and its case had been preserved so well in a chamber of the catacombs that had been sealed by "layers of bones" (67). Because this twenty-first century historian knows how depressed Andi is, he is delighted that the guitar inspires her to play her music. But the eighteenth-century diary Andi finds inside the secret base of the guitar proves to be even more important to her healing because of the story she learns about another teenager who has cared for someone who is like a brother to her.

The novel moves into its third and most intricate narrative level in ways that are also motivated by issues of caring. Andi has made friends with a group of musicians, including one named Virgil, on whom she has a crush. He leads her into the catacombs where he wants her to play with his band—which includes a friend named Charon, so the intertextual references to Dante's *Divine Comedy* are clear. (The book is also divided into three parts: Hell, Purgatorio, and Paradise, with everything prior to Andi's time travel corresponding to Hell; her time travel to eighteenth-century France signifying Purgatory, and her return back home being Paradise.) At the catacombs party where Andi descends into the underworld of eighteenth-century Paris, she tells readers that she has taken way too many of her antidepressants, and so she should not have drunk the wine she drinks at the party—which proves to be not unlike ingesting forbidden pomegranate seeds. She knows that her antidepressants do not mix well with alcohol, and the combination leads her to be so befuddled that she concusses herself while running away from a police raid.

Andi returns to consciousness in Paris in 1795. The brooding and Byronic musician Malherbeau himself serves as the person who saves her. After several days in which Andi can't decide if she's having bad dreams or a "vision quest" or is in a coma, Andi comes to believe that she really is in eighteenth-century Paris and that it is Alexe's spirit who has drawn her back into the past so that Andi can finish the work that Alexe has left undone with her death. Andi takes over the role of one-caring for Louis-Charles: she plays guitar under his window and sets off fireworks to cheer him. Andi knows that he will die in six days, so she realizes that Alexe is asking her to be the one-caring for the Dauphin only temporarily. Nonetheless, Andi has herself entered another dark underworld. In the catacombs, she sees and smells stacks of headless, rotting corpses. She is attacked by lewd revelers when she plays her guitar to make money for herself and Malherbeau to eat. And she witnesses first-hand the brutality and corruption of the guillotine and Robespierre's era of the Revolution. The imagery surrounding Andi's sojourn to the past depicts Paris as dark, dank, rank, and sinister.

The Duc d'Orléans has told Alexe, "The world goes on, as stupid and brutal tomorrow as it was today" (344), but inspired by Alexe's guidance, Andi realizes that, although the world may go on being stupid and brutal, she does not need to be stupid and brutal herself.

> It goes on, this world, stupid and brutal.
> But I do not.
> *I* do not. (471, italics in the original)

Andi has despaired, and she has grieved—as Alexe has—that the Dauphin—a boy as young as Truman—"lies dying. Alone. In the dark. Insane. In pain. Afraid" (446). Andi wants "to scream. To howl. . . . to wake up the priest in the rectory. The people in their houses. The whole street. The city. I want to tell them about Louis-Charles and Truman. I want to tell them about the Revolution" (447). And then she utters the statement that is the core of this novel's ethics of care: "I want to make them see that nothing is worth the life of a child" (447). Andi has come to value her own life and is no longer suicidal, but she can also perceive that children are the group most vulnerable to the tumult that revolutions create. Malherbeau has told her that "the orphanages of Paris are full now. . . . [The orphans'] parents were guillotined, perhaps, or their fathers killed in the wars. Danton and Desmoulins, fathers both, tried to stop the worst of Robespierre's excesses. . . . But Robespierre, Saint-Just, Couthon—none of them had children, only ideas, and there is little mercy in ideas" (385). Malherbeau creates a false equivalence in equating ethics only with parenthood; people without children can be ethical (just as people with children are not always ethical). Donnelly's concern, however, seems to be more with child safety than with parenting, especially in her insistence that children are even more vulnerable to the ravages of war and corruption than adults.

Similarly, the crazed man Max who has pulled Truman to his death under a twenty-first century delivery truck in Brooklyn has done so in the name of "the Revolution"; Max, who suffers from schizophrenia, wants "to kill the rich and give the city back to the people" (368). But in Paris, Virgil teaches Andi that, although "life's all about the revolution," the real revolution is "the one inside" (471). Andi learns from many people in her descent into the underworld: Alexe and Malherbeau are particularly instrumental in teaching her how to be emotionally generous again. But her greatest source of comfort comes from Virgil, who himself is willing to serve as one-caring for Andi.

Not insignificantly, by the end of the novel, Andi is reunited with her mother, who checks herself out of the psychiatric ward and begins to heal emotionally from her "collapse" (370). Andi's worry for a long time has been that her mother's heart is not holding together. She reminds her father of Truman's favorite fairy-tale, "The Frog Prince," in which the prince is turned into a frog, and so his beloved servant's heart breaks and can only be held together by "three iron bands" (91). Andi's father bluntly tells Andi that it is not the daughter's place to try to heal her mother: "You think you can fix it. Fix her" (91), but Andi makes it clear that she wishes she "could make it heal" (157). And, indeed, Andi has written a song for her mother called "Iron Band":

> If I had coal and fire
> And metal fine and true
> I'd make an iron band
> An iron band for you
> I'd pick up all the pieces
> From where they fell that day
> Fit them back together
> And take the pain away (157)

At the end of the novel, Andi is still estranged from her Byronic father, but she is reunited with her grieving mother, who tells her daughter that "I was her iron band all along, didn't I know that?" (467). Demeter and Persephone are reunited, and in their reunion, they can serve as one-caring for each other and finally begin to heal from the grief of Truman's death: "Truman is part of the picture now, not the whole picture anymore. There's room for other things in my mother's life again. There's room for me. Which is nice. Because I need her now. I'm really busy" (467). Thus, on three narrative levels, *Revolution* demonstrates how Blackford's theory about the Demeter-Persephone cycle is still at work in twenty-first century feminist fantasy YA novels—and how intertwined that cycle is with feminist ethics of care.

Kerry Mallan demonstrates another strand of the relationship between caring and narrative structure in her book *Secrets, Lies and Children's Fiction*. Mallan identifies as the "key concepts" in her work "secrets, lies and deception" and she notes that these concepts are "linked by a notion of survival" (*Secrets* 11). In other words, like Lissa Paul, Mallan observes the fundamental relationship between deceit and survival; like Paul, Mallan also writes about interrelationships—because lies and secrets are fundamentally communal activities that involve how people interact with others in ways that are both self-protective and protective of others. Mallan identifies as a central metaphor in her work the veil as a "material object as well as a trope that evokes multiple interpretations. It hides a mystery and signifies a host of oppositional binaries: difference or recognition, exotic or traditional, freedom or oppression . . . the veil, as both a noun and a verb, can reveal or conceal truth" (*Secrets* 15–16). Mallan notes how diverse the purposes are of the veil for "striptease performers, dancers of the seven veils, *femme fatales*, nuns, Muslim women and girls"—and of course, the veil here is entirely gendered as a feminine material object (*Secrets* 15).

In a related essay, Mallan expressly links survival to gender issues, explaining that she is "interested in how literature for young people depicts survival as a complex activity that negotiates silence, subjugation and subjectivity"; she is also "interested in how secrets and femininity are theoretically linked with truth and concealment"; as she adds, she is seeking to identify the connections among "truth, femininity, fiction, and concealment" ("On Secrets" 36, 38). She argues that "texts that thematize secrecy work to withhold and disclose their secrets as part of the process of narrating and sequencing" ("On Secrets" 38). She perceives secrets as "fall[ing] between truth and lies, copying a kind of limbo"; in this economy, secrets do not serve as the active agents that lies are (*Secrets* 213). Marjane Satrapi's *Persepolis* memoirs serve as two of her most vivid examples: in order to survive, the narrator must learn how to lie effectively to other Muslims, to her parents, and even at times to herself. Her family keeps secrets from the neighbors; she keeps secrets from her family; and the government keeps secrets from its citizens. The literary goal of depicting all of this lying and all of these secrets, ironically enough, is to move the reader towards a greater understanding of truth and what it means to Marjane to survive and be true to herself.

Mallan observes that "truth is often regarded as something that can be discovered, revealed or hidden. This suggestion implies that truth has a tangible quality, a core essence, which is both problematic and impossible . . . truth is not monolithic, and . . . the connection between unveiling and the truth is a tenuous one" (*Secrets* 41). Mallan's project thus intersects with material feminism in at least two ways: in her observation that too often truth is falsely depicted in children's literature as having a "tangible quality" and also in her observation that the metaphors that surround truth-telling and deceit, such as veiling or cloaking, are indeed very material. Mallan's narrative theory invites us to "complicate" what she reveals to be the "simplistic idea of concealment as deception, and unveiling as truth, by taking into account how subjects transform themselves in their quest to find the truth" (*Secrets* 16).

The ethics of care is also at work here because deceiving and self-deceiving characters are relational beings whose deceptions involve interacting with others, often in relationships of care, and because self-knowledge (as opposed to self-deception) is linked to Noddings's principle that ethical caring requires the one-caring to also be self-caring. "Self-deception has the potential to destroy the ethical ideal. The one-caring, then, must look clearly and receptively on what is there-in-herself. This does not mean that she must spend a great deal of time self-indulgently 'getting to know' herself before reaching out to others. Rather, she reflects on what is inside as she relates to others" (Noddings 108). Few scholars of children's literature would portray any young person's efforts to know themselves as "self-indulgent," but when connected with Mallan's work on self-deception, this principle from feminist ethics of care has validity for children's literature. Mallan identifies a "paradox of self-deception" that occurs when we lie to ourselves because "the lies we tell ourselves may bring short-term feelings of psychological well-being, and enable us to adapt to a situation, but do not change anything in the long run" (*Secrets* 159).

Mallan also notes that survival often includes the liar protecting someone else, especially when the one-caring must lie to ensure the survival of the cared-for: "In these instances, the truth could harm; it could be dangerous or lethal to speak. In circumstances of oppression, unspeakable trauma or a dying loved one, truth is swept under the cover of deception" (*Secrets* 213). I thus combine the idea of the relational self as the one-caring with Mallan's narratological inquiry into secrets, lies, and truth to examine the way that they function as narrative structures. Kate DiCamillo's *Flora & Ulysses* provides a clear example of a girl protagonist who lies but who also finds strength in allowing herself to be both the one-caring and the cared-for—and to become in her process of growing more relational.

In *Flora & Ulysses*, Flora's next-door neighbor, Mrs. Tickham, accidently vacuums a squirrel up with her new "Ulysses" brand vacuum-cleaner; the traumatic brain injury the squirrel experiences gives him the powers of a super-hero, including super-strength, being able to fly, and being able to type poetry. Flora names him Ulysses, after the source of his super-powers, and decides to keep him. (The book is a playful parody of comic books; therefore, many of its conceits involve super-hero tropes, including the trope of a super-hero having a secret identity.) Flora lies to her mother about Ulysses, just as she lies to her mother about not reading comic books.

Flora also requires Mrs. Tickham to lie to Flora's mother about the squirrel's super-powers. Flora's mother is a novelist who does not think a squirrel has a place in their home, a situation that necessitates the narrative element of lying: Ulysses's only real chance at survival requires Flora to lie because otherwise, her mother will have Ulysses killed. Flora justifies herself by thinking about "doing impossible things, *surviving* when the odds were against her and her squirrel" (84, italics added). Flora's mother eventually forces Ulysses to type a lie to Flora, and Ulysses thinks, "It was as if typing the lies, the wrong words, had depleted him of all ability to act" (183). When Flora reads the lie that Ulysses has "chosen" to run away, she thinks, "it was the biggest lie that Flora had ever read in her life" (186). In this moment, she knows that her mother is attempting to kill Ulysses—and, of course, Flora's mother has lied to her daughter about not having murderous motives. When she confronts her mother about this lie, Flora says, "It's the truth" (149). Her mother does not disagree.

Another important form of deception in this novel, however, is self-deception. Flora deceives herself into believing that she is a cynic. Flora loves to read comic books and frequently thinks about the lessons she learns from them about controlling the "criminal element" because these stories reinforce her sense of herself as cynical (53). These stories also teach her that "the human heart is a deep, dark river with hidden currents" (91). Nevertheless, she is deceiving herself because it's clear that she *wants* super-heroes to exist: "Not that Flora really believed in superheroes. But still" (9). Flora's reasons for feeling cynical emerge from her relationship with her mother. Because Flora's mother is self-absorbed and seems to perform the role of mother in a perfunctory way that emerges more from a sense of obligation and more as a misguided perception of ethical-caring than natural-caring, Flora convinces herself that she, Flora, is a cynic who expects little from the universe and nothing from her mother. "Flora's mother had often accused Flora of being a 'natural-born cynic.' Flora suspected that this was true. . . . *Yep*, thought Flora, *that's me*." (6, italics in the original); "'Do not hope; instead, observe' were words that Flora, as a cynic, had found useful in the extreme" (33). Flora does not allow herself to hope, to believe, or to have faith in much of anything because she is not able to participate as the object of her mother's caring, as the cared-for in their relationship. And Flora deceives herself into believing she is not affected by her mother's apathy.

Flora's cynicism and lack of faith in her mother is reinforced by a material object—an ugly shepherdess lamp that her mother has named "Mary Ann" (80). Flora is convinced that Mary Ann is the daughter her mother has always wanted. The lamp has been ordered from a store in London, and when it arrives, Flora's mother says, "Oh, she's so beautiful. Isn't she beautiful? I love her with all my heart" (30). Flora thinks to herself, "Flora's mother never called Flora beautiful. She never said that she loved *her* with all her heart. Luckily, Flora was a cynic and didn't care whether her mother loved her or not" (30, italics in the original). Flora, of course, is lying to herself. "Sometimes she felt as if Mary Ann knew something that she didn't know, that the little shepherdess was keeping some dark and terrible secret" (30); Mary Ann has "a look on her face that said, *I know something you don't know*" (141, italics in the original). Flora hates Mary Ann for having the kind of secret that Mallan argues is implicated in the relationship between gender and survival. Mary Ann—a lamp—is thus the material object onto which Flora can project her anger, her sense of injustice, and her own dishonesty.

Two secrets emerge, however, that affect Flora's relationality and allow her to begin to have faith and hope again. First, she learns that her father—who is divorced from her mother—misses Flora terribly and grieves that he no longer lives with his daughter. His neighbor, Dr. Meescham, delivers this news to Flora, telling her that her father is "capacious of heart" (129). Hearing these words brings Flora almost to tears, but she stops herself from crying by remembering "I'm a cynic!" Dr. Meescham tells the girl, "Bah. . . . Cynics are people who are afraid to believe" (129). Flora, however, believes her mother has been harboring another secret when she hears her mother say that it would make "my life much easier" if Flora would just move in with her father (150). Only once her mother truly despairs that Flora has run away does the woman reach out for her daughter, calling her "my baby," demonstrating the type of love that seems to feel to Flora like natural-caring (225). Flora cries tears of joy, and it is clear that the girl has learned to have faith in her mother and hope for herself again. She is now completely willing to believe in "the possibility of impossible things" (171).

If lies, self-deception, and secrets shape the narrative form of this novel, the search for truth resides in the novel's ethical core. For example, when Ulysses is confronted with his first word-processor, he knows he can type, but he does not know what to write. He thinks to himself:

> What could he do? . . .
> There was nothing he could do except to be himself, to try to make the letters on the keyboard speak the *truth* of his heart, to work to make them reveal the essence of the squirrel he was.
> But what was the *truth*? (62, italics added)

Flora has also learned from her comic books that people can learn truths from listening. She has read in a comic book, "All words at all times, true or false, whispered or shouted, are clues to the working of the human heart" (72). Additionally, Dr. Meescham talks about truth, telling Flora that in the village of her youth, "the words on the sign were often not the truth. And I ask you: What good does it do you to read the words of a lie?" (117). When Flora wants a typewriter so that Ulysses can tell them what Flora's mother has done, she says, "We need a typewriter so that we can get to the truth," but her friend, William Spiver, tells her, "The truth . . . is a slippery thing. I doubt that you will ever get to *The* Truth. You may get to a version of the truth. But *The* Truth? I doubt it very seriously" (221, italics in the original). One conceit driven by the novel's embedded narrative level—a pastiche of comic-books—is the false binary that implies all criminals are dishonest and non-criminals are honest. Flora must learn exactly what William Spiver asks her to recognize: that truth is complex—and it may even include the fact that dishonesty is sometimes the best strategy for survival in certain situations.

Symbolically, as the novel ends, Flora finds herself "wedged" so that she no longer slides off Dr. Meescham's horsehair sofa; she is wedged between her mother and Mrs. Tickham's great-nephew, William Spiver, who has become a good friend (226). William Spiver is another self-deceiving character; he believes he is blind, even though he is not. He insists that he is telling the truth: "I am telling the truth, my truth. I cannot see" (205). When Flora asks him to take his dark glasses off, he maintains that they've been glued to his head: Flora responds: "You lie," and he admits: "Yes. No. I don't. I do. I'm engaging in hyperbole" (81). His blindness is a metaphor for another type of cloaking or veiling; he cannot allow himself to see the truth that he is the person who has damaged his own relationship with his mother (by pushing his stepfather's truck into a pond). William Spiver is highly articulate and occasionally annoying; nevertheless, Flora grows to care about his opinion and to trust him. At one point, she is surprised to learn that she misses him (174) and even more surprised to realize that she trusts him (187). By the end of the novel, she is holding his hand, telling him not to "squeeze" her hand so tightly, but still herself holding on tightly to him (230).

William Spiver and Flora have a reciprocal relationship in that they take turns being the one-caring and the one cared-for. The same is true of Flora in her relationship with Ulysses. Initially, Flora is the one-caring for Ulysses as she nurses him back to health, but she thinks in relational terms:

"Together, she and Ulysses could change the world. Or something" (39). By the end of the novel, Ulysses is caring for her and loving her beyond measure.

Metaphors about relationality and the human heart occur when Flora takes time to place her hand on her father's chest so she can feel his capacious heart and when she and William Spiver later fall down together and she feels his beating heart. The fall breaks his glasses, so they no longer cloak him in the darkness that allows him to convince himself he is blind, so he, too, is freed from self-deception and now more free to love. Readers also learn that Flora's mother has been motivated to protect Flora from the "strangeness" of Ulysses because she does not want her daughter to "end up unloved and all alone in the world," as she fears herself to be (196). In the novel's most poignant image, Dr. Meescham explains that her late husband painted a giant squid devouring a lone boat on the ocean to symbolize the loneliness of the human heart: "The giant squid is the loneliest of all God's creatures. He can sometimes go for the whole of his life without seeing another of his kind," Dr. Meescham tells Flora—who proclaims the squid a "villain" (124). And Dr. Meescham answers her: "Yes, well, loneliness makes us do terrible things" (124)—such as perhaps valuing a lamp more than one's daughter or saying hurtful words to her or trying to kill her dearest friend, just because he's a squirrel. The wise woman Dr. Meescham articulates many of the novel's themes about love and relationality, including one about the reason to open a door hopefully: "Always . . . you opened the door because you could not stop hoping that on the other side of it would be the face of someone you loved" (219–20). In this novel, no relationship is perfect, especially not the fraught mother-daughter relationship, but relationality, nonetheless, is valued as the highest ethic. Paradoxically enough, as Mallan's work demonstrates happens often in children's literature, secrets and lies help lead the way to that truth. The metaphors about relationality in *Flora & Ulysses*, in particular, demonstrate how saturated children's and adolescent literature can be, as Mary Jeanette Moran has established, with the rhetoric of feminist caring.

NARRATIVE INTIMACY AND ETHICS OF CARE

Sara K. Day defines "narrative intimacy" as a textual construct by which "many contemporary American novels for and about adolescent women actively encourage . . . blurring of boundaries" between reader and narrator "by constructing narrator-reader relationships that reflect, model, and reimagine intimate interpersonal relationships through the disclosure of information and the experience of the story as a space that the narrator invites the reader to share" (*Reading* 3). Day's work involves both narrative theory and reader-response theory. She is especially interested in the relationality between narrator and reader.

Day observes that the core element of narrative intimacy is "the creation of an emotional bond based on trust and disclosure" (*Reading* 4). When a text relies on narrative intimacy, the narrator generally expresses a desire to share intimate details with the reader, and that narrator generally is reluctant to share those feelings with characters in the book, which creates a narrative bond between narrator and reader based on trust, knowledge, vulnerability, and power (Day, *Reading* 4–6). Relying on the work of psychologists Carin Rubenstein and Philip Shaver, Day demonstrates how gendered American concepts of intimacy are because young women "have historically been raised to nurture and care"; female adolescence has historically been a time in which young women were indoctrinated to prepare for adult roles as wives and mothers (Day, *Reading* 9). Narrators and readers, of course, can never really "know" one another, so Day focuses on Seymour Chatman's distinction between the narrator and the real reader and the "logical gap" that Peter Lamarque perceives separating them (Day, *Reading* 18; Lamarque 114–15). Without directly saying so, Day implies that an interest in ethics is at the heart of her argument because in the relationship of narrative intimacy, "the reader may experience intimacy without risk, just as the narrator seeks to do"—which creates a paradox in suggesting "that the only 'safe' space within which to fully explore the possibilities of intimacy is the impossible narrator-reader relationship" (*Reading* 28).

Day analyzes a variety of novels, such as Sarah Dessen's *Keeping the Moon* (1999), Natasha Friend's *Perfect* (2004), and Lizabeth Zindel's *The Secret Rites of Social Butterflies* (2008), to demonstrate how narrators create intimacy; she concludes that these books reflect a *Zeitgeist* that intense adolescent friendships prepare teenaged girls for intimate adult relationships—but that they do so depicting friendship as a "double-edged sword" that can both empower and disempower a female (*Reading* 30). "The implicit relationships between narrator and reader in these novels . . . [model] a sort of 'ideal' interpersonal relationship—the narrator may reveal anything and everything to the reader without fear of being betrayed or facing unexpected consequences. The very boundary between fictional narrator and real reader . . . actively reinforces contradictory messages about intimacy" (*Reading* 63). At the core of Day's argument is an ethics that questions any relationship that *cannot* be reciprocal, given that the real reader cannot meaningfully affect a narrator. As Noddings argues, "Each of us is dependent upon the other in caring and moral relationships"; even when relationships are asymmetrical, ethical care includes at least some measure of mutuality and reciprocity (48). Since the narrator cultivating intimacy cannot engage in mutuality, Day is implying that such novels do not and cannot engage in a feminist ethics of care.

Linda Sue Park's *Project Mulberry* attempts to grapple with the ethics of narrative intimacy, albeit not altogether successfully. The narrator, Julia Song, directly addresses the reader to establish their relationship, saying things like, "I always want to thread a needle on my first try—it's a thing with me" (8–9) and telling the reader that, after a kid on the playground in elementary school yelled "Chinka-chinka-Chinamen" at her, "it made me feel really bad inside—so bad that I hated thinking about it" (29). Julia and her best friend, a white boy named Patrick, want to work together on a project for a club much like 4-H. Patrick thinks they should work on silkworms, but Julia doesn't know how to tell him that would be "too *Korean*"; she wants "a nice, normal, All-American, red-white-and-blue kind of project" (29, 30, italics in the original). As she tries to find ways to throw up obstacles for embarking on this project, she begins to think of herself as a "secret agent working undercover—thinking one thing while acting and saying the opposite" (53). Rather than confiding her doubts in Patrick, she confides in the reader, establishing what Day would identify as narrative intimacy—and as Mallan might note, Julia establishes that intimacy through secrecy and deceit. Eventually, however, Julia works through her doubts, and the friends do work on a silkworm project. Some level of reciprocity occurs between Patrick and Julia when she discovers late in the novel that he has also been keeping a secret from her: he has a "worm phobia" (157). Patrick, however, confides this to Julia, not directly to the reader.

Park complicates the issues of Julia and reciprocity with a series of interstitial dialogues between herself-as-the-author and Julia-as-a-character. The dialogues are written in the form of a play script, with Julia still narrating in the first person, underscoring the artifice at work here: Park may be the author, but readers are interacting with her as a character in her own novel. Moreover, Park is depicting the author and the character as having a reciprocal relationship. Julia frames the first section, telling readers, "I've got another story to tell you, and I'm going to do it here, between the chapters. Every story has another story inside, but you don't usually get to read the inside one.... if you're interested in learning how this book was written ... you've come to the right place.... It's mostly conversations between me and the author, Ms. Park. We had a lot of discussions while she was writing" (12). The conceit is that Julia is both a muse to Ms. Park and has, as a character, taken on her own life.

> **Me:** Do you want my opinion? I am not happy with the way things are going here. I hate the project idea....
>
> **Ms. Park:** Actually, no—I don't want your opinion. In fact, I have to admit, this is weird for me. I've written other books, and only *once* has a character ever talked to me. You talk to me *all the time*, and I'm finding that hard to get used to....
>
> **Me:** Well, I don't care whether you want my opinion or not—you're getting it. *That was a terrible chapter.*
>
> **Ms. Park:** Would it help if I said I'm sorry you're having such a hard time....
>
> **Me:** But it's *my* story. I should have a vote. (34–35, italics in the original)

In a nod towards Julia's ontological status, when Julia tells Ms. Park that she wants "plenty of time in the story to practice my embroidery," Ms. Park answers Julia as if she were a real child: "It's your responsibility. You have to organize your schedule, get your homework and your chores done, and not dilly-dally around. You should have plenty of time to do embroidery if you plan your time efficiently" (44). Park seems to be shifting Julia's ontological status precisely to demonstrate that their interactions have reciprocity, even though they don't.

Julia, however, purportedly believes Ms. Park has too much agency because she accuses her of being bossy, and Ms. Park explains, perhaps coyly, "Neither of us is the boss. The story is the boss.... It's kind of hard to explain. Sometimes the story takes over, and I end up writing things I didn't expect" (45). Park is playing into Romantic constructions of creativity with her insistence that the story "tells itself." Julia asks the fictionalized author, "even though I'm part of your imagination, I'm my own person, too?"—to which Ms. Park responds, "You think I'd deliberately invent a character who was as much trouble as you are?" (97). Park will grant herself the agency of making revisions—"I *like* finding my mistakes and trying to make the story better—changing little things here and there, taking some words out, choosing others" (127), but she maintains the fiction (one that could perhaps be considered deceitful) that Julia is somehow *real* throughout their dialogues.

Only through this false attempt to establish ontological reality can Park demonstrate any sense of reciprocity in their relationship. Ms. Park, too, has a secret, which Julia ostensibly discovers: like Patrick, the author also has a phobia of worms that she has kept hidden from Julia (and the reader).

When Julia doesn't like the way the story is going, she gives Ms. Park the silent treatment for a month. After Julia begins to talk again, she pleads with Ms. Park to end the story right there with an inderminant ending. Ms. Park then shifts the ontological source of reciprocity, telling Julia: "You have to care about the readers. Because without them, you won't exist.... You exist while the story is being written ... but pretty soon the story will get made into a book. And after that, it's the readers who will bring you to life" (191). While it's true that readers "bring Julia to life" when they read, the relationship is still unidirectional. The author can change who Julia is and what she does, but readers cannot. This is what Day refers to as the "impossible narrator-reader relationship" (*Reading* 28).

Day's concept of narrative intimacy can be tied in this novel to a certain type of knowledge. Park asserts that readers who can deal with the complexity of how a book is written, especially one with multiple narrative levels, will have a cognitive advantage over readers who take everything in a book at face value:

> **Ms. Park:** I think it's good for people to know that there *is* an inside story, and to decide for themselves when it's important to know.
> **Me:** Isn't it always important?
> **Ms. Park:** That's a tough one. I think ... in life, yes. The more you know about things, the more you can appreciate them. (219)

Through the dialogues between Julia and Ms. Park, Linda Sue Park—the (real) author—intensifies levels of narrative intimacy. Julia has confided in the reader, and Ms. Park confides in Julia, reinforcing what Day says about the interrelated nature of disclosure, vulnerability, trust, and intimacy (Day, *Reading* 62–63). Moreover, Park emphasizes the mutuality of the creative process: books require readers to complete the meaning. Nevertheless, despite Park's attempts to protest otherwise, the ethics of reciprocity can never be complete because no reader can make herself vulnerable to Julia by trusting her with the intimate details of the reader's own confidences. The relationality of a novel is a one-way street.

Day argues convincingly that "the complicated and often contradictory messages about intimacy that are propagated by contemporary culture shape representations and experiences of interpersonal relationships across genres, as well as across age, gender, race, and class" (*Reading* 202). Drawing from fiction, fanfiction, film, and self-help books, Day shows how teenaged girls "have become one of the groups most immediately influenced by the understanding that intimacy simultaneously depends upon disclosure and represents a threat *because of* disclosure" (*Reading* 202, italics in the original). When she talks about "disclosure," Day is referring to how girls make themselves vulnerable with their honesty. Day concludes:

> Ultimately, because the content of these novels so frequently presents warnings about disclosure within interpersonal relationships even as they construct narrator-reader relationships based upon the assumption that the narrator can confide all of her thoughts, feelings, and experiences to the reader, *narrative intimacy particularly acts as an embodiment of contradictory expectations regarding disclosure and discretion in young women's relationships.* (*Reading* 203, italics added)

Day's work is particularly useful in helping us examine one specific way that the ethics of feminist care can never be enacted successfully as a narrative device: the creation of narrative intimacy is always already a non-reciprocal relationship, even when the text creates the illusion of what Day might refer to as "trust" through disclosure.

CONCLUSION

When I realized that many of the feminists I most respect are writing about preadolescent and adolescent literature in terms that evoke the ethics of care, I was at first surprised. While it seems logical to me that disabilities rights advocates would focus on care, it seemed more unusual to me that narrative theorists would. In retrospect, I should not have been surprised. Blackford, Mallan, and Day all focus demonstrably on narrative structures that involve relationality. The net effect surfaces the inherent feminist ethics of care at work among those adolescent literary theorists interested in rhetorics of disability, narrative structures, and reader response theory.

After conducting this study, I have become convinced that material feminism and ethics of care are mutually implicated in shaping twenty-first century children's and adolescent literature as both a genre and as a field of study. Moreover, the relationship between material feminism and ethics of care is reflected in Nel Nodding's belief that "it is the recognition of and longing for relatedness that form the foundation of our ethic" (6). Material feminists also insist on the primacy of relationality. For example, in Chapter 1, I wrote about how Barad's theories of intra-activity depend on the ongoing relational processes by which meaning is defined. In Chapter 2, I demonstrated that Critical Race Theorists acknowledge how forms of oppression are multiplied by the relationality between people, especially as they are classified into groups in terms of social identities. Chapter 3 shows how ecofeminists' insistence on the interactionisms among people, living beings, and the environment involve fundamentally ethical acts. I personally find speculative fictions that emphasize individuality over the relationality of the collective to be unethical, as I observe in my critique of neoliberal interpretations of embodiment in Chapter 4. Chapter 5 examines sexuality, orientation, and gender identity as a function of embodiment and human relationships. And this chapter has openly linked relationality to narrative constructions that include novels implicated in Disability Studies and the work of various narrative theorists in children's literature.

My own inquiry into material feminism began with a study of how cognitive theory can better help us understand children's literature, but I soon realized cognition is an embodied activity, which lead me to learn more about materiality. Cognition, embodiment, the environment, and the meaning-systems by which we interact with each other and our world are interdependent, processual, and cannot be understood in terms of discourse alone. In *Flora & Ulysses*, William Spiver makes an observation that evokes the most basic principles of material feminism when he says, "My mother says that . . . I live in my head as opposed to living in the world. But I ask you: Don't we all live in our heads? Where else could we possibly exist? Our brains *are* the universe" (191, italics in the original). Without our embodied cognition and without perception, we would have no relationship to the universe. The squirrel Ulysses underscores the necessary connection between relationality and the universe in the final poem of the novel. Ulysses has learned from William Spiver that the universe is always expanding, so he writes his love to Flora with the words: "You are the ever-expanding universe to me" (233). The universe in this novel is defined in terms of relationality and care.

The legacy of various feminisms in twenty-first century preadolescent and adolescent literature includes the emphasis on relationality, especially those that resonate among embodiment, the environment, technology, and discourse. Novels that acknowledge intra-activity, interrelationships, and the importance of social support systems may well empower cis and trans girls far better than the twentieth-century feminist model that emphasized discourse as the primary form of empowerment. Discourse is, indeed, an imperative element of empowerment, but it is not the only factor involved in creating feminist literature for the young. Novelists and critics alike in the twenty-first century have become increasingly aware of our relationship to what DiCamillo calls the "ever-expanding universe" (*Flora & Ulysses* 233). The result is a lens through which we can view the many ways empowerment enacts itself in relational interactions with other people, with the environment, with technology, with our own embodiment and embodied cognition, and with our social identities. All of these concepts promise to complicate and expand how gender issues manifest themselves in children's and adolescent literature for many years to come.

1. Curry further connects ecofeminism to caring in the following passage: "If a feminist ethic is to re-envisage environmental thinking—most ecofeminists argue—it must do so by establishing conceptual frameworks that are non-oppressive and nonsubordinating and effectively freed from oppositional thinking. Such an ethical re-visioning must confront the cultural normativity of a masculinised public sphere and a feminised private sphere, and interrogate the political context and conditions of knowledge production" (74). Curry also critiques "the tendency in justice ethics towards the abstract and universal" (76).

2. According to Moran, "Maternal care ethics has enormous potential to help us rethink cultural attitudes toward mothers and to reshape relationships and institutions according to a model of care" ("Mother" 195).

3. Victoria Flanagan asserts that "one of the most notable achievements of *Cinder*" involves "the way in which [its] consideration of the 'othered' posthuman body advocates a variety of ethical social transformations" (*Technology* 60).

4. Flanagan links Cinder's cyborg foot to the ancient Chinese practice of manipulating the structure of the human body through foot-binding (*Technology* 62–63).

"FAÇON": WOMEN'S FORMAL AND INFORMAL WORK IN THE GARMENT INDUSTRY IN KAVALA, GREECE

Joanna Hadjicostandi

This is a regular day for me: get up at 5:30 A.M to prepare breakfast, and sometimes the main meal so my husband can have lunch. Then I have to prepare my son for school and the baby for his grandmother's home. I am lucky that my Petros [her husband] drops them off, so I can be at work by seven. When I get home after work, I have to take care of the rest of the housework tasks, prepare for dinner, and help my son with his homework. I usually do not go to bed before 12 midnight. (Hadjicostandi 1987)

The 1985 Nairobi International Women's Conference, which marked the end of the United Nations Decade for Women and its World Plan of Action, underscored the need for a more careful assessment of changes in women's participation in world economic development. Despite the U.N.'s commitment to women's equality and the many proposals aimed at women in development, numerous reports have revealed that, although a few women have entered high-paying, high-status occupations, there has been little improvement for most women in the Third World or for lower-class women in the "developed" world. Given that women have indeed been integrated in some fashion in the economies of their countries, the problem is not the lack of integration into the development process but the manner in which they are being integrated in production (as well as politics and reproduction).

Since the mid-1960s, industrial production has been internationalized at an increasingly rapid pace. Through direct investment or subcontracting arrangements, corporations from the United States and other industrialized countries have shifted many of their labor-intensive operations to low-wage export processing zones (EPZs) in Third World countries.[1] The availability of cheap female labor has become the primary criterion for investment, especially in garment manufacturing, textiles, electronics, and food processing (Enloe 1983; Fernandez-Kelly 1983; Fuentes and Ehrenreich 1983; Lim 1983a; Nash 1983; Safa 1981; Elson and Pearson 1981a). The introduction of large-scale commodity production outside the home, as well as the establishment of waged labor as the main source of family income, accounts for the increasing availability of women's waged labor in the international division of labor and in changes in the gender division of labor within the family (Beneria and Sen 1981). On the local level, existing divisions of labor have been transformed unevenly. Nonetheless, despite the increase in women's participation in the waged labor force in both "developed" and Third World countries, women still hold a disproportionate number of jobs in low-status occupations, many of which are in the low-paid "informal" labor market. These jobs are usually underrecorded in official statistics (Rollins 1986; Arizipe 1977; Jelin 1977). Helen Safa (1981) notes that the wage levels, working conditions, stability, and possibilities for occupational mobility offered Third World women by industrial employment could simply amount to a new form of exploitation and subordination. The statement quoted at the beginning of the chapter is representative.

Gender has become central in refining theories of development in the past three decades and has been incorporated as a key variable in the examination of women's changing status and sociopolitical and economic roles in both industrialized and Third World countries. This examination has taken place within two distinct paradigms. On the one hand, modernization theories that derive from classical and neoclassical economics explain women's status chiefly

---

1. Export processing zones are areas that attract foreign capital investment because of the many benefits provided, including the low-wage labor, minimal tax requirements, and few or no trade union demands for safety and health standards.

in terms of the degree to which they participate in production roles outside the home. As a result, such modernization theorists stress individualist solutions such as increases in education or factory work as most important in changing women's roles and status (Inkeles 1983; Marshal 1978). On the other hand, theorists within a Marxist tradition emphasize the effects on women of changes brought about by capitalist relations of production and class antagonisms, especially in societies where precapitalist relations still exist.

Women's conditions are very specific to their national economies, and, although domestic activities are overwhelmingly performed by women across countries, the differences are quite clear. Also, female and male workers are absorbed into the international political economy at different rates and under different conditions. Thus the new relations, while influential, can transform neither existing techniques of production contained in the division of labor nor family relations into "modern" ones. The particular way in which capitalist production is articulated with precapitalist modes of production is an important determinant of the economic action necessary to sustain people.

Given the different nature of women's participation in both the labor market and the domestic sphere, we need to understand the complexity of articulation between the existing modes of production and between production and reproduction to explain the gender division of labor as well as changes in women's status (Hen 1988; Beneria and Sen 1981; Deere 1986; Safa 1981).[2]

Garment manufacturing for export, based on foreign capital investment, has expanded during the past twenty-five years in northern Greece, and the industry employs predominantly women. In this chapter the impact of industrial expansion on women's status in the northern Greek city of Kavala is evaluated. The data were obtained in 1986 from a sample of sixty women who worked in the garment manufacturing industry in Kavala. In-depth interviews with factory workers (formal economy) and with home piece workers ("informal" economy) and nonparticipant observation provided a wealth of in-

---

2. Women's work is largely assumed to be within the sphere of social reproduction. This includes reproduction of the labor power on a daily basis (domestic work or daily maintenance activity) and the reproduction of labor over time (biological and child rearing).

formation about the women's background, family position, economic participation in the family, and trade union participation, as well as other detailed economic, attitudinal, and behavioral information.[3] The selection of the samples from both the formal and "informal" economy had a twofold purpose: first, to make possible an evaluation of the differences and similarities between the two groups of women, using the home piece workers as a control group; and second, to shed light on the little researched area of home piece-work employment known in Greece as "façon."[4] In both cases the women did the same type of work, assembling garments, but their conditions and circumstances were distinctly different. The factory workers were restricted to a specific, closely supervised environment, whereas the piece workers worked at home or in a small workshop attached to the home and considered an extension of it.

This study analyzes women's integration into international development by addressing the interconnections between international capital accumulation, class formation, and gender relations within a theoretical framework based on the articulation between modes of production and between production and reproduction.

WOMEN IN THE GREEK LABOR MARKET AND FAMILY

The turn of the century found Greece economically stagnant and politically devastated. Feudalist relations of production still persisted despite the expansion of trade and the establishment of small-scale manufacturing. The majority of Greek women and men were peasants and strongly tied to the land. The state, first the Ottoman and then the Greek, supported feudalist production because it owned

---

3. The formal economy is defined as paid work that is state regulated and in which employees have access to Social Security and fringe benefits. The informal economy here refers to *paid* work done outside the arena of the formal, regulated economy. It usually escapes official record keeping and can be poorly paid, irregular, unprotected, nonunionized, and has no Social Security or other fringe benefits. There is an ongoing debate in the literature over the formal versus informal economy (see Portes and Sassen-Koob 1987; Redclift and Mingione 1985; Hadjicostandi 1983, 1987; Bromley 1978; Moser 1978).

4. *Façon* is the French word for *subcontracting*. It is used very commonly in Greece with reference to piece work.

the largest part of the land. The transition from feudalism to capitalism, which began in the late 1800s, was very slow. According to Pandelis Agianoglou (1982:12), the beginning of the change was generated by class contradictions that arose as a result of the redistribution of about three-quarters of the arable land in 1871. Before the 1922 war in Asia Minor, which displaced thousands of Greeks both inside Greece and in Asia Minor, local and diaspora capital were invested in trade, not manufacturing. Many historians, economists, and other social analysts see this as the main reason Greek capitalist "development" was so delayed. Only after 1927 was investment capital poured into industrial development, and this was linked more to changes in the objective structural conditions within Greece itself than to the shift in capital investment from trade to industry (Agianoglou 1982:13–14). Nicos Mouzelis (1978:3–29) argues that Greek capitalism did not really take off until the interwar and postwar years.

Today Greece stands in the gray area between "developed" and Third World countries. Its economy is usually classified as semiperipheral, meaning that it has many of the contradictions and social characteristics of both advanced and Third World countries. Women, who were at the forefront of the long war of independence from the Ottoman empire, not only constituted the main agricultural force in the beginning of the century but also held an important role as a source of cheap labor during the early years of industrialization. During the mechanization and commercialization of agriculture, however, increasingly more men were employed in agriculture, and peasant women were led to industrial employment. By 1928, about 23 percent of the economically active population in manufacturing was female. Women thus were on the front line of capitalist expansion, especially in textile, tobacco, and soft-drink manufacturing. The gender inequalities in the labor market had already been clearly established (Mears 1928), for women were underpaid and unprotected by the state.

Women's position in the labor force did not alter dramatically until sharp changes occurred in the Greek economy during the period following World War II.[6] But although postwar industrial devel-

6. See Papandreou 1981 for elaboration on multinational expansion in Greece. See Mousourou 1985 for further information on women's position in Greece.

opment was impressive, it did not mean the end of small, low-productivity industrial (i.e., footwear, clothing, and leather products) units, which usually employed women at very low wages. Meanwhile, capitalist economic development failed to support agricultural development and allowed family-based, low-productivity units to continue to exist (Mouzelis 1978:122). Furthermore, postwar economic growth was accompanied by heightened income inequalities, persistent unemployment, massive flight to the cities, foreign migration, and increased dependence on the United States and western Europe. Capitalist expansion did not destroy all preexisting forms of labor organization. On the contrary, a coexistence of capitalist and noncapitalist ways of production is observed. According to Nicos Mouzelis, those engaged in agriculture became progressively worse off as agricultural per capita income dropped from 83.3 percent of the average income to 51.1 percent from 1951 to 1970 (1978:122–23). The mass exodus of the rural population to the cities and then to the European countries in search of better living conditions is thus understandable.[7] Has industrialization provided for the improvement of people's condition? How has it affected women's position and status?

A limited number of empirical studies have been done on the effect of industrialization on the status of women in Greece. Joanna Lambiri-Dimaki (1965) pioneered this line of work in her research on women factory workers in the town of Megara. She concluded that, despite the economic benefits it offered, the new work environment had affected women's ideas and values more than it had provided them with an independent way of life and position in the patriarchal family. She further found that women still adhered to the "traditional" values of obeying their families, marrying early, and acquiring a dowry. Thus any changes that did occur were in the women's ideas rather than in their social actions. A study by Magda Nikolaidou (1975) of the same town and factory fifteen years later confirmed many of Lambiri-Dimaki's findings. Nikolaidou argues that a "cultural lag" was created because it took so long for the society to accept the change in women's occupational roles. Although

---

7. For elaboration on the migration movements in Greece, see Kassimati 1984 (in Greek); Filias 1975; Kudat and Nikolinakos 1975; Lianos 1975; Nikolinakos 1974 (in Greek).

paid employment enabled women to shake some traditional roles, their roles within the family remained the same. Nikolaidou further noted that the way the dowry was accumulated had changed: originally, all of it was given by the father, whereas now women worked for it. Finally, she concluded that women worked out of economic necessity. Such conditions are not evidence of drastic changes in their status, however, since traditional values and roles were constantly being reproduced in the workplace. I examined several of the findings from these earlier studies in my study, which took place in Kavala.

WOMEN IN THE KAVALA GARMENT INDUSTRY

Kavala, in northern Greece, is one of the most rapidly industrializing cities in the country, although its people still hold preindustrial ("traditional") values. In the early 1960s, Kavala's industrial infrastructure was minimal. Production was based on the processing of tobacco products and to a lesser extent on small-scale fish processing based on local fishing, olive-oil refinement, and textile manufacturing. Most of the industries were small and employed women on a seasonal basis, while men were usually occupied in small commercial enterprises. A chemical fertilizer plant, established a few miles from the city in 1960, employed men from Kavala and the surrounding area as unskilled laborers, mostly in construction. This did not solve the unemployment and underemployment problem, however, and in the 1960s the town witnessed staggering exoduses of both men and women laborers to various parts of Europe (i.e., Switzerland, France, and especially Germany) and to other parts of the world. This trend culminated in the 1970s when German and Greek migration policies changed. Migrants thus returned to Greece, mostly to big cities close to their villages. Many invested in businesses that had subcontracting arrangements with firms in Europe, especially Germany.[8] The garment industry provided many such opportunities. Cloth, usually

---

8. Upon their return to Greece, the workers, of course, hurried to buy their own houses, comfortable furniture, and other consumer goods. This appeared to be the ultimate dream of many migrant workers. Not surprisingly, very few emigrants returned to their villages to assume agricultural pursuits.

precut, was imported to Greece for assembly only and then exported as finished or semifinished products. Frequently, accessories for the assembly of clothes, such as thread and buttons, accompanied the shipment. This increase in export manufacturing provided employment for local Kavala women.

Government policies concerning subcontract manufacturing (similar to those in most export processing zones) prevent the sale of the garments in the local market. Subcontractors are thus parasites of the Greek economy: as a whole, manufacturers utilize almost no goods produced in the national market, and the final product is exported immediately. Subcontractors have a secure and stable income as long as they can guarantee good and reliable service to their foreign partners. And because they do not have to supply the local market, they are free of its irregularities. Statistics obtained from the records of the Union of Garment Export Manufacturers of East Macedonia and Thrace indicate that in 1983, 40 percent of the export garment factories of Macedonia and Thrace were established in the county of Kavala (34 percent in Drama, 11 percent in each of the areas of Komotini and Xanthy, and 5 percent in Evros).

The first sample of 50 women for my study was randomly drawn from a population of 206 women employed in two garment factories in Kavala. The second sample of 10 home piece workers was selected from the population of Kavala through informants.

The informal nature of home work and the absence of any official records made selection of the home workers a herculean task. The population of home workers in the greater Kavala area was not explored nor were home workers outside the garment industry. Data were obtained through in-depth interviews and through nonparticipant observation.

Garment Workers and the Household Economy

My findings indicate that there were no great differences in marital status, age, family size, household composition, social conditions, or family background between the home workers and the factory workers. The majority of women in both samples were between twenty-five and forty years old and married.

Before obtaining their present jobs, the majority of women in both samples either had been at home taking care of housework and other family-related duties (about one-third were not old enough to work) or had occasional jobs in other factories. Four women, two from each sample, reported having worked in factories in Germany and had found the experience rewarding. They pref erred the working conditions abroad but had found the work to be more intense and alienating.

Those factory and home workers who had worked on the land were all married and older than twenty-five. Very few still had any agricultural duties. Two of the factory workers had been involved in office work before securing their present jobs, and two had been attending high school. One home worker told of washing clothes for wealthy households, but since the families had purchased washing machines, this had become an increasingly unstable activity and she had sought alternative means of earning an income. The majority of women considered these earnings as "pocket" money, however. The length of employment (or lack thereof) before seeking work in the factory appeared to be of crucial significance when correlated with other demographic factors, such as age or marital status. Most of the women had unstable incomes before they took their present positions, and most had relied on their parents or husbands for pocket money.

When asked about their motives in seeking their present work, most of the women were surprised and considered the reasons to be quite obvious: women had to seek jobs outside the household out of economic necessity. The overwhelming majority of the women came from working-class families where one wage was not enough to sustain the family. A high percentage of the spouses of both the factory and home workers were involved in seasonal work (41 percent and 43 percent respectively) and thus had unstable incomes; 27 percent and 43 percent owned small businesses such as restau-rants or retail stores; and 29 percent and 14 percent were white-collar workers. Only 3 percent of the factory and none of the home workers' husbands were full-time farmers. This is not surprising, however, considering migration from and to the city of Kavala.

Eighty percent of the respondents revealed that family economic support or the capacity to supplement the family income was the main motive for seeking employment. Only 6 percent of the factory workers and none of the home workers decided to work to escape family pressure. Fourteen percent of the factory workers and 20 percent of the home workers decided to seek work to achieve both economic and personal independence. One can thus conclude that economic instability rather than personal independence led the women to seek paid employment.

For the factory workers at least, the meager thirty thousand to forty thousand drachmas[9] a month the women earn represent a fairly steady monthly income. The home workers confront hardships because of the instability of their income, which is dependent on each woman's daily piece-work production and the needs of the supplying manufacturer. Popi, a forty-year-old home worker described the situation very vividly:

> When you work very fast the pay is good. A young woman who is just starting can earn 2,000 to 3,000 drachmas a day. Someone who works very fast may make even 5,000 a day. It depends on the hours she devotes and the productivity. When you spend sixteen hours working at home at least nine have to be pure work if you really want to break even. You see, one has a lot of expenses to take care of, like thread, electricity, machine maintenance, and sometimes rent. I personally spend 1,200 a day on expenses. If I earn 2,000 it is too little. A woman in the factory earns at least 2,000 to 2,500 a day, so I have to make at least that to be satisfied.

The possibility of not making enough money and the flexibility to pursue more work may explain why home workers on average earn more than factory workers. More research is needed on this question.

Two major points emerged, however, to explain why home workers did not seek employment in factories. The first related to their degree of control over their labor, and the second to their family situations. They said that they did not want any "bosses over their head" and extended that to not having to deal with other women. Most important, they liked the flexibility of working at home. "I have to take care of my seven-year-old daughter," one woman said. Her answer reflected that of most of the other married workers and is one that is common to most studies on home work.

---

9. In 1986, there were approximately 130 to 150 drachmas to the dollar.

In addition, the investment in one or more machines and their installation in the home worker's kitchen, back room, or adjacent basement made switching to other types of work difficult. Ninety percent of the home workers owned their machines; approximately 50 percent had bought them second-hand at factory sales or through friends or relatives. The other women claimed that buying a new machine was a better investment since one did not have to worry about repairs or costly maintenance. Only one woman did not have her own machine. She rented it for a minimal monthly fee from the manufacturer for whom she worked. What would become of her machine if the woman decided to stop this work? "You'll be lucky if you find someone who would want to buy it," one woman said. She added, "Today if you are to do this type of work, you are better off buying a new machine. Who would want my old machine? I am probably the only one who can handle it. We know each other."

One woman said that she could only start thinking about working outside her home in another seven years, when her son began school, and even then she would need to think seriously about it: "I really want to have him under my supervision when he is out of school; otherwise he'll play soccer all day long and not study."

The majority of women in both samples were not satisfied with the wages they received. They had minimal buying power and thus could hardly afford necessities, especially if they had children. In response to a question about her buying power, Mary, a factory worker, asked, "What buying power are you talking about? This money is nothing. To give you an idea, yesterday I went to buy shoes. These cost five thousand drachmas. I earn seven thousand a week. You can imagine the rest."

In conclusion, my findings corroborate those of previous studies of Greece that women are still dominated by economic instability. Pressured by need, they seek employment in industrial production, which hardly ever provides the channels for occupational mobility and improvement of status.

Contribution to the Family Budget

Economic independence has often been equated with social independence, but how much more independent do women become when they earn a wage? One way to examine this question is to look at the way women spend their earnings: how much they keep for their own expenses, and how much they contribute to the family budget. Consistent with other findings of my study, I found that the majority of the married women in both samples contributed all of their wages (thirty-two thousand to forty thousand drachmas a month) to their families' budgets. Of the women who said that they kept all of their money for themselves, only one was married. Four women were separated and lived alone, four were engaged, and three were single. Those who were single or engaged indicated that they were saving some of their money for the future (they did not say for a dowry).

The pattern of contribution became clearer when they discussed the way household decisions were made regarding spending. Fifty-six percent of the factory workers and 60 percent of the home workers, the majority of whom were married, stated that financial decisions were made with their husbands or fathers, based on the needs of the household. They confirmed that they were free to purchase anything they wanted at any time, yet they never failed to mention the difficulties they faced in making ends meet. Twenty-six percent of the factory and 20 percent of the home workers stated that they made decisions alone regarding how money was to be allocated. This contrasts with 18 percent of the factory and 20 percent of the home workers (the majority of whom were married or engaged) who indicated that their husbands or fathers made such decisions.

Recognizing their double burden, most of the women admitted that they would stop working if they had economic independence. Mary, a factory worker, for instance, stated, "I wouldn't mind stopping work if he [her husband] had quite a lot of money and we could live comfortably." Sofia replied firmly, "If he has an income that would support us comfortably, I would stop because I am very tired. I've been working for too many years." When I asked her if she would consider advancing her education she replied, "I am already forty years old. It is impossible to do anything like that now." Other married women said that it would be "easier to take care of their kids" without having to work or that they were tired and wanted to escape the double and often triple burdens. But Katie, a factory worker, disagreed: "I have a sense of fulfillment when I'm working.

I wouldn't stop for anything in the world. I do think that women should have a job and keep it. In this way they are more respected in the family, since they contribute economically." She voiced the position of another five women who saw their jobs as a form of security.

Gender Relations within the Family

Changes in gender relations within the family, although not dramatic, were more pronounced than earlier studies found. The gender division of labor was altered, especially in families where the wife worked either in a factory or at home. Working outside the home for eight hours a day, five (sometimes six) days a week, or spending between eight and fifteen hours at a sewing machine objectively limited the amount of time the women could devote to housework. Most families were nuclear, so although parental help with household chores and care of grandchildren was evident, it was limited. In many families the husbands did some of the housework. A high percentage of the women stated that their husbands "helped" with chores (62 percent of the factory workers and 86 percent of the home workers). Nonetheless, the range of men's activities was quite limited, and 90 percent of the women saw them as "help." Typically, the husband helped when the wife did not "feel well" or was "very tired" or had a heavy task to accomplish (i.e., airing the carpets). One factory worker, however, said,

> He really helps a lot. He washes clothes, airs clothes; in general, he helps with everything. I don't want him to wash the dishes. He doesn't know how. I wouldn't allow it anyway. However, since we are both working he has to help out.

A twenty-eight-year-old woman who had been divorced for a year and had two children (ages two and five) said,

> I didn't really mind doing more work. I always had to do everything for him anyway. I was actually cooking two dishes every day because he was very peculiar with his food and the children did not get enough nourishment. He beat me up. The last time he beat me was in front of the children.

My oldest son then assured me that when he grew up he'd take care of him!

Most of the men helped with the children by taking them out of the house. "He takes the child to the park so I can do my work without being interrupted," one woman said. Another added that "sometimes he takes the child for a walk, and other times he helps with the housework."

These accounts illustrate that, although they "helped out," the men as a group did not assume any real responsibility for what was still viewed as "women's work." As a result, the married women had to combine their paid labor with domestic work and child care. And, as the women noted, many had yet another set of responsibilities, a "triple" burden, such as taking care of elderly parents or close relatives.

When single women were asked if they would expect their husbands to "help" around the house, the majority (in a pattern similar to that of the married women) responded that they would expect the husband to "help" (81 percent of the factory workers and 67 percent of the home workers). They often couched their answers by saying they wanted the help "when it is needed." A twenty-four-year-old factory worker said, "I don't want to be sitting when he is working around the house, like some other women do. Yes, I'd like him to help, but when I really need it."

Only one woman, twenty-eight-year-old Katie, said that her marriage was completely egalitarian. She explained that not only did she and her husband both have jobs but that they were also active in political meetings of the Greek Communist party (KKE) and therefore had to use their time efficiently. She said, "He helps with everything. Sometimes when I come home after working late I find everything ready. He is involved in everything. He is particularly good with our daughter, even when she was a baby." Political affiliation needs to be studied carefully as a variable in determining changing gender roles within the family.

The finding that working-class Greek women bear a double and often triple burden does not come as a surprise, since patriarchal relations supporting gender inequalities predominate in most capitalist societies. "Domestic" functions are still maintained in the private sphere rather than in the public. Thus, despite attempts by the government or the entry of women into waged employment (accompanied by slight changes in gender relations within the family), women's positions as well as their attitudes and behavior have not changed to a great extent. Most of the women did not mention or discuss dowries, but they were concerned with saving money for their new households. Furthermore, the need for increased decision making, respect for their opinions, independence, and changes in the power relations in the family were not discussed at any length.

Work Problems and Control

The problems home workers faced were different from those facing the factory workers. Most of the home workers complained about the long hours they worked and the difficulties of adapting to this schedule. A forty-year-old woman who had started working in her early twenties said,

> Yes, I faced a lot of problems. When I first started I was working nineteen hours a day to be able to pay for the machines. You see, I did not have any capital when I started and had to pay the machine off quickly so that I could make some profit for myself.

This woman's response touches on two of the most important problems the home workers face: the long and irregular hours that comprise their workday and the need to acquire and maintain their means of production. On the average, the women reported working twelve hours a day and at any time (day or night) when they were free from housework. In most cases, other members of the family worked with them. The advantage of home work, they said, was that they had total control over their time. In contrast, the major problem facing the factory workers was child care. Their schedules made it difficult for them to attend to their children's needs.

Health problems caused by sitting for long periods, poor lighting, and the lint and fluff were common among both the home and factory workers. In the case of the home workers, the problem was extended to the whole family.

Lisa expressed the factory workers' concerns about supervision and control:

I am really satisfied because I am able to work [whether I am alone or with others]. Of course, when you have so many people above you controlling you and treating you like a "thing," then you realize that the only loser is you. When I'm at work sometimes I am appalled by women screaming and swearing at each other, especially when it involves a fifty-year-old woman. I see the injustice and feel that I have to try to change things.

Lisa was referring to the supervisor, who did not hesitate to use foul language to keep the women "in line." According to the owner, the supervisor was the best example of a good worker, because she was efficient and had taken only one sick day in ten years. She appeared to be friendly, but her mood could change in seconds. Her presence, coupled with the tight production quota that the women had to meet to receive full wages, discouraged any lengthy discussions during worktime. Moreover, a bonus system offered the opportunity to earn extra money by exceeding the set production quota. The women thus made every effort not only to meet the tight quota but to surpass it by working during their breaks or staying after work to get their "prim."[10] The "prim" is usually set by the German manufacturers. Greek managers, however, often find it necessary to modify the time needed to perform a certain task because of differences in the German and local machines and in the level and experience of the women involved.

In conclusion, through discussions with factory workers, it became apparent that patriarchal relations predominated in the workplace and traditional values and roles were constantly reproduced. The majority of the workers indicated, for example, that the best way to solve their problems was to "discuss them with the boss," as opposed to union representatives. This led to yet another form of dependence on an authority figure.

---

10. Derived from the word *premium,* the "prim" is a bonus based on the time spent on each garment, in fractions of a minute.

SUMMARY AND CONCLUSIONS

Contrary to assumptions about "modernization," factory work is not really providing the bridge to "modernity" and development for working-class women in Greece, as evidenced by the lack of significant differences between the women working in the factory and the women working at home. The historical comparison did not indicate dramatic changes, either.

The overwhelming majority of the respondents indicated that their decision to obtain waged or home work was economically motivated. The women saw waged work as an "unavoidable" but "temporary" necessity that would benefit their family in the future or improve the family's current standard of living. Although the women's responses indicated that "traditional" roles in the family have been shaken, the division of labor in the household has not changed significantly. Women are still burdened with the major responsibility for household tasks and child care. One change since Lambiri-Dimaki's and Nikolaidou's reports is that there is a decreasing emphasis on dowry. Does this mean that women have become more independent? Any answer should be given with great caution, since there is much evidence that women's dependence is reproduced in several ways, not the least of which is, as my findings have shown, their almost total responsibility for social reproduction.

Although one would expect that working outside the household would increase women's interactions with other individuals, thus affecting their attitudes, I found that this held true for very few of the factory workers. The double burden of work and home responsibilities makes "leisure" a male right. Further, in many cases the double burden becomes a triple burden when women have to finish their work at home or have to maintain households for their elderly parents.

Tight control over the women in the workplace, as a technique for meeting production norms, allows for very little interaction among them. Discussions with factory workers about the union and their political participation indicated that, although they were not indifferent or unaware of their condition, they were not ready to engage in any form of practical resistance. They were more concerned with receiving their wages, suggesting at times, "Let others do the changing. I need my day's wages." The attitudes of the home workers did not differ much from those of the factory workers. They indicated on several occasions that they were dissatisfied with their conditions but were also thankful to have work.

The paternalistic attitude toward women and women's unequal position vis-à-vis men was carried onto the factory floor, so that relations of dependency and subordinate female roles were clearly reproduced. The women's wages were considered "supplementary" to the family budget, and hence their attitude was that they would resign when "things get better at home."

This study has opened the way for two very important larger-scale investigations. The first would address the relation of export processing, which usually utilizes women's labor, to Greece's overall economy and consequently to the changes in women's and men's conditions. Questions concerning economic development and its impact on individuals need to be asked on a large scale. Are export-processing factories catalysts for the development of indigenous industry through technology diffusion (Nikolinakos 1983)? Can they serve as substitutes for primitive accumulation? Development is time-based. To trace the consequences of any particular articulation of modes of production, longitudinal research is critical.

The second investigation that is needed is an exploration of a most prominent and ever-expanding phenomenon, informal economic activity and its consequences on employment. What is the role of informal activity for development in Greece? Do informal activities expand in response to domestic demand? Or are they state-supported efforts to overcome a chronic lack of good jobs? Under what conditions are the rewards of informal activity greater for women?

Questions related to improvements in women's status and position must be explored through macro and micro interchange. Women's equality presupposes changes in the socioeconomic structure concomitantly with changes in the social construction of that structure. These changes must necessarily be part of the ongoing struggle for political emancipation from all forms of exploitation and oppression, be it class, gender, race, age, handicap, or sexual preference.

Border Arte:
Nepantla, el Lugar de la Frontera

Gloria Anzaldua

This essay, like "Bearing Witness: Their Eyes Anticipate the Healing" (in part 3), illustrates another side of Anzaldúa: her intense interest in the world of visual art. Originally published in the San Diego Museum of Contemporary Art's *La Frontera/The Border: Art about the Mexico/ United States Border Experience* (1993), "Border Arte" describes Anzaldúa's experience viewing "AZTEC: The World of Moctezuma" exhibition at the Denver Museum of Natural History. In addition to offering important insights into Anzaldúa's shaman aesthetics, "Border Arte" contains her first extensive description and interpretation of Coyolxauhqui (Ko-yol-sha-UH-kee) as well as elaborations on her theories of el cenote, nepantla, and autohistoria. This piece also demonstrates Anzaldúa's shift from borderland to nepantla theory and her ongoing interest in revisionist mythmaking, trans issues, and the relationship between identity, nationalism, and art. Although some readers, particularly those who identify as "white," as male, and/or as members of the dominating culture, have felt as though Anzaldúa excludes them from portions of this piece, "The New Mestiza Nation" and other later writings indicate that the aesthetics and artists she describes here are inclusionary, and apply to other artists as well.

Border Arte

Nepantla, el Lugar de la Frontera

The gatekeeper at the museum takes our ticket. We enter the simulation of the Aztec capital city, Tenochtitlán, as it was thought to exist before the European colonizers destroyed it. It is opening day of the "AZTEC: The World of Moctezuma" exhibition at the Denver Museum of Natural History. El legado indígena. Here before my eyes is the culture of nuestros antepasados indígenas. Sus símbolos y metáforas todavía viven en la gente chicana/mexicana. I am again struck by how much Chicana/o artists and writers feel the impact of ancient Mexican art forms, foods, and customs. We consistently reflect back these images in revitalized and modernized versions in theater, film, performance art, painting, dance sculpture, and literature. La negación sistemática de la cultura mexicana-chicana en los Estados Unidos impide su desarrollo haciendo esto un acto de colonización. As a people who have been stripped of our history, language, identity, and pride, we attempt again and again to find what we have lost by digging into our cultural roots imaginatively and making art out of our findings. I ask myself, What does it mean for me, esta jotita, this queer Chicana, this mexica-tejana to enter a museum and look at indigenous objects that were once used by her ancestors? Will I find my historical Indian identity here, along with its ancient mestizaje? As I pull out a pad to take notes on the clay, stone, jade, bone, feather, straw, and cloth artifacts, I am

281

disconcerted with the knowledge that I too am passively consuming and appropriating an indigenous culture. I, and the Chicano kids from Servicio Chicano Center I walked in with, are being taught our cultural roots by whites. The essence of colonization: rip off a culture, then regurgitate the white version of that culture to the "natives."

This exhibit bills itself as an act of good will between North America and Mexico, a sort of bridge across the border. The Mexico/United States border is a site where many different cultures "touch" each other, and the permeable, flexible, and ambiguous shifting grounds lend themselves to hybrid images. The border is the locus of resistance, of rupture, implosion and explosion, and of putting together the fragments and creating a new assemblage. Border artists cambian el punto de referencia. By disrupting the neat separations between cultures, they create a culture mix, una mezcla in their artworks. Each artist locates her/him self in this border "lugar," and tears apart and rebuilds the "place" itself.

The museum, if it is daring and takes risks, can be a kind of "borderlands" where cultures co-exist in the same site, I think to myself as I walk through the first exhibit. I am jostled amidst a white middle-class crowd. I look at videos, listen to slide presentations, and hear museum staff explain portions of the exhibit. It angers me that all these people talk as though the Aztecs and their culture have been dead for hundreds of years when in fact there are still 10,000 Aztec survivors living in Mexico.

I stop before the dismembered body of la diosa de la luna, Coyolxauhqui, bones jutting from sockets. The warrior goddess with bells on her cheeks and serpent belt calls to mind the dominant culture's repeated attempts to tear the Mexican culture in the U.S. apart and scatter the fragments to the winds. This slick, prepackaged exhibition costing $3.5 million exemplifies that dismemberment. I stare at the huge round stone of la diosa. To me she also embodies the resistance and vitality of the Chicana/mexicana writer/artist. I can see resemblances between the moon goddess' vigorous and warlike energy and Yolanda López's *Portrait of the Artist as the Virgin of Guadalupe* (1978), which depicts a Chicana/mexicana woman emerging and running from the oval halo of rays with the mantle of the traditional virgen in one hand and a serpent in the other. *Portrait* represents the cultural rebirth of the Chicana struggling to free herself from oppressive gender roles.[1] The struggle and pain of this rebirth is also represented eloquently by Marsha Gomez in earthworks and stoneware scuptures such as *This Mother Ain't For Sale*.

The sibilant whispery voice of Chicano Edward James Olmos on the walkman interrupts my thoughts and guides me to the serpentine base of a reconstructed sixteen-foot temple where the human sacrifices were flung down, leaving bloodied steps. Around me I hear the censorious, culturally ignorant words of the whites who, while horrified by the bloodthirsty Aztecs, gape in vicarious wonder and voraciously consume the exoticized images. Though I, too, am a gaping consumer, I feel that these artworks are part of my legacy. I remember visiting Chicana tejana artist Santa Barraza in her Austin studio in the mid-1970s and talking about the merger and appropriation of cultural symbols and techniques by artists in search of their spiritual and cultural roots. As I walked around her studio I was amazed at the vivid Virgen de Guadalupe iconography on her walls and drawings strewn on tables and shelves. The three "madres," Guadalupe, La Malinche, y La Llorona are culture figures that Chicana writers and artists "re-read" in our works. And now, sixteen years later, Barraza is focusing on interpretations of Pre-Columbian codices as a reclamation of cultural and historical mestiza/o identity. Her "códices" are edged with milagros and ex votos.[2] Using the folk art format, Barraza paints tin testimonials known as retablos, traditional popular miracle paintings on metal, a medium introduced into Colonial Mexico by the Spaniards. One of her devotional retablos is of La Malinche with maguey (the maguey cactus is Barraza's symbol of rebirth). Like many Chicana artists her work explores indigenous Mexican "symbols and myths in a historical and contemporary context as a mechanism of resistance to oppression and assimilation."[3] Once more my eyes return to Coyolxauhqui. Nope, she's not for sale and neither are the original La Lupe, La Llorona, and La Chingada and their modern renditions.

Olmos's occasional musical recitations in Náhuatl further remind me that the Aztecs, their language, and indigenous cultures are still very much alive. Though I wonder if Olmos and we Chicana/o writers and artists also are misappropriating Náhuatl language and images, hearing the words and seeing the images boosts my spirits. I feel that I am part of something profound outside my personal self. This sense of connection and community compels Chicana/o writers/artists to delve into, sift through, and rework native imagery.

I wonder about the genesis of el arte de la frontera. Border art remembers its roots—sacred and folk art are often still one and the same. I recall the nichos (niches or recessed areas) and retablos (altar pieces) that I had recently seen in several galleries and museums such as the Denver Metropolitan State College Art Museum. The altar pieces are placed inside open boxes made of wood, tin, or cardboard. The cajitas contain three-dimensional figures such as la virgen, photos of ancestors, candles, and sprigs of herbs tied together. They are actually tiny installations. I make mine out of cigar boxes or vegetable crates that I find discarded on streets before garbage pickups. The retablos range from the strictly traditional to the modern more abstract forms. Santa Barraza, Yolanda M. López, Marsha Gomez, Carmen Lomas Garza, and other Chicanas connect the everyday life with the political, sacred, and aesthetic with their art.[4]

I walk from the glass-caged exhibits of the sacred world to the Tlatelolco, the open mercado, the people's market, with its strewn baskets of chiles, avocados, nopales on petates, and ducks in hanging wooden cages. I think of how border art, in critiquing old, traditional, and erroneous representations of the Mexico/United States border, attempts to represent the "real world" de la gente going about their daily lives. But it renders that world and its people in more than mere surface slices of life. If one looks beyond the obvious, one sees a connection to the spirit world, to the underworld, and to other realities. In the "old world," art was/is functional and sacred as well as aesthetic. At the point that folk and fine art separated, the metate (a flat porous volcanic stone with rolling pin used to make corn tortillas) and the huipil (blouse)[5] were put in museums by the western curators of art. Many of these officiators believe that only art objects from dead cultures should end up in museums. According to a friend[6] who recently returned from Central America, a museum in Guatemala City solely houses indigenous clothing as though they were garments of the past. There was little mention of the women she saw still weaving the same kind of clothing and using the same methods as their ancestors. However, the men in the Guatemalan community, Todos Santos, wear red pants while men from another area wear another color. Indigenous peoples were forced to wear clothing of a certain color so that their patrones could distinguish "their" peons from those of other bosses. The men's red pants reflect a colonization of their culture. Thus, colonization influences the lives and objects of the colonized and artistic heritage is altered.

I come to a glass case where the skeleton of a jaguar with a stone in its open mouth nestles on cloth. The stone represents the heart. My thoughts trace the jaguar's spiritual and religious symbolism from its Olmec origins to present-day jaguar masks worn by people who no longer know that the jaguar was connected to rain. Who no longer remember that Tlaloc and the jaguar and the serpent and rain are tightly intertwined.[7] Through the centuries a culture touches and influences another, passing on its metaphors and its gods before it dies. (Metaphors *are* gods.) The new culture adopts, modifies, and enriches these images, and it, in turn, passes them on. The process is repeated until the original meanings of images are pushed into the unconscious. What surfaces are images more significant to the prevailing culture and era. However, the artist on some level still connects to that unconscious reservoir of meaning, connects to that nepantla state of transition between time periods, and the border between cultures. Chicana/o artists presently are engaged in "reading" that cenote, that nepantla, and that border.

Art and la frontera intersect in a liminal space where border people, especially artists, live in a state of "nepantla." Nepantla is the Náhuatl word for an in-between state, that uncertain terrain one crosses when moving from one place to another, when changing from one class, race, or sexual position to another, when traveling from the present identity into a new identity. The Mexican immigrant at the moment of crossing the barbed wired fence into a hostile "paradise" of el norte, the U.S., is caught in a state of nepantla. Others who find themselves in this bewildering transitional space may be the straight person coming out as lesbian, gay, bi, or transsexual, or a person from working-class origins crossing into middle-classness and privilege. The marginalized starving Chicana/o artist who suddenly finds her/his work exhibited in mainstream museums or sold for thousands in prestigious galleries, as well as the once neglected writer whose work is in every professor's syllabus, for a time inhabit nepantla.

I think of the borderlands as Jorge Luis Borges's Aleph, the one spot on earth which contains all other places within it. All people in it, whether natives or immigrants, colored or white, queers or heterosexuals, from this side of the border or del otro lado are personas del lugar, local people — all of whom relate to the border and to the nepantla states in different ways.

I continue meandering absently from room to room, noticing how the different parts of the Aztec culture are partitioned from others and how some are placed together in one room and a few feet apart but still seem to be in neat little categories. That bothers me. Abruptly I meet myself in the center of the room with the sacrificial knives. I stand rooted there for a long time, thinking about spaces and borders and moving in them and through them. According to Edward Hall, early in life we become oriented to space in a way that is tied to survival and sanity. When we become disoriented from that sense of space we fall in danger of becoming psychotic.[8] I question this — to be disoriented in space is the "normal" way of being for us mestizas living in the borderlands. It is the sane way of coping with the accelerated pace of this complex, interdependent, and multicultural planet. To be disoriented in space is to be en nepantla. To be disoriented in space is to experience bouts of dissociation of identity, identity breakdowns and buildups. The border is in a constant nepantla state and it is an analog of the planet. This is why the borderline is a persistent metaphor in el arte de la frontera, an art that deals with such themes of identity, border crossings, and hybrid imagery. "Imágenes de la Frontera" was the title of the Centro Cultural Tijuana's June 1992 exhibition.[9] Malaquías Montoya's *Frontera Series* and Irene Pérez' *Dos Mundos* monoprint are examples of the multi-subjectivity, split-subjectivity, and refusal-to-be-split themes of the border artist creating a counter art.

The nepantla state is the natural habitat of artists, most specifically for the mestizo border artists who partake of the traditions of two or more worlds and who may be binational. They thus create a new artistic space— a border mestizo culture. Beware of el romance del mestizaje, I hear myself saying silently. Puede ser una ficción. I warn myself not to romanticize mestizaje—it is just another fiction, something made up like "culture" or the events in a person's life. But I and other writer/artists of la frontera have invested ourselves in it.

There are many obstacles and dangers in crossing into nepantla. Border artists are threatened from the outside by appropriation by popular culture and the dominant art institutions, by "outsiders" jumping on their bandwagon and working the border artists' territory. Border artists also are threatened by the present unparalleled economic depression in the arts gutted by government funding cutbacks. Sponsoring corporations that judge projects by "family values" criteria are forcing multicultural artists to hang tough and brave out financial and professional instability. Border art is becoming trendy in these neo-colonial times that encourage art tourism and pop culture rip-offs, I think, as I walk into the Aztec Museum shop. Feathers, paper flowers, and ceramic statues of fertility goddesses sell for ten times what they sell for in Mexico. Of course, there is nothing new about colonizing, commercializing, and consuming the art of ethnic people (and of queer writers and artists) except that now it is being misappropriated by pop culture. Diversity is being sold on TV, billboards, fashion lines, department store windows, and, yes, airport corridors and "regional" stores where you can take home Navaho artist R.C. Gorman's *Saguaro* or Robert Arnold's *Chili Dog*, a jar of Tex-Mex picante sauce, and drink a margarita at Rosie's Cantina.

I touch the armadillo pendent hanging from my neck and think, frontera artists have to grow protective shells. We enter the silence, go inward, attend to feelings and to that inner cenote, the creative reservoir where earth, female, and water energies merge. We surrender to the rhythm and the grace of our artworks. Through our artworks we cross the border into other subjective levels of awareness, shift into different and new terrains of mestizaje. Some of us have a highly developed facultad and may intuit what lies ahead. Yet the political climate does not allow us to withdraw completely. In fact, border artists are engaged artists. Most of us are politically active in our communities. If disconnected from la gente, border artists would wither in isolation. The community feeds our spirits and the responses from our "readers" inspire us to continue struggling with our art and aesthetic interventions that subvert cultural genocide.

A year ago I was thumbing through the *Chicano Art: Resistance and Affirmation* catalog. My eyes snagged on some lines by Judy Baca, Chicana muralist: "Chicano art comes from the creation of community. . . . Chicano art represents a particular stance which always engages with the issues of its time."[10] Chicana/o art is a form of border art, an art shared with our Mexican counterparts from across the border[11] and with Native Americans, other groups of color, and whites living in the vicinity of the Mexico/United States border or near other cultural borders elsewhere in the U.S., Mexico, and Canada. Both Chicana/o and border art challenge and subvert the imperialism of the U.S., and combat assimilation by either the U.S. or Mexico, yet they acknowledge its affinities to both.[12]

"Chicana" artist, "border" artist. These are adjectives labeling identities. Labeling impacts expectations. Is "border" artist just another label that strips legitimacy from the artist, signaling that s/he is inferior to the adjectiveless artist, a label designating that s/he is only capable of handling ethnic, folk, and regional subjects and art forms? Yet the dominant culture consumes, swallows whole the ethnic artist, sucks out her/his vitality, and then spits out the hollow husk along with its labels (such as Hispanic). The dominant culture shapes the ethnic artist's identity if s/he does not scream loud enough and fight long enough to name her/his self. Until we live in a society where all people are more or less equal and no labels are necessary, we need them to resist the pressure to assimilate.

I cross the room. Codices hang on the walls. I stare at the hieroglyphics. The ways of a people, their history and culture put on paper beaten from maguey leaves. Faint traces in red, blue, and black ink left by their artists, writers, and scholars. The past is hanging behind glass. We, the viwers in the present, walk around and around the glass-boxed past. I wonder who

I used to be, I wonder who I am. The border artist constantly reinvents her/himself. Through art s/he is able to re-read, reinterpret, re-envision, and reconstruct her/his culture's present as well as its past. This capacity to construct meaning and culture privileges the artist. As cultural icons for her/his ethnic communities, s/he is highly visible. But there are drawbacks to having artistic and cultural power—the relentless pressure to produce, being put in the position of representing her/his entire pueblo and carrying all the ethnic culture's baggage on her/his espalda while trying to survive in a gringo world. Power and the seeking of greater power may create a self-centered ego or a fake public image, one the artist thinks will make her/him acceptable to her/his audience. It may encourage self-serving hustling—all artists have to sell themselves in order to obtain grants, get published, secure exhibit spaces, and receive good reviews. But for some, the hustling outdoes the artmaking.

The Chicana/o border writer/artist has finally come to market. The problem now is how to resist corporate culture while asking for and securing its patronage and dollars without resorting to "mainstreaming" the work. Is this complicity on the part of the border artist in the appropriation of her or his art by the dominant dealers of art? And if so, does this constitute a self-imposed imperialism? The impact that money and making it has on the artist is a little explored area though the effect of lack of money has been well-documented (as evidenced in the "starving artist" scenario).

Artistic ideas that have been incubating and developing at their own speed have come into their season—now is the time of border art. Border art is an art that supercedes the pictorial. It depicts both the soul of the artist and the soul of the pueblo. It deals with who tells the stories and what stories and histories are told. I call this form of visual narrative *autohistorias*. This form goes beyond the traditional self-portrait or autobiography; in telling the writer/artist's personal story, it also includes the artist's cultural history. The altars I make are not just representations of myself; they are representations of Chicana culture. El arte de la frontera is community- and academically-based—many Chicana/o artist have MAs and PhDs and hold precarious teaching positions on the fringes of universities. To make, exhibit, and sell their artwork, and to survive, los artistas band together collectively.

Finally, I find myself before the reconstructed statue of the newly unearthed el dios murciélago, the bat god with his big ears, fangs, and protruding tongue representing the vampire bat associated with night, blood sacrifice, and death. I make an instantaneous association of the bat man with the nepantla stage of border artists—the dark cave of creativity where they hang upside down, turning the self upside down in order to see from another point of view, one that brings a new state of understanding. I wonder what meaning this bat figure will have for other Chicanas/os, what artistic symbol they will make of it and what political struggle it will represent. Perhaps like the home/public altars, which expose both the United States' and Mexico's national identity, the murciélago god questions the viewer's unconscious collective and personal identity and its ties to her/his ancestors. In border art there is always the specter of death in the backgrounds. Often las calaveras (skeletons and skulls) take a prominent position—and not just of el día de los muertos (November 2nd). De la tierra nacimos, from earth we are born, a la tierra retornamos, to earth we shall return, a dar lo que ella nos dió, to give back to her what she has given. Yes, I say to myself, the earth eats the dead, la tierra se come a los muertos.

I walk out of the Aztec exhibit hall and turn in the walkman with the Olmos tape. It is September 26, mi cumpleaños. I seek out the table with the computer, key in my birthdate, and there on the screen is my Aztec birth year and ritual day name: 8 Rabbit, 12 Skull. In that culture I would have been named Matlactli Omome Mizuitzli. I stick my chart under the rotating rubber stamps, press down, pull it out, and stare at the imprint of the rabbit (symbol of fear and of running scared) pictograph and then of the skull (night, blood sacrifice, and death). Very appropriate symbols in my life, I mutter. It's so raza. ¿y qué?

At the end of my five-hour "tour," I walk out of the museum to the parking lot with aching feet and questions flying around my head. As I wait for my taxi, I ask myself, What direction will el arte fronterizo take in the future? The multi-subjectivity and split-subjectivity of border artists creating various counter arts will continue, but with a parallel movement where a polarized us/them, insiders/outsiders culture clash is not the main struggle, where a refusal to be split will be a given.

The border is a historical and metaphorical site, un sitio ocupado, an occupied borderland where single artists and collaborating groups transform space, and the two home territories, Mexico and the United States, become one. Border art deals with shifting identities, border crossings, and hybridism. But there are other borders besides the actual Mexico/United States frontera. Juan Dávila's (a Chilean artist who has lived in Australia since 1974) *Wuthering Heights* (1990) oil painting depicts Juanito Leguna, a half-caste, mixed breed transvestite. Juanito's body is a simulacrum parading the phallic mother.[13] Another Latino artist, Rafael Barajas (who signs his work as "El Fisgón"), has a mixed media piece titled *Pero eso sí . . . soy muy macho* (1989). It shows a Mexican male wearing the proverbial sombrero taking a siesta against the traditional cactus, tequila bottle on the ground, gunbelt hanging from a nopal branch. But the leg protruding from beneath the sarape-like mantle is wearing a high-heeled shoe, hose, and garterbelt. It suggests another kind of border crossing—gender-bending.[14]

As the taxi whizzes me to my hotel, my mind reviews image after image. Something about who and what I am and the 200 "artifacts" I have just seen does not feel right. I pull out my "birth chart." Yes, cultural roots are important, but I was not born at Tenochitlán in the ancient past nor in an Aztec village in modern times. I was born and live in that in-between space, nepantla, the borderlands. There are other races running in my veins, other cultures that my body lives in and out of, and a white man who constantly whispers inside my skull. For me, being Chicana is not enough. It is only one of my multiple identities. Along with other border gente, it is at this site and time, where and when, I create my identity along with my art.

Notes

I thank Dianna Williamson, my literary assistant, for her invaluable and incisive critical comments and suggestions, Natasha Martínez for copyediting this essay. Gracias also to Servicio Chicano Center in Denver for the pricey and hard-to-get ticket to the opening of the Aztec exhibition.

1. See Amalia Mesa-Bains's article "El Mundo Femenino: Chicana Artists of the Movement—A Commentary on Development and Production," in the catalog, CARA, *Chicano Art: Resistance and Affirmation*, eds. Richard Griswold Del Castillo, Teresa McKenna and Yvonne Yarbro-Bejarano (Los Angeles: Wight Art Gallery, University of California, 1991).

2. See Luz María and Ellen J. Stekert's untitled art catalog essay in [the catalog for the exhibition] "Santa Barraza," March 8–April 11, 1992, La Raza / Galería Posada, Sacramento, California.

3. Santa Barraza, quoted in Jennifer Heath's, "Women Artists of Color Share World of Struggle," *Sunday Camera*, March 8, 1992, 9C.

4. See Carmen Lomas Garza's beautifully illustrated children's bilingual book, *Family Pictures / Cuadros de familia* (San Francisco: Children's Book Press, 1990), in particular "Camas para soñar / Beds for Dreaming." Garza has three pieces in "La Frontera / The Border: Art About The Mexico / United States Border Experience" exhibition of the Museum of Contemporary Art and El Centro Cultural de la Raza in San Diego, California.

5. The Maya huipiles are large rectangular blouses which describe the Maya cos-

mos. They portray the world as a diamond. The four sides of the diamond represent the boundaries of space and time; the smaller diamonds at each corner, the cardinal points. The weaver maps the heavens and underworld.

6. Dianna Williamson, June 1992.

7. Roberta H. Markman and Peter T. Markman, eds., *Masks of the Spirit: Image and Metaphor in Mesoamerica* (Berkeley: University of California Press, 1989).

8. The exact quote is: "We have an internalization of fixed space learned early in life. One's orientation in space is tied to survival and sanity. To be disoriented in space is to be psychotic." Edward T. Hall and Mildred Reed Hall, "The Sounds of Silence," in *Conformity and Conflict: Readings in Cultural Anthropology*, eds. James P. Spradlley and David W. McCurdy (Boston: Little, Brown and Co., 1987).

9. The exhibition was part of El Festival Internacional de la Raza 92. The artworks were produced in the Silkscreen Studios of Self Help Graphics, Los Angeles and in the Studios of Strike Editions in Austin, Texas. Self Help Graphics and the Galería Sin Fronteras, Austin, Texas, organized the exhibitions.

10. See *Chicano Art: Resistance and Affirmation*, eds. Richard Griswold Del Castillo, Teresa McKenna, and Yvonne Yarbro-Bejarano (Los Angeles: Wight Art Gallery, University of California, 1991), 21. For a good presentation of the historical context of Chicana/o art see Shifra M. Goldman and Tomás Ybarra-Frausto's "The Political and Social Contexts of Chicano Art," in CARA, 83–95.

11. For a discussion of Chicano posters, almanacs, calendars, and cartoons that join "images and texts to depict community issues as well as historical and cultural themes," metaphorically link Chicano struggles for self-determination with the Mexican revolution, and establish "a cultural and visual continuum across borders," see Tomás Ybarra-Fausto's "Gráfica/Urban Iconography" in the art catalog *Chicano Expressions: A New View in American Art*, April 14–July 31, 1986 (New York: INTAR Latin American Gallery, 1986), 21–24.

12. Among the alternative galleries and art centers that combat assimilation are the Guadalupe Cultural Arts Center in San Antonio, Mexic-Arte Museum and Sin Fronteras Gallery in Austin, Texas, and the Mission Cultural Center in San Francisco.

13. See Guy Brett, *Transcontinental: An Investigation of Reality* (London: Verso, 1990). The book, which accompanied the exhibit at Ikon Gallery in Birmingham and Cornerhouse, Manchester, explores the work of nine Latin American artists: Waltercio Caldas, Juan Dávila, Eugenio Dittborn, Roberto Evangelista, Victor Grippo, Jac Leirner, Cildo Meireles, Tunga, Regina Vater.

14. See "ex profeso, recuento de afinidades colectiva plástica contemporánea: imágenes: gay-lésbicas-eróticas," put together by Círculo Cultural Gay in Mexico City and exhibited at Museo Universitario del Chopo during la Semana Cultural Gay de 1989, junio 14–23.

Unit VI. Creating Culture: Women in the Arts, Music, Literature

THE BOOTY DON'T LIE / PLEASURE, AGENCY, AND RESISTANCE IN BLACK POPULAR DANCE

Takiyah Nur Amin

And the booty will always tell the truth of a given situation. *You can always tell what a community or a person truly believes by studying the actions of their booties at any given time.* They can claim to love this other person or culture or believe in this peaceful god, or really want freedom but do their actions prove it? Their actions, what their booties do, or don't do, that tells you the truth. · JANELLE MONÁE (Emphasis added)

People are known by the records they keep. If it's not in the records, it will be said that it did not happen. That's what history is, a keeping of records. · ALICE WALKER

Black Dance: Beyond Taxonomy, Beyond Pathology

Black dance—both concert and vernacular, sacred and secular—has been explored in a variety of ways in contemporary scholarship. Citing Black dances in the diaspora as a repository of African aesthetics, Kariamu Welsh, Brenda Dixon-Gottschild, and others intervened in dance studies by situating the movement vocabularies of Black dancing bodies at the center of scholarly inquiry to expose African retentions and characteristics, both subtle and overt.[1] Susan Manning, John Perpener, and Thomas DeFrantz have engaged Black dance—particularly as it relates to the landscape of twentieth-century American concert dance—as a crucial site for historical research and the development of new considerations in performance theory.[2] Notably, as Black choreographers began to create for the concert stage, many celebrated artists imported, restaged, and made use of Black vernacular or popular dance forms in their work. Katherine Dunham's *Barrelhouse Blues* (1938) made use of popular dances of the period and is centered around the "Slow-Drag," a pelvis-to-pelvis couple's dance made popular in jook joints at that time. Alvin Ailey's *Blues Suite*, his first evening-length work, premiered in 1958 and showcased stylized versions of Black popular dances derived from his youth in rural Rogers, Texas. The staging and repurposing of Black popular dance informs much of the backbone of contemporary Black concert dance today, with the work of Camille A. Brown, Rennie Harris, Ronald K. Brown, and others as testimony. Similarly, familiar movement traditions that are today celebrated as theatrical dance forms, including tap and jazz dance, are rooted very specifically in the social dances that emanated from newly emancipated Black communities in the United States, as seen in the work of Jacqui Malone and Katrina Hazzard-Donald.[3] Hip-hop dances have had a similar migratory path, from the urban Black and Latino communities of their origin to the concert stage, music video, film, and television.

Despite the pervasive presence and generative impact of Black popular dance, it is often cited as confirmation or evidence of Black deviance and the unsuitability of Black people for the project of citizenship. The ongoing push to criminalize Black youth for breakdancing in subway cars, for example, is justified by highlighting the dance as the domain of vagrants who endanger passengers with their antics.[4] Similarly, the suspension and punishment of students from a San Diego high school for creating and posting a video of students twerking suggests the heightened anxiety that Black popular dance can bring to those in mainstream positions of authority: surely, dancing *that way* is evidence of the students' aberrant and hypersexual behavior.[5] Even the National Football League has taken a stand on the matter, updating their 1984 rule to decry "choreographed celebrations" or "excessive celebration" on the field when a player has had a successful outcome or touchdown, suggesting that the presence of popular dance is read as unsportsmanlike behavior. Players have been punished with fines and other penalties for ignoring this rule.[6] These readings of popular dances that emanate from Black communities affirm the notion that Black bodies, in which these dances have their genesis, are best understood as the site and source for every negative human behavior; these readings suggest that bad habits or behavior somehow reach their zenith in the very personhood and physicality of Black people. Undoubtedly, racism and white supremacy hinge on the notion that it is not structural or political barriers that impinge on Black life but the very culture and habits—dance included—that reside within Black bodies that are, in fact, the problem. To that end, Black bodies are always already wrong—troubled, tainted, unworthy, dispossessed. By extension, Black dancing bodies are an even larger problem as both the dances and the bodies in which they find their origin are deemed pathology in motion. The terror and indignities of kidnapping, chattel slavery, lynching, stop and frisk, mass incarceration, and misogynoir are all forms of violence levied against the very being and materiality of Black flesh as a way to tame, discipline, and/or punish Black bodies for being purveyors of deviant culture; they are convicted by their speech, dress, hair, skin color, and dance. Perhaps the lack of sustained critical engagement with Black popular dance in both public and academic scholarship is rooted in the collective trauma of the shaming, exploitation, and abuse of Black bodies. *Why, after all, would anyone want to study something that emanates from a body so worthy of ridicule and disdain?* When this perspective is considered in light of the Western notion that dance is a "feminized" act and therefore inherently less valuable as a site of knowledge production, it is not a surprise that discussions of Black popular dance very seldom find themselves at the center of rigorous public scholarship or thoughtful public discourse.[7]

I contend that there is another way. Building on the existing work of dance scholars noted above, I posit that we might understand Black popular dances and the possibility they embody by moving beyond taxonomy, beyond pathology. Writing about Black popular dance for the sake of cataloguing its characteristics is perhaps too simple; the act of merely looking at the body to truncate and disassemble it can rob us of the dance and leave our understanding in tatters. This act of classification and dismemberment (i.e., What is the head doing? What are the hips doing?) distills Black dances into easily consumable parts that belie the complexity of the whole and obscure any sense of the ideas that are residing within the movement. Engaging Black popular dance demands resistance to the tendency to boil the dances down to a laundry list of cultural characteristics. These aesthetic markers are points of departure for sure, but what needs tending is the ways in which Black popular dances embody ideas, concepts, and memory. What are the ideas that are implicated and alluded to when we "pop, lock, and drop it"? What ideologies are implicated in a body roll? Beyond any negative readings that have been projected onto these movement vocabularies and the bodies from which they emanate, it is possible to read Black popular dances as more than confirmations of cultural deviance. I propose that these dances are sites for bodily enactments of pleasure, agency, and resistance, and consider that moving one's body in the manner of one's choosing is perhaps as revolutionary an act as many others. Black popular dances are resistive precisely because they push back against that idea that Black bodies are best when used to service the needs of a system that has little regard for their existence. These dances are a harvest, a bounty of meanings that require thinking beyond thick movement description or the mere capture of dance on film or video. Engaging and perpetuating the value of Black vernacular dance requires a consideration of the ideas and meanings therein and an intimacy with the nuances that the dances themselves represent.

Black Popular Dance as Possibility

I define "Black dance" as the multiple movement idioms that arise in Black African culture and those that emerge as they are filtered through the experiences of Black people as a result of assimilating various cultural influences. I understand social and popular dances to be those that are generally recognizable, easily accessed, and widely acceptable, even if that last descriptor is up for some debate when considering Black popular dance.[8] When I think of my own experiences doing Black popular dances, those movements are tethered inextricably to memories—places, sensations, experiences whose meanings ultimately become a part of the "stuff" of the dance itself. As the sociologist Paul Connerton writes, "the past, as it were, [is] sedimented" in the body.[9] Gesture, movement, and dance are ways to get at, to reengage, to remember; dancing is an act of putting the body back together, from a truncated analysis into a complex, integrated whole, composed of an ever-changing flurry of ideas that are at once deeply personal and informed by the contexts from which they emanate. The anthropologist Janet Goodridge explains that "kinesthetic memories . . . may range from snapshot impressions to short or longer sequences of movement" and that "kinesthetic memory of movement behavior [can arise] from what is learned in social and ritual contexts."[10] This suggests that there are other ways of knowing and of accessing knowledge that resides in the body, a notion that highlights Brenda Farnell's idea that "memory [or the past] remains with us not only in words but also in our neuromuscular patterning and kinesthetic memory."[11] Without a consideration of the ideas and knowledge that reside in the dancing body, understandings of Black popular dance are rendered incomplete. Beneath imposed readings of Black bodily enactment lie memories and experiences that exist within those movements. Critical engagement with Black popular dance becomes a way to challenge prevailing assumptions, reshaping collective narratives and equipping one to get in between, up under, around, and through the readings of Black popular dance that are meant to devalue and oversimplify. In this sense, the record or history of both individual Black and collective experiences, memories, and knowledge resides within the body and is manifest, in part, through Black popular dance. The dances become a way to give voice to Black dancing bodies as repositories of trauma and pleasure, abuse and agency. Popular dances function as a means by which to connect across history and diaspora through the recognition of diverse cultural experiences. Dance challenges the contours of what we know, of what is knowable, of how we know. As human beings shape and inform cultural systems and processes through their practices, Black popular dances must be considered as formative, not just as reactive or as unchanging archives. The question becomes: How do Black popular dances shape, inform, and record experiences and speak ideas? What new possibilities are presented as movement vocabularies continue to emerge?

Pleasure, Agency, and Resistance

Given that Black dance has and continues to be a source for mainstream conceptions of the popular, it is all the more important not to diminish it in its vernacular form as a pop fad that can be reduced to a singular narrative or experience. There is no one single authoritative reading of any particular dance, and contested meanings might reside within the same embodied enactment, juxtaposing hot and cool, pleasure and pain, and conflicting representations of the self. No single story is sufficient for the understanding of

Black popular dances, and the presence of tensions and dichotomies needn't be reconciled; all can arise in time and space to occupy the dance. No single narrative encompasses the lived experiences of Black people, and as such, no single story is our dancing. As a scholarly project, engagement with Black popular dance must be expansive, challenging the false boundaries of nation, geography, and academic discipline. By rethinking disciplinary and national boundaries we have the potential to engage with Black popular dance as "vital acts of transfer, transmitting social knowledge, memory and a sense of identity through reiteration." If we accept that performance—the repetition of acts that constitute our citizenship, gender, ethnicity, sexual identity, and so on—functions as epistemology, then dance specifically offers a way of meaning-making.[12] Dance can communicate concepts, deliver pronouncements and indictments of social structures, embody memories, and carry within it the possibility of shaping and reconsidering notions of the self. The Black popular dances twerking, the Harlem Shake, and J-Setting embody these possibilities.

While twerking only recently entered mainstream consciousness, its roots stretch back to at least the early 1990s in Black communities in New Orleans. It was 1993 when DJ Jubilee first made use of the term in the New Orleans bounce anthem "Do the Jubilee All," directing partiers to "twerk baby, twerk baby, twerk, twerk, twerk" in response to his music. Later popularized by queer artists Katey Red and Big Freedia, twerking as an accompanying dance to the Big Easy's indigenous bounce music was familiar to many well before Miley Cyrus's attempt to perform the dance on MTV's 2013 Video Music Awards. Popularized a decade earlier by Atlanta rap duo the Ying Yang Twins in their debut single, "Whistle While You Twerk" and by other hip-hop artists, including Cheeky Blakk, Bubba Sparxxx, and Timbaland, mainstream pop artists such as Justin Timberlake and Beyoncé referenced twerking in their song lyrics as well.[13]

While variations on the dance abound, the execution of twerking requires bent knees and the relaxed but persistent and jubilant shaking of one's backside; alternatively, one's buttocks may be alternated and isolated in twerking. Twerking can be executed in standing, squatting, or bent-over positions and in some instances is carried out standing on one's head. The dance's iconic movement demonstrates kinship with West African movement aesthetics and shows a strong resemblance to Mapouka. Known in Côte d'Ivoire as "la dance fussier" or the dance of the behind, Mapouka is executed in both traditional and ceremonial contexts and more recently as a popular dance among Ivoirian youth. Of Mapouka, Maureen Monahan writes:

The more modern version—and the one most closely related to twerking—is considered obscene and suggestive by some, and its traditional roots haven't immunized it against controversy. In fact, the public performance of modern Mapouka by groups such as Les Tueuses (The Killers), was outlawed in the 1980s; the Ivoirian government cited lewdness as the reason for the ban. After that government was toppled by a military coup around 2000, Mapouka performances were rendered legal once again. However, despite (or possibly due to) its prohibition, the infectious dance style had already spread throughout coastal West Africa and even taken up roots in the U.S.[14]

Similar indictments of twerking have not been enacted in the United States, though "twerking" was added to the Oxford English Dictionary in 2013.

Beyond the booty shaking that is central to twerking, it is a dance that, due to its concentration in the lower regions of the body, upsets traditional Black respectability politics that privilege chastity. Hampton University went so far as to use a PowerPoint slide during a student orientation stating that "ladies do not twerk" and that "Hampton men do not take twerkers home to their mothers."[15] In a blog post on the Crunk Feminist Collective on August 29, 2013, the feminist scholar Brittney Cooper (Professor Crunk) writes, "There is [a] time and place for sexy gyration with wild abandon, and Black folks should never concede that this isn't a part of our inheritance. We recognize as we participate that ratchet is a part of who we are, but not the whole picture. And it is a part of our experience that made the blues and jazz and hip hop necessary, not just for entertainment but for survival."

Cooper's words animate some of the ideas and possibilities within twerking. The persistent presence of this kind of movement evidences an understated truth: *this dance feels good*. The relaxed posture of the lower body needed to execute twerking liberates the body from being tightly held at the base of the spine. Twerking expresses a connection to the diaspora through movement with its emphasis on polycentrism in the body (movement emanating from multiple centers), polyrhythm, and the use of a bent or soft knee posture to execute the dance. Black dance scholars have written at length about the ways in which these markers of African-derived movement vocabularies find themselves remixed and recycled within the context of Black social dance and movement practice.[16] It is plausible that the currents that suggest a connection between Mapouka and twerking in terms of their execution are not necessarily a result of immigration or U.S. residents traveling to the continent per se, but are more likely the result of the persistence of West African movement aesthetics surfacing and resurfacing in social dances in the United States, as with the movements that made up jazz dance at the turn of the twentieth century. Moreover, this insistence in twerking on "freeing up" the parts of the body—the release of the spine and freedom of the hip girdle and pelvis—needed for reproduction and regeneration of a community hints at a kind of resistance to persistent puritanical ideals about sex that suggest the body as the site for deviance: twerking often literally turns this notion upside-down by privileging the unfettered movement of the body below the navel. Given the ways in which Black reproduction has been controlled, exploited, and commodified through enslavement, forced sterilization, and other means of violent control, it is perhaps no wonder that these same communities would develop—as a resistive technology—movement vocabularies that celebrate their ability to reproduce themselves, even within the context of state violence and inhumane treatment. In the twerk there is a possibility for pleasure, for cultural connection, and for freedom of movement that pushes back against social domination. While such meanings may not be articulated by all of its practitioners, the dance itself suggests a complexity that is about much more than the shaking of one's backside.

Similar to the mainstream fascination with twerking, the Harlem Shake is a dance form that has recently captured imaginations, albeit as a result of gross misrepresentation. In 2013, short videos were posted to YouTube of riotous, often costumed partiers shaking and bouncing their torsos to the song "Harlem Shake" by Baauer, an electronic musician from the United States. As these viral videos caught the attention of news stations and college campuses across the country, residents of Harlem and others familiar with the dance's origins and iterations began to speak out on YouTube and in interviews about the history of what was being touted as a "new" dance form.[17]

The Harlem Shake was initiated by Albert Leopold Boyce, a resident of the northern city, on basketball courts some three decades before its recent resurgence. Boyce would perform the dance as a part of half-time entertainment at basketball tournaments at the world-famous Rucker Park. In a rare interview, Boyce noted, "It's a drunken shake, it's an alcoholic shake, but its fantastic, everybody loves it and everybody appreciates it. And it's glowing with glory. . . . It was a drunken dance, you know, from the mummies, in the tombs. That's what mummies used to do. They was all wrapped up and taped up. So they couldn't really move, all they could do was shake."[18]

Boyce, who died of heart failure in 2006, suggests that while the dance began with him as a drunken reverie it also hinted at the way mummies would move if awakened from death, trying to remove their bandages. The dance includes popping-style movements in the upper body, with emphasis on the shoulder and side-to-side locking movements. Practitioners may infuse other movements on top of the basic Harlem Shake structure, including splits and isolations of the head and neck. First known in the community as the "Al. B.," the Harlem Shake first garnered broader recognition in G. Dep's music videos for "Special Delivery" and especially "Let's Get It." Both videos featured Harlem native, music mogul, and G. Dep's former producer Sean "P. Diddy" Combs executing the dance. The Harlem Shake has also been referenced in music lyrics by hip-hop artists Missy Elliott and Nelly.[19]

The persistence of Harlem community residents in decrying the meme-style iteration of the Harlem Shake first popularized in 2013 suggests that the dance itself is about more than Boyce as an individual; that it is a dance that represents community identity. Taken together with other dances emanating from Harlem in the past three decades, including the Chicken Noodle Soup, the Harlem Shake functions as a text for what it means to be from that particular community. While the dance is surely executed by persons from other locales, its origins were critical enough for community members to declare it as their own and dismiss the meme as "inauthentic." This dance is intimately tied to "place"; it "belongs" to a community that in the past thirty years has seen the worst of urban blight and gentrification. Extending Boyce's drunken-mummy-shake metaphor the dance embodies a desire to shake loose what is holding one in, to throw off one's constrictive bandages and receive new life. The Harlem Shake suggests an act of claiming one's beloved origins while embodying a desire for self-determination and a breaking of boundaries, self-imposed or otherwise. This embodied push to combat being held back or held down points to an embodied agency in the dance; the Harlem Shake becomes emblematic of the capacity of a particular community to act independently and make their own choices.

Originating in the 1970s, J-Setting is another increasingly popular Black dance form. The name is derived from the majorettes at Jackson State University, known as the Prancing J-Settes. Originally known as the Prancing Jaycettes, the group was first developed under the leadership of Shirley Middleton, who sponsored and advised the group from 1970 to 1975. Middleton, a former majorette and ballet dancer, approached the university's sixth president, Dr. John A. Peoples, to ask that the majorettes be allowed to "put the baton down," removing the centrality of twirling from their routines to focus on developing and executing more intricate dance routines. Referred to as "the thrill of a thousand eyes," the Prancing J-Settes have performed on national television, and their dance style has spawned today's J-Setting dance phenomenon.[20]

J-Setting has a call-and-response structure, whereby the leader of the group initiates dance steps first and is then joined or followed by the others. The dance performance includes intricate formations, similar to those used by a collegiate marching band; the group will also march in rows organized by height. One critical aspect of J-Setting is marching with high knee lifts or "high stepping": in this style of march, alternating legs lift with a bent knee but the foot must be brought up to the height of the opposite knee before returning to the ground. J-Setting also makes use of what the Philadelphia-based choreographer Jumatatu Poe calls "sharp explosive movements choreographed in tightly executed routines."[21]

While J-Setting has found its way into the mainstream, being deployed in music videos by Beyoncé ("Single Ladies") and on the Lifetime Channel's popular show *Bring It!*, the dance has become popular as a kind of competitive dance among men in the gay African American club scene. During the late 1970s, male students observed the practice sessions and performances of the Prancing J-Settes, bringing the dance movement back to their own local communities. Today groups like the Prancing Elites compete in J-Setting dance-offs with groups at various gay cultural events across the country.

What to make of the J-Setting phenomenon, which finds its genesis on an HBCU campus and moves into Black queer club culture? When Middleton took over sponsorship and advising of the Prancing J-Settes in 1971, she established requirements for the team such as academic standards, attire, and deportment; no member of the all-female auxiliary was allowed to "display any mannerism and stature of anything less than a model citizen."[22] This remains a core value of the Prancing J-Settes today. By promoting perfection and precision in both the dance routines and public demeanor of the auxiliary members, Middleton inculcated within J-Setting culture an emphasis on crisp, high-quality execution of steps, good-natured competition, and a focus on self-presentation as art. The existence, predominantly in the South, of Black, all–male J-Setting groups alongside the presence of the original Prancing J-Settes and other female teams of varying ages suggests that the dance creates a space for the queering of gendered identities. Male J-Setting teams wear costumes that are very similar to the ones worn by the women's group, including knee-high white boots, capes, and leotards. The dance opens a space to resist socially acceptable and stereotypical notions of gendered identities: Black gay men who J-Sett can push back against social scripts about what is appropriate or suitable for men to engage in. Similarly, the hyperstylized, hyperfeminine deportment of Black women who J-Sett (as evidenced by the emphasis on long, flowing hair and movements designed to highlight the curvature of the hips, buttocks, and breasts) creates a space where they can access markers of beauty and femininity that are often reserved for non-Black women.

While the presence of predominantly Black, gay male J-Setting groups has grown to include the widely known Prancing Elites as well as the Memphis Elite, J-Phi (Atlanta, Georgia), X-Men (Grambling, Louisiana), and Detroit Danz Zone, their presence hasn't eclipsed Black women who are proficient in the form. The Prancing J-Settes at Jackson State University have maintained their visibility for over thirty years and have performed not only at football games with the JSU marching band but also in music videos and at the NAACP Awards. Similar groups abound at other historically black colleges including Howard University's Ooh La La! Dance Line, which performs movements similar to the classic interpretation of the Prancing J-Settes. The popular television show *Bring It!* showcases the work of the entrepreneur, teacher, and choreographer Dianna Williams and features the Dancing Dolls and other predominantly Black girl dance teams in the U.S. South competing in hip-hop, J-Setting, and other dance vocabularies.

The J-Setting done by the all-male Prancing Elites and similar groups shouldn't be read as merely an appropriation and reembodiment of Black female performance. It is important to remember that at its origin, the context out of which J-Setting emerges privileges the space as single-gender and homosocial. Moreover, the aspects of J-Setting that privilege hyperstylized deportment is perhaps better understood when taken on by gay men as a desire to embody and express this aspect of southern football culture. As J-Setting becomes a site where dancers are celebrated and accepted by viewers willing to be entertained and inspired by the form, it is telling that gay men who may be perceived as deviant take up the dance to challenge the boundaries of social acceptance. Read in this way, the existence of the Alabama State University Honey Beez, a group of plus-size Black women dancers who perform with the school's marching band, suggests that J-Setting can function as a site whereby those considered outside of or beyond the confines of narrow readings of beauty can challenge those dominant social assumptions.

Taken collectively these readings of specific Black popular dances, though not exhaustive, demonstrate an interest in the meanings and ideas embodied in the movement of these vernacular dances. More than "steps," Black popular dances can function as a site for multiple representations of pleasure, agency, and resistance.

Conclusion

Black dances are more than a repository of aesthetics or cultural characteristics. They are ideas and meaning in motion. Sustained, critical engagement with Black vernacular dances is an opportunity to consider those ideas more thoroughly and access the collective meanings they embody, not in an effort to reassert some grand narrative to which all Black people ascribe but as a means by which we might uncover voices and experiences that have been understudied or undertheorized. Whose voices and experiences have been left out of the dominant narrative? Dance is an act of remembrance, a chance to incorporate ideas from the fringes of our consciousness into our understanding of Black life, past and present, without sacrificing the complexity of our own lived experience. In endeavoring to write about Black popular dance, we have a ripe possibility to reassemble ideas and ways of knowing that are articulated beyond language. In writing about Black vernacular dances in particular—street dances, bad dances, nasty dances—there is an opportunity to consider not only the ideas embodied therein but what aspects of ourselves we might have overlooked, ignored, or disavowed. Who might we disinherit by not including these dances in the grand project of thinking seriously about Black history in general and Black popular culture in particular? Our embodied ideas, memories, and experiences act as a counternarrative to oversimplified, derisive, watered-down, and inaccurate tellings of Black people's story. We should take seriously what the author Jonathan Holloway, writing on the work of choreographer Alvin Ailey, called "embodied retellings of collective memory," not as a confirmation of the sameness of all Black people but as a means by which to question that which is silent in the usual retelling of our history. In this way, sustained engagement with Black popular dance functions as a way to push the boundaries of community to be more inclusive and to wrestle with complex ideas. By approaching Black vernacular dance as a site for ideas, experiences, and memories, one can pull in from the edges of one's awareness those persons, places, things that one might rather turn away from because the complexity therein troubles notions of identity and the self. Sustained engagement with Black popular dance is a subversive act because it offers up other ways for thinking about bodily enactment, with all of its complexity and tension, as sources of new ways of conceiving of ourselves, of reconstituting the Black (dancing) body, of rescuing the embodied archive from pernicious attacks on its existence. In this sense, we might proceed by dancing, writing, and documenting ourselves into the future.

Notes

Epigraphs are from "About Janelle Monáe" and "A Keeping of Records."

1 Welsh-Asante, "Commonalities in African Dance," 71–82; Dixon-Gottschild, *Digging the Africanist Presence.*
2 Manning, *Modern Dance*; Perpener, *African-American Concert Dance*; DeFrantz, *Dancing Many Drums.*
3 Malone, *Steppin' on the Blues*; Hazzard-Gordon, *Jookin'.*
4 Smith, "Yes."
5 Garcia, "Twerking YouTube."
6 Jones, "So You Think You Can Dance?"
7 Burt, *The Male Dancer*, 22.
8 Vissicaro, *Studying Dance Cultures.*
9 Connerton, *How Societies Remember*, 72.
10 Goodridge, "The Body," 121.
11 Farnell, " Moving Bodies," 353.
12 Taylor, *The Archive*, 2, 3.
13 Lynch, "A Brief History."
14 Monahan, "What Is the Origin."
15 Jacobs, "Hampton University."
16 See Dixon-Gottschild, *Digging*; Hazzard-Gordon, *Jookin'*; Malone, *Steppin' on the Blues.*
17 Schlepp Films, "Harlem Reacts."
18 "Inventor of Harlem Shake Interview."
19 Gregory, "It's a Worldwide Dance Craze."
20 "Origins and Development."
21 Quoted in Alvarez, "How J-Setting Is Changing Pop Culture."
22 "Origins and Development."

References

"A Keeping of Records: The Art and Life of Alice Walker." Accessed May 15, 2014. https://www.theguardian.com/books/2009/apr/28/exhibition-color-purple-walker.
"About Janelle Monáe." Accessed May 15, 2014. https://www.laphil.com/musicdb/artists/3679/janelle-monae.
Alvarez, Alex. "How J-Setting Is Changing Pop Culture." *ABC News*, April 26, 2013. https://abcnews.go.com/ABC_Univision/Entertainment/sette-dance-moves-loved-knowing/story?id=19041546.
Alvin Ailey American Dance Theater. "Ailey Repertory: Blues Suite." Accessed May 24, 2014. http://www.alvinailey.org/about/company/alvin-ailey-american-dance-theater/repertory/blues-suite.

Burt, Ramsay. *The Male Dancer: Bodies, Spectacle and Sexuality*. New York: Routledge, 1995.

Connerton, Paul. *How Societies Remember*. New York: Cambridge University Press, 1989.

DeFrantz, Thomas F. *Dancing Many Drums: Excavations in African-American Dance*. Madison: University of Wisconsin Press, 2002.

Dixon-Gottschild, Brenda. *Digging the Africanist Presence in American Performance: Dance and Other Contexts*. Santa Barbara, CA: Praeger, 1998.

Dunham, Katherine. "Barrelhouse Blues." In *Dancing in the Light: Six Compositions by African-American Choreographers*. DVD. 1938; Red Bank, NJ: Kultur, 2007.

Farnell, Brenda. "Moving Bodies, Acting Selves." *Annual Review of Anthropology* (1999): 341–73.

Garcia, Saudi. "Twerking YouTube: San Diego High School Students Suspended for Twerking Video." *Arts.Mic*, May 2, 2013. http://mic.com/articles/39229/twerking-youtube-san-diego-high-school-students-suspended-for-twerking-video.

Goodridge, Janet. "The Body as Living Archive of Dance/Movement: Autobiographical Reflections." In *Fields in Motion: Ethnography in the Worlds of Dance*, edited by Dena Davida. Waterloo, Ontario: Wilfrid Laurier University Press, 2011.

Gregory, Kia. "It's a Worldwide Dance Craze, but It's Not the Real Harlem Shake." *New York Times*, February 28, 2013. http://www.nytimes.com/2013/03/01/nyregion/behind-harlem-shake-craze-a-dance-thats-over-a-decade-old.html?pagewanted=all&_r=1&.

Hazzard-Gordon, Katrina. *Jookin': The Rise of Social Dance Formations in African-American Dance*. Philadelphia: Temple University Press, 1990.

"Inventor of Harlem Shake Interview." *Inside Hoops*, August 13, 2003. http://www.insidehoops.com/harlem-shake-081303.shtml.

Jacobs, Peter. "Hampton University Allegedly Lectured New Students About the 'Dangers' of Twerking." *Business Insider India*, August 29, 2013. https://www.businessinsider.in/Hampton-University-Allegedly-Lectured-New-Students-About-The-Dangers-Of-Twerking/articleshow/22148733.cms.

Jones, Jonathan. "So You Think You Can Dance? NFL Coming Down Harder Than Ever on TD Celebrations." *Sports Illustrated*, September 23, 2016. https://www.si.com/nfl/2016/09/23/nfl-excessive-celebration-penalties-antonio-brown.

Lynch, Joe. "A Brief History of Twerking." *Fuse*, August 28, 2013. http://www.fuse.tv/2013/08/brief-history-of-twerking.

Malone, Jacqui. *Steppin' on the Blues: The Visible Rhythms of African American Dance*. Champaign: University of Illinois Press, 1996.

Manning, Susan. *Modern Dance, Negro Dance, Race in Motion*. Minneapolis: University of Minnesota Press, 2006.

Monahan, Maureen. "What Is the Origin of Twerking?" *Mental Floss*, July 27, 2013. http://mentalfloss.com/article/51365/what-origin-twerking.

"Origins and Development of the Prancing J-Settes." Sonic Boom of the South. Accessed July 15, 2014. http://websites.one.jsums.edu/sonicboom/?page_id=522.

Perpener, John O., III. *African American Concert Dance: The Harlem Renaissance and Beyond*. Champaign: University of Illinois Press, 2005.

Schlepp Films. "Harlem Reacts to the Harlem Shake. Do the Harlem Shake. Harlem Shake Dance Original (v1)." YouTube, February 18, 2013. https://www.youtube.com/watch?v=IGH2HEgWppc.

Smith, Mychal Denzel. "Yes, Arresting Subway Dancers Is Still a Way of Criminalizing Black Youth." *The Nation*, July 8, 2014. http://www.thenation.com/blog/180569/yes-arresting-subway-dancers-still-way-criminalizing-black-youth#.

Taylor, Diana. *The Archive and the Repertoire: Performing Cultural Memory in the Americas*. Durham, NC: Duke University Press, 2003.

Vissicaro, Pegge. *Studying Dance Cultures around the World: An Introduction to Multicultural Dance Education*. Dubuque, IA: Kendall Hunt, 2004.

Welsh-Asante, Kariamu. "Commonalities in African Dance: An Aesthetic Foundation." In *African Culture: The Rhythms of Unity*, edited by Kariamu Welsh-Asante. Trenton, NJ: Africa World Press, 1989.

Audre Lorde, Presente!

Bettina Aptheker

At the Fourth Berkshire Conference on the History of Women held at Mount Holyoke College in August 1978 I heard Audre Lorde read her essay, "Uses of the Erotic, the Erotic as Power." The experience transformed my life. It wasn't the essay alone. It was Audre Lorde's presence, the quality of her voice, the clarity of sound, her thoughts propelled with such precision and confidence. It was also the story of how the panel got to happen and the audience response to it.

There were three participants. They had titled their session "Lesbians and Power." The program committee at the Berks unilaterally changed the title to something innocuous, deleting the word "lesbian," and scheduled it in a small room. Audre Lorde and her co-panelists were outraged. They printed a flyer (this is in the day before cell phones, computers, and email), reclaimed the word "lesbian" in their title, and secured the largest auditorium on the campus.

Two thousand women came. We listened with rapt attention. At the end of each paper there was robust applause. Then the floor was opened for discussion. A woman rose and told the story of the panel's titled obscurity and near demise. She asked if all the lesbians in the room would please stand. Almost the entire audience rose.

In August 1978 I had only recently separated from my husband, and while we had joint custody of our two young children, they lived with me. I had been struggling to come out for years, trying to overcome the terror induced by near-constant FBI and police surveillance because I was a member of the U.S. Communist Party and because I was a prominent activist in movements for civil rights, peace, and social justice. I also had been physically brutalized. I remained seated in that moment, too frightened to stand. It occurred to me that the few other women still sitting may well have also been closeted lesbians!

However, I understood the politics of solidarity. I knew that those two thousand women were not all lesbians; and I knew that Audre Lorde and her sister organizers had presented me with a miraculous moment. One year and two months later I met the love of my life, and gradually over the next several years I came out to more and more people, until I was finally able to join my two other fully "out" colleagues at the University of California, Santa Cruz, in 1983. By then I had left the Communist Party. I am immensely grateful to my students and a broad spectrum of faculty and staff for their warm support and encouragement and as grateful for the unconditional love of my partner. Still, the pivotal moment of consciousness-raising, as we used to call it, was with Audre Lorde at that panel at the Berks.

Later I wrote to Audre and asked her to send me a copy of the paper on the erotic. She did, along with a note of immense kindness. When I began teaching an introduction to feminism course at the UCSC in the winter of 1980 that essay was on my syllabus as required reading. After Lorde's book *Sister/Outsider* was published in 1984 I used it as a text, adding "Poetry Is Not A Luxury" and "The Transformation of Silence into Language and Action" as essential course readings. I taught that class through the fall of 2008, also sometimes reading selections from Lorde's poetry aloud to my students. The students loved her writing.

I taught my introductory course from a multiracial, multicultural, and, later, transnational perspective. It was explicitly antiracist. It adopted an intersectional analysis of gender, race, class, and sexuality, using the Combahee River Collectives Statement as its bellwether text, and later incorporating the work of Kimberlee Crenshaw. The course embraced lesbian and gay sensibilities, again expanding and incorporating queer and transgender perspectives as these issues emerged. It was interdisciplinary, with a range of perspectives from the humanities and social sciences and with occasional forays into the sciences, using the work of Donna Haraway, for example, or the story of the Nobel Prize–winning founder of molecular biology, Barbara McClintock.

The class had an annual enrollment of 475 to 500 students, and I worked with between twenty-six and thirty graduate and undergraduate assistants. The paid teaching assistants were graduate students, but I was never allotted more than two or three, not nearly enough for a class of that size. To compensate and so we could hold small weekly sections, I developed a system of using undergraduates and offering them five units of credit. They enrolled in my seminar Feminist Methods of Teaching, and the graduate students helped me to mentor them.

The students powered the class with their attention, enthusiasm, and oft-demonstrated courage. Lorde's writing was a key motive force that allowed it to work. Early in the quarter I had them read "Poetry Is Not A Luxury" and "The Transformation of Silence . . ." Through these readings and complimentary lectures we opened a space in which students could safely give voice to their experiences. Then came a more difficult task. Again, using Lorde as an exemplar of the method, we worked to show the students how to *connect* their experiences to a larger schema that would allow for political and theoretical analysis. Not everyone got there; not everyone was willing to make the effort. It meant close readings of additional assigned texts by, for example, feminist sociologists, historians, cultural critics, or political theorists and applying their insights into those the students had gleaned from their own experiences. However, those students who made the effort learned a way to hone their own skills of critical analysis and to gain a voice of confidence and increasing sophistication.

At the end of the quarter I asked the TAs and undergraduate assistants to write a "learning analysis" to reflect on their teaching experiences. I also encouraged them to give me feedback about course readings and lectures. Here's an excerpt from a typical paper from an undergraduate assistant in 2003:

> Audre Lorde's essay, "Poetry Is Not a Luxury," was a central tenet to the structuring of my section. For me, the fusion of creative and analytical writing is essential to developing critical writing that has both emotional and academic impact. Holding creative and analytical writing separate denies the whole existence of the author. Because of the nature of the subject matter covered in class this quarter, I emphasized experimenting with merging poetry and analytical essay writing as a way of not only engaging in Audre Lorde's project, but the project of the class as a whole. And while I was hesitant to entrust a space that could potentially backfire for many, the twenty students in my section blew me away with their work.

Students used the invitation to consider poetry as "the distillation of experience" and as a way to explore that experience, sometimes without having to literally name it because they could envelop it in a kind of imaginative context. Many who had not written poetry were inspired to do so. Sometimes the poetry was not really a poem, but prose strung together on a page to look like a poem, and sometimes we got a real juxtaposition of images and an invocation of sounds and moments and visions that broke long held silences and erasures. At times we even got new insight and a new way of understanding.

The permission to "transform silence into language and action" sometimes opened a floodgate of unexpected articulation, of performance pieces, paintings, sculptures, choreography, monologues at the end of the quarter in student presentations that transfixed me, the class, and the TAs: the enactment of the violence of rape was "without mercy" she said; "he was without mercy," and her words were w/ringing in our hearts. Birth, both a literal and metaphoric birthing, danced with such grace and passion it took our breath away. A monologue by a young man who had survived years of child sexual abuse reading the letter he had written to his mother, no longer in the voice of the abandoned and conquered child, but with the confidence of an adult, comprehension about the relationship between power and abuse, erasure and censure, articulation and healing dawning. A young Iranian woman talking about the Jewish woman who was her love, and how to handle the censure she knew would come from her family (or worse) and yet, she said, Lorde's words empowered her speech, and she felt a sense of confidence that she would figure out the best thing to do. This was their work, not mine. I felt that I simply opened a space into which they had chosen to walk.

I saved Lorde's essay "Uses of the Erotic" until the end of the quarter. In a final lecture I gave a sort of spiritual compendium by offering ways to think about movements for radical social change that were filled not so much with righteous anger as with compassion and a joyous, steady perseverance. I wanted students to think about their own best work, where they excelled, and what they most enjoyed. I analyzed Lorde's essay, suggesting the ways in which she used the *feeling* of sexual satisfaction and pleasure as an *experience* that might be replicated in nonsexual but equally erotic ways. One could think about the pleasure of writing or painting, of dancing or theorizing, of designing a building or gardening or effectively arguing a legal point, whatever it was that gave one pleasure and a deep and abiding satisfaction. This was, in Lorde's idea, erotic knowledge, and it could become "a lens through which we scrutinize" our lives, in order to do our best and most meaningful work. I joked with students that they could perhaps see that for me teaching was such an erotic experience.

I discovered that many students had not understood Lorde's essay when they first read it because they had only ever thought of the erotic in sexual terms. They got lost in its allusions, indeed, in its principle argument about the uses of the erotic and the power of the erotic. I also found, however, that one paragraph particularly spoke to them and I often read it aloud. This was the one that began "The principal horror of any system which defines good in terms of profit rather than human need . . . is that it robs our work of its erotic value, its erotic power and life appeal and fulfillment." The paragraph ends with a clear statement about the "profound cruelty" of such a system.

I think the students identified with this, perhaps because they were witness to many of their parents' unfulfilled dreams and desires or aware of their own experiences learning by rote and memorization rather than for the pleasure of discovery on its own terms, for its own sake. Whatever the reason, it seemed as though at some point in that discussion, in lecture, in section, in hearing Lorde's words read aloud and in a different context, so much came into focus for them.

Audre Lorde always described herself with multiple identities: Black, Feminist, Lesbian, mother, warrior, woman, lover, poet. She taught us that the "master's tools would never dismantle the master's house," and I thought about that as I worked intellectually and emotionally, politically and personally to break myself out of orthodox Marxist theory. She wrote the first personal/political memoir about cancer in *The Cancer Journals*, opening a floodgate for thousands, politicizing medical trauma. She embraced the struggle against apartheid in South Africa, *Leaving Our Dead Behind Us* moving us beyond grief into a vision of national and feminist liberation. She lived just long enough to see Nelson Mandela walk out of prison after twenty-seven years. Thinking about Audre Lorde now, in this retrospective, it is not only the content of her work that matters. After all, women's studies itself, and the social movements that gave rise to it, have shifted ground, this action resembling the way fissures opened by an earthquake reveal new layers of geologic meaning and interpretation. The categories of "gender," "race," "sexuality," "identity," and "global politics" have imploded, transformed, extended. Lorde's legacy is in the content of her work, but also, most important, in the fearlessness of her process; the brilliance of her mind; the relentless productive probing; digging so deep into herself; scooping out nuggets of memory and meaning, connection, and kaleidoscopic insight. This process remains for us today her precious political and intellectual legacy.

Eduardo Bonilla-Silva

2011 KEYNOTE ADDRESS

THE INVISIBLE WEIGHT OF WHITENESS: THE RACIAL GRAMMAR OF EVERYDAY LIFE IN AMERICA

I know many of you have read my book, <u>Racism Without Racists</u>, and are expecting a talk on that subject. But I have decided to present material from a book-in-progress because it better fits this year's theme, "Navigating Intersectionality." In the book project, tentatively titled "The Invisible Weight of Whiteness," I argue that racial domination necessitates something like a grammar to normalize the standards of white supremacy as the standard for all sorts of everyday transactions rendering domination almost invisible. Although racial power is defended in the last instance through coercion and violence—and I just finished an edited book on the importance of coercion and violence in everyday transactions (Jung, Vargas, & Bonilla-Silva, 2011)—coercion and violence are not the central practices responsible for the reproduction of racial domination in contemporary America (Omi & Winant, 1994). Instead, I contend racial domination generates a grammar that helps reproduce the "racial order" as just the way things are. Racial grammar helps accomplish this task by shaping in significant ways how we see or do not see, how we frame, and even what we feel about race-related matters. Racial grammar, I argue, is a distillate of racial ideology and, hence, of white supremacy. Interested parties can read what I have written about racial ideology in general (2001), and color-blind racism (2010), in particular.

To facilitate the discussion today, I want you to keep in mind the following three elements about racial grammar—and please know I am using the notion of grammar as a conceptual metaphor. First, if racial ideology furnishes the material that is spoken and argued, the racial grammar provides the "deep structure" or the "logic" and "rules" for proper composition of racial statements and, more importantly, what can be seen, understood, or even felt about racial matters. Second, although we learn "proper grammar" in school, grammar is truly acquired through social interaction and communication (Crystal, 2003). Accordingly, we absorb what I call "racial grammar" mostly through social intercourse. Third, no racial grammar completely rules any linguistic field and, if its "speakers" rebel, the grammar may change or collapse altogether. Thus, if there is a ruling racial grammar, there is always a counter-grammar and fractures that make change possible.

Before I get into my material, I am going to challenge all of you here to help me expand the scope of my original argument. I want you to think about the existence of a *social grammar*, that is, the idea that racial, class, gender, and sexual domination produce a collective grammar that allows domination on all fronts to be normalized. Although my examples today are based on racial considerations, many are, like life itself, not purely race-based. Hence, I hope I stimulate your imagination so that at the end, you can think about examples of the social grammar dealing with gender, class, or sexual orientation.

The catalyst for this project was a very pedestrian and somewhat silly incident. I was part of a *Weight Watchers* group, and we were told we had to begin our diet with an "accurate" assessment of our weight. My wife and I decided to go to the local GNC store to weigh ourselves because they had a very reliable scale. After I provided my age, sex, and height, the scale printed the following morsel in a tiny piece of paper for me: "You weigh 235 pounds and need to lose fifty pounds to reach your ideal weight." I am a tall, muscular, large-framed man, so the verdict of the scale seemed inappropriate. I believed I needed to lose *some* weight, but fifty pounds…come on! Yet, the cold, seemingly "factual" verdict remained. According to this scale, I was fat and far off my ideal weight. In fact, my Body Mass Index, or BMI, was 31, which was one unit above the lower range of those classified as "obese."

At least initially, this scale's dictum depressed me, as reaching my "ideal weight" seemed impossible! But suddenly, it hit me! Did my African ancestry have anything to do with the whole thing (I am a handsome black man from Puerto Rico)? And how does this scale determine one's "ideal weight"? First, people of African descent in the USA *seem* to be, as African Americans say, "big boned," that is, our bones are anywhere between 5 to 15% denser than the bones of white people

(Hubbard, 1995). And please know I am not reifying or biologizing race. I am just making a probability statement and limiting it to the USA. In the future we will have to study the interaction of environmental factors and genetics to explain why this is the case. Second, and most important, the scale made an assessment about my "ideal weight" based on presumably universal data. However, the "universe" used as the standard for the original notion of "ideal weight" was elite white people in Europe. The formula for calculating ideal body weight was developed in 1871 by the anatomist Dr. Paul Broca—it is known as the "Broca Index." But what many of the people who use this formula today do not know is that Dr. Broca, like many "men of science" of his time, was in the business of measuring physical differences between "nationalities," "races," and men and women to demonstrate the presumed superiority of elite European men (Gould, 1981). On his work measuring crania, Broca said:

> In general, the brain is larger in mature adults than in the elderly, in men than in women, in eminent men than in men of mediocre talent, in superior races than in inferior races....Other things being equal there is a remarkable relationship between the development of intelligence and the volume of the brain (as cited by "Widely Used Body Fat Measurements Overestimate Fatness In African-Americans, Study Finds," 2009, p. 83).

Recent research suggests that Blacks have, on average, more muscle (Grace, 2008), which makes the BMI and waist circumference measure less reliable for determining all sorts of things.

This incident, and my quest to understand what shaped it, made me think long and hard about the idea that something like a grammar is affecting, if not altogether directing, our cognition and emotions on all sorts of racial matters. And I wondered whether such grammar is ultimately *as important* as all the visible structures and practices associated with white supremacy.

BEAUTY AND THE BEAST

Let me offer a few examples of how the racial grammar of contemporary America organizes a racialized field of interpretation and vision. The subject of one of the chapters in the book, titled "Beauty and the Beast," came out of an "Aha" moment. I was watching the *Nancy Grace* show one night when she said the following:

Breaking news tonight! At yet another college campus, a beautiful 22-year-old president of the UNC Chapel Hill student body, double major, biology, poli sci, last seen 1:30 AM doing homework, 5:00 AM, shots fired, 22-year-old Eve Carson found dead out in the intersection near campus, multiple gunshot wounds. (Santos, 2007)

Did you catch the problem with this statement? The problem, as a few of you guessed, is with the adjective "beautiful." TV hosts such as Nancy Grace seem to always describe a missing or murdered young white woman as "beautiful." We checked transcripts of Grace's show and other similar crime shows such as FOX's *Greta Van Susteren* to see if there was a pattern, and we found that in cases dealing with the disappearance or murder of young white women, the adjective was there, but when the victim is a black or Latino woman, (1) they are seldom discussed in the first place (although they too are victims of violence)[1] and (2), when discussed, the adjective is not there.

The underrepresentation of minority female victims, by the way, has been discussed by journalists, media critics, and minority victims' group advocates. Roy Peter Clark, vice president and senior scholar at the Poynter Institute, a training center for journalists in St. Petersburg, Fla., said: "Sex sells, kidnapping sells, but not every kidnapping is equal" (Bobo, 2006). Sheri Parks, Professor of American Studies at The University of Maryland, calls it the "missing white woman syndrome" and adds that: "since we can't solve all the problems, since we can't save all the women, this woman becomes a symbol...and...for a few days, we are OK" (Samuels, 2001).

The notion of racial grammar helps us understand the structure of this unsavory "racial situation." First, stories about whites become universal stories about all of us. This is how whites frame these stories symbolically but, of course, this is not the case in reality. When Laci Peterson (the woman killed by her husband in Modesto, CA) disappeared in 2002, Evelyn Hernandez, a Salvadorean woman went missing, and like Peterson, her decapitated torso was also found in the San Francisco Bay.

---

[1] The most recent victimization survey shows that black women endure a rate of 23.3 per 100,000 compared to white women's rate of 16.7. See Table 6 in U.S. Department of Justice, "Criminal Victimization in the United States, 2008 Table," (Bureau of Justice Statistics, 2011).

In 2005, the year Natalee Holloway disappeared, LaToyia Figueroa, a black Puerto Rican pregnant woman from Chester, PA, also disappeared—but no one has heard of her. Second, the beauty element in these stories reflects what Toni Morrison has articulated so well in novels such as *The Bluest Eye*, "that all modes of representation in our current culture tend to idealize the desire for whiteness and devalue the presence of blackness" (Goldberg, 1993, p. 8). This social fact remains despite years of symbolic and practical struggle against white supremacy. Normative whiteness is still the not-so-hidden standard—the cultural essence of 500 years of "racist culture" (Sala-Molins, 2006), a culture that since Kant, Voltaire, Hume, and all the other enlightened white men of Europe and America, has depicted nonwhites as ugly and *particular* and whites as beautiful and *universal* (hooks, 1996).

WATCHING WHITENESS

Now I provide examples from another chapter titled, "Watching Whiteness: White Movies and White TV Shows." The idea for this chapter came from a conversation I had 14 years ago with Tyrone A. Forman, then a student at Michigan and now a professor at Emory University. He declined to join a group of us to go out for a movie because he did not enjoy watching "*white* movies." I gave him what I now regard as a white line—"Man, you see racism in everything!" Like most whites, I thought, "This dude is hypersensitive. A movie, after all, is just a movie." I now realize he was right and I was wrong; I now realize how deeply I was affected by the racial grammar which prevented me from appreciating the depth of whiteness in movies.

In terms of movies, bell hooks has suggested that "to experience the pleasure that cinema [can offer, blacks have] to close down critique, analysis; they [have] to forget racism" (hooks, 1996, p. 203) (2003, p. 203). Our visual culture expects (maybe even demands) that people of color suspend belief and become white-like, otherwise "no soup for you" (no pleasure for you). On movies and TV shows, we have plenty of work from scholars such as Hernán Vera (Denzin, 2002), Norman Denzin (2004), Herman Gray (2005), Darnell Montez Hunt (2005), and Stephanie Greco Larson (2009). Both Vera and Denzin provide a historical interpretation of the "cinematic racial order"—an order that evolved from civilizational racism (*Birth of the Nation* to *Gone with the Wind*) and almost total whiteness to the modern-day cultural racism where people of color appear mostly in secondary, stereotypical roles.

I will not delve on this subject deeply: however, I will say a few general things. First, racial minorities are still underrepresented in movies and TV. Even in movies where we should be, we are not or are appear in a twisted way (the movie *21* (2008)). Second, when minorities appear in mainstream movies, they still are given mostly stereotypical roles (e.g., thugs, buffoons, & angry people). And Hollywood folks seem to never get it right, so even in so-called "progressive" movies, such as *Avatar* (2009), depicted as an anti-colonialist film, or *The Blind Side* (2009), sold as an anti-racist film, Hollywood reproduces the racial order of things. In the former, the colonized are saved by a Neo-Tarzan white character (Hollywood never dares have us liberating ourselves in movies), while in the latter, race conflicts are portrayed as simple misunderstandings that can be settled by the "great white hope" played by Sandra Bullock (similar to *Mississippi Burning* (1998)).

Another stereotypical way in which black characters appear in movies is when they play the role of "magical negroes" --black people who are given some "power" and whose job in the plot of a movie is helping whites navigate their lives (Prosise & Johnson, 2004). Examples abound: Will Smith in *Hancock* (2008), Whoopi Goldberg in *Ghost* (1990), Morgan Freeman in *Bruce Almighty* (2003) and *Evan Almighty* (2005) (you can play God in a movie and, if you are black, still be second banana), and Michael Clark Duncan (recently deceased) in *The Green Mile* (1999).

Third, the storylines in films and TV shows tend to a) reinforce racial boundaries, b) bolster the racial status quo, and c) present a felicitous view of racial affairs. We see examples of racial boundary-setting in TV shows like *Friends* (1994-2004), *Cheers* (1982-1993), *Everybody Loves Raymond* (1996-2005), *How I Met Your Mother* (2005-), where minority characters seldom appear and, when they do, last but a few episodes. Or in movies like *Hitch* (2005)—with Will Smith and Eva Mendes, since white-black romantic comedies are still a no-no (Cole, 2006) and black-on-black romance is still regarded as a black movie, so whites will not see it; thus, their choice for a black man with a light-skinned Latina (but not too light; they did not choose Cameron Diaz). These storylines also bolster the racial order, as in crime shows like *America's Most Wanted* (1988-), *COPS* (1989-) *(Dixon, 2008)*, and the local news (Malanowski, 2002), all of which distort the reality of crime and "criminals". In reality TV shows, people of color are hard to find and, when they are there, are usually portrayed as pushy or hard to get along with, like in the case of Omarosa in *The Apprentice* (2004-) or most minorities on *Big Brother* (1999-) or *The Biggest Loser* (2004-). Lastly, these shows present a felicitous, simple-minded view of racial affairs in buddy movies such as *48 Hours* (1982), *Lethal Weapon* (1987), *I Spy* (2002), *White Men Can't Jump* (1992), and almost all Jackie Chan movies: they create the impression that if we just get to know each other, we can become friends because "racism" is simply a matter of not knowing one another well, and, more problematically, a property we all have (as in *Crash* (2004)). As an aside, if you want to know why interracial buddy movies are made by the dozen, the answer is *money*! Movie critic Jamie Malanowski calculated in 2002 that "the average gross of black-and-white buddy movies is $101,939,175 while the average gross for all buddy movies is $67,081,163" (Sykes, 2004).

Before I move on, I must confess that I am addicted to movies and watch several per month. But the racial grammar that makes white movies seem universal (for everyone), while black movies are framed as particular (for black folks only), is getting to me. White folks do not watch good movies such as *Obsessed* (2009), *Why Did I Get Married Too*, *For Colored Girls…*(2010), or *The Heart Specialist* (2010). Instead, they watch buffoon movies such as *Big Momma's House* (2000), or movies that reinforce racial stereotypes such as *Precious* (2009), or movies that present whites as heroes and distort history, such as *The Help* (2011).

ALL OF OUR CHILDREN

Let me now discuss material from a chapter titled "All of Our Children," in which I address the matter of child abductions. Most of us here probably recognize the names Elizabeth Smart, from Utah, or the "adorable" Kyron Horman from Oregon. But who amongst us recognizes the names Alexis Patterson, Laura Ayala, or Anthony Thomas? The latter are names of minority children abducted in the last few years and only Alexis' case, the Milwaukee girl abducted seven years ago, received any serious media attention. But the abduction of Elizabeth Smart, which happened at the same time as Alexis', received six times more news coverage (Menifield, Brewer, Winfield, & Homa, 2002).

Is this because minority children are not likely to be kidnapped? Actually, 20% of all "stereotypical child kidnappings" (Glassner 2010) involve minority children, so one would expect that about 1 out of every 5 child abduction news stories would involve minority children. To sum up the issue here, I cite Alexis Patterson's stepfather, who stated before the 2002 National Association of Black Journalists' convention that

We have nothing against the other kids that have been missing... We know their parents hurt the same way we do and are grieving the same way. We want the same attention for our child so we can have just as much a chance of getting [Alexis] back as they do. (Wise, 2001)

BAD BOYS, BAD BOYS: SCHOOL SHOOTINGS IN WHITE, BLACK, AND BROWN

Now I discuss examples from a chapter titled, "Bad Boys, Bad Boys: School Shootings in White, Black, and Brown." Although 9 out of 10 children killed in schools die in urban schools, and although violent acts are 11.5 more likely in urban, relative to rural and suburban, schools,[2] white America is only morally distraught by tragedies such as the one in Columbine. Why is this the case? Eugene Kane, a writer for the Milwaukee Journal Sentinel, said it best in a 2006 piece after a shooting in Cazenovia, WI, and an alleged plot in Green Bay:

When tragedy hits a small town or city, the sympathy swells up for all involved. When young people die in Milwaukee's central city, too often the reaction from outsiders is to point fingers and blame residents for tolerating the violence.

He then added,

Suburban and rural white students caught in gunfire get immediate grief counselors dispatched to the scene. Black and brown city kids surrounded by violence have to resolve their emotional issues all by themselves. (Kane, 2006)

For those who believe these shootings are, in fact, different events and thus ought to be treated differently, Menifield et al. (1998) clearly suggest this is not the case. The authors document that even when one compares similar types of school-shooting events, the media coverage is

---

[2] For a robust study on school shootings, see Katherine S. Newman, Cybelle Fox, David Harding, Jal Mehta, and Wendy Roth, *Rampage: The Social Roots of School Shootings* (New York: Basic Books, 2004).

disproportionally weighted toward white schools. More significantly, the authors find that the tone of the coverage is different: articles dealing with shootings in white schools report the news in ways to elicit the sympathy of their readers, whereas articles dealing with shootings in urban schools portray these shootings as examples "of the usual violence in urban America" and betray a concern with accountability.

And if your racialized imagination is telling some of you, "Well, I am not a racist, but…aren't minority kids more likely to be involved in drugs, alcohol abuse, and bringing weapons to schools than white children, so…" you are in for a surprise. Antiracist activist Tim Wise, who is white, citing data from the Center of Disease Control, stated:

> …white high school students are seven times more likely than blacks to have used cocaine; eight times more likely to have smoked crack; ten times more likely to have used LSD and seven times more likely to have used heroin. … What's more, white youth ages 12-17 are more likely to sell drugs: 34% more likely, in fact than their black counterparts. And it is white youth who are twice as likely to binge drink, and nearly twice as likely as blacks to drive drunk. And white males are twice as likely to bring a weapon to school as are black males. (Provasnik & Shafer, 2004)

These sobering facts led Wise to state: "I can think of no other way to say this, so here goes: white people need to pull our heads out of our collective ass" (2004). Although this is a very cute statement, it is a sociologically flawed one. "Facts" matter very little on the things I have been discussing today. What ultimately counts in the real world weaved by race is whites' *perceptions* about blacks—specifically, their perception of black men as criminalblackmAn, to use Katheryn Russell-Brown's term (1996). And the same racial grammar prevents whites from accepting the fact that it is their children who are more likely to use drugs and bring weapons to school than black and brown children.

HWCUs

Now I discuss an example that is closer to home: H*W*CUs. The "racial" character of H<u>B</u>CUs is tattooed in their very name. We believe that these colleges are all-black institutions (although non-black faculty account for 45% of faculty at HBCUs (Turner, 1994)) and that they have a Black agenda. However, "we" never ponder about the whiteness of the places in which we labor; we rarely question the history and practices that created and maintain these institutions white. Instead, we conceive of them in universalistic terms, that is, as *just* colleges and universities. However, these colleges have a history, demography, curriculum, climate, and a set of symbols and traditions that embody, signify, and reproduce whiteness. For example, most traditions in HWCUs, such as homecoming, predate their so-called "integration" and thus are exclusionary. And while some traditions are almost innocently exclusionary, such as Friday afternoon tea at Smith College or yearbooks, some are highly racialized, as with offensive, anti-Indian mascots (Fenelon, 2000).

The demography of these places is such that a black student interviewed by Feagin, Vera, and Imani in their book, *The Agony of Education,* stated, after visiting a private college in the Northeast, that "I was only there for two days, and after one day I wanted to leave. And I mean, really, it just reeked everywhere I went, reeked of old white men, just lily whiteness, oozing from the corners!" (2000, p. 5) The demography and symbols in HWCUs create an oppressive racial ecology where just walking on campus is unhealthy; where minority students feel, as one observer commented, as "guests [who] have no history in the house they occupy. There are no photographs on the wall that reflect their image. Their paraphernalia, paintings, scents, and sounds do not appear in the house" (Parenti, 2007, p. 356)

This oppressive ecology is worse in college towns, as the businesses in the area reproduce/reflect the whiteness of HWCUs. Hence, local businesses and even local people cater to white interests—a practice that leads to a "defending one's turf" mentality. For example, four years ago, an employee at Ed's Express, in Madison, WI, approached a group of black students eating dinner and told them, "I'm sick of you people leaving piles of shit all over our tables," and added, "I want you to leave the premises. I don't want you here" (Gendall, 2005).

CONCLUSION: WHY SHOULD WE CARE ABOUT "RACIAL GRAMMAR"?

In the book I will write about other things such as "Be Nice to Me as I Buy Your Stuff Too" (race and selling commodities), "We the (White) People" (race and citizenship), a chapter on "When Whites Love a Black Politician" (race and Obama), a chapter on "I Want to Adopt a (White or Asian) Baby" (race and adoptions), and a chapter on "Race and Academia" (Sociology). However, I must conclude now to leave some time for discussion and debate. Therefore, let me articulate why studying the contemporary racial grammar of the USA is so important and suggest what we can do to fight this grammar, which, as Marx said, "weighs like a nightmare on the brains of the living" (Alexander, 2010). Racial grammar must be challenged because, like air pollution, it is hard to see clearly, yet it is out there poisoning us all. It affects people of color deeply. It affects our cognitive map as well as our sense of self and even how we view and what we do to our bodies (hair politics), what we do to our skin and eyes (bleaching creams), and what we do to other parts of our body (including cosmetic surgery).

Needless to say, the racial grammar shapes whites' racial cognitions, too, and more deeply than it does folks of color. More importantly, the racial grammar prevents whites from truly empathizing with people of color. Otherwise, when our votes are stolen (as they were in the 2000 election (Parenti, 2007)), when the death penalty is applied to us at unbelievably high rates (Alexander, 2010), or when our children are abducted and their stories are not mentioned by the media, our white brethren would be up in arms, as they would regard "an injury to one" as "an injury to all." This human solidarity, unfortunately, does not happen because these horrid things are not processed by whites as they are for folks of color. In short, these things are, for whites, *ungrammatical*.

But all forms of domination generate resistance (Garner, 2007). First, as I pointed out at the outset, the racial grammar has not completely ruled the grammatical field of the nation. Segregation has always provided what historian Lawrence Levine (2011)has labeled the "necessary space"—the schoolyard—for people of color to see the racial world differently than whites. And within this space, people of color have been able to develop an alternative racial grammar that has prevented them from absolute "mental slavery." Through that partial alternative grammar, people of color have posed challenges to things such as the white normative beauty standard and provided counter-standards, such as "Black is beautiful." They have made movies such as 2007's *The Great Debaters*, produced by Oprah Winfrey and directed by Denzel Washington, in which unlike classic so-called anti-racist movies (e.g., *Mississippi Burning, AMERICAN X* (1988), or *Crash*), the heroes were not whites but blacks themselves. Even the recent B-movie, *MACHETE* (2010), directed by Richard Rodriguez with Danny Trejo as the leading man, provided an important counter-narrative to the contemporary discourse on immigration. On TV, we have had shows such as *In Living Color* (1990-1994), the short-lived *David Chapelle's Show* (2003-2006), and five years of HBO's *The Wire* (2002-2008). And, yes, all of these efforts have had serious limitations (e.g., *In Living Color*'s rampant sexism), but they all provided frontal challenges to the dominant racial common sense. On the importance of challenging ruling racial dogmas, David Simon, *The Wire*'s creator and writer, said in his farewell letter:

> We tried to be entertaining, but in no way did we want to be mistaken for entertainment. We tried to provoke, to critique and debate and rant a bit. We wanted an argument. We think a few good arguments are needed still, that there is much more to be said and it is entirely likely that there are better ideas than the ones we offered. But nothing happens unless the shit is stirred. That, for us, was job one. (Simon, 2008)

Accordingly, we need to get busy to get "job one" done. We must develop an epistemology of racial emancipation as a necessary corrective to the racial grammar that fosters and reflects the "moral economy of whiteness" (Garner, 2007). But please know that epistemology and counter-ideological struggles alone have not liberated *anyone* in history! Thus the task at hand for us in this peculiar and contradictory moment in America's racial history is to organize a movement of racial liberation; to work towards change we can *truly* believe in. Dominant grammars collapse when the oppressed fight back! Then, and only then, will the grammar of America be multicultural, democratic, and reflect the views, interests, and feelings of all of us in our America.

REFERENCES

Alexander, M. (2010). *The New Jim Crow: Mass Incarceration in the Age of Colorblindness*. New York: The New Press.

Bobo, L. (2006). *Prejudice in politics : group position, public opinion, and the Wisconsin treaty rights dispute*. Cambridge, MA: Harvard University Press.

Bonilla-Silva, E. (2001). Anything but Racism: How Social Scientists Limit the Significance of Racism. *Race and Society, 4*, 117-131.

Bonilla-Silva, E. (2010). *Racism Without Racists: Color-Blind Racism and the Persistence of Racial Inequality in the United States*. Lanham, MD: Rowman and Littlefield Publishers, Inc.

Cole, S. (2006). The Skin Game: Why can't Denzel Washington score with white women on screen? Retrieved September 18, 2012, from http://www.cbc.ca/arts/film/skingame.html

Crystal, D. (2003). *The Cambridge Encyclopedia of Language* (2nd ed.). Cambridge, MA: Cambridge University Press.

Denzin, N. (2002). *Reading Race: Hollywood and the Cinema of Racial Violence*. New York: Sage.

Dixon, T. (2008). Crime News and Racialized Beliefs: Understanding the Relationship Between Local News Viewing and Perceptions of African Americans and Crime. *Journal of Communication, 58*, 106-125.

Feagin, J. R., Vera, H., & Imani, N. (1996). *The Agony of Education*. New York: Routledge.

Fenelon, J. V. (2000). Indian Mascots in the World Series of Racism. In P. Batur, J. R. Feagin & G. Moute (Eds.), *The Global Color Line* (Vol. 6, pp. 25-45). New York: JAI Press.

Garner, S. (2007). *Whiteness: An introduction*. New York: Routledge.

Gendall, M. (2005, March 16). Protesters Rally at Ed's Express. *Badger Herald*. Retrieved from http://badgerherald.com/news/2005/03/16/protesters_rally_at_.php

Glassner, B. (2010) *Culture of Fear, Revised:Why Americans Are Afraid of the Wrong Things Crime, Drugs, Minorities, Teen Moms, Killer Kids, Mutant Microbes Plane Crashes, Road Rage, & So Much More*. New York, NY: Basic Books

Goldberg, D. T. (1993). *Racist Culture: Philosophy and the Politics of Meaning*. Malden, MA: Wiley-Blackwell.

Gordon, A., & Vera, H. (2003). *Screen Saviors: Hollywood Fictions of Whiteness*. Lanham, MD: Rowman and Littlefield.

Gould, S. J. (1981). *The Mismeasure of Man*. New York: W.W. Norton & Co.

Grace, N. (2008). UNC Student Body President Found Shot to Death Near Campus. *CNN Transcripts* Retrieved 9/6/12, from http://transcripts.cnn.com/TRANSCRIPTS/0803/06/ng.01.html

Gray, H. (2004). *Watching Race: Television and the Struggle for Blackness*. Minneapolis, MN: University of Minnesota Press.

Greco Larson, S. (2005). *Media & Minorities: The Politics of Race in News and Entertainment*. Lanham, MD: Rowman and Littlefield.

hooks, b. (1996). *Reel to real: Race, sex, and class at the movies*. New York: Routledge.

Hubbard, R. (1995). *Profitable Promises: Essays on Women, Science, and Health*. Monroe, ME: Common Courage Press.

Hughey, M. (2009). Cinethetic Racism: White Redemption and Black Stereotypes in "Magical Negro" Films. *Social Problems, 56*(3), 543-577.

Jung, M.-K., Vargas, J. C., & Bonilla-Silva, E. (2011). *The State of White Supremacy: Racism, Governance, and the United States*. Palo Alto, CA: Stanford University Press.

Kane, E. (2006, October 3). Violence has no color or ZIP code. *Milwaukee Journal Sentinel*.

Malanowski, J. (2002, November 10). Colorblind Buddies in Black and White. *New York Times*. Retrieved from http://www.nytimes.com/2002/11/10/movies/colorblind-buddies-in-black-and-white.html

McLellan, D. (Ed.). (2000). *Karl Marx: Selected Writings*: Oxford University Press.

Menifield, C., Brewer, A. K., Winfield, R., & Homa, J. (2002). The Media's Portrayal of Urban and Rural School Violence: A Preliminary Analysis. *Deviant Behavior, 22*, 447-464.

Montez Hunt, D. (Ed.). (2005). *Channeling Blackness: Studies on Television and Race in America*. Cambridge, MA: Cambridge University Press.

Omi, M., & Winant, H. (1994). *Racial Formation in the United States: From the 1960s to the 1990s*. New York: Routledge.

Parenti, M. (2007). The Stolen Presidential Elections. from http://www.michaelparenti.org/stolenelections.html

Prosise, T., & Johnson, A. (2004). Law enforcement and Crime on Cops and World's Wildest Police Videos: Anecdotal Form and the Justification of Racial Profiling. *Western Journal of Communication, 68*(1), 72-91.

Provasnik, S., & Shafer, L. L. (2004). *Historically Black Colleges and Universities, 1976 to 2001*: NCES, US Department of Education--Institute of Education Sciences.

Russell-Brown, K. (1998). *The Color of Crime: Racial hoaxes, white fear, black protectionism, police harassment, and other microaggressions*. New York: New York University Press.

Sala-Molins, L. (2006). *Dark Side of the Light: Slavery and the French Enlightenment*. Minneapolis, MN: University of Minnesota Press.

Samuels, R. (2001). *Writing Prejudices: The Psychoanalysis and Pedagogy of Discrimination from Shakespeare to Toni Morrison*. New York: SUNY Press.

Santos, M. C. (2007). Missing People Face Disparity in Media Coverage. *MSN Lifestyle*.

Simon, D. (2008). A final thank you to The Wire fans, from show creator David Simon. *HBO The Wire Interviews*, fromhttp://www.hbo.com/the-wire/inside/interviews/article/finale-letter-from-david-simon.html

Sykes, L. J. (2004, May 1). Public interest in finding missing girl dims: but after 2 years, some maintain hope that Alexis Patterson will be found. *Milwaukee Journal Sentinel*.

Turner, C. S. (1994). Guests in Someone Else's House: Students of Color. *The Review of Higher Education, 17*(4), 350-370.

Widely Used Body Fat Measurements Overestimate Fatness In African-Americans, Study Finds. (2009, June 22). *Science Daily*.

Wise, T. (2001, March 5). School shootings and white denial. *AlterNet*.

Unit VII. Violence Against Women

Anti-Black Sexual Racism: Linking White Police Violence, COVID-19, and Popular Culture

Tamari Kitossa

Half a century ago, James Baldwin (1965), Frantz Fanon (1967), and Joel Kovel (1971) asserted that erotic and sexual racism is fundamental to the pleasure principle of power; quite specifically, the pleasure of sadistic sexual power in colonialist and racist regimes. At the point of existential articulations of the imperatives of White supremacist institutions and systems, racist sexual dominance remains a current running through arrests, beatings, murders, surveillance, strip searches, and stop and frisks of Black people. Equally, sadistic sexual racism is canalized by malignant neoliberal policies of racism that choke, chop, imprison, starve and sicken Black individuals, families and communities (Curry 2017; Foster 2019; Kitossa 2021; Lemelle 2010; Roberts 2011; Thomas 2007; Wynter 1994).

Consistent with sexual racism, a variety of population control mechanisms, including criminalization, mass imprisonment, segregation, sterilization and toxic exposure, express the anti-Black genocidal imperatives of capitalism and White supremacy (Dillon 2012). By means of the bureaucratic administration of Black death-making, the "necropolitical state" (Mbembe 2003) empowers manifest and latent White supremacists (conservatives and liberals alike) to seek Black submission through the enforcement of ordinary rules of social organization. But what has (White) police and vigilante violence and COVID-19 to do with the sadistic sexual racism of (White) individuals and the White racial state?

Here we turn to the murders of George Floyd and Breonna Taylor by police this year—but we must go beyond the incidental that George Floyd and Breonna Taylor were both AfricanAmericans. Relevantly, Floyd's autopsy revealed he was COVID-19 positive, and Taylor was soon to be a nurse, bringing into sharp relief the realities of the pandemic, since the virus disproportionately affects Black communities and since many Black women are in caregiving positions at high risk of contracting the virus. But neither Floyd nor Taylor were understood as human beings made vulnerable to the virus through racisms and deserving support during the pandemic. Rather, they were seen only as threats to be literally eliminated through murder, a deadly truth that speaks to the persistence of sexualized anti-Black racist tropes—him as *Predator* and her as *Alien*.

The Predator

What makes Black men killable (Van Natta 2011), rapable (Brenner 2007; England 2017), torturable (Guarino 2013), castratable (Heggs 2014; Holcombe and Moon 2020) and demonized (Campbell 2020) by White cops and vigilantes? There is Ahmaud Arbery, killed in Brunswick, Georgia by a retired cop, Gregory McMichael, and his son, Travis McMichael. There is George Floyd, killed by Minneapolis police officer Derek Chauvin. And the list goes on... As Douglas Flowe (2020), Tommy Curry (2017), Vincent Woodard (2014) and Greg Thomas (2007) all demonstrate, each of their murders form part of a pattern of search and destroy since transatlanticslavery.

Plantations, slave ships and the auction block—sites for the manufacture of exploitable labour—set the trend. While the myth that Black men (and women) did not feel pain emerged during slavery (Washington 2006), the myth that Black men are superhuman did not fully develop until the 1930s Tuskegee syphilis experiment (Randall 1996). 50 years after this medically sanctioned experiment on Black men, the 1987 Hollywood film launched the *Predator*series (Travis 2018), depicting a big, dark, "dreadlocked" and super virile male. White art converges with White medical science and White history to reconfigure anti-Black White supremacist violence as justifiable, anticipatory self-defense against violent Black men incapableof feeling pain.

So great a portent of danger were Black children believed to be that in 2005 William "Bill" Bennett, former Secretary of Education for President Ronald Reagan and a popular radio talk-show host, suggested aborting them, if crime reduction were the political objective (Faler 2005). Making this comment on his syndicated talk show, Bennett was only following through on the genocidal logic implicit in an earlier, written declaration about young Black men. Along with his co-authors John DiIulio and John Walters, he asserted in race-coded language that (African American) youth are "super predators": "radically impulsive, brutally remorseless youngsters, including ever more pre-teenage boys, who murder, assault, rape, rob, burglarize, deal deadly drugs, join gun-toting gangs, and create serious communal disorders" (Bennett et al.1996: 27). Clearly prenatal genocide was more efficient than throttling Black babies in their cribs; Black infant deaths are routinely manufactured through racist policies that breed disease, poverty and starvation among Black families. Prenatal genocide is more efficient, as well, than the more laborious task of police murdering Black children, youths and adults in the streets.

Although considered controversial at the time, Bennett's views are not extreme, but part of long established traditions in the highest circles of American politics. In 2006, Hillary Clinton praised her spouse President Bill Clinton's 1994 Crime Bill for its containment of those she referred to as "super predators" with "No conscience, no empathy" (C-Span 2016), in vocabularies saturated with anti-Black connotations. Joe Biden, Democratic senator in Delaware in 1994 and now President-elect of the United States, was an enthusiastic supporter of Bill Clinton's "get tough on crime" policies. Like the Clintons, Biden mobilized the trope of dangerous Black men to justify draconian anti-welfare and pro-criminalization policies, launching the mass incarceration of young Black men in the United States. It is ironic that in hindsight the dispute is whether Biden used the term "predator" or "super predator" (see Reuters2020). Does it matter?

The Alien

Across the United States, the murder and physical assault of Black women by police (Crenshawand Ritchie 2015; Williams 1987) is a pattern, similar to the violence suffered by Black men butinformed by different gendered, racialized imaginaries from American popular culture. Among the most recent deaths of Black women caused by the police is Breonna Taylor, murdered in a "no knock raid" by Louisville police officer Brett Hankison (Boynton 2020), supported by officers Myles Cosgrove and Jonathan Mattingly. There are between 50,000 and 80,000 paramilitary home invasions by the police in the United States each year (Balko 2014; Barnett and Alongi 2011)—as many invasions as there are people attending an average National FootballLeague game. Too often, these police home invasions result in unaccountable slaughter. Citizensin the United States and around the world need to ask hard questions about the "full spectrum dominance"—to borrow a term used to justify irregular American warfare abroad (Ryan 2014)—regularly mobilized against Black people by the police in these home invasions.

The roots of such anti-Black brutality are multiple and deep. First, there is the classist and White supremacist so-called "war on drugs", which is the prime rationale for police forces to kick down people's doors

(Bauer 2014). From Harry Anslinger (Smith 2018) through to Richard Nixon (Baum 2016), anti-Black racism has always been the prime justification for the "war on drugs". Second, and relatedly, through the modern architecture of civil asset forfeiture pioneered in 1983 by now President-elect Joe Biden (Calton 2019), police routinely shakedown US citizens for all they are worth (Miller 1996; Nunn 2002); assets ranging from cash to property are seized from (Black) citizens who are presumed guilty of involvement in the illegal drug trade or other criminal activity. Third, the totalitarian National Defense Authorization Act (Barrett 2020; Goodman 2012; United States Congress 2020) enables the Pentagon to funnel millions of dollars of "outmoded" military hardware to police forces across the country. And finally, but not exhaustively, there is an ever complicit and pliant judiciary (what else could they be?) who enable police thugs to operate under what is euphemistically called the "rule of law" (see Klasfeld 2013; Plakas v. Drinski 1994). The rule of law permits secrecy in policing; secrecy in policing permits unaccountability; and unaccountability in policing is the essence of legalized lawlessness by the state against its own Black citizens.

These practices have long histories of justification at the highest levels of American politics. In 1980, when then Presidential candidate Ronald Reagan took a page from Richard Nixon's playbook and relaunched the "Southern Strategy" campaign to win the American South, he combined regressive neoliberal economic policies with White supremacist dog whistle tropes about poor African Americans and the myth of the Black welfare "queen" (Inwood 2015). But the White politics of the Reagan campaign did not stand alone. Before Reagan, there was Daniel Moynihan's (1965, 1970) grotesque rendering of Black women as a super-fecund castrating, domineering, poor and modern ghetto plantation animal—the Black woman of the neoliberal White imaginary.

Both Reagan and Moynihan's tropes of sexual racism have a metaphorical parallel in Ridley Scott's 1979 film *Alien*: a constantly breeding and feeding Black female monster. *Alien* spoke to the anti-Black zeitgeist of White America, with its imagery of a carbon-Black, devious, roach-like resilient and unkillable *Alien* who threatened the White body (politic) with her womb, hence the need for continued sterilization (Roberts 1993; Waweru 2019). Artistic culture and political culture under White supremacy mesh and merge, belying the myth that they are separate. The fear of the *Alien*'s reproductive capacity, palpable in Moynihan's (1965, 1970) missives, is that she will continue to produce and (mis)socialize poor and socially excluded, disaffected young Black boys and men: imagined as useless eaters who, along with fecund Black women, endanger the White Republic.

We need not imagine this is a case of American exceptionalism. The anti-Black artistic and popular culture and exclusionary immigration policies of the United Kingdom and its colonial off-shoots (Australia, Canada, Aotearoa New Zealand, and South Africa) have not only been historically anti-Black and pro-White, there is now a palpable fear of so-called "genetic extinction", the idea that a White "race" is not reproducing as quickly as Black and racialized Americans so leading to the end of White "race" (Jacobs 2019). Where Blackness is defined as the essence of the problem, genocide is implicit: so, why not simply kill the mother alien before she really gets going, and wage total war on the predators who "stalk" the streets?

Sexual Sadism and Anti-Black Racism

When the federal government in the United States socialized slavery with the 13th Amendment, it asserted the property status of African Americans as public rather than privately fungible. Police and prisons, thereafter, took on the status of overseers and the whole of the United States became a plantation. Lynch mobs linked the state and the White masses in an orgy of sadistic anti-Black sexual terror. Today, the diseasing of Black America through genocidal policies of benign indifference that have made COVID-19 rife among African Americans, clasps hands with the malign intent of the criminal industrial complex. As Baldwin (1965), Fanon (1967) and Kovel (1971) insisted, unless we pay attention to the psychosexual pathology of White supremacy, materialist analyses, no matter how excellent, will not explain the sexual sadism at the heart of anti-Black social determinants of police violence and manufactured Black vulnerability to the pandemic.

Acknowledgments

Thanks to Jennifer Adkinson, Wesley Crichlow, Adisa Deliovsky, Katerina Deliovsky, EricaLawson, and Delores Mullings.

References

Baldwin J (1965) *Going to Meet the Man*. London: Michael Joseph

Balko R (2014) Shedding light on the use of SWAT teams. *Washington Post* 17 February https:// www.washingtonpost.com/news/the-watch/wp/2014/02/17/shedding-light-on-the-use-of-swat-teams/ (last accessed 28 November 2020)

Barrett B (2020) The Pentagon's hand-me-downs helped militarize police: Here's how. *Wired* 2 June https://www.wired.com/story/pentagon-hand-me-downs-militarize-police-1033- program/ (last accessed 28 November 2020)

Barnett R and Alongi P (2011) Critics knock no-knock police raids: The increasing use of surprise tactic raises privacy, risk questions. *USA Today* 14 February https://usatoday30.usatoday.com/news/nation/2011-02-14-noknock14_ST_N.htm (lastaccessed 28 November 2020)

Bauer S (2014) The making of the warrior cop. *Mother Jones* 23 October https://www.motherjones.com/politics/2014/10/swat-warrior-cops-police-militarization-urban-shield/ (last accessed 3 December 2020)

Baum D (2016) Legalize it all: How to win the war on drugs. *Harper's Magazine* April https://harpers.org/archive/2016/04/legalize-it-all/ (last accessed 28 November 2020)

Bennett W J, DiIulio J J and Walters J P (1996) Body Count: Moral Poverty…and How to WinAmerica's War against Crime and Drugs. New York: Simon & Schuster

Boynton S (2020) Breonna Taylor death: Fired police officer shot "blindly" in "reckless conduct", chief says. *Global News* 23 June https://globalnews.ca/news/7099793/breonna- taylor-police-officer-fired-actions/ (last accessed 28November 2020)

Brenner M (2007) Incident in the 70th Precinct. *Vanity Fair* 16 January https://www.vanityfair.com/magazine/1997/12/louima199712 (last accessed 28November 2020)

Calton C (2019) How a young Joe Biden became the architect of the government's asset forfeiture program. *Foundation for Economic Education* 9 March

https://fee.org/articles/how-a-young-joe-biden-became-the-architect-of-the-governments-asset-forfeiture-program/ (last accessed 28 November 2020)

Campbell J (2020) NYPD defends "challenge coins" that call East Flatbush Precinct "Fort Jah".

The Gothamist 30 August https://gothamist.com/news/nypd-defends-challenge-coins- dubbing-east-flatbush-precinct-fort-jah (last accessed 28 November 2020)

C-Span (2016) 1996: Hilary Clinton on "superpredators". 25 February https://www.youtube.com/watch?v=j0uCrA7ePno (last accessed 30 November 2020) Crenshaw K W and Ritchie A J (2015) "Say Her Name: Resisting Police Brutality against Black

Women." African American Policy Forum and Center for Intersectionality and Social Policy Studies https://aapf.org/sayhernamereport/ (last accessed 28 November 2020)

Curry T J (2017) *The Man-Not: Race, Class, Genre, and the Dilemmas of Black Manhood.* Philadelphia: Temple University Press

Dillon S (2012) Possessed by death: The neoliberal-carceral state, Black feminism, and the afterlife of slavery. *Radical History Review* 112:113–126

England C (2017) French police say "anal rape" of suspect with officer's truncheon was an accident. *The Independent* 10 February http://www.independent.co.uk/news/world/europe/french-police-anal-rape-suspect-truncheon-paris-officer-accident-sodomised-expandable-baton-theo-a7572581.html (last accessed 28 November 2020)

Faler B (2005) Bennett under fire for remark on crime and Black abortions. *The Washington Post* 30 September http://www.csun.edu/~bashforth/155_PDF/BennettBlackBabiesandAbortion.pdf (last accessed 28 November 2020)

Fanon F (1967) *Black Skin, White Masks* (trans C L Markmann). New York: Grove

Flowe D J (2020*) Uncontrollable Blackness: African American Men and Criminality in Jim Crow New Yor*k. Chapel Hill: University of North Carolina Press

Foster T A (2019) *Rethinking Rufus: Sexual Violations of Enslaved Men.* Athens: University of Georgia Press

Goodman A (2012) Journalist Chris Hedges sues Obama Administration over indefinite detention of US citizens approved in NDAA. *Truthout* 18 January https://truthout.org/articles/journalist-chris-hedges-sues-obama-administration-over-indefinite-detention-of-us-citizens-approved-in-ndaa/ (last accessed 28 November 2020)

Guarino M (2013) Chicago Mayor Rahm Emanuel apologizes for two decades of police torture.

The Christian Science Monitor 12 September https://www.csmonitor.com/USA/Justice/2013/0912/Chicago-Mayor-Rahm-Emanuel- apologizes-for-two-decades-of-police-torture (last accessed 28 November 2020)

Heggs D (2014) Sexual assault by police equals ruptured testicle for high schooler. *Liberty Voice* 23 January http://guardianlv.com/2014/01/sexual-assault-by-police-equals-ruptured-testicle-for-high-schooler/ (last accessed 28 November 2020)

Holcombe M and Moon S (2020) A Black activist who trained police officers on implicit bias was injured with rubber bullet during protest. *CNN* 9 June https://www.cnn.com/2020/06/09/us/san-jose-police-training-activist-rubber-bullets-trnd/ index.html (last accessed 28 November 2020)

Inwood J F (2015) Neoliberal racism: The "Southern Strategy" and the expanding geographies of White supremacy. *Social and Cultural Geography* 16(4):407–423

Jacobs T (2019) A fear of "White extinction" is provoking racial bias among American Whites. *Pacific Standard Magazine* 3 June https://psmag.com/news/a-fear-of-white-extinction-is- provoking-racial-bias-among-american-whites (last accessed 28 November 2020)

Kitossa T (2016) Making sense of repression in police studies: Whither theorizing in the descenttoward fascism. *Radical Criminology* 6:247-321 http://journal.radicalcriminology.org/index.php/rc/article/view/79/pdf (last accessed 28 November 2020)

Kitossa T (ed) (2021) *Appealing Because He Is Appalling: Black Masculinities, Colonialism, and Erotic Racism.* Edmonton: University of Alberta Press

Kovel J (1971) *White Racism: A Psychohistory.* New York: Pantheon Books Lemelle A J (2010) *Black Masculinity and Sexual Politics.* New York: Routledge Mbembe A (2003) Necropolitics. *Public Culture* 15(1):11-40

Miller R L (1996) *Drug Warriors and Their Prey: From Police Power to Police State.* Westport:Praeger

Moynihan D P (1965) "The Negro Family: The Case for National Action." Office of Policy Planning and Research, United States Department of Labor https://www.dol.gov/general/ aboutdol/history/webid-moynihan (last accessed 28 November 2020)

Moynihan D P (1971) "Memorandum for the President, 16 January." Richard Nixon Presidential Library and Museum https://www.nixonlibrary.gov/sites/default/files/virtuallibrary/documents/jul10/53.pdf (last accessed 28 November 2020)

Nunn K B (2002) Race, crime, and the pool of surplus criminality: Or why the "war on drugs"was a "war on Blacks". *Journal of Gender, Race, and Justice* 6(2):381–446

Plakas v. Drinski (1994) "No. 93-1431, 19 F.3d 1143; Argued 1 November 1993, Decided 21 March 1994; United States Court of Appeals, Seventh Circuit." http://www.caselaw4cops.net/ cases/plakas_v_drinski_19f3d1143_7cir_1994.html (lastaccessed 28 November 2020)

Randall V R (1996) Slavery, segregation, and racism: Trusting the health care system ain'talways easy!—An African American perspective on bioethics. *St. Louis UniversityPublic Law Review* 15(2):191–235

Reuters (2020) Fact check: Hillary Clinton, not Joe Biden, used the term super predator in 1990s. 26 October https://www.reuters.com/article/uk-factcheck-hillary-clinton-biden-super-idUSKBN27B1PQ (last accessed 28 November 2020)

Roberts D E (1993) Crime, race, and reproduction. *Tulane Law Review* 67:1945-1977

Roberts D E (2011) *Fatal Invention: How Science, Politics, and Big Science Re-create Race in the 21st Century.* New York: New Press

Ryan M (2014) "Full spectrum dominance": Donald Rumsfeld, the Department of Defense, and US irregular warfare strategy, 2001–2008. *Small Wars and Insurgencies* 25(1):41–68

Smith L (2018) How a racist hate-monger masterminded America's War on Drugs. *Timeline* 28 February https://timeline.com/harry-anslinger-racist-war-on-drugs-prison-industrial- complex-fb5cbc281189 (last accessed 28 November 2020)

Thomas G (2007) *The Sexual Demon of Colonial Power: Pan-African Embodiment and Erotic Schemes of Empire*. Bloomington: Indiana University Press

Travis B (2018) The *Predator* synopsis promises genetically upgraded predators. *Empire Online* 27 April https://www.empireonline.com/movies/news/predator-synopsis-promises-genetically-upgraded-predators/ (last accessed 25 November 2020)

Van Natta D (2011) Race issues rise for Miami Police. *The New York Times* 22 March https://www.nytimes.com/2011/03/23/us/23miami.html (last accessed 28 November2020)

Waweru N (2019) The disturbing history of forced sterilisation of Black women in US. *Face2Face Africa* 19 January https://face2faceafrica.com/article/the-disturbing-history-of-forced-sterilisation-of-Black-women-in-u-s (last accessed 24 November 2020)

Washington H (2006) *Medical Apartheid: The Dark History of Medical Experimentation on Black Americans from Colonial Times to the Present*. New York: Doubleday

Williams P (1987) Spirit-murdering the messenger: The discourse of fingerpointing as the law's response to racism. *University of Miami Law Review* 42(1):127–157

Woodard V (2014) *The Delectable Negro: Human Consumption and Homoeroticism within US Slave Culture* (eds J A Joyce and D A McBride). New York: New York University Press.

Wynter S (1994) "No humans involved": An open letter to my colleagues. *Forum N.H.I.:Knowledge for the 21st Century* 1(1):42–73

ANGELA Y DAVIS AND ASSATA SHAKUR AS WOMEN OUTLAWS: RESISTING U.S. STATE VIOLENCE[1]

Mechthild Nagel
State University of New York, Cortland

Abstract

Angela Yvonne Davis and Assata Olugbala Shakur share histories of struggle and outlaw status in the face of intense state repression. Both revolutionary freedom fighters were captured after spending time underground as a result of intense surveillance and being marked for outlaw status, in part for their participation in solidarity work for imprisoned Black Panther members. In sexist language, they were typecast as "mother hens" of their respective organizations and thus singled out for the FBI's Most Wanted "criminals" or "terrorists" list. Despite their experiences with state violence, Angela Davis, now a distinguished professor with international stature, and marooned activist Assata Shakur continue to speak out against racist and sexist injustices as well as against global capitalism and inspire a new generation of activists.

Introduction

Nothing gives us x-ray vision to the ills of society like the daunting experience of incarceration, especially the horror of solitary and death row, as well as the intense stress of anticipating or being subjected to torture or extra-legal execution. During much of her pre-trial incarceration (of sixteen months) Angela Davis was kept in solitary confinement. The other activist woman featured in this essay, Assata Shakur, was broken out of prison precisely because she feared for her life—not by other prisoners, but by the state's agents. It would have been extremely difficult to receive justice after flawed trials that intended to show that she was guilty of murdering a white state trooper, even though there was no evidence that could corroborate such motive or deed. In fact, the post-Ferguson photo montages and demonstrations with protestors' hands raised symbolically and shouts of "hands up, don't shoot" could have easily been used as rallying cry to demand Shakur's acquittal. In all likelihood, she had her hands raised while being shot into her right hand, making it impossible for her to hold a gun, let alone to shoot what was not meant to be. At the height of a secret and illegal government program COINTELPRO, which the FBI mounted to destroy the Black Panther Party (with which both Davis and Shakur worked) and all other organizations which protested state terror and imperialist warfare, Shakur was found guilty by a white jury not of her peers (Shakur, 1987).

Prisons have always served the role of social control (Kurshan, 1996), but they are also tremendous sites of cultural, social and political activity, namely as diasporic sites (Nagel, 2008). Nobody has more acutely theorized about the function of imprisonment than political prisoners, thus they find themselves singled out for acute repression and women are equally targeted. Part of it may be the authorities' fear of such prison intellectuals' savvy critique of hegemonic ideologies and uncanny ability to see through the level of disinformation by elite corporate media. This ability often is borne inside the dungeon. For my purposes here, political prisoners include people convicted due to their resistance to repressive state policies and politics and those who become politicized while facing detention and/or long prison sentences. Many political prisoners such as Assata Shakur and Angela Davis have engaged in prisoners support work *before* they were incarcerated themselves. For opposing the state, they face further reprisals by the prison authorities. For instance, if a prisoner complaints "we are treated like slaves!" within earshot of guards, she may get time in the "hole"—weeks in solitary confinement, as if she had committed the act to call for a slave insurrection. Ironically, the complainant is simply stating the obvious: The U.S.

Thirteenth Amendment to the Constitution, which putatively abolished slavery, describes prisoners as legal slaves. Therefore, they do not enjoy freedom of speech or freedom to assemble peacefully within a total institution. However, the US government denies confining people for political convictions and that all so-called political prisoners are duly convicted of a (terrorist) crime. Yet, the US government's claim is hardly credible, in particular in light of CIA run prisons, which defied even U.S. Supreme Court rulings, notably Abu Ghraib in Iraq and Guantánamo Bay, Cuba. In addition, the state routinely disappears prisoners who are not a security threat into supermax prisons, which contribute to (mental) health abuse and premature death (Amnesty International, 2014).

Much mainstream reporting or prison literature ignores the gendered nature of prisons (and ignores writings by revolutionary prison intellectuals altogether). For instance, the mass media did not focus on Iraqi women prisoners who had also been sexually abused, raped, humiliated and even disappeared, as the human rights groups International Women Count Network, Black Women's Rape Action Project, and Women against Rape have charged (Groves, 2004). Such "disappearance" of women is disturbing, especially in light of the dramatic media display of U.S. personnel's torture against Iraqi male detainees. Women and feminist prisoners' rights activists the world over report that women's imprisonment is always considered an afterthought (cf. Nagel, 2013). Some of it has to do with the demographics, since most countries' incarceration rate of women hovers around six percent, whereas in the U.S. manages it is nine percent of a total population of 2.3 million prisoners. However, as Angela Davis (2003) has reminded us, the rate of women, especially Black women, has increased in the U.S., Canada and other countries around the world due to the global war on drugs.

This article foregrounds two revolutionary women's autobiographies and highlight their importance as neo-slave narratives. Their analysis is not reducible to a liberal human rights critique of appalling prison conditions, since they also give us a conceptual framework to understand prisoners' resistance to repression akin to enslaved people's insurrections within the U.S. historical context. Angela Y Davis and Assata Shakur, two iconic Black women and former imprisoned intellectuals, specifically address the racialized and gendered carceral aspects of capitalist "justice." Both evaded capture by the state for some time in the 1970s, and, in the case of Shakur, she continues to be marooned in Cuba, which does not have an extradition agreement with the United States. How is it that both these women, passionate in their pursuit for social justice for oppressed peoples became political outlaws? Having experienced criminal injustice, their analyses, written in the tradition of neo-slavery narratives, are able to give us important insights about a) the function of the penal system and its policing/enforcement mechanisms within a capitalist system; b) the paradox of utilizing legal procedures; and c) the importance of political organizing and of envisioning abolitionist alternatives to challenge state sponsored criminal injustice.

I want to highlight Davis and Shakur's biographies to make light of their radicalization and anti-racist activism within the Black Power movements in the 1960s and 70s (and beyond), which engendered their reputation as "outlaws." However, their activism in the Black Panther and Black Liberation Army was short-lived, critiquing the organizations for hierarchical, male-dominant posturing, as much as they were also aware of governmental infiltration (before the FBI's nefarious scheme was made public). They both wrote their autoethnographic books within a decade after their imprisonment and trials at a relatively young age. Both women have been at one point on the FBI's Most Wanted list; in Shakur's case, she made the Most Wanted Terrorist list, which even notes that she is the first woman on that list (http://www.fbi.gov/wanted/wanted_terrorists).

It is also noteworthy to point that that it is rare for female political prisoners to publish their experiences (cf. Dearey, 2010, p. 97). By contrast, everybody is familiar with Nelson Rohlihlahla Mandela, "prisoner number one" turned statesman, and his book *Long Road to Freedom* (1995) turned into a Hollywood movie, his wife Winnie Madikizela-Mandela's writing is forgotten. The title of her book *Part of my Soul Went with Him* (1985) already focuses on the relationship and her fierce loyalty to her imprisoned husband, rather than alluding to her own struggle and resistance against apartheid. Winnie Mandela experienced repeatedly imprisonment and house arrest and bore the extra pressure of caring for their children. In the U.S., students read Dr. King's celebrated "Letter from Birmingham Jail" or his "I have a Dream" speech, but it is doubtful that they would be treated to Professor Davis's provocative essay "From the prison of Slavery to the Slavery of Prisons" (in James, 1998). One reason is the officially sanctioned ideology that with the end of Jim Crow all vestiges of chattel slavery have been extinguished from the legal canon: prisons houses only those who are duly convicted of a crime, and students receive no explanation what the exception clause means embedded in the 13th Amendment to the U.S. constitution: prisoners are deemed slaves (of the state). These main-streamed students probably will not view Cuban filmmaker Gloria Rolanda's (1997) moving film *Eyes of the Rainbow* about Cuban resident-in-exile Ms. Shakur—of course, it does not help that the film is no longer commercially available; nor will students know of her radio address (1973) "To my people" while she was imprisoned. In her appeal, she explains the continuation of systemic racism even while racism seems forbidden *de jure*. In other words, neither Davis nor Shakur present a vision of the following optimism: Racism will disappear if a policy of colorblindness is pursued. Their work resists the selective re-reading of a prophetic "Dream" speech: Dr. King, of course, talked about the need of reparations, of economic justice for Black people; none of that makes its way into political stump speeches today. Instead, the opportunistic focus is on the utopia of postracial unity among Black and white children, which is a palatable vision in a white supremacist polity.

Both Davis and Shakur's writings represent unique *neo*-slave narratives. They are written as provocation: to defy a white supremacist, triumphalist pedagogy of American history, which simply teaches that slavery is relegated to the past. As Joy James (2005) argues Black radical intellectuals' analyses differ from liberal perspectives by focusing on abolitionism rather than on reform of the prison system. Theirs is a clarion call to acknowledge the continuation of chattel slavery within the capitalist, carceral structure of the prison (and "free" society) in the United States of the 20th Century. I argue that prison critics, especially white critics, collapse all Black women's writings into one ideological perspective, as if there were no theoretical and programmatic difference between Michelle Alexander's bestseller *The New Jim Crow* (2010), which presents a liberal view on "mass incarceration," and Angela Davis's *Abolition Democracy* (2005), which by contrast seeks to abolish "the prison industrial complex." However, Davis and Shakur's writings tend to be obscure because they challenge the state's legitimation as "penal democracy" (cf. James, 2007). In Shakur's case, the threat is even greater, since she continues to be depicted as a "cop killer" (sic), and the Fraternal Order of Police succeeded in getting her framed as a domestic terrorist.

In the following, I present biographical sketches of Davis and Shakur to show that these Black women political prisoners aptly theorize the paradox of using the law for revolutionary struggle against white supremacy, patriarchy and capitalism. Their political engagement in service to others presents a clue how they defy a description of heroic iconization (*pace* James, 1999). Instead, Davis aptly puts their agenda of collective transformation in the following way:

> Social meanings are always socially constructed, but we cannot leave it up to the state to produce these meanings, because we are always encouraged to conceptualize change only as it affects individuals. There is a dangerous individualism that is not unrelated to the possessive individualism of capitalism. And it is bound to transform these collective victories we win. If we imagine these victories as community victories and they are transformed into individual victories, then what happens is that we seek heroic examples, we seek individuals. There is a whole

array of people like [Alberto] Gonzales, [Clarence] Thomas, and [Condoleezza] Rice. And then what happens is that we forget about the structural changes that were actually intended by those struggles. (Davis, 2012, p. 132)

I will briefly mention a comparison of an unlikely couple, namely of two Birmingham women who have made history: Angela Davis and Condoleezza Rice, before linking Davis's Southern with Shakur's North Eastern struggle against injustice.

Defying the Odds: Angela Yvonne Davis

By all foreseeable measures, Prof. Angela Y Davis ought to have followed Condoleezza Rice's biographical trajectory rather than Assata Shakur's, namely by joining the ranks of the Talented Tenth (cf. James, 1997). Or, perhaps Rice should have followed Davis's revolutionary example. Both Davis (born 1944) and Rice (born 1954) grew up in the Jim Crow South, in a particularly violent city, Birmingham, Alabama, where Black homeowners were terrorized by the Klan. Birmingham became known as "Bombingham," and they were shaken by the news of their playmates (Rice) or friends of the family (Davis) being murdered in a church basement in 1963, while engaging in civil rights activism. Both of them had teachers as parents who instilled in them a passion to excel in education despite the intense challenges of a segregated, inferior public school, and as teenagers, they left the South permanently to study at private highschools. They learned to speak French fluently, and then later in life another language: Davis studied German in Frankfurt and Rice Russian in Moscow for their respective postgraduate education. In some ways, both have been decried as "outlaws"—and this is where the similarities end: Rice's parents shielded her from participating in the children's marches in Birmingham, while Davis's parents actively participated in anti-racist progressive struggles and had ties to Communist Party members (Maloney, 2014; James, 1998; Davis, 2011). Serving as state department official during the G.W. Bush administration, Rice was heavily criticized for condoning water boarding of terrorist suspects; in other words, she is accused of participating in various aspects of state violence (including supporting the Iraq invasion in 2003), if not state-sponsored terrorism. However, Rice's reputation has not been diminished as she continues to be a member of the elite capitalist class (member of corporate boards and think tanks) and a professor at Stanford University (Maloney, 2014). Occasionally, she faces protests as university students protest her appearance as commencement speaker because they consider her a war criminal (Democracy Now!, 2014). So, ironically, for a person who benefited from racial uplift, sheltered education, Prof. Rice has now become a "persona non grata"—in fact, a moral outlaw due to students' moral outrage. By contrast, as a former political outlaw, Prof. Davis's intellectual star power could not be greater: her alma mater, Goethe University, Frankfurt, installed an Angela Y Davis Visiting Professorship for international Gender and Diversity Studies in 2013 (Cornelia Goethe Centrum, 2014).

Davis's outlaw status emerges in the following biographical account. Her experience as an activist (and ultimately, as "outlaw" activist) began at home receiving encouragement from her parents, as well as family friends, and her Quaker educators in New York city. They imparted upon her that it is ethically important to engage in solidarity work with those who were fighting for social justice and against state repression. Her mother Sally Davis was a key Southern organizer in the NAACP and providing support for the Scottsboro Boys who were decades in prison before being cleared of charges of rape (McDuffie, 2012). Angela Davis (2012) acknowledges her own support work for political prisoners as a pre-condition for becoming a political prisoner herself. This certainly was the case for many activists, including Assata Shakur (see below). Upon her return to the United States, Davis followed her Brandeis University mentor Herbert Marcuse to University of California at San Diego, to study the meaning of freedom (Kelley, 2012) and providing legal support for a court-marshaled Black Navy officer (James, 1998). After attaining her M.A. and beginning her doctoral studies at the

University of California at San Diego, she immersed herself in solidarity work for political prisoners, which she continued as assistant professor of philosophy at the University of California at Los Angeles (UCLA). Davis had other job offers but accepted UCLA's offer, so that she could live in a Black community (Neumann, 2008); she had felt quite isolated during her studies in Southern France (Kaplan, 2012) and in Germany, which was one of the reasons why she didn't pursue her doctoral work with Theodor Adorno in Frankfurt. However, Davis voices surprise that she was the most experienced organizer when she arrived on UCLA's campus (Davis, 1974; Davis, 2012).

Davis found herself caught up in Cold War anti-Communist controversies by being publicly identified as a member of the Communist Party USA; in fact, she joint the Che-Lumumba Club, one of the few Black branches of the CP. (In the same year, she had also joined the Panthers, but that membership lasted for a mere two years.) She lost her assistant professor position, only to be reinstated after much public outcry and collegial support, an important lesson about the limits of abstract rights (freedom of speech or academic freedom) and the power of organized protest. Davis courageously defended her membership publicly; at the same time, she pointed out that this question regarding her membership was illegal. However, the victory was short-lived, since she refused to back down as a political activist, as other junior academics would have done. Davis became Los Angeles chair of the Soledad Brothers Defense Committee for Black prisoners at Soledad State Prison, accused of killing a white guard. This was the final straw as her activism was deemed unbecoming of a university professor (and certified her status as "outlaw"). UCLA fired activist scholar Davis in 1970 and drew censure from the American Association of University Professors (Neumann, 2008). Then-Governor Reagan infamously declared that she would never again be hired in the state university system (Kautzer et al., 2004). Due to her imprisonment, she was not able to complete her doctorate in philosophy, but Davis received an honorary doctorate in philosophy from the Karl Marx University, Leipzig (German Democratic Republic) in 1972 (Kaplan, 2012).

In 1991, after twenty years working as part time instructor, Davis was appointed a professor in the History of Consciousness Program at UC Santa Cruz and became presidential chair of African and Feminist Studies in 1994 (Feminist Studies, 2014). However, this professorship did not proceed without a fight: after all, Reagan's vow was remembered by the Board of Regents who raised severe objections to her professorship in the California system. Furthermore, when she opposed a state-wide anti-affirmative action policy, which in turn was championed by Regent Ward Connolly, he castigated her for her progressive stance and demonized her for her past: "your record as a revolutionary is not merely disturbing but it may impair your effectiveness as a member of the faculty of one of this nation's most highly respected academic institutions" (James, 1998, n.19, p. 22). Connelly's rhetoric unleashed a longstanding, acceptable tradition of redbaiting in light of Davis's affiliation with the Communist Party which included candidacy as Vice President in 1980 and 1984. In the 1990s, she broke with the Communist Party and joined with like minded reformists the Committees of Correspondence before accepting the full professor position. Clearly, Professor Davis is not a Black woman academic who has learned her civic lessons well, namely that it is more opportune to collude with state power (Rice's example) than to oppose it.

Davis's most important collision was in 1970, when she became the third woman (and first philosopher?) to appear on the FBI's Most Wanted List. She was charged with conspiracy, kidnapping, and homicide, due to her alleged participation in a prisoners' escape attempt from Marin County Hall of Justice. Allegedly, Jonathan Jackson, younger brother of prison inmate and *cause célèbre*, George Jackson, had taken the guns from Davis's home to use in the escape attempt. She evaded the police for two months before being captured in New York city, tried, and against the odds, acquitted of all charges eighteen months later. While being held in the Women's Detention Center in New York City,

Davis got on well with other inmates and with the help of her outside supporters was able to mobilize the prisoners, in particular, helping to initiate a bail program for indigent prisoners. Even as prisoner, Davis was an incessant organizer!

For much of her incarceration, Davis was segregated from the general population in deplorable conditions, but with the help of her excellent legal team she obtained a federal court order squashing that practice (Davis, 1988 [1974]). The administration's excuse was that prisoners might be hostile to her, but, as in Shakur's case, most of the other prisoners were friendly and supportive. The state tends to be punitive against political prisoners, and enormous resources have to be spent to mount a legal defense, over and above what is necessary for preparing for trial. In 1972, Angela Davis was exonerated on all charges by an all-white jury after a world wide campaign to "Free Angela," which also sparked a cultural forms of expression. Prior to her aquittal, several musicians including the Rolling Stones's song "Sweet Black Angel" brought awareness to her trial (Moussaoui, 2013). So, political organizing clearly increases in effectiveness (this is especially true in the age of social media) when moral outrage against injustice is buttressed through playful, symbolic interventions.

Davis, now distinguished professor emerita of UC Santa Cruz, continues to be active in political prisoners' campaigns, notably Mumia Abu-Jamal's, and in the prison abolitionist movement. Recently, writing about the legacy of Assata Shakur, she alerts us to the state's language of violence, labelling a revolutionary thinker as "terrorist":

> Four decades after the original campaign against her, the FBI decided to demonise her once more. Last year, on the 40th anniversary of the New Jersey turnpike shoot-out during which state trooper Werner Foerster was killed, Assata was ceremoniously added to the FBI's Ten Most Wanted Terrorist list. To many, this move by the FBI was bizarre and incomprehensible, leading to the obvious

question: what interest would the FBI have in designating a 66-year-old black woman, who has lived quietly in Cuba for the last three and a half decades, as one of the most dangerous terrorists in the world – sharing space on the list with individuals whose alleged actions have provoked military assaults on Iraq, Afghanistan and Syria? (Davis, 10/1/14)

As activist and participating in her own legal defense team as well as countless others, Davis is of course mindful about the power of the state to *invent* punitive procedures to castigate undesirable members, especially revolutionaries. The offshore prison Guantánomo Bay, an area illegally seized from Cuba, which cages Prisoners of War as "enemy combattants" (including teenagers) is a dramatic case in point.

Davis answers the question why Shakur's struggle is important to us today:

The global response to the police killing of a black teenager in a small midwestern town suggests a growing consciousness regarding the persistence of US racism at a time when it is supposed to be on the decline. Assata's legacy represents a mandate to broaden and deepen anti-racist struggles. In her autobiography published this year, evoking the black radical tradition of struggle, she asks us to "Carry it on. / Pass it down to the children. /Pass it down. Carry it on … / To Freedom!" (Ibid., 2014)

With prescient foresight, Davis writes about Shakur's importance to the freedom struggle only a few months before the official détente and renewed diplomatic relations between Cuba and the U.S. Shakur's autobiography was republished in 2014 along with Angela Davis's foreword. Independent publishing houses such as Africa World Press find themselves targeted, first by the fraternal order of police, who wages its PR war against those who it blames for killing police officers (e.g., Abu-Jamal and Shakur), secondly, by the IRS following up with expensive audits, because these presses dare to publish voices which break the silence about state and corporate violence.

References:

Adewunmwi, B. (July 13, 2014). Assata Shakur: From civil rights activist to FBI's most-wanted. *The Guardian.* Accessed 2/22/15 from: http://www.theguardian.com/books/2014/jul/13/assata-shakur-civil-rights-activist-fbi-most-wanted

Abu-Jamal, M. (1996). *Live from death row.* New York: Harper Perennial.

Amnesty International. (2014). Entombed: Isolation in the federal prison system. Accessed 3/6/15 from *Solitary Watch*: http://solitarywatch.com/2014/07/16/federal-supermax-prison-violates-international-law-amnesty-international/

Assata Speaks. (2010). Comrade Marilyn Buck. Accessed 12/28/14 from: http://www.assatashakur.org/marilyn.htm

Assata Speaks. (2006). Comrade Silvia Baraldini is free! Accessed 12/28/14 from: http://www.assatashakur.org/silvia.htm

Baraldini, S., M. Buck, S. Rosenberg, and L. Whitehorn. (1996). Women's control unit. In E. Rosenblatt (Ed.) *Criminal injustice: Confronting the prison crisis.* Boston: South End Press.

Barr, M. (2007). Some Facts and Anecdotes of Women Arrested and Imprisoned in the United States. In M. Nagel and S. Asumah (Eds.), *Prisons and punishment: Reconsidering global penality.* Trenton, NJ: Africa World Press.

Change.org. (2014). President Barack Obama: Remove Assata Shakur from the FBI's "Most Wanted Terrorists" List.

Cornelia Goethe Centrum. (2014). Rückschau auf die Angela Davis-Gastprofessur. Accessed 3/27/15 from:

http://www.cgc.uni-frankfurt.de/angeladavis.shtml

Davis, A. Y. (November 1, 2014). From Michael Brown to Assata
    Shakur, the racist state of America persists. *The Guardian*.
    Accessed 12/28/14 from:
    http://www.theguardian.com/commentisfree/2014/nov/01/mich
    ael-brown-assata-shakur-racist-state-of-america

Davis, A. Y. (2012). *The meaning of freedom: And other difficult
    dialogues*. San Francisco: City Light Books.

Davis, A. Y. (2003). *Are prisons obsolete?* New York: Seven
    Stories Press.

Davis, A. Y. (1988 [1974]). *Angela Davis—An autobiography*.
    New York: International Publishers.

Davis, A. Y. (1981). *Women, race, and class*. New York: Random
    House.

Davis, A. Y. (1971). *If they come in the morning: Voices of
    resistance*. New York: The Third Press.

Day, S. (2001). Cruel but not unusual: The punishment of women
    in U.S. prisons: An interview with Marilyn Buck and Laura
    Whitehorn. *Monthly Review*, July-August.
    Accessed 2/24/15 from:
    http://mrzine.monthlyreview.org/2010/day050810.html

Deary, M. (2010). *Radicalization: The life writings of political
    prisoners*. New York: Routledge.

Democracy Now! (May 15, 2014). "War Criminals Shouldn't Be
    Honored": Rutgers Students Nix Condoleezza Rice from
    Commencement Speech. Accessed 3/13/15 from:

http://www.democracynow.org/2014/5/5/war_criminals_should
nt_be_honored_rutgers

Dodge, L. M. (2002). *"Whores and thieves of the worst kind": A study of women, crime, and prisons, 1835-2000*. DeKalb, IL: Northern Illinois University Press.

Elijah, J. S. (2007). Political prisoners in the U.S.: New perspectives in the new millennium. In M. Nagel and S. Asumah (Eds.), *Prisons and punishment: Reconsidering global penality*. Trenton, NJ: Africa World Press.

Feminist Studies Dept. (2014). Angela Y Davis. Accessed 2/24/15 from:
http://feministstudies.ucsc.edu/faculty/singleton.php?singleton
=true&cruz_id=aydavis

Groves, S. (2004). News and views. The prison issue. *Feminist Studies* 30(2), 535-540.

Honan, William H. (April 12, 1995). Two scholarships given new names after controversy. *The New York Times*. Retrieved 6/14/15 from: http://www.nytimes.com/1995/04/12/us/two-scholarships-given-new-names-after-controversy.html

James, J. (Ed.). (2007). *Warfare in the American Homeland: Policing and Prison in a Penal Democracy*. Durham, NC: Duke University Press.

James, J. (2005). Introduction: Democracy and Captivity. In J. James (Ed.), *The new abolitionists: (Neo) slave narratives and contemporary prison writings*. Albany: SUNY Press.

James, J. (Ed.). (1998). Introduction. *The Angela Y. Davis reader*. Malden, MA: Blackwell.

James, J. (1997). *Transcending the talented tenth: Black leaders and American intellectuals*. New York: Routledge.

James, J. (1999). *Shadowboxing: Representations of black feminism*. New York: St Martins Press.

Johnson, P. (2003). *Inner lives: Voices of African American women*. New York: New York University Press.

Jones, A.J. (December 23, 2014). Cuba won't let FBI or Christie have Assata Shakur back. *The Intercept*. Accessed 12/28/14 from: https://firstlook.org/theintercept/2014/12/23/fbis-desperate-pursuit-assata-shakur-continues-u-s-cuba-talks/

Kaplan, A. (2012). Dreaming in French: On Angela Davis. *The Nation*. Accessed 3/12/15 from: http://www.thenation.com/article/166784/dreaming-french-angela-davis

Kautzer, C. and E. Mendieta. (2004). Law and resistance in the prisons of empire: An interview with Angela Y. Davis. *Peace Review* 16(3), 339-347.

Kelley, R. (2012). Foreword. In A.Y. Davis, *The meaning of freedom: And other difficult dialogues*. San Francisco: City Light Books.

Kurshan, N. (1996). Behind the walls: The history and current reality of women's imprisonment. In E. Rosenblatt (Ed.) *Criminal injustice: Confronting the prison crisis*. Boston: South End Press.

Law, V. (2012). *Resistance behind bars*, 2nd ed. Oakland: PM Press.

Mandela, N.R. (1995). *Long Road to Freedom*. Back Bay Books.

Maloney, C. (2014). Condoleezza Rice. *Encyclopedia of Alabama.* Accessed 3/12/15 from: http://www.encyclopediaofalabama.org/article/h-2541

McDuffie, E. (2012). *Sojourning for freedom: Black women, American communism, and the making of black left feminism.* Durham, NC: Duke University Press.

Moussaoui, R. (May 1, 2013). Angela Davis: The Iconic "Sweet Black Angel" at l'Humanité. *TruthOut.* Accessed 3/14/15 from: http://www.truth-out.org/opinion/item/16105-angela-davis-the-iconic-sweet-black-angel-at-lhumanite

Nagel, M. (2013). Review essay of eight books on imprisoned women. In *Wagadu*, Vol. 11. Wagadu.org

Nagel, M. (2008). Prisons as diasporic sites: Liberatory voices from the diaspora of confinement. *Journal of Social Advocacy and Systems Change*, 1, March,1-31.

Nagel, M. (2007). Witness to injustice. Special Issue: Scholar's symposium: The work of Angela Y. Davis, *Journal of Human Studies*, 30, 281-90.

Neumann, C. (2008). Angela Davis. *Encyclopedia of Alabama.* Accessed 3/11/15 from: http://www.encyclopediaofalabama.org/article/h-1427

Nixon, R. (1991). Mandela, messianism, and the media. *Transition*, 41, 42-55.

Shakur, A. (2010). Assata: Exile since 1979. Hands off Assata campaign. Accessed 12/28/14 from: http://www.assatashakur.com/

Shakur, A. (2009). *Assata: In her own words: I have advocated and I still advocate revolutionary change.* Stone Mountain, GA: Talking Drum Collective.

Shakur, A. (2005). Women in prison: How we are. In J. James (Ed.), *The new abolitionists: (Neo) slave narratives and contemporary prison writings.* Albany: SUNY Press.

Shakur, A. (1987). *Assata: An autobiography.* Chicago: Lawrence Hill Books.

Shakur, A. (1973). To my people. *The Talking Drum.* Accessed 2/22/15 from:
http://www.thetalkingdrum.com/tmp.html

Ozemebhoya, E. D. (December 23, 2014). Assata Shakur's journey in her own words. *The Root.* Accessed 12/28/14 from:
http://www.theroot.com/articles/culture/2014/12/assata_shakur_s_journey_in_her_own_words.html?wpisrc=obinsite

Wahad, D. B.; Shakur, A., & M. Abu-Jamal. (1993). *Still black, Still strong*: Survivors of the U.S. war against revolutionaries. Semiotext(e)

Williams, E. (1993). *Inadmissible evidence: The story of the African-American trial lawyer who defended the Black Liberation Army.* Brooklyn, N.Y.: Lawrence Hill Books.

Zed Books. (October 8,2014). Watch: Assata launch event at Black Cultural Archives. Accessed 12/28/14 from:
http://zed-books.blogspot.co.uk/2014/10/watch-assata-launch-event-at-black.html

Still Brave? Black Feminism
as a Social Justice Project

Patricia Hill Collins

REFLEXIVE ESSAY: *In spring 2010, I attended a conference that focused on examining the thirty-year history of Black women's studies' in the academy. Many attendees were familiar with the 1982 publication of the groundbreaking anthology,* But Some of Us Are Brave: All the Women Are White, All the Blacks Are Men: Black Women's Studies. *For many of us, that book was a bible that helped shape our entry into Black women's studies. We gathered to mark the publication of a follow-up volume titled* Still Brave: The Evolution of Black Women's Studies. *I appreciated the commemoration, yet, for me, something was missing. I was far more interested in developing action strategies for the next thirty years than in celebrating the past ones. My efforts to rethink the issue of whether Black feminist thought within academic settings is "still brave" catalyzed this essay. I consider the core question that anchors the essay—What will it take for Black women to be free?—as fundamental to scholarship in service to social justice. This essay highlights the significance of audience—Who is our work for?*

W HAT WILL IT TAKE for Black women to be free? This core question lies at the heart of Black feminism, shaping its themes, theories, and politics. Just has times have changed, so too have the conceptions of freedom pursued by women of African descent. For Black women, the forms that oppression takes vary tremendously from one society to the next and from one historical period to the next. The specificities of identities or experiences may differ, yet the overarching experience of oppression is essential. This fundamental theme of Black women's oppression simultaneously results in economic and social disadvantages and drives the need for and the contours of Black feminist theory and politics. Yet basic questions concerning freedom define Black women as a transnational Black population and forms of political action that Black women embrace and/or reject.

Oppression constitutes an unjust situation where over time one group systematically denies another group access to the resources of society. An individual can experience the effects of oppression, but oppression itself is an institutional phenomenon that characterizes a given social system. Social justice projects routinely aim to address social inequalities among groups that result from oppression. In the United States, for example, an individual can experience the *effects* of intersecting oppressions of race, class, and gender, and sexuality, primarily because those systems are important in the U.S. context. Similarly, while social justice projects require individual initiative, they are best viewed as heterogeneous, group-based responses to the myriad forms that oppression can take historically, cross-culturally, and/or within one social location.

Black feminism is a social justice project advanced by African American women and their allies in defense of the interests of African American women. Black women as individuals need not claim an identity as an "oppressed" person, yet each Black woman grapples with varying aspects of domestic and global social structures that routinely place Black women as a collectivity at the bottom of the social hierarchy. In this context, African American women have characteristic experiences that catalyze recurring political responses to their oppression in the U.S. context that may resemble and differ from those of Afro-British women, African women in Nigeria, or women of African descent in Venezuela. Although Black women's political responses carry different names, in the United States, Black feminism constitutes one generally accepted term that emerged in the late twentieth century to describe these oppositional political and intellectual responses. This grounding of U.S. Black feminism in African American women's quest for freedom positions Black feminism as a social justice project within a broader array of similar intellectual and political projects. Quite simply, if African American women were "free," there would be no need for Black feminism.

This quest toward freedom in contexts of oppression is what Black feminism has been in the past. But what forms might Black feminism as a social justice project take today? What challenges face contemporary U.S. Black feminism in moving Black women closer to social justice? What might it take to meet these challenges?

Challenges Facing U.S. Black Feminism as a Social Justice Project

U.S. Black feminism rests on a synergistic relationship among three distinguishing features, namely: (1) Black women's everyday, lived experiences; (2) Black women's analyses of the meaning and significance of those experiences; and (3) Black women's actions that stem from and shape both experiences and analyses. Each of the three distinguishing features makes important contributions to the effectiveness of Black feminism writ large. Each feature stands on its own as a vital part of feminism, with patterns of relationship among these three concepts of experience, thought, and action varying from one historical era to the next, as well as across social settings.

First, African American women's experiences with oppression have been central to Black feminism. These experiences have been shaped by U.S. Black women's position within race, class, gender, and sexuality as systems of power.

The self-defined knowledge that African American women have produced to conceptualize their experiences, or Black feminist thought, constitutes a second distinguishing feature of U.S. Black feminism. Analyzing Black women's experiences with oppression has been vital to Black women's empowerment as well as to the stimulation of new knowledge about oppression itself. Knowing that Black women's freedom struggle necessarily proceeds on several fronts, against racism, sexism, class exploitation, and heterosexism in particular, has been central to this knowledge. The idea that Black women can never be free without addressing race, class, gender, and sexuality as systems of oppression that mutually construct one another has been a key tenet of Black feminist analysis. The framework of race/class/gender studies and its accompanying paradigm of intersectionality also emerge within this quest for freedom, because it was clear that gaining one kind of "freedom" (race or gender or class) would not free Black women.

A third distinguishing feature of U.S. Black feminism concerns African American women's politics or political action in response to oppression. Black women have approached their specific experiences with oppression not only by analyzing it but also by taking action. An everyday feminism, although it was rarely called such, characterized African American women's everyday struggles for survival, a long-term, albeit often unnamed, Black feminist politics. Ideas about Black women as the backbone of black communities and views of women as strong, self-reliant, and able to take care of themselves are part of this everyday politics about what it means to be a strong woman.

This everyday Black feminist politics also shaped patterns of African American women's political behavior across several social movements. In the 1950s to 1970s, for example, African American women were active participants within multiple social movements (Civil Rights; Black Power; women's movement; anti-war movement; gay/lesbian liberation movement), and modern U.S. Black feminism was shaped by these social movements. Not only did these movements affect one another but individual African American women also moved among them, often participating in more than one. These patterns of engagement framed initial expressions of modern Black feminism.

African American women who were intellectual leaders for modern Black feminism of the 1950s, 1960s, and 1970s typically participated in this synergistic and dynamic relationship among Black women's experiences, self-defined knowledge regarding those experiences, and a Black feminist politics. It's hard to categorize them as being either scholars or activists because they often were both. Toni Cade Bambara, Shirley Chisholm, Pauli Murray, Audre Lorde, June Jordan, Alice Walker, and many others drew on their own personal lived experiences as African American women. Yet Black feminist intellectual leaders also participated in organized political activities that enabled them to see beyond their own personal points of view. Building on their individual and collective experiences in Black women's politics, they used experiences to develop theoretical analyses of the intersectional nature of Black women's oppression. Moreover, they engaged in a Black feminist politics that was simultaneously free-standing (organizations for Black women) and that permeated other organizations (working with feminist organizations or Black nationalist organizations, for example) that incorporated these ideas.

From the social location of this synergistic relationship among experiences, analyses, and actions, these Black women intellectuals were able to look beyond the specificity of time and space to build on the ideas and actions of African American women from the past as well as Black women in transnational contexts. When it comes to questions of sexual violence, one can see links between the earlier work of researcher, journalist, and activist Ida Wells-Barnett and the later work of late-twentieth-century African American feminists. Angela Davis's groundbreaking work on sexual violence under slavery builds on Wells-Barnett's analyses of unmasking the violence visited on Black men as a site of racial and gender oppression that upheld class inequalities. Davis shifts the lens from Black men to Black women, pointing out how Black women have been raped by both white and black men, and that the control of Black women's bodies has been a terrain of struggle for masculinity. She also examines institutionalized rape as a tool of public policy, for example, the refusal of local municipalities to prosecute the rapes of Black women. When it comes to self-defined knowledge, modern Black feminists identify silences within African American communities as well as within dominant discourse as significant in minimizing sexual violence targeted toward African American women. More recently, sexual violence against Black women as a form of entertainment, the burgeoning pornography sites, is a new area of investigation. Modern Black feminists did not originate this type of analysis, nor will it stop with them. Because they crafted political responses to sexual violence as shaped within these power relations, this issue will persist as long as this expression of oppression continues to affect women of African descent.

Contemporary U.S. Black feminism faces many challenges that, if neglected, promise to leave this rich period of Black feminist intellectual production and politics marooned without ties to past movements or comparable cross-cultural initiatives. Staying the course of celebrating Black feminist accomplishments of the past few decades fosters a blindness to challenges. Many of the challenges faced by contemporary U.S. Black feminism require taking a hard look at shifts in U.S. society, the content and practices of Black academic feminism, and complacency within the U.S. context toward the issues that African American women continue to face. In essence, U.S. Black feminism is not a finished social justice project. Instead, it is one in the making, whose challenges reflect a weakening of the ties among experiences, analysis, and action.

One challenge concerns the need to refocus U.S. Black feminism on the everyday realities of Black women's lives. African American women who are working in community organizing roles are well aware of the list of social issues that face African American women and girls. At the same time, if the American media is to be believed, one could easily conclude that African American women are a privileged group that no longer needs Black feminism. Certainly, media figures such as Oprah Winfrey and political figures such as and Michelle Obama suggest that U.S. Black feminism has experienced some success in that some African American women are doing far better than the majority of U.S. citizens of all races.

Academia constitutes another important environment where Black feminism seems to be celebrated in order to be dismissed. This treatment of Black feminist thought within academia reflects pressures on scholars to sever our intellectual work from the group-based, social justice projects that initially stimulated them. We are encouraged to replace robust, empowering forms of knowledge that were developed within social movement contexts with narrow, individualistic, market-based solutions to social problems. This is the first historical juncture in U.S. politics where it is possible to have Black feminist analyses with neither substantive connections to Black women's lived experiences nor expectations that one would engage in Black feminist politics.

The visibility of prominent African American women within higher education, mass media, and electoral politics can be held up as an example of Black feminist accomplishments. Yet how deeply has the incorporation of Black feminist ideas actually penetrated in shaping the content of curriculum offerings, news and entertainment media content and public policy? The large numbers of Black women and girls who continue to face a litany of social problems suggest that considerable distance remains to be traveled.

In this context, a second challenge facing Black feminism concerns paying careful attention to how the language of Black feminism is being used, often in ways that are antithetical to Black feminist politics. Take, for example, the differences between the Combahee River Collective's statement on identity politics in the context of Black feminist politics of the 1980s and its redefined meanings within contemporary academic settings. The Combahee River Collective's approach to *identity politics* drew on the concept of the personal as political in ways that linked individual identity to collective political social location. Experiences were honed in this space, linking the individual and the collective, or the personal and the political. This concept was highly empowering for African American women, who often lacked a language that explained social inequality in ways that generated avenues for action. The major insight of the Collective also lay in identifying how African American women were positioned within multiple systems of power—their politics necessarily involved grappling with race, class, gender, and sexuality as intersecting systems of power that shaped individual identity and personal experience. The Collective advanced a powerful theory of action, one grounded in analysis and experience, with "identity politics" as the phrase that captures these complex relationships. In contrast, contemporary approaches to identity politics rely on an individualist notion of identity: identity as freedom from social constructions, no matter the power relations.

A third challenge concerns developing new standards for evaluating the effectiveness of Black feminism as a social justice project within a greatly changed political environment. What would an effective Black feminist politics look like now? Many people see the visibility of highly competent African American women as evidence of the effectiveness of Black feminism. Whereas the accomplishments of successful Black women should be applauded, seeing a Black female face in a highly ranked position as a proxy for African American women's economic, social, and political progress may be misguided.

Gaining visibility is not the same thing as exercising power. Many Black women who occupy positions of power and authority and who are trying to advance a social justice agenda continually find their way blocked. Take, for example, the impressive career of Congresswoman Eleanor Holmes Norton, an eleven-term representative of the District of Columbia in the U.S. House of Representatives. Despite being a nonvoting member of Congress, Norton has been a tireless advocate for the rights of children, women, Blacks, poor people, and the disenfranchised, all target populations of her congressional district. Her career illustrates the challenges that face even the most gifted and accomplished Black women who work on behalf of social justice. Moreover, the absence of accountability standards for Black women who claim to be leaders speaks to the disconnect between African American women as a group and the array of Black women who claim to speak for them.

African American women and their allies might benefit from a clear social issues agenda that is easy to understand, reflects issues that are important to African American women as a group, and can be used to shape Black feminist politics. This kind of clarity would make it far easier to evaluate whether a media figure or a newly hired Black woman professor is contributing to Black feminism as historically understood or is using it for her own career or personal gain. Such an agenda would also enable Black women and our allies to recognize and support the exemplary leadership of Eleanor Holmes Norton and numerous women whose Black feminism is not confined to the academy.

Confronting the Challenges: Revitalizing Black Feminism as a Social Justice Project

The continued relevance of Black feminism as a social justice project lies in its ability to reconnect with its traditional core, namely, the synergistic and dynamic relationship among Black women's experiences, self-defined knowledge regarding those experiences, and a Black feminist politics. Because many action strategies can address these challenges, here I sketch out three actions that I see as being especially pressing. They are: (1) setting a new social justice agenda that links African American women's social issues in the U.S. context with the concerns of global social justice initiatives; (2) reaching neglected constituencies by making African American girls and working-class women central as audiences for contemporary Black feminism; and (3) building coalitions *among* African American women who share a commitment to a social issues agenda yet are differentially positioned in relation to it.

Setting a New Social Justice Agenda

Highlighting a global social justice agenda identifies a list of social issues that concern social justice projects in general. They are: (1) struggles for political rights, especially citizenship; (2) struggles for economic rights, such as housing, food, and health; (3) struggles for economic rights issues of employment, poverty, and education; and (4) issues of bodily integrity, such as reproductive rights and elimination of violence. Whereas all social justice projects have a stake in this broad-based agenda, the work of U.S. Black feminism might lie in highlighting African American women's specific connections to this agenda. This would create space to see areas of consensus and conflict with other social justice projects and could form the foundation for new dialogues.

Here global feminism, especially a transnational Black feminism that embraces an intersectional framework, has much to offer African American women. Social issues that disproportionately affect African American women and girls in the United States—female-headed families, poverty, inadequate health care, and HIV/AIDS—also disproportionately affect women and girls of African descent in a global context. Black women in a global context do not reject issues of women's empowerment as women ("feminism," as a shorthand term). While they too often reject the term "feminism," they do see the need for female solidarity. African American women have greater difficulty achieving this solidarity because pushing for women's rights (especially if claimed under the banner of feminism) is seen as "white" and is often dismissed. Rather than confining U.S. Black feminism primarily to the terrain of race relations, the proverbial question, "Black and white women—can we get along?"—developing links between African American women and women of African descent in a transnational context creates space for new issues and points of view.

For example, reproductive rights—retaining one's own bodily integrity—are a fundamental premise of women's rights in a global context. Yet this social issue takes varying forms for women who have different social locations within racism, sexism, heterosexism, class exploitation, age, and religious fundamentalism. Fighting for the rights of Black women is central to much broader debates concerning reproductive rights. In this regard, given Mississippi's history as a staunch opponent of the rights of African Americans, Mississippi voters' rejection of the personhood amendment is extremely noteworthy. The amendment had implications beyond banning all abortions—if implemented, it had the potential to ban many forms of birth control and fertility treatments. How were Black women positioned in relation to this decision?

There would be no need for a transnational Black feminism if women of African descent as a collectivity were well housed, healthy, educated, well fed, employed, and safe from violence, and had loving relationships with their partners, family members, and friends. The core of a transnational Black feminism must begin not with discussions of who can participate in such a movement but rather by acknowledging that a disproportionate percentage of people who are poor, homeless, and hungry are women, are black, and are young. The convergence of systems of racism, sexism, class exploitation, age discrimination, citizenship, and heterosexism converge most intensely to create a global population of people called "Black women." Most certainly, there is significant social and cultural variation in how groups of Black women experience these social issues. But it also is important to remember that there would be no need to discuss Black feminisms of any kind in the absence of these kinds of social issues.

Here, the challenge is to take the main ideas of U.S. Black feminist thought, many of which are now theoretical frameworks and cultural analyses that are developed within academic settings, and use this framework to rethink the social issues that are of most concern to African American women. These issues include violence, education, health care, jobs, housing, family, body politics/sexuality, and a whole host of other social issues that threaten the vitality of Black communities. A Black feminist social issues agenda will recognize that some of these issues take gender-specific forms. For example, a responsive Black feminist agenda would critique violence against African American men at the hands of the police state, while recognizing that much of the violence experienced by African American women (and all women?) is at the hands of men. Thus, a crucial component of this social issues agenda lies in bringing U.S. Black feminism more in line with these social justice initiatives as they are articulated within the global women's movement. At the same time, a parallel component is to make sure that the global women's movement is attentive to the specifics of African American women's experiences. Women may share a common global position, yet building a global women's movement against women's poverty and powerlessness cannot come at the cost of ignoring how racism and heterosexism also affect women.

Women who are concerned with the need to create a common social issues agenda responsive to the heterogeneous social context in which Black women live form the backbone of transnational Black feminism. Transnational black feminism can share how other ways of living provide a different interpretive context for the same social issues experienced by African American women. Extracting the social issues of Black women from the race relations paradigm of the U.S. context and positioning such issues instead in a context of transnational Black feminism would be an important first step in addressing the challenges that currently face U.S. Black feminism.

Reaching Neglected Constituencies: Working-Class Black Girls as a Target Audience for Black Feminism

Black feminism currently reaches a far broader constituency than African American women. At the same time, the patterns of access to a discourse whose very reason for being is to advance social justice and whose specific form resists racism, sexism, class exploitation, and heterosexism are shaped by these very same systems of power. Within this broader constituency, are African American women still target audiences for Black feminism?

If Black feminism were reaching a broad constituency of African American women, one would assume that African American girls, the next generation of Black feminist intellectual leaders, would know about it and value its contributions to bettering their lives. Yet African American women and girls, the population on whose behalf Black feminism emerged and whose lives were supposed to be changed by this work, typically remain remarkably unaware of Black feminism. Moreover, if they have even heard of Black feminism, they reject it. In this context, I have become increasingly concerned about who exactly gets to develop Black feminist ideas as well as who has access to those ideas. Black feminism cannot be effective if those who are aware of this history hold distorted understandings of it. Black feminism has a limited future if it is invisible to Black girls and to the working-class African American women they are likely to grow up to be.

Currently, Black feminism is carefully rationed, with women and girls from already privileged groups gaining access to its ideas, primarily through college and university classrooms. Yet Black feminism in the academy decreasingly reaches college-age African American women, in part, because they form a shrinking percentage of students on elite college campuses. Black women must continue to do high-quality scholarship across many academic disciplines. However, we must ask ourselves, does our scholarship speak to the concerns of African American women, or are we increasingly addressing issues that reflect academic agendas? Should our intellectual talents be devoted to yet another dissertation, journal article, or book on well-trod academic topics, for example, the maternal politics of Toni Morrison's *Beloved*? Surely Morrison's work is of tremendous value for understanding motherhood, captivity and resistance. Yet who are the intended audiences for our dissertations, journal articles, and books on Morrison and for the current preoccupation of academic Black feminism?

If Black women intellectuals both inside and outside the academy considered ways of reaching Black girls and working-class Black women as neglected target audiences for our work, we might develop organizational capacity for reaching African American boys and Black men. Black feminism argues that gender matters in shaping the experiences of African American women. This does not mean that gender means girls. It does mean that Black feminism would think about Black women and men as target audiences for our work. This is an issue of need.

How would we go about building organizational capacity? Most likely, we would pay more attention to schools and similar social institutions that facilitate Black feminism or serve as gatekeepers. Black girls, especially poor and working class African American girls, need a critical education, which public schools are unlikely to provide. One important challenge that confronts Black feminism still aiming to be brave as a social justice project lies in educating Black youth not to fit into existing social hierarchies, but rather to challenge them. Education has long been the central theme of African American politics, and Black feminism that ignores this fact does so at its own peril.

Schooling is the social justice battleground for Black girls. Black feminism has made some progress into classrooms of higher education, but even there Black feminism remains contained within Women's Studies, Cultural Studies, and to a lesser extent, Black Studies programs. The works of individual African American intellectuals may be incorporated into the mainstream curriculum, yet a robust treatment of Black feminism remains rare. K–12 education shows even less interest in Black feminism, beyond teaching material on Black women worthies like Sojourner Truth. However, incorporating the ideas of Black women is no substitute for recruiting, educating, and graduating Black girls, especially girls from poor and working-class backgrounds, from colleges and universities.

The handwriting has been on the wall for some time concerning the steady pressure to exclude African American students from elite colleges and universities. The next Black feminist frontier must be K–12 education, not simply a watered down "shero" curriculum modeled on the "hero" curriculum for boys. Talk of "sheroes" and heroes assume that Black girls and boys are unaware of the accomplishments of African Americans and that they need accomplished role models to encourage them not to be like the people in their families and communities. Role model approaches assume that Black youths lack an analysis of their own situation, have low self-esteem, and can be motivated by exposure to images of African Americans who have "made it." Just because Black boys know about Tiger Woods doesn't mean that they are going to take up golf.

There is nothing wrong with exposing Black girls to images (if not actual) Black women who have achieved. Yet a Black feminist "shero" curriculum that urges modeling one's life after Black women worthies without also helping girls further develop their own analyses of their lives remains incomplete. Black girls will be encouraged to better themselves one at a time, often by leaving their families and communities behind. Instead of this curriculum, I'd suggest using the broader social justice agenda discussed earlier to strategize how Black girls fit into it. A critical education would expose them to a kind of Black feminism that fuses experiences, thought, and action. If we asked Black girls to engage in projects where they examined their own lives (and not primarily in relation to the "sheros" of Black women worthies), what experiences would they share, what analyses might they offer, and what would they plan on doing with their knowledge? Stated differently, Black girls would not be consumers of Black feminism—instead they would create it.

How can we put poor and working-class Black girls at the center of Black feminism? Their lives are not marginal to intersecting power relations of race, class, gender, sexuality, and age. Rather, they are central to the future of Black feminism. Keep in mind that Black girls are over-represented among the poor. They disproportionately attend inferior public schools, have children young, and do not finish high school. They are more likely to end up as single mothers. They are more likely to grow up to be working class, if not poor. Their gendered lives occur primarily through their relationships with African American men as fathers, friends, brothers, sexual partners, husbands, sons, and grandsons. Any Black feminism worth its salt would not squander its resources on the children of elites. Instead, it would recognize that poor and working-class Black girls who are situated in families and communities are its special ground zero in the early twenty-first century.

Organizing Differently: Strengthening Coalitions among African American Women

Three important groups of contemporary U.S. Black women are positioned to make important contributions in meeting the challenge of developing a new social justice agenda and reaching out to working-class Black girls. Each group is differently situated within the U.S. context and brings a different skill set and experiential base to Black feminism. All three groups understand the existential question, "What will it take for Black women to be free?" but they interpret the question itself and its possible responses differently.

Black women community leaders constitute the first and, in many ways, the most foundational group. This is the group with skills of grassroots community organizing and a deep-seated commitment to developing African American communities. They are the ones dealing with recalcitrant schools, intrusive social service bureaucracies, and overzealous police. This is the group whose gender analyses include men, mainly because they see first-hand how the combination of race and gender places young Black men at risk. This is also the group that is least likely to claim Black feminism, even though their work embodies Black feminism's social justice agenda.

The second group consists of young women who personally identify with Black feminism. Most are introduced to Black feminism through Women's Studies classrooms and have had access to the rich idea base of an increasingly global feminism. Black feminism in the academy is often situated within Women's Studies, a field that has made tremendous strides in diversifying its study and staff. Within this area, young feminists of color discover each other as African American, Latina, and Asian American women and see the connections between what may have been understood in their home communities as separate struggles. They access a different, coalitional social justice ethos within the academic field of Women's Studies. Feminism advances an individual rights discourse, one that resonates well with the generational logic of young Black feminists.

Self-defined "hip hop feminists" may constitute a third group for a coalition among African American women. This group provides another forum of Black feminist politics with the potential to bridge feminist and nationalist strategies while encouraging African American women to develop, expand, and/or create new social institutions that house Black feminist praxis.

Building coalitional politics among these three groups of African American women would go far toward revitalizing Black feminism as a social justice project. Each has a distinctive angle of vision on Black feminism's traditional core, namely, the synergistic and dynamic relationship among Black women's experiences, self-defined knowledge regarding those experiences, and a Black feminist politics that reflects a broader social justice ethos. Yet this coalitional politics cannot happen without building organizational capacity that fosters such coalitions. To this end, Black women's organizations and organizations that have identifiable, internal Black women's caucuses might develop structural initiatives that are designed to bring together key agents from these three groups. It's not that one group contributes unexamined experiences and the other offers up theoretical knowledge that explains those experiences. Rather, all three have distinctive perspectives on the intersecting power relations that shape Black women's experiences. They also may propose different strategies for Black women's empowerment that stem from their placement in lived social relations. Moving the ideas and actions of U.S. Black feminism closer together might revitalize African American women's politics.

Still Brave?

Looking ahead, what direction and shape should Black feminism take? The answer brings the discussion back to the core question framing this essay: What will it take for Black women to be free? This question is straightforward, yet infinitely complex, and this essay has explored some of that complexity. I want to finish this presentation by revisiting this question in light of the previous discussion.

The meaning of "to be free" is important because freedom and social justice are deeply intertwined. *Freedom from* the social injustices that are structured by intersecting systems of oppression? This sense of the idea of freedom references issues of citizenship and emancipation, a widespread belief up until now that political freedom would yield tangible social benefits. With the growing disenchantment with representative democracy, it seems clear that political remedies, while crucial, are not enough. Freedom now must be recast through ideas about the economy. *Freedom to* live our lives as we want, with imagination and personal choice, to think what we want, go where we want, love whom we want, and dream big dreams that have some possibility of coming to fruition?

The heart of the issue concerns *what will it take*? Identifying examples from Black feminism that required women to be brave, to tackle thorny social problems that weighed more heavily on Black women than on other groups, reveals the multiple strategies that have been deployed to try to bring about this freedom. The need to ask the question at all suggests that this project is unfinished. This is a core existential question for Black women. I have also stressed African American women in my presentation, using Black women's experiences as a touchstone for broader social issues.

I remind you that the framework of intersectionality encourages an opening up of this question beyond the specific case of African American women. We need multiple cases, grounded within intersectional analyses that examine how this same question affects individuals and groups in a global context. For example, as refracted through the category of nation-states, one might ask, "What will it take for all young women citizens of South Africa to be free?" For stateless peoples, the question becomes, "What will it take for Palestinians to be free?" For subjugated ethnic groups, "What will it take for the Dhalit to be free?" For subordinated segments of national populations, the question might be, "What will it take for *beur* youth in Parisian suburbs to be free?"

Collectively, these questions remind us that "What will it take for us all to be free?" may be the existential question of human experience. Despite our disparate starting points, in moving along a path toward freedom, we might all tell ourselves from time to time, "Be brave," if only in a whisper. Yet we might be better served by remembering Fannie Lou Hamer's unshakable commitment to social justice. She found a way to "be brave."

ADDITIONAL RESOURCES

Combahee River Collective. 1995. "A Black Feminist Statement." In *Words of Fire: An Anthology of African American Feminist Thought*, pp. 232–240, ed. Beverly Guy-Sheftall. New York: New Press.

Davis, Angela Y. 1981. *Women, Race, and Class.* New York: Random House.

Hernandez, Daisy, and Bushra Rehman, eds. 2002. *Colonize This! Young Women of Color on Today's Feminism.* New York: Seal Press.

Hull, Gloria T., Patricia Bell Scott, and Barbara Smith, eds. 1982. *But Some of Us Are Brave: All the Women Are White, All the Blacks Are Men: Black Women's Studies.* New York: The Feminist Press.

James, Stanlie, Frances Smith Foster, and Beverly Guy-Sheftall, eds. 2009. *Still Brave: The Evolution of Black Women's Studies.* New York: The Feminist Press.

Norton, Congresswoman Eleanor Holmes. http://www.norton.house.gov/index.php?option=com_content&view=frontpage&Itemid=121. Accessed: June 24, 2012.

Pough, Gwendolyn D. 2004. *Check It While I Wreck It: Black Womanhood, Hip-Hop Culture, and the Public Sphere.* Boston: Northeastern University Press.

Ransby, Barbara. 2003. *Ella Baker & the Black Freedom Movement: A Radical Democratic Vision.* Chapel Hill: University of North Carolina Press.

Unit VIII. Activism, Change, and Feminist Futures

Eco-Feminism: Plants as Becoming-Woman

Prudence Gibson

Much of the writing of this book has been a concerted effort to discuss artworks that speak with the major issues of critical plant studies and as a means of reintroducing ourselves (as humans) to nature. Wastelands, hybrids, robotany, ethics, rights and moral contracts, have monopolised the conversation to this point. But there is another element of this discourse which fires the hearts of many plant lovers and will be developed in this chapter – eco-feminism, a mainstay of the plant contract. My interests are led by Irigaray's thesis that a separation of the human from nature is a kind of non-thinking and causes a lack of living energy. By focusing on a return to the elements of nature – in this case the myriad possibilities that plant life can show us – humans have a means of returning to careful thought. Irigaray says 'from being alone in nature to being two in love.'[1]

The female, in an emergent state of radical reinterpretation of vegetal life, sits at the nexus of art/plant research and a *plant contract*. Nature has conventionally been cast as a womanly figure. Nature is a mother, a fecund vessel, within which life (that is, the human) can grow. This casting of nature as female, however, can be seen as delimiting and may not serve the purposes of becoming woman, of fulfilling both an independent and a collective state of being. That is, constant growth. This chapter acknowledges the history of feminising the planet but reanimates and recasts that process by introducing the water lily as a breathing becoming-woman. The flower, especially the water lily, is an eco-feminist object and has been a motif in art. This chapter refers to French modernist artist Claude Monet's water lily and also the olfactory experience of artist Cat Jones' 2017 *Scent* performance (See figure 8).

An addition to the historical mythologising of the natural world as a woman, there is the chronicle of botanical study in the 19th century. There was an efflorescence of female interest in botanical studies and its scholarship in Britain at the time. Women, for this short period of British history (mostly under strict controls and without the possibility of publication of their own work), were allowed to investigate botany from the safety of their home environments. However, it soon became clear that the sexual information that women

---

1   Luce Irigiary and Michael Marder, *Through Vegetal Being.* New York: Columbia University Press 2016, 84.

FIGURE 8   *Cat Jones. Scent of Sydney 2017. Performance, sound, biotic matter. Carriageworks, Sydney Festival 2017.*

accrued via this plant science knowledge was not deemed beneficial for them and limitations of access were widely imposed by the end of the 19th century in the interests of social morality.[2]

Botany has been a domain of thought and scholarly engagement that has a marginal female heritage. These restrictions and constraints are still reflected in the male-dominated publication numbers, papers written by philosophers and scientists, which are now in the canon of history. These unequal representations cut across philosophy as well as botany. In one of his books, Michael Marder writes essays on philosophers who have written on plants and trees such as Aristotle's wheat, Leibniz's blades of grass and Derrida's sunflowers.[3] Marder follows ten male philosophers, but only refers to one female: Luce Irigaray.

Since that publication of plant philosophers, Marder and Irigaray have worked together on different texts, both scholarly and journalistic, focussing

2   Ann Shtier, 'Botany in the Breakfast Room: Women and Early Nineteenth Century British Plant Study' in Pnina Abir-Am and Dorinda Outram (eds) *Intimate Lives: Women in Science 1789–1979*, London: Rutgers University Press, 1987.

3   Michael Marder, *The Philosopher's Plant,* New York: Columbia University Press, 2014.

on plants or vegetal being.[4] Irigaray always had a deep connection with plants. She has said that thought needs 'to be ready to listen to nature, to the sensible.'[5] By this she refers to the importance of being aware of physical surroundings and material differences between elements in nature. Irigaray draws out the 'nothing of nature in growing' as a taking on of the void which refers to the life of the vegetal world beyond utility and beyond a human understanding of 'nothing.' She warns her readers to distance themselves from experiences that are only immediate, from not always mastering the real. Rather than seeing plant life as objects, only there for our subjective experience, we can think of different time scales and the possibility of different non-immediate experience. By breathing, she suggests, we can continuously re-open the possibility of new growth for life, for desire, for culture and for love.[6] There is a requirement for breath, Irigaray's philosophical legacy, even in this writing of the water lily as a becoming-woman. Plants breathe out and in, contrary to humans' in and out. The synergy is something that humans yield rather than vice versa. Humans gain from plant life, yet plant life yields little from the human.

Sexuality versus the Sexuate being

In terms of sex, plants often have a male and a female part in the one plant. Some mosses have male plants and female plants working together. Some conifers have two types of cones; one is the stamen cone, the second catches the pollen if the wind is howling right. Certain flowers have both stigma and stamen in the one plant. These last self-fulfilling processes of reproduction have enormous significance for a culture where gender and sexual politics are a constant source of queering change and fluidity. A greater awareness of plant difference creates potential provocations for a re-thinking of the world – where individual species have hybrid, undetermined or multiple sexualities.

This text addresses plants and art as provocateurs in a discourse, and in this chapter focuses on the water lily as a plant with aggregated representations, histories, significance and feminist properties. The water lily is a metaphor for woman. It is an allegorical device for drawing attention to the vegetal world. Women and the vegetal world have much in common. The water lily is also a

---

4 Luce Irigaray and Michael Marder, *Through Vegetal Being*, Columbia University Press, New York, 2016.

5 Luce Irigaray, *I Love to You* New York: Routledge 1996, 139.

6 Luce Irigaray and Michael Marder, *Through Vegetal Being*, Columbia University Press, New York, 2016, 96–97.

sexuate being. In this text, I refer to sexuate as the way plants are situated and how they independently exist in terms of sexuality, without being reduced to their sexual processes. Luce Irigaray believes 'cultivation of our sexuate surges is crucial for our becoming able to behave as a living being among other different living beings without domination or subjection.'[7] This is relevant to the water lily and artistic representations that relate to sexuate being and plants. Being relieved of domination allows writers to consider the water lily and its effects on humans as something that can constantly close and open, much like Irigaray's notion of breath.[8]

Approaching this subject matter within the context of the feminine is specific. Humanity's place in the world is centralised. This anthropocentric 'bind' is why, according to Claire Colebrook, 'becoming-woman' is still required.[9] This could be a human-plant alternative, a 'shaking of the tree' to create new political and cultural units of thought. Or it could be a quiet listening for the breath of plants. This is not a frequency that humans can hear but it is a process by which we can become more aware, more respectful.

Luce Irigaray's choice of plant, as discussed by Marder, is the water lily. The water lily has roots and it also floats across the water, a fluidly female surface. It reproduces asexually with the help of insects carrying seed from the anther to the stigma. The water lily cannot be tied down and requires the help of an entire ecological community to thrive. This is an important model for living or for fully expressing life. Breathing through the skin with the whole body, as Buddha contemplates the lily,[10] can be aligned to the way a plant's nodes open and close with each breath of wind. This allows the thing that we are attentive to, to become attentive of us.[11]

Water lilies flourish in clusters and chemically communicate to one another within their community.[12] They can self-reproduce and move across watery surfaces, being both rooted in the earth and waterborne. I am proposing here that if there is a capacity to find metaphorical connections between human culture and natural life, then this allows a space to introduce the water lily as a feminist plant. In a social and political context, the water lily relies on no

---

7   Luce Irigaray and Michael Marder, *Through Vegetal Being*, Columbia University Press, New York, 2016, 87.

8   Luce Irigaray and Michael Marder, *Through Vegetal Being*, Columbia University Press, New York, 2016, 21.

9   Claire Colebrook, *Sex After Life*, Open Humanities Press, 2013, 158.

10   Michael Marder, *The Philosopher's Plant*, New York: Columbia 2014, 224.

11   Ibid, 214.

12   Monica Gagliano, 'The Mind of Plants: Thinking the Unthinkable.' Communicative and Integrative Biology, 2017. http://www.tandfonline.com/doi/full/10.1080/19420889.2017.128 8333.

individual authority, nor is it dictated to by its male counterparts. As with most plants, it has been marginalised and treated as unequal or ontologically less relevant in the past. Vilified for being too passive and too silent, disparaged for having inferior abilities and condemned for being immobile, the water lily nevertheless defies these denigrations.[13] The water lily is a feminist plant.

Luce Irigaray believes we have moved away from the vegetal world and neglected what being alive presupposes. She suggests that it has taken our planet being threatened to finally realise what the basic conditions of living mean.[14] If speaking can't ever be neutral, should we not speak? In terms of the water lily as a feminist plant, it is time to speak. Speak via eco-transmissions. Speak via chemical releases. Speak via the movement of flowers across the water. Speak, irrespective of whether there is a human there to listen. So, the plant contract speaks.

All plants create oxygen through photosynthesis and they absorb carbon dioxide. All animals breathe oxygen and exhale carbon dioxide. Most of us remember learning this basic fact in primary school science. Yet still we have forgotten these crucial points. Plants and humans breathe together. When did we forget this? Irigaray warns of trying to make animals our partners in the universe or, worse still, a kind of human-like version.[15] Humans can't write of things outside our comprehension. However, we can write a response to the independent agency of the water lily.

The Whole Water Lily

The water lily ecology is both an element in nature and an entire environmental structure in itself. Gaia is a concept developed by James Lovelock to engender a form of the living earth, a form that might be seen from space.[16] This concept comprises an earthly 'it' that is alive and moving, constantly decaying and dismantling. The earth's self-making and its limits are intrinsic to the Gaian hypothesis. Donna Haraway acknowledges the mythological elaboration of

---

13   Michael Marder, *Plant Thinking: A Philosophy of Vegetal Life*. New York: Columbia, 2013.

14   Luce Irigaray and Michael Marder, *Through Vegetal Being*, Columbia University Press, New York, 2016.

15   Luce Irigaray, 'Animal Compassion' in M. Collarco and P. Atterton (eds) *Animal Philosophy: Essential Readings in Continental Thought*, Continuum, London 2004, pp. 195–201.

16   James Lovelock, 'Atmospheric homeostasis by and for the biosphere: the Gaia Hypothesis,' *Tellus* XXVI 1974.

Gaia and the Anthropocene but she also articulates its limitations.[17] These limits might include the descriptions of the earth as a she, as Earth Mother, as Terra Mater. I prefer 'it' or the genderless pronoun 'hen.' The earth is a gender-neutral being that is constantly changing, a system of being that is in a never-ending flux of experience. Symbiosis, developmental phenomena and change through time, Haraway says, were not dealt with in biology in the early twentieth century. Economy and ecology and world-being in the third age of carbon require a different view of Gaia.[18] Gaia is not a 'she,' then, but a 'we,' or an everything.

Referring these Gaian and anthropocentric ideas back to the water lily, the presentation of the lily as a feminist plant may indeed fall into this trap of anthropomorphism – the binding process of only seeing and understanding the world through human eyes – but it is intended as an allegory. Can allegorical or metaphorical thinking be seen as limiting, and does it have the capacity to reduce the importance of learning from plant life? There is a force in 'story' and in 'metaphor' that avoids this danger and carries the relevance of vegetal life, just as the wind carries seeds across the globe, propagating and disseminating dangerous plant ideas.

The water lily is the plant of choice, here, as a way to discuss vegetal relevance to contemporary cultural thought, because it has an idealised history as the Nymphea bride or 'veiled one.' Its long history of representation has created its iconic status and its associated meaning of purity. The cycle of life and enlightenment still reverberate in illustrations, engravings, stories and architecture. It is the divine, the female and the otherworldly.[19] Rather than becoming frustrated by the gendered issues of the bride, Michael Marder, in his reading of Luce Irigaray's writing on the water lily, harnesses and expands them: 'Through attentive fidelity, we become the betrothed of what or whom we follow.'[20] This is a re-appraisal of the history of representation, beyond a mere attempt at de-substantiation. We cannot redress the way the water lily has been identified in history but we can lengthen that discussion into the long now, meaning a view of the future that has longevity. Can we all become collective brides of the material earth? Can we show allegiance to the dirt and stones, the rivers and forests? Can we commit an honourable agreement, a pact of loyalty? Irigaray suggests that consciousness and thoughtful attention, free from cumbersome 'understanding' is exactly this form of fidelity. It follows a

17   Donna Haraway, Anthropocene, Capitalocene, Plantationocene, Chthulucene: Making Kin, *Environmental Humanities*, Vol 6 2015: 159–165.

18   Ibid.

19   Michael Marder, *The Philosopher's Plant*, New York: Columbia 2014, 216.

20   Ibid, 224.

deliberate alliance with Aristotlian ideas of growth. The space to be nourished and to grow is implicit to a feminist modality of being.[21]

Despite the conceivable beauty of the water lily as symbol of female deity, other worldliness and fertility, this concept falls short. So too, according to Marder, has our history of humanity: 'In what amounts to a self-betrayal, and a betrayal of one another, we have historically opted for a cunning synecdoche, according to which one half of humanity – men – is interchangeable with human, as such.' Speech, like the 'mutilated-beyond-recognition' state of nature has wandered away from being.'[22] Where Marder refers to men's breathless aspiration to get to the top of the tree, he speaks of an inability to become. The water lily – despite its history of otherness, femaleness and as divine nymph or goddess – reminds us that breath is a respiration, not to be confused with mere aspiration. The motion moves in and out.

Representation and Expression

While carrying this 'otherworldly' divine significance, it is interesting to remember that the iconic images of the water lily in art, culture and design are flat images. Think of religious icons and Buddha contemplating the water lily. So on the one hand, the waterlily is 'idealised' and revered for its iconic value, and yet, on the other hand, its true earthly essence and sexual versatility are kept 'flat' – immobile and static like a picture.[23] Culturally, women have experienced the same. Women have been 'idealised' and revered as icons, yes, but their feminine essence and sexual versatility have been also kept 'flat' within this cultural/social trap, like the water lily.

Irigaray defies the history of divination, marginalisation and fetishisation by breathing the water lily: writing it, thinking it and thereby giving plants, women and earth-care the room to grow and become. This story, woven by Irigaray and Marder, requires a new construction of the character of the lily within a *mise en scène* – where its activities and behaviours can be understood by humans as a condition of living that can be admired and even emulated, not as object but as fellow participant.

The capabilities and capacities of water lilies, aside from representation, are further evidence that plants require critical and cultural examination as

---

21   Michael Marder, *The Philosopher's Plant,* New York: Columbia 2014, 219.

22   Ibid, 225.

23   Gibson, P. and Gagliano, M. 'The Feminist Plant: Changing Relations with the Water Lily.' *Ethics and the Environment*, Vol 22, Issue 2, 2017.

companion species, and that plants require an accompanying shift in human perception of their vegetal status. By addressing the feminist nature of the water lily, I hope to develop a connection between plant biology and art for a better understanding of plants, via a feminist perspective.

This leads us to the community-focused example of an art-plant hybrid that many humans around the world have encountered – that is, Claude Monet's series of 250 paintings, *Nympheas*. Bioart scholar Monika Bakke says 'art can explore the post natural condition that is typical of modern human-plant relationships.'[24] While the *Nympheas* paintings are not bioart (contemporary art using biological matter, process and methodology) they are nevertheless precursors of the bioart genre in their microscopic detail and alchemical painterly process.

At the original Musee de L'Orangerie gallery in Paris, Monet's *Nympheas* were installed in a lower level oval-shaped gallery space. These paintings of water lilies circled around the viewer, creating a privileged community among those art visitors who saw it, and who shared a love for its beauty at that venue and at all subsequent exhibition spaces. Perhaps it was the way Monet created depth and shallowness at once and how this engendered a sensory affect not experienced before. Or was it the movement of colours in kaleidoscopic propositions that continues to work on human neurobiology in chemical ways? There is a strange and forceful power in these paintings of seemingly prosaic subject matter – a force of energy, a tension between the naturalistic details of the natural plant specimens and the matter of the painted surfaces. The lilies sit on the top of the painting ground, floating over the gesso-primed canvas on board – part of the overall picture but also spontaneously independent of it too, a sensation of natural complication. Deleuze says 'sensation is vibration' and the subject in process of becoming is facilitated by the vibrations in the natural world.[25]

The *Nympheas* are known to have a sensory effect on viewers, both as individuals and as a group. Spurred on by communication of their experiences to one another, the art world's love for the *Nympheas* spread since the painting of them in the modernist era. This fame resulted in prints and posters being hung up in every second (or so it seems) doctor's surgery across the developed world. An epidemic of water lilies. Emotions can vary, but it is not unusual to see a fellow viewer become teary or even choked up with emotion by the lilies. This is the spirit or force of the vegetal artwork; the flat surface, made endlessly

---

24   Randy Laist (ed), *Plants and Literature: Essays in Critical Plant Studies,* New York: Rodopi 2013, 181.

25   Elizabeth Grosz, *Chaos, Territory, Art,* New York: Columbia University Press, 2008, 84–86.

ecological via layers of applied paint, reminds the viewer of nature but from a distance.

This is an important point when considering what art can do to change our values about nature. How can art show humanity the harm we have done to the planet, the contract we have broken and whether there are any possibilities for remediation of the agreement? Art is more than a representation, more than a means to uplift (although it can do that too). When art is good, it instills a commemorating force. When we view the *Nympheas* today, we see the reminder of what once was. The legacy. The force of this memory is as strong as the cleverly manipulated forces of painting technique that Monet used – colour as mood, layers of paint as an illusory device, and the haze of light that reveals and conceals in a soothing yet antagonistic way. These are the forces exerted by the artist in his studio. They are used not to disrupt but to bind, like an evangelical aesthetician calling together a community of lookers, an aggregate of people who are bound by a connection to the earth's produce and bounty.

The water lily's roots nestle in the silt below the water but its leaves and flowers are mobile, floating across the reflective water surface. The conventional criteria for considering plants as less relevant than the human species, since the era of 18th century nature classifier Karl Linnaeus, are based on vegetal lack of mobility and sentience.[26] It is possible to undermine this latter convention, based on recent discoveries in plant science that support the concept of plant intelligence, cognitive sensing and learning.[27] Mobility and sentience are scrutinised as legitimate criteria for relevance.

Water lilies have capacities and qualities that support a feminist life due to their adaptive option to self-reproduce, and provide an ideal model for inter-species, non-hierarchical ways of living. We can learn models of appropriate ethical and political behaviour from the vegetal world by raising the status of plants from sub-species to co-species. This suggests a model of thought where vegetal life is equal to human life and where the 'feed' or ecology of dependence is a human reliance on plants for survival – rather than mistakenly perceiving the reverse. This is, in part, a reference to the production and harvesting of plant life, its manufacture and economy. Humans perceive the relationship between humankind and crop plants as a process of dutiful and/or technological care (processes such as water reticulation, bug spraying and artificial nutrients) and that these crops survive only if supported by constant human attention.

---

26   Michael Marder, *The Philosopher's Plant*, New York: Columbia 2014, 63.

27   Monica Gagliano, 'In a green frame of mind: perspectives on the behavioural ecology and cognitive nature of plants.' *AOB* 7, 2015.

The current state of agricultural affairs makes this true in the sense that our practices have selectively reduced both the genetic and phenotypic variability of those plant species we grow as crops. By constraining them into obligate annuals designed for uninhibited sex and early death, the process of converting wild species into tamed plants fit for human consumption has enfeebled them, stripping them of their ability to communicate effectively to protect themselves from pests and diseases.[28]

As Gagliano writes:

> In fact as a result of breeding for increased growth or yield in modern agricultural systems, many modern crop cultivars such as cacao, corn and cranberry, to name a few, have lost their ability to produce adequate quantities of volatile organic compounds to maintain the integrity of their precious relationships with the arthropod community, which includes beneficial insects pollinating them and controlling their pests.[29]

Gagliano explains that plants are no longer able to 'cry for help' or emit key chemical information when they are under attack or are suffering root damage, which means they become susceptible. This then continues into a decline, where yearly yield loads are reduced by the billions.[30] That being said, it can also be argued that this perception is skewed and we have forgotten, due to our cultivated urban relationships with plants, that the natural processes of growth occur with or without human contact. The longevity of ancient clonal plants such as the water lilies, whose cells and tissues can survive impeccably for millennia, is indeed an excellent example to illustrate this point. Thus it can be argued that plant life, without human intervention, provides valuable lessons of adaptation and sustainability for co-species living.

We can develop human strategies for how to focus on the processes of being and becoming by observing how plants are and how they change. This establishes a way to understand that being rooted in the earth does not necessarily correspond to being immobile or lacking in the associated processes of reason or decision-making. It discusses how to participate in a linguistic exchange

---

28   Gibson, P. and Gagliano, M. 'The Feminist Plant: Changing Relations with the Water Lily.' *Ethics and the Environment*, Vol 22, Issue 2, 2017.

29   N. Dudareva, A. Klempien, J.K. Muhlemann, I. Kaplan, 'Biosynthesis, function and metabolic engineering of plant volatile organic compounds' *New Phytologist* 198, 2013: 16–32.

30   Gibson, P. and Gagliano, M. 'The Feminist Plant: Changing Relations with the Water Lily.' *Ethics and the Environment*, Vol 22, Issue 2, 2017.

that exists outside human meaning and it seeks to find a way of being that is not hierarchical and not gender specific, but is instead a return to an inner earth, as opposed to the de-privileging notions of 'Mother Earth.'

We see plant or vegetal writing to be a form of feminist writing, a means to develop the idea of the plant world outside of heteronormative values and outside a generalist community. Humans have ignored the hardships of plant life – just as we have ignored the plight of women in terms of equal pay, equal work opportunities, the right to work outside the domestic home and shared parenting duties. These are socially perceptive conditions that women and plants have in common. That is, vegetal writing sits alongside the growth of plants and acknowledges the wealth of knowledge and capabilities of plant life – it does not operate within an authoritative hierarchy, it appreciates active co-species qualities and it understands that all species thrive when they function as communities.

The Woman Moves

Gagliano says:

> In his world-wide famous opera *Rigoletto*, Giuseppe Verdi entrusts one of his most remarkable arias, "La donna e' mobile," to one of his most despicable characters, the Duke of Mantua. While he sings what becomes his signature tune about the woman being fickle, it is ironically, he blissfully unaware who personifies the volatile and fickle character in the opera. With a surprisingly feminist element, the catchy aria illuminates the arrogant and condescending attitude towards a feminine, whose apparent lack in groundedness ('qual piuma al vento'/ 'like a feather in the wind') and inwardness ('Muta d'accento e di pensier'/ 'She changes her voice and her mind' or alternatively translate as 'She does not speak nor think'), relegate it to a place of inferiority and even unconsciousness. By offering a comic moment in the story with the Duke boasting about his superiority to women in the area of stability, could the aria disclose the idea that the declared feminine fickleness and lack of awareness is a projection of a masculine inner instability? If this was the case, we may expect the unstable masculine character of our culture to unnaturally consign its feminine counterpart to a ground of limited or no movement – if successful, the woman is mobile no more.

> Women have suffered from conventions of immobility. Whether bound by domesticity, motherhood or the workplace glass ceiling, these

experiences have been adequately documented already. What is less known is how plants too have experienced a de-privileging associated with an apparent lack of movement. The perception of plants as immobile objects in space and time emerges from the superficial and impatient glances of humans and it is – in Francis Hallé's words (personal communication) – "an extremely deluded impression on the part of us animals." Indeed, this perception has very little to do with reality in general, where "nothing happens until something moves" – as pointed out by Einstein. And in actuality, something is always happening in a constant flow of beginning and becoming that makes life. If plants were truly immobile as prescribed by conventional wisdom, then plant life would not be *happening* – there would be no beginnings and certainly, no becomings. And yet, the growth of plants through space and their rhythmic changes across time stand as an unquestionable testimony to the mere appearance, rather than actual truth, of plant immobility.[31]

Much vegetal life has the appearance of immobility due to their rootedness in the soil. This stable, fixed (but certainly *not* immobile) position on the earth's surface can be seen as doubly advantageous, particularly if there is a duality to that rootedness. It suggests a secured position from which to courageously swing to and fro in surrender, swaying flowers and rattling leaves at a tempo dictated by the breeze. All this swaying and rattling is no poetic figure of speech but actual adaptation for successful plant reproduction and defence.

The apparent immobility of plants also suggests a firm position from which to emerge, described by Elizabeth Grosz as the beginning: a chaotic and unpredictable movement of forces. Grosz develops the idea that sexual selection, the consequence of sexual difference, is the source of endless generation but is also the source of indeterminate taste, pleasure and sensation.[32] I would like to extend this idea of a beginning to the plant world. Plants' capacity to use both sexual and self-production generates multiple alternatives. Different types of sexual selection and production increase reproductive success. Plants such as the water lily adopt both types of reproduction mechanisms; moving between the two means to achieve maximum outcomes. In several species of water lilies, the female and male functions overlap, enabling self-pollination.

---

31 Gibson, P. and Gagliano, M. 'The Feminist Plant: Changing Relations with the Water Lily.' *Ethics and the Environment*, Vol 22, Issue 2, 2017.

32 Elizabeth Grosz, *Chaos, Territory, Art*, New York: Columbia University Press, 2008, 6.

Gagliano explains that the vast majority of species, however, have bisexual flowers with female and male functions more or less separated in time, where flowers open one day in the receptive female phase to then close and reopen the following day in the male phase.[33] In some water lily species, the stigma (the female part of the flower) becomes hidden by bending itself over the center of the flower or by being covered by the stamens (the pollen-producing male part of the flower), which bend over it.[34] All this movement is agile and adaptive. To move is to think, to experience, to learn.[35]

So the act of moving and the facility of mobility stems from the 'beginning' of life. As Grosz says, sexual selection, a convention of evolution, also opens up a body of sensory activities such as 'taste and pleasure.'[36] Here, Grosz is referring to conditions associated with the sublime. However, I prefer to redirect attention to plant biology as ready-made models for better living, rather than reverting to transcendental mechanisms that remove humans (subjects) from nature (objects). Instead, I hope to suggest that water lilies and their processes of sexual or natural selection are open and emergent: they are beginnings and becomings.

And all this movement in space is also done in good time because plants know the importance of aligning their internal circadian clocks with external environmental signals. Showing a remarkable ability to adjust the speed of starch consumption in response to changes in day length, plants are able to maintain efficient photosynthesis during the day as well as optimal use of reserves during the night.[37] Clearly, time-keeping is crucial to the immediacy of plant survival, but also to its reproductive success, to ensure the continuation of the species. The opening and closing time of flowers, for instance, varies between species and has coevolved in synchrony with the presence and activities of animals. Among the water lilies, some species bloom exclusively by day and others by night. Day-blooming species are usually characterised by brightly coloured flowers that are sought out as a pollen and nectar source by insects such as bees and flies. These flowers are at most only moderately fragrant.

---

33 J.H. Wiersema, 'Reproductive biology of *Nymphaea* (Nymphaeaceae),' *Annals of the Missouri Botanical Garden* 75, 1988: 795–804.

34 G. Hirthe, S. Porembski, 'Pollination of *Nymphaea lotus* (Nymphaeaceae) by rhinoceros beetles and bees in the northeastern Ivory Coast,' *Plant Biology* 5, 2003: 670–676.

35 Monica Gagliano, co-written journal paper with Prudence Gibson, under peer review, pending.

36 Elizabeth Grosz, *Chaos, Territory, Art,* New York: Columbia University Press, 2008, 6.

37 A. Graf, A.M. Smith, 'Starch and the clock: the dark side of plant productivity,' *Trends in Plant Science* 16, 2011: 169–175.

Plant Protests and Smell

In terms of the fragrance of plant life and the sensory and phenomenological experience of plant olfaction, I must include a short discussion of Australian artist Cat Jones' work. Although the 2017 performance was not specifically on the water lily, its olfactory sensations were intense and vastly connected to the concept of a becoming-woman, a feminist and a political protest.

As part of the Sydney Festival in January 2017, Cat Jones created an experience room at Carriageworks Sydney (see figure 8). In the space were five tables with upturned cups. Each table had a theme – landscape, competition, democracy, extravagance, resistance – and there were headphones to listen to stories told by various Sydney characters, talking about how they relate to the idea of scent in Sydney. These stories related to the themes as well as olfactory memories and how the two interrelate.

So the experience for a participant, such as myself, was to wander and sit at the tables, smell the aromas Cat had made and infused in the upturned cups and listen to stories. Afterwards, I was given the chance to talk with a roaming artist-crew member who helped me formulate my own scent of Sydney and to talk about why those smells are important to me.

After being interviewed by the artist/crew member – who was also a friend, Sumugan Sivanesan – it turns out that the scents I associate with Sydney are storm-driven seaweed rotting on the beach, mould growing on garden soil, newly cut grass, the burning off from the incinerator in our back yard (where my dad burned off the garden refuse) and dead rats. I didn't intend my overall Sydney scent to be quite so fetid and manky but that's how the story of the smell of Sydney evolved for me.

The reason I liked Jones' format was because it occurred to me that the scents I had identified were all related to the artist's fifth theme of 'resistance.' Seaweed expelled from the ocean and ruining the perfect crescent of the beach; rats being killed by human-laid poisons but leaving a fetid stench far worse than their scampering could ever be; the white cobwebs of mould creeping across the soil in my back garden. These are all examples of defiance, resilience, resistance to order, resistance to human control and our desire for pristine perfection.

These smells of biotic matter that I associate with the place of my birth and my home city are plant-based. The olfactory memory of plants is strong, but their defiance of humans is stronger still. They persevere and they move, they linger and they defy.

Plant and Female Mobility

To move from fragrance, one kind of vegetal elusiveness, back to the mobility of plants, another kind of elusiveness, is to keep mobility high. Pigeon-holing plant life into non-mobility (as a representation of the supposed vegetal inability to make cognitive decisions or enact a will) is to misunderstand the concepts of nature's workings. Although much plant life is made static in their earthy position, nevertheless root systems can move for many kilometres to reach water or minerals. It is also a misreading of the ecology of vegetal matter. Bees, beetles and moths move to pollinate and then, mostly, fly away.

So the mobility of plants may appear to be limited, that is, by virtue of mostly being rooted in the ground and not being able to 'run away' from prey. However, the rapid and effective communication and movement of information within the plant itself represents an alternative form of mobility. As Aristotle says in *De Anima*, plants exhibit three of the four types of movement. They alter their state, grow and decay. The only mobility it does not have is changing its position.[38] To define mobility only in terms of a changed position in space strikes me as more limiting than being rooted in the soil. In addition, water lilies defy this fourth type of movement by being able to change position in space, via floating flowers across water. This, then, effectively places the water lily in a position of higher relevance than previously thought.

Gender-Neutrality

Plants function without organs, without a brain, yet they survive aggressive attacks, extreme weather conditions and food shortages. These, surely, are attributes of a species to pay more attention to. Plants have been associated with many gender-specific and pre-feminist narratives. Likewise, women have regularly been associated with the blooming of flowers and the blossoming of buds – the genitalia of flowers as being female with the male stamen rising up out of it.

This desire to eschew gendered preoccupations, for instance reconsidering the water lily as sexualised female deity, provokes a context within nature-culture that requires a 'becoming-other.' Can we follow the true spirit of vegetal life (its self-reproduction and interspecies reproductive assistants – beetles,

---

38   Michael Marder, *The Philosopher's Plant,* New York: Columbia 2014, 20.

moths and bees) and disrupt the notion of earth as reductively female and re-place it with fluidly female? Can we reclaim nature and plant life as a queering place, where gender is as irrelevant as the human, but difference is allowed? Claire Colebrook engages with queer theory as it relates to logics of survival. This survivalist theorising is important when discussing the specific qualities of vegetal life to grow, decay, revive, and become. She writes against a generative model of life and instead discusses whether queer theory reflects on being queer or suggests that the changing nature of being queer affects the way we theorise.[39]

I would like to extend this point to posit that the emergent possibilities of plant life and their hidden skillsets affect the way we theorise on nature. Cole-brook's Queer Vitalism proposes that what life ought to be must emerge from what life is. The 'self as it is formed in the social unit of the family (with the self, taking on either male or female norms) fail to account for the emergence of the self and the genesis of the family.'[40] In contrast, Colebrook maintains that passive vitalism is queer in its difference and distance from constituted images of life as fruitful and generative and humanly organized. Colebrook believes this passive vitalism has implications for aesthetics in terms of the creation of monuments rather than work. The body emerges and is formed through encounters with the sensual.

Community

To subvert old habits, to show audiences the potential for change, is the key to new philosophical thinking surrounding vegetal life. The concept of community focuses on the communication, growing patterns and rhythmic being of the water lily as a case study for how we can learn from vegetal life. The water lily is female but fluidly female and communally female. It is a sexuate difference that is on the brink of change, rather than contained, discrete and bound.

Donna Haraway quotes Don Ihde in her book *When Species Meet*. Ihde says 'In this interconnection of embodied being and environing world, what hap-pens in the interface is what is important.'[41] Haraway proceeds to investigate the intersections of non-human marine animals, human marine scientists, cameras and National Geographic and television documentaries. Her point

39   Claire Colebrook, 'Queer Vitalism,' in *Sex After Life*, Open Humanities Press, 2014, 236.

40   Ibid, 101.

41   Donna Haraway, *When Species Meet*, Minneapolis: University of Minnesota Press, 2008, 249.

is that these experiences and things are both inter-related and compounded (both a composite and an enclosure). They are parts and wholes that are conjoined and separate at the same time. The water lily community is similar. It can reproduce alone or together, it can move and remain stationary. The research and writing into the water lily community – the mythological significance of water lilies as feminine spirits and Luce Irigaray's writing on water lilies –are wholes and parts of wholes, communities and individuals that gather as part of a community.

As Deleuze/Guattari said, 'Follow the plants: you start by delimiting a first line consisting of circles of convergence around successive singularities; then you see whether inside that line new circles of convergence establish themselves, with new points located outside the limits and in other directions ... in nature, roots are taproots with a more multiple, lateral, and circular system of ramification, rather than a dichotomous one.'[42] Humans see the single flower, the single tree and, based on our conventional reliance on nature for our spiritual and contemplative meaning, cannot see beyond that singularity. The subterranean language of plants is a series of chemical emissions and receptions. Deleuze and Guattari's concept that language can be broken down into internal structural elements and is not fundamentally different from a search for roots strikes an accord with what new science now shows – that there is rhizomic assemblage multiplicity rather than unity or units of measure.[43]

The multiple, then, is not a single rose growing on its own, nor is it a single woman gazing upon that one rose. The multiple is the community of plants, its ecosystem of like species among other species. Fungi help to send messages from root to root. Beetles and moths help pollinate at night. Various roots from various plants search for nutrients and water and communicate their findings. This, then, is not a male patriarchal or hierarchical system of politics. It is an aggregated and equalized community.

There is a desire among plants to survive, to flourish. Like the concept of becoming woman, this could be considered a desire to communicate and contribute to the lives of our neighbours as much as ourselves. Could this model of vegetal behaviour be worth more than we previously thought? Perhaps more urgently, does this desire to flourish change our preconceptions of plants as inert, immobile and incapable of thought processes or decisions-making? If so, what effect does this epiphany have for culture, for communities, for women?

42   Felix Guattari and Gilles Deleuze, A Thousand Plateaus, Minneapolis: Minnesota Press, 1987, 26, 34.

43   Ibid, 29.

For the feminist woman, a plant that self-reproduces, works as a team member and is mobile beyond human definitions could be a revelation of political force. Plants are the becoming of the becoming of each other.

A quality of being among a community is the ability to care. From insemination to dissemination, animal to plant, the reproduction of plants relies on winds and inter-species.[44] From the structure of an animal co-species, from the words of Donna Haraway, comes a plant co-species test. Where Haraway speaks of seeing again, holding in regard, to esteem and pay attention, she is speaking of humanity's relationship with dogs. Here I apply that respect to plant species, particularly water lily.[45]

Her concept of becoming woman is that every woman is an 'actualisation of the potentiality to be female.' For a group of humans, this means the energy lies in the force of that potentiality. Nothing has arrived, it is in flux. *The plant contract* is a radical re-thinking and a celebration of what differences there might be. Beneath these stories of artworks and of women is a tacit agreement, a contract, to pay more attention to the plant stories within each moment.

---

44   Elaine Miller, *The Vegetative Soul: From Philosophy of Nature to Subjectivity in the Feminine*, Albany: SUNY Press, 2002, 184.

45   Donna Haraway, *When Species Meet*, Minneapolis: University of Minnesota Press, 2008.

Resisting Racism,
Writing *Black Sexual Politics*

Patricia Hill Collins

REFLEXIVE ESSAY: *In* Black Sexual Politics, *my thesis was that African American anti-racist projects would remain limited until sexism and heterosexism were made central to Black intellectual analysis. The difficulty I faced in writing the book was that African Americans were firmly wedded to race-only analyses, primarily because intersectional analyses of Black experiences were scarce. I realized that I could not concentrate solely on the ideas of my argument but also had to attend to the process I used in writing it. Because I envisioned* Black Sexual Politics *as scholarship that was placed in service to social justice, I faced decisions about not only the purpose of the book but also its intended audiences, content, and form (prose). Working with, for, and/or on behalf of oppressed groups raises a distinctive set of concerns that shape the choice of topics, research methods, and intended audiences. In this essay, I examine how these broader concerns affected the approaches I decided to take in* Black Sexual Politics.

BLACK SEXUAL POLITICS: *African Americans, Gender, and the New Racism* illustrates one site of my intellectual activism, where I place my scholarship in service to social justice. In this volume, I use the experiences of African Americans to examine the contradictions and tensions that surround anti-racist politics. I argue that African Americans must make gender and sexuality more central features of anti-racist political agendas. In essence, African

Americans need an adequate analysis of the new racism as well as new political strategies to deal with it.

In the book, I present the following set of ideas: (1) Black sexual politics consists of a set of ideas and social practices shaped by gender, race, and sexuality that frame Black men's and women's treatment of one another, as well as how African Americans are perceived and treated by others; (2) Black sexual politics lies at the heart of beliefs about black masculinity and black femininity, gender-specific experiences of African Americans, and the new racism in the post–Civil Rights era; (3) to confront social inequality, African Americans need an analysis of black masculinity and black femininity that questions the links between prevailing Black sexual politics, the connection to black gender ideology, and struggles for African American empowerment in response to the new racism; (4) taking into account the new challenges of the post–Civil Rights era, such an analysis would strive to point the way toward a more progressive Black sexual politics within African American communities; and (5) this politics in turn might both catalyze a more effective anti-racist politics and contribute to a broader social justice agenda. Collectively, this analytical framework shapes the core arguments advanced in the book.

Readers often think that ideas such as these fall from the sky and that the craft of writing a book matters little in relation to the final product. Yet when it comes to scholarship in service to social justice, the processes of intellectual production can be just as important as the ideas that find their way into print. For *Black Sexual Politics,* I was trying to engage in anti-racist intellectual activism during a period when the contours of racism itself were undergoing considerable change. It is difficult to analyze change, write about change, and try to effect change when you are living with the contradictions of change itself.

The challenges that I encountered in writing *Black Sexual Politics* illustrate broader issues associated with scholarship in service to social justice. The overarching goal of scholarship in service to social justice is not to explain social inequality or social injustice, but to foster social justice, to bring about some sort of change. Social injustice and social inequality are not necessarily the same thing. Situations of social inequality may or may not be unjust. Social inequalities exist that may be justified (e.g., power over young children to protect them from harm). In contrast, social justice traditions challenge *unfair, unjust,* or *unethical* social inequalities. For example, the abuse of children hiding behind ideologies that defend abuse with claims that it's natural to discipline them *does* qualify as a situation of social injustice. I use the term "oppression" to refer to the unjust structures, practices, and ideas that catalyze social inequality. Via its questions, methods, findings, and/or intended audiences, scholarship in service to social justice is against oppression.

We should ask how scholarship in service to social justice differs from traditional mainstream scholarship. Traditional mainstream scholarship is based on the quest for truth—the phrase "knowledge for knowledge's sake" captures this sensibility. Traditional scholarship has been extremely helpful to social justice projects, yet, because such scholarship sees knowledge as an end in and of itself, it need not be placed in service to social justice agendas. Much traditional scholarship, in fact, has been far more complicit with social injustice than is typically acknowledged. In part, traditional scholarship must play by a set of rules where neither ethics nor politics is deemed suitable for scholarship endeavors—these are seen as introducing bias into the scholarly process. In contrast, scholarship in service to social justice places ideas and the "truths" that emerge from mainstream scholarship in dialogue with broader ethical and/or political concerns. Such scholarship constitutes a tradition of engaged research designed to help people envision and build more equitable and fair societies, not to help them better fit into things the way they are. In essence, scholarship in service to social justice constitutes harnessing the power of ideas in service to social justice.

In this sense, there is an important distinction between scholarship *in support of* social justice and scholarship *in service to* social justice. Scholarship *in support of* social justice implies a lack of accountability on the part of the scholar—others are engaged in social justice projects and the thinker in question aims to make a contribution but is not held accountable for how his or her contribution works out. In contrast, scholarship *in service to* social justice invokes the responsibilities that are associated with the idea of service itself, namely, that service should be unpaid, freely chosen, altruistic, and may involve sacrifice. Positioning one's scholarship within a service framework by doing scholarship in service to social justice may mean being underpaid or even not getting paid at all, making choices that put one at odds with prevailing academic norms, having one's altruism mistaken for a passion for service, and/or assuming the risks of censure, failure, persecution, and other negative outcomes.

The specific decision points I encountered while writing *Black Sexual Politics* shed light on the challenges of engaged scholarship generally, and scholarship in service to social justice, in particular. Two overarching questions guided this project. First, what is the purpose of this book? Second, who make up its intended audience? These dimensions of purpose and audience are simultaneously intellectual and political. Together they define the context for the work. Let me address each in turn.

Purpose: Engaged Anti-Racist Scholarship

I had three main reasons for writing *Black Sexual Politics*. My first and most fundamental reason was to resist racism by writing a book about racism. I actually began working on *Black Sexual Politics* as a continuation of the analysis I advanced in *Black Feminist Thought* (1990). Then as now, I saw the need for a Black feminist analysis of the gender politics within African American communities that addressed the ways in which the politics helped or hindered anti-racist projects. My sense was that African American conceptions of both black masculinity and sexuality as ideological constructions weakened Black politics. In the 1990s, the scholarship that I needed to write *Black Sexual Politics* was in its infancy. Considerable scholarship existed on African American men, yet much of it was neither analytical nor considered masculinity as a gendered structure. Similarly, work on sexuality did challenge homophobia, yet racial analyses were scarce in the literature. Analytical arguments of black masculinity and/or sexuality that reflected robust intersectional frameworks were not fully developed.

The broader scholarly context of the 1990s also influenced my sense that my vision for *Black Sexual Politics,* namely, resisting racism by writing a book about racism, would be an uphill battle. I increasingly encountered scholars who were safely housed in elite academic institutions and simply had little interest in actual politics. From my perspective, many of these people engaged in "race" talk (always in quotations to suggest that they knew that race wasn't real), yet refused to walk the race walk at their own institutions. During this decade, historical and empirical research on racism that had inspired me morphed into decontextualized, abstract discussions that endlessly pointed out how race was an invalid construct. For some of my colleagues, talking about race meant constructing it, and for still others, such talk meant that one was "racist." I almost gave up on academia because it seemed to be moving away from my interest in engaged scholarship. The version of Black feminism that I espoused was under attack. Despite my anger at the growing disregard for the ideas of Black women (but not actual individual Black women who, ironically, were much in demand as visible entities within a new multicultural, colorblind racism), I could not write *Black Sexual Politics* in that intellectual and political environment. I would have to wait. In the meantime, I took on other projects that enabled me to track and learn the literatures of black masculinity and sexuality.

My second reason for writing *Black Sexual Politics* is related to the first. I aimed to develop an intersectional analysis of racism that did not rely on a race-only lens, but instead showed how it only made sense via intersectional analyses. Despite an outpouring of scholarship in the 1980s and 1990s that argued that race, class, and gender as intersecting systems of power shaped everyone's lives, the predilection to see certain topics (and groups of people) through race-only, or gender-only, or class-only lenses, for example, persisted. When I set out to explore how racism was alive and well, I joined a legion of scholars who were writing about the new colorblind racism. My contribution was to provide a theoretical argument about how the gendered and sexual dimensions of racism had also been reconfigured in the post–Civil Rights era. *Black Sexual Politics* provides an intersectional analysis of how race, gender, and sexuality as systems of power mutually construct one another. These systems take center stage in the book. Yet *Black Sexual Politics* also incorporates an intersectional analysis of class and nationality (explored via globalization) categories as well. Thus, the book focuses on racism, yet via its intersectional lens, it challenges monocategorical analyses.

A third reason why I decided to write *Black Sexual Politics* was to develop arguments that might be useful to people working in political projects for racial justice. Academics routinely produce reams of articles, books, and conference presentations for one another that address pre-existing questions in scholarly literature. Yet we often seem far less interested in investigating the concerns of everyday people who are involved in social justice projects in their families, neighborhoods, schools, and places of employment. We study them for our own reasons, but we express less interest in studying what they want to know.

In *Black Sexual Politics,* by examining how African Americans confronted new forms of social injustice, I wanted to encourage readers to imagine new possibilities in their everyday lives. *Black Sexual Politics* is not a handbook about how to engage in political action. Rather it is a diagnostic tool that suggests that, when we think about the world differently, we often see different ways of being in it. One of the difficulties of writing "solutions" is that people want easy answers to hard questions when there are none.

In my own work, I have found that one important component of intellectual activism lies in learning how to ask good questions and drawing on the best ideas from many points of view in answering them. In *Black Sexual Politics,* I continued to engage a core existential question that guides my work: "What will it take for Black people to be free?" This question defies easy answers and formulaic thinking. For this particular project, this question pointed me toward gender and sexuality, and the kinds of political action that would be needed to move toward freedom in an era of colorblind racism. I needed to refine my question. A shift as simple as asking, "What will it take for African American men to be free?" or "What will it take for African American women to be free?" yields more nuanced answers to the question of freedom. This simple shift lies at the heart of *Black Sexual Politics,* and it is a shift that should catalyze new angles of vision on African American realities.

When it comes to the theme of scholarship in service to social justice, is this focus on the specificity of African Americans and freedom, even when refracted through intersectional arguments, enough? Many people think that engaging in social justice scholarship requires a direct connection with existing social movements and political activism. Yet scholarship in service to social justice suggests a bottom-up stance, one that respects the specificity of group experience while trying to see commonalities across differences. Many groups have had experiences that resemble those of African Americans, yet no group has had exactly the same experiences. Continuing to ask the same question with different groups at the center—"What will it take for Latinas to be free?" or "What will it take for youth in South Africa to be free?"—keeps the broader question in play, yet produces ideas that might be useful to the specific populations at hand. When placed in dialogue, the ideas developed from these multiple standpoints, each examining freedom from its own point of view, produce a whole that is greater than the sum of its parts. Social justice need not be an explicit theme. But it does need to be incorporated into the process of deciding what will count.

Black Sexual Politics is situated at this juncture between the specificity of one group's experiences and the universal themes that resonate throughout those experiences. I tell a story that is *both* specific *and* universal, working contrapuntally between the specific and the universal, trying to remain in an in-between space that allows me an angle of vision in both directions. Staying in this in-between space and using it creatively meant looking in both directions, namely, *both* to the specificity of African American experience *and* to the contributions of contemporary social theory. Moreover, each of these spaces has a variety of audiences attached to it, each of whom can have varying standards for what they deem to be important. Many authors resolve this difficulty by choosing one audience and writing to it, for example, writing a scholarly paper for publication in a refereed journal with the intention of writing a companion piece for the general public, or by writing directly for the public with the intention of figuring out how to make the ideas travel to the academic elite. *Black Sexual Politics* is written in both registers—two subtexts, one for the everyday people (in this case, African Americans and college undergraduates) and the other for scholarly elites. Rather than resolving the seeming contradictions between these two audiences, I choose to see how placing them in dialogue might shape the book. In practicality, maintaining this in-between space meant that I had to consider navigating multiple audiences.

Navigating Heterogeneous Audiences

The question of intended audience was crucial to *Black Sexual Politics,* framing virtually every decision I made in the research, writing, publication, and marketing of the volume. My target audiences consisted of scholars and academics, African Americans, both everyday and politically engaged, and a general public with an interest the themes of the book. Having multiple audiences that were very different meant that answers to my guiding questions shifted, depending on the actual topic, available material, and resources. I asked: "What are the concerns and issues of the intended audiences for *Black Sexual Politics*? What do they consider to be credible evidence and convincing arguments? What knowledge do they bring to this project? What is the best way to organize the content in regard to the concerns, issues, and worldviews of the intended audiences?"

Typically, these questions are recast as technical issues of writing style and reading level, yet, when it comes to the theme of intellectual activism, they are simultaneously intellectual questions and questions with profound political implications. Most scholars rarely stop and consider these questions, mainly because they need not do so. Most of us who produce engaged scholarship must confront these questions, primarily because we often have to work to create the conditions that make our own work possible. Scholarship that strives to step outside the seemingly objective standards of Western science must meet a higher standard of excellence, often by critiquing those standards and advocating new ones.

As writers and scholars, we can identify the integrity of the project and the challenges that might face us in writing for multiple audiences, but how do we frame what we really want to say? For this project, one danger lay in selecting examples that were too far removed not only from the everyday experiences of African Americans but also from their interpretation of those experiences. A related danger lay in making the arguments too "academic," typically received by people outside the academy as dense and boring. How sad it would be to bore people with a book about their own experiences! I was confident about my ability to write to the narrow specialty audiences of academia—but writing for a broad, heterogeneous public without unduly weakening one's argument is a challenge.

Let me share an example of what it actually meant to write for heterogeneous audiences and the public conversations that accompany this process. Recall the points of the working definition of Black sexual politics introduced early in this essay. This working definition works well with academic readers, but some of the main ideas prove to be far more relevant than others for different audiences. This became especially clear to me the first time I went on Black talk radio to "discuss" my book. One of the first questions stopped me in my tracks—"Do you think that Black men should date white women?" the caller asked, with a note of disapproval clearly expressed in the tone of her voice. The calls came hot and heavy afterward, with a heated debate about the merits of interracial dating. I never got a chance to make *any* of the "main points" of my book. Rather than blaming the callers, after that endlessly long hour was over (it was an early hour—morning Black talk radio!)—I reviewed my careful definition of Black sexual politics and realized that I needed to find different ways to discuss the material with different audiences or I had written the book for a select few who already lived in my academic world. "*Black Sexual Politics* 101" (Chapter 3) presents the polished version of the themes that were left standing as I returned repeatedly to *Black Sexual Politics,* mining the volume for themes that resonated with diverse audiences.

Yet another danger of writing for multiple audiences consists of pivots on rejecting epistemological frameworks of dominant groups. If Black intellectual production does not make sense to them or challenges dominant points of view too aggressively, that scholarship can be devalued and even suppressed. For example, within the framework of U.S. race relations, African Americans are typically studied in relation to whites, as a "minority" group or as a marginalized population, and not as a population with a set of interests, issues, and concerns that may be separate from those of whites. This has at least three common outcomes. First, it casts African American experience as a list of social problems (e.g., the issues that most concern whites are at the center of how African Americans are studied, such as unwed mothers, teen criminals, welfare cheats, racial gaps in test scores). Second, it assumes that African American experience can only provide evidence for some larger theory or perspective (white women have it bad as unwed mothers, but African American women have it really bad). Third, it assumes that African American experience is so exotic that it belongs in another category of analysis altogether (cultural deviance: "sexual practices of black folk" or the "natural predilection for violence").

Refracting African American experience through these lenses encourages African American thinkers either to do more "objective" work within a race relations framework or to move to the seemingly universal place of topics that are unrelated to people of African descent and/or that address issues that concern the general public. Currently, this first set of pressures suggests doing away with a black/white paradigm of race relations in favor of a more "modern" and seemingly theoretically complex analysis of difference. But what are the concerns of the general public? Who is this imagined general public? Within both of these strategies, African American concerns become subordinate to putatively more important issues.

The politics of knowledge that creates practices such as pushing the U.S. race relations' paradigm informs the specific decisions that I made in *Black Sexual Politics* concerning the overall purpose of the book, my imagined audiences of academics, African Americans and an interested general public, as well as the specific choice of topics. I explicitly centered on the experiences of African Americans, especially by identifying selected social issues that are important to Black people, and examined how they cannot be adequate addressed without attending to issues of gender and sexuality. Casting my argument in this fashion was designed to show how African Americans were negatively situated at the intersections of racism, sexism, and heterosexism as intersecting systems of power. Thus, when it comes to the question, "What will it take for Black people to be free?" answers that do not take all three systems of power and their intersections into account will be limited. How effectively I achieved my purpose of resisting racism by speaking to heterogeneous audiences through *Black Sexual Politics* remains to be seen.

ADDITIONAL RESOURCES

Angelou, Maya. 2009. *I Know Why the Caged Bird Sings*. New York: Ballantine.
Bell, Brenda, John Gaventa, and John Peters, eds. 1990. *We Make the Road by Walking: Conversations on Education and Social Change*, by Myles Horton and Paulo Freire. Philadelphia: Temple University Press.

"BLACK LIVES MATTER"

Structural Violence, Agency, and Resiliency in Black Transgender Women's Communities

Leo Wilton and Ellen L. Short

I have come to believe over and over again that what is most important to me must be spoken, made verbal and shared, even at the risk of having it bruised or misunderstood. That the speaking profits me, beyond any other effect.

—-Audre Lorde (*Sister Outsider*, 1984)

It wasn't until I was a young adult that I realized that my life would be very different from what I had imagined. I had no idea that I would face brutal violence and structural oppression simply for existing. I had no idea that I could be legally denied access to medical care, housing and employment... I thought the fight for Black folk to obtain civil rights in this country happened over 45 years ago. What I realized is that fight was not for the liberation of the Black Trans Woman.

—-Lourdes Ashley Hunter (*Huffpost Black Voices*, 2015)

It is not a woman's duty to disclose that she's trans to every person she meets. This is not safe for a myriad of reasons. We must shift the burden of coming out from trans women, and accusing them of hiding or lying, and focus on why it is unsafe for women to be trans.
—-Janet Mock (*Redefining Realness: My Path to Womanhood, Identity, Love, & So Much More,* 2014)

INTRODUCTION

Islan Nettles, a 21-year-old Black transgender[1] woman, was murdered adjacent to a police precinct on the streets of Harlem on August 17, 2013. According to media reports, while walking with two other Black transgender women friends, Nettles was stridently attacked by James Dixon, a 24-year-old Black man, who was accompanied by a group of male cisgendered[2] friends (Murphy, 2014). Before the events that occurred, the group of young Black men engaged in verbal sexual harassment in the form of jeering and taunting Nettles and her friends, initially identifying them as cisgendered women. After the young men recognized that Nettles and her friends were Black transgender women, homo(trans)phobic comments were made by them to the group of women. Thereafter, media accounts noted that Dixon "punched Nettles in the face, causing Nettles' head to hit the pavement so hard that she incurred a serious brain injury that left her unconscious… Dixon allegedly continued to punch Nettles even while she lay on the ground motionless" (Eromosele, 2015). Nettles was taken to Harlem Hospital where, in a coma, she was placed on life support, and died a few days later as a result of the brain trauma. The activism of Dolores Nettles, the mother of Islan Nettles, her family, and Black transgender women's (LGBT) communities through the Trans

FIGURE 8.1.   This Photo Illustrates the Community Organizing and Mobilization That Occurred in Response to the Hate Crime and Murder of Islan Nettles.

Women of Color Collective[3] along with other supporters addressed the egregious hate crime that was committed against Nettles—an aspiring and talented fashion designer—including the legal structural barriers involving the mishandling and long delays of the legal case of Nettles, which resulted in the indictment of Dixon (Kellaway, 2015).

Tiffany Gooden, a 19-year-old Black transgender woman, was murdered as the result of being stabbed several times and found in an abandoned building on the west side of Chicago on August 14, 2012 (Jenkin, 2012). One of the residents in the Chicago neighborhood commented, "They said it was a male dressed like a female that they found in the house." It is important to note this description of Gooden did not portray her as an individual, nor as a person, but as an "it," who was "a male dressed like a female." This description denied Gooden's humanity and her choice to express her gender identity in a way that was meaningful to her in life and in death. Moreover, Gooden's body was found a few blocks away from where one of her friends, Paige Clay, a 23-year-old, Black transgender woman, was murdered by a gunshot wound to the face and found in an alley a few months earlier on April 16, 2012. Clay, an "'outgoing and determined' young woman, who had experienced gender-based violence, was recognized for her involvement in the house ball community[4] in Chicago (Kostek, 2013). There have been no arrests or charges in the cases of Paige and Clay and there is a void in information about the circumstances of their murders, which illustrates the persistent erasure, silencing, and invisibility related to the enactment of violence against Black transgender women's communities. In the 2012 article published on The Root entitled, "Transgender Deaths: Where is the Outcry?" the executive director of National Coalition of Justice, Sharon Lettman-Hicks cited a level of indifference and inaction towards violence perpetrated towards trans women. The article cited that Black and civil rights communities were "shamefully silent when victims of violence were [B]lack and transgender." The article identified the Trans People of Color Coalition, a national social-justice organization promoting the interests of transgender people of color as urging civil rights and community leaders to join their appeal to "consciousness and action" and to the Department of Justice to establish a task force to investigate the systemic murders of multiple transgender women of color who they cited as being "attacked for living their truth" (McLeod, 2012).

The murders of Islan Nettles, Tiffany Gooden, and Paige Clay are part of a larger, ongoing, and systemic problem of racialized and gendered violence perpetrated against women who are Black and transgender. This chapter will examine multi-layered structural inequalities embedded in acts of violence for Black transgender women. The domains of stigma, marginalization, and structural inequalities will be explored from an intersectional conceptual framework. A specific emphasis will be placed on contemporary contexts of violence directed against Black transgender women's communities. Another salient component of the chapter will explore how Black transgender women's communities respond to violence and enact a sense of agency and resiliency in addressing this understudied domain.

THE CONTEXT OF BLACK LIVES MATTER

"Our lives begin to end the day we become silent about things that matter."
Martin Luther King, Jr.

There has been an evolving public discourse about structural violence embedded in Black communities that emerged based on the case of Trayvon Martin, a 17-year-old, Black cisgendered male high school student who was racially profiled and murdered by George Zimmerman in Florida while walking home from the store in the evening on February 26, 2012; Zimmerman was not indicted in the killing of Martin (Alvarez, 2015). The Trayvon Martin case received (inter) national media attention involving ongoing protests and outcry in Black communities, which culminated into the Black Lives Matter Movement. Founded in 2012 by Alicia Garza, Patrisse Cullors, and Opal Tometi, three Black queer women, the Black Lives Matter movement—a call to action that affirms Black communities and addresses structural violence—engages the salience of social justice and human rights implications in the lives of Black people (Black Lives Matter, n. d.). Following the Trayvon Martin case, several occurrences of the murders of Black cisgendered men have been the focus of public discourse in the construction of this ideological framework, such as Eric Garner, John Crawford III, Walter Scott, and Freddie Gray, Jr. On July 17, 2014, Eric Garner, a 43-year-old, Black cisgendered man was placed in an illegal choke-hold by New York City police for allegedly selling "loosies" (i.e., individual cigarettes), which resulted in him indicating "I can't breathe" and subsequently dying on the street in Staten Island (Goodman & Baker, 2014). His death was classified as a homicide. John Crawford III, a 22-year-old, Black cisgendered male was shot and killed by Sean Williams, a White police officer, while handling a toy BB gun in a Walmart store in Dayton, Ohio on August 5, 2014 (Connolly, 2015). Michael Brown, an 18-year-old, Black cisgendered man was killed by White police officers for allegedly taking cigarillos in a convenience store in Ferguson, Missouri (Buchanan et al., 2014). Walter Scott, a 50-year-old Black cisgendered man, who was unarmed, was shot in the back by a White police officer while he was running away after a routine traffic stop for a non-working brake light in North Charleston, South Carolina on April 4, 2015 (Glinder & Santora, 2015). Freddie Gray, Jr., a 25-year-old, Black cisgendered man was arrested by the Baltimore Police Department for allegedly concealing a switchblade. Gray, Jr., while in police custody in a police van, died due to spinal cord injuries (Pérez-Peña, 2015).

According to the Black Lives Matter Movement, "When we say Black Lives Matter, we are broadening the conversation around state violence to include all of the ways in which Black people are intentionally left powerless at the hands of the state. We are talking about the ways in which Black lives are deprived of our basic human rights and dignity....How Black women bearing the burden of relentless assault of our children and our families is state violence. How Black queer and trans folks bear a unique burden from a hetero-patriarchal society that disposes us like garbage and simultaneously fetishizes us and profits off of us, and that is state violence..." (Black Lives Matter, n. d.). Nonetheless, one of the contradictions related to how the Black Lives Matter movement was created from an intersectional ideological framework by three Black queer women has involved the anchoring of this grassroots human rights intervention in a hetero-normative, male-centered discourse that places gendered analyses on the periphery. One glaring example of this erasure is the ongoing void and neglect in public discourse about structural violence embedded in Black communities pertaining to Black cisgendered women who experience gender-based violence (Richie, 2012).

Recent egregious illustrations of how Black cisgendered women have experienced multiple forms of violence include the cases of Rekia Boyd, Ersula Ore, and Chalena Cooks. In 2012, Rekia Boyd, a 22-year-old, Black cisgendered woman, was shot in the head and killed by Dante Servin, a White detective, who fired several shots with an unregistered gun into a large group of people while he was off duty, in Chicago. Servin inaccurately assumed that one of the people walking in the group of Black folks had a gun when, in actuality, was a cellphone. Although Servin was charged with involuntary manslaughter, he was acquitted of these charges (Schmadeke & Gorner, 2015). In 2014, Ersula Ore, an English professor at Arizona State University, a Black cisgendered woman, was subjected to excessive force by Stewart Ferrin, a White cisgendered male university police officer for "jay-walking" during the evening. Ore reported that she walked across the middle of the street due to construction. She was confronted by Ferrin and following a discrepancy between them was thrown to the ground and arrested by him, with some of her clothing being unveiled in public. Arizona State University initially supported Ferrin's actions but he later resigned from his position based on the University's intent to terminate his employment due to policy violations (Blinder, 2015). In 2015, Charlena Cooks, a Black pregnant woman, was wrestled to the ground by White police officers following a disagreement with a White woman regarding parking. When confronted by the police and asked for her name, Cooks only provided a first name and was subjected to this severe physical violence (Goodman, 2015).

Furthermore, these pervasive acts of police-related violence have been experienced by Black cisgendered girls. For example, Dajerria Becton, a 15-year-old Black girl, while at a graduation pool party in Texas, was violently thrown to the ground, placed faced-down with a knee in her back, and her braids being forcefully pulled by Eric Casebolt, a White cisgendered male corporal police officer on June 5, 2015; this extreme act of aggression and dehumanization was accompanied by Casebolt wielding his gun at other Black youth (Cole-Frowe & Fausset, 2015). The police indicated that community members in the majority White province of McKinney reported [inaccurately] that youth did not have permission to use the pool following an alleged altercation between White parents and some Black youth (Gross, 2015). These cases highlight how Black cisgendered women and girls have been disproportionately impacted by numerous acts of violence including but not limited to sexual assault (e.g., rape), intimate-partner, and police-related violence and are one of the least protected groups from these horrific assaults (Richie, 2012).

The marginalization of gendered analyses in the public formulation of the Black Lives Matter movement can be linked to that of Black transgender women, who have experienced multiple forms of exclusion embedded in structural disenfranchisement and subordination based on the intersection of race, gender, and class domains. For example, Kimberlé Crenshaw (2014) notes that "These [inequalities] are sometimes framed as distinctive and mutually exclusive axes of power, for example racism is distinct from patriarchy which is in turn distinct from class oppression. In fact, the systems often overlap and cross each other, creating complex intersections at which two, three, or four of these axes meet" (p. 17). The ongoing killing of Black transgender women, as will be further described later, is connected to structural violence in the form of legal, political, economic, health, and educational disenfranchisement, for example, as illustrated in the cases of Nettles, Gooden, and Clay. According to Master and Sherouse (2015), "These [murders] occur at the intersection of racism, transphobia, misogyny and homophobia—forms of discrimination that work together to force transgender people of color into poverty; deny them employment, housing, access to health care and fair treatment from law enforcement..." Therefore, the critical role of understanding multi-layered processes embedded in power relationships based on structural subordination is pivotal to addressing micro-level processes that occur in the everyday lived experiences of Black transgender women's communities.

EXPERIENCES OF VIOLENCE FOR BLACK TRANSGENDER WOMEN

Black transgender women experience increasing disproportionate rates of violence in the United States (US) (Graham et al., 2014). According to a national report on hate violence from the National Coalition of Anti-Violence Programs (NCAVP) (2015), which documented the experiences of lesbian, gay, bisexual, transgender, queer, and HIV-affected communities, Blacks represented the highest rate of hate violence with homicides (60%) as compared to Latino/as (15%) and Whites (15%). The NCAVP report also showed that 55% of the hate violence-related homicides were transgender women, with 50% representing transgender women of color (NCAVP, 2015), and the majority of these cases were Black transgender women (O. Ahmed, personal communication, June 8, 2015). Notably, transgender women of color reported elevated rates of police-related violence, including physical violence, as compared to White cisgendered individuals (NCAVP, 2015).

Furthermore, Grant et al. (2011) conducted a national survey, *Injustice at Every Turn: A Report of the National Transgender Discrimination Survey*, on the discrimination experiences of transgender communities in the US (n=6,436). Importantly, related to police-related violence, findings indicated that Black transgender individuals (n=290) reported the highest rates (38%) of police harassment and assault as compared to other racial/ethnic groups (the data presented in this report was not disaggregated by gender identity for Black respondents). Grant et al. (2011) also observed higher percentages of Black transgender respondents with a household income of less than $10,000 per year (38.0%) and a history of homelessness (41.0%), which is indicative of living below the federal poverty level. The survey respondents with a history of homelessness reported being denied access to shelters (40.0%) and experiencing harassment (61.0%), physical assault (32.0%), and sexual assault (31.0%) within the shelters. Earlier work on discrimination in Black LGBT communities demonstrated that the most common bias reported by survey respondents at Black pride events related to racial and ethnic identity (53%), followed by sexual orientation (42%) (Battle et al. 2002); Black transgender individuals indicated that bias related to gender identity (e.g., transgender) was the most common bias type (58%). Moreover, the overall sample noted that the most important issues experienced by Black LGBT communities related to HIV/AIDS (64.0%), hate crime violence (42.0%), and marriage/domestic partnerships (30.0%); however, Black transgender individuals reported that job discrimination/lack of jobs (45.0%) and HIV/AIDS (45.0%), followed by hate crimes (35.0%) and drugs (33.0) were their primary concerns. Taken together, these findings highlight the severe and pervasive impact of violence for Black transgender women's communities. These acts of violence are highly invisible in national media coverage, policy considerations, and structural prevention interventions (Grant et al., 2011; NCAVP, 2015). These findings must be situated within multi-layered forms of structural violence and disenfranchisement embedded in social, economic, legal, political, and educational systems. These acts of violence also occur within the context of intersectional frameworks of institutional racism, poverty, (trans) homophobia, and sexism.

STIGMA, MARGINALIZATION, AND STRUCTURAL INEQUALITIES

A critical component for interrogating and addressing violence for Black transgender women's communities involves the development and application of theoretical frameworks that are nested within culturally relevant conceptualizations. A critical analytic framework for violence research—based on theory, methodologies, and praxis—incorporates a connection to the intersection of racial, gender, sexuality, and social class politics (Cohen, 2004). In this context, a fundamental dimension of this work calls for a paradigm shift that links violence within interdisciplinary and intersectional frameworks that coalesce with socio-structural factors that are relevant to the life experiences of Black transgender women. Notably, the concepts of stigma, marginalization, and structural inequalities provide a theoretical framework to examine the multi-layered manifestations of structural violence, as located in the everyday, lived experiences of Black transgender women.

The overarching theoretical construct of marginalization, as articulated by (Cohen, 1999), can be applied to violence. Building on the work of Cohen (1999), these fundamental ideas provide a theoretical framework for addressing asymmetrical power relationships (i.e., power inequalities) in Black communities, including those that incorporate socio-historical and –political experiences of "exclusion and marginalization" based on race/ethnicity, gender, sexuality, and social class, for example. Moreover, according to Cohen (1999), a major component of these critical analyses pertain to the duality of examining macro (e.g., external processes) and micro (e.g., internal processes) structures that have an impact on Black communities in relation to articulations of violence. For example, macro level processes relate marginalization associated with larger social structures (e.g., structural inequalities based on legal, political, economic, and educational structures such as institutionalized racism) and micro level processes relate to "secondary marginalization" within Black communities (e.g., based on gender and sexuality) (Cohen, 1999). Therefore, the integration of transformative discourses in addressing structural domains that provide intersectional analyses serve as fundamental interventions in the work on violence. As such, this scholarly work must be at the center of the discourse through incorporating critical, innovative, and transformative analyses that interrogate and challenge hegemonic, Eurocentric, patriarchal, and hetero-normative discourses that pathologize Black transgender women's communities.

Building on intersectional theoretical approaches, an integral component to the study of violence in Black transgender women's communities is the incorporation and application of epistemological/theoretical frameworks and methodologies based on cultural studies (e.g., African Diaspora Studies), gender studies, queer/lesbian/gay/bisexual studies, and sexuality studies. One of the objectives in utilizing the scholarly work of these areas in the study of violence relates to the development of epistemological/theoretical frameworks that provide the basis for incorporating the socio-historical, -political, -economic, and –cultural contexts that have been integral in Black transgender women's communities. As such, theoretical and methodological approaches based on these scholarly areas work to juxtapose theory and practice that is grounded in culturally relevant conceptualizations, which are fundamental to the lived experiences of Black transgender women's communities. These areas provide a critical approach to the work on violence that engage a critique at macro- and micro-levels with respect to the sociopolitical processes that influence structural inequalities in Black transgender women's communities. This paradigm shift has the promise of providing opportunities to engage rigorous dialogues regarding the centrality of social justice perspectives as well as the interrogation of knowledge to incorporate intersectional approaches within the domain of violence.

REFERENCES

Alvarez, L. (2015, February 24). U.S. won't file charges in Trayvon Martin killing. *New York Times*. Retrieved from http://www.nytimes.com/2015/02/25/us/justice-dept-wont-charge-george-zimmerman-in-trayvon-martin-killing.html?_r=0

American Psychiatric Association. (2013). *Diagnostic and statistical manual of mental disorders* (5th ed.). Arlington, VA: American Psychiatric Publishing.

Austin, A., & Craig, S. L. (2015). Transgender affirmative cognitive behavioral therapy: Clinical considerations and applications. *Professional Psychology: Research and Practice, 46,* 21–29.

Bailey, M. M. (2013). *Butch queens up in pumps: Gender, performance, and ballroom culture in Detroit.* Ann Arbor, MI: University of Michigan Press.

Battle, J., Cohen, C. J., Warren, D., Fergerson, G., & Audam, S. (2002). *Say it loud: I'm Black and I'm proud; Black pride survey 2000.* New York, NY: The Policy Institute of the National Gay and Lesbian Task Force.

Belluardo-Crosby, M., & Lillis, P. J. (2012). Issues of diagnosis and care for the transgenderpatient: Is the DSM–5 on point? *Issues in Mental Health Nursing, 33,* 583–590.

Bissinger, B. (2015, July). Introducing Caitlyn Jenner. [Web log post] *VF Hollywood*. Retrieved from http://www.vanityfair.com/hollywood/2015/06/caitlyn-jenner-bruce-cover-annie-leibovitz

Black Lives Matter. (n. d.). *Black Lives Matter: Not a moment, a movement.* Retrieved from http://blacklivesmatter.com/

Blinder, R., (2015, February 17). Arizona State University police officer resigns after caught on video slamming professor to the ground for jaywalking. *New York Times*. Retrieved from http://www.nydailynews.com/news/national/asu-resigns-throwing-jaywalking-prof-ground-article-1.2118181

Brockenbrough, E. (2015). Queer of color agency in educational contexts: Analytic frameworks from a queer of color critique. *Educational Studies, 51,* 28–44.

Buchanan, L., Fessenden, F., Lai, K. K. R., Park, H., Parlapiano, A. Tse, A., et al. (2014). *What happened in Ferguson?* Retrieved from http://www.nytimes.com/interactive/2014/08/13/us/ferguson-missouri-town-under-siege-after-police-shooting.html

Centers for Disease Control and Prevention. (2015). *HIV surveillance report, 2013, 25,* 1–82. Retrieved from http://www.cdc.gov/hiv/pdf/g-l/hiv_surveillance_report_vol_25.pdf

Chapman, R., Wadrop, J., Freeman, P., Zappia, T., Watkins, R., & Shields, L. (2012). A descriptive study of the experiences of lesbian, gay and transgender parents accessing health services for their children. *Journal of Clinical Nursing, 21,* 1128–1135.

Cohen, C. (1999). *The boundaries of Blackness: AIDS and the breakdown of Black politics.* Chicago, IL: University of Chicago Press.

Cohen, C. (2004). Deviance as resistance: A new research agenda for the study of Black politics. *Du Bois Review, 1,* 27–45.

Cole-Frowe, C., & Fausset, R., (2015, June 8). *Jarring image of police's use of force at Texas pool party.* Retrieved from http://www.nytimes.com/2015/06/09/us/mckinney-tex-pool-party-dispute-leads-to-police-officer-suspension.html

Connolly, N. D. B. (2015, May 1). Black culture is not the problem. *New York Times*. Retrieved from http://www.nytimes.com/2015/05/01/opinion/black-culture-is-not-the-problem.html

Crenshaw, K. (2014). The structural and political dimensions of intersectional oppression. In P. R. Grzanka (Ed.), *Intersectionality: A foundations and frontiers reader* (pp. 16–21). Boulder, CO: Westview Press.

Currah, P., Juang, R. M., & Minter, S. P. (2006). *Transgender rights.* Minneapolis, MN: University of Minnesota Press.

Dooley, S., Dawson, M., Zak, L., Ng, C., Effron, L., & Keneally, M. (2015, April 24). *Bruce Jenner: 'I'm a woman.'* [Web log post]. Retrieved from http://abcnews.go.com/Entertainment/bruce-jenner-im-woman/story?id=30570350

Erdely, S. R. (2014, July 30). The transgender crucible. *Rolling Stone*. Retrieved from rollingstone.com

Eromosele, D. (2015, March 4). NYC man indicted for fatally beating transgender woman. *THE ROOT*. Retrieved from http://www.theroot.com/articles/news/2015/03/james_dixon_is_indicted_for_fatally_beating_transgender_woman_islan_nettles.html.

Farmer, P., Nizeye, B., Stulac, S., & Keshavjee, S. (2006). Structural violence and clinical medicine. *PLOS ONE, 3*, e449. Retrieved from http://www.plosmedicine.org/article/fetchObject.action?uri=info:doi/10.1371/journal.pmed.0030449&representation=PDF

Follins, L. D., Walker, J. J., & Lewis, M. K. (2014). Resilience in Black lesbian, gay, bisexual, and transgender individuals: A critical review of the literature. *Journal of Gay & Lesbian Mental Health, 18*, 190–212.

Glinder, A., & Santora, M. (2015, April 8). Officer who killed Walter Scott is fired, and police chief denounces shooting. *The New York Times*. Retrieved from http://www.nytimes.com/2015/04/09/us/walter-scott-shooting-video-stopped-case-from-being-swept-under-rug-family-says.html

Goodman, A. (2015, May 29). *Barstow, CA police slam 8-month pregnant women to ground for failing to provide last name*. Retrieved from http://www.democracynow.org/2015/5/29/headlines/video_barstow_ca_police_slam_8_month_pregnant_woman_to_ground_for_failing_to_provide_last_name

Goodman, J. P.., & Baker, A. (2014, December 3). Wave of protests after grand jury doesn't indict officer in Eric Garner chokehold case. *New York Times*. Retrieved from http://www.nytimes.com/2014/12/04/nyregion/grand-jury-said-to-bring-no-charges-in-staten-island-chokehold-death-of-eric-garner.html

Graham, L., Crissman, H. P., Tocco, J., Lopez, W. D., Snow, R. C., & Padilla, M. (2014). Navigating community institutions: Black transgender women's experiences in schools, the criminal justice system, and churches. *Sexuality Research and Social Policy, 11*, 274–287.

Grant, J. M., Mottet, L. A., Tanis, J., Harrison, H., Herman, J. L., & Keisling, M. (2011). *Injustice at every turn: A report of the national transgender discrimination survey*. Washington, D.C.: National Center for Transgender Equality and National Gay and Lesbian Task Force. Retrieved on 1/11/16 from http://www.endtransdiscrimination.org

Gross, K. (2015, June 10). We must make police brutality against Black women an issue in 2016. *THE ROOT*. Retrieved from http://www.theroot.com/articles/politics/2015/06/we_must_make_police_brutality_against_black_women_an_issue_in_2016.html

Haas, A. P., Rodgers, P. L., & Herman, J. L. (2014, January). *Suicide attempts among transgender and gender non-conforming adults: Findings of the National Transgender Discrimination Survey*. Retrieved from http://williamsinstitute.law.ucla.edu/research/suicide-attempts-among-transgender-and-gender-non-conforming-adults/.

Hadjimatheou, C. (2012, November 30). Christine Jorgensen: 60 years of sex change ops. *BBC News Magazine*. Retrieved from http://www.bbc.com/news/magazine-20544095.

Herbst, J. H., Jacobs, E. D., Finlayson, T. J., McKleroy, V. S., Neumann, M. S., Crepaz, N., & HIV/AIDS Prevention Research Synthesis Team. (2008). Estimating HIV prevalence and risk behaviors of transgender persons in the United States: A systematic review. *AIDS & Behavior, 12*, 1–17.

Hightow-Weidman, L. B., Phillips, G. II, Jones, K. C., Outlaw, A. Y., Fields, S. D., Smith, J. C., & YMSM of Color SPNS Initiative Study Group. (2011). Racial and sexual identity-related maltreatment among minority YMSM: Prevalence, perceptions, and the association with emotional distress. *AIDS Patient Care & STDs, 25*, S39–S45.

Hunter, L. A. (2015, February 6). Every breath a Black trans woman takes is an act of revolution. *Huffpost Black Voices*. Retrieved from http://www.huffingtonpost.com/lourdes-ashley-hunter/every-breath-a-black-tran_b_6631124.html.

I AM: Trans people speak. (n. d.). [Web log post]. Retrieved from http://www.transpeople-speak.org

Jenkin, M. (2012, August 17). Trans teen stabbed to death in Chicago. *Gay Star News*. Retrieved from http://www.gaystarnews.com/article/trans-teen-stabbed-death-chicago170812.

Kellaway, M. (2015, March 4). *Suspect indicted in beating death of N.Y. Trans woman Islan Nettles.* Retrieved from http://www.advocate.com/politics/transgender/2015/03/04/suspect-indicted-beating-death-ny-trans-woman-islan-nettles

Kleinman, A. (2000). The violences of everyday life: The multiple forms of dynamics of social violence. In V. Das, A. Kleinman, M. Ramphele, & P. Reynolds (Eds.)., *Violence and subjectivity* (pp. 226–241). Berkeley, CA: University of California Press.

Koken, J. A., Bimbi, D. S., & Parsons, J. T. (2009). Experiences of familial acceptance-rejection among transwomen of color. *Journal of Family Psychology, 23*, 853–860.

Kostek, J. (2013, January 7). Trans Woman who thrived in ball scene murdered on west side. *DNAinfo*. Retrieved from http://www.dnainfo.com/chicago/20130107/west-garfield-park/transgendered-woman-murdered-on-west-side.

Lawrence, A. A., (2007). Transgender health concerns. In I. H. Meyer & M. E. Northridge (Eds.), *The health of sexual minorities: Public health perspectives on lesbian, gay, bisexual, and transgender populations* (pp. 473–585). New York, NY: Springer Press.

Lorde, A. (1984). *The transformation of silence into language and action. Sister outsider: Essays & Speeches*. Freedom, CA: The Crossing Press.

Master, S., & Sherouse, B. (2015, January 30). As Black transgender women continue to die, it's time for a call to action. *THE ROOT*. Retrieved from http://www.theroot.com/articles/culture/2015/01/time_to_stop_end_the_violence_against_transgender_people.html

McDonough, K. (2014, January 7). Laverne Cox flawlessly shuts down Katie Couric's invasivequestions about transgender people. *Salon* [Web log post]. Retrieved from http://www.salon.com

McLeod, K. (2012, September 1). *Transgender deaths: Where is the outcry.* Retrieved from: http://www.theroot.com/articles/culture/2012/09/transgender_women_killings_advocates_urge_doj_to_investigate.html

Mock, J. (2013, September 12). Essays by Janet Mock: How society shames men dating Trans Women & how this affects our lives. [Web log post]. Retrieved from http://janetmock.com/2013/09/12/men-who-date-attracted-to-trans-women-stigma/

Mock, J. (2014). *Redefining realness: My path to womanhood, identity, love & so much more*. New York, NY: Atria Books.

Morgan, S. W., & Stevens, P. E. (2012). Transgender identity development as represented by a group of transgendered adults. *Issues in Mental Health Nursing, 33*, 301–308.

Murphy, T. (2014, March 4). Who cares about Islan Nettles? *Huffpost Gay Voices*. Retrieved from http://www.huffingtonpost.com/2014/03/06/islan-nettles-trans_n_4913663.html.

National Black Justice Coalition (NBJC). (n. d.). *Black, trans and proud* [Web log post]. Retrieved from http://nbjc.org/black-trans-and-proud

National Coalition of Anti-Violence Programs. (2015). *Lesbian, gay, bisexual, transgender, queer, and HIV-affected hate violence in 2014*. New York, NY: New York City Gay and Lesbian Anti-Violence Project.

Neighbors, H. W., Trierweiler, S. J., Ford, B. C., & Muroff, J. R. (2003). Racial differences in DSM diagnosis using a semi-structured instrument: The importance of clinical judgment in the diagnosis of African Americans. *Journal of Health and Social Behavior, 43*, 237–256.

Nemoto, T., Bodeker, B., & Iwamoto, M. (2011). Social support, exposure to violence and transphobia, and correlates of depression among male-to-female transgender women with a history of sex work. *American Journal of Public Health, 101*, 1980–1988.

Nuttbrock, L., Bockting, W., Rosenblum, A., Mason, M., Macri, M., & Becker, J. (2011). Gender identity conflict/affirmation and major depression across the life course of transgender women. *International Journal of Transgenderism, 13*, 91–103.

Obama, B. (2015). *Remarks by the President in State of the Union Address*. Washington, D.C.: White House. Retrieved from https://www.whitehouse.gov/the-press-office/2015/01/20/remarks-president-state-union-address-january-20-2015

Pérez-Peña, R. (2015, May 21). *Six Baltimore officers indicated in death of Freddie Gray*. Retrieved from http://www.nytimes.com/2015/05/22/us/six-baltimore-officers-indicted-in-death-of-freddie-gray.html?gwh=D12E9F365FE903DBD37E148FE3318C78&gwt=pay

Raspberry, C. N., Morris, E., Lesesne, C. A., Kroupa, E., Topete, P., Carver, L. H., & Robin, L. (2014). Communicating with school nurses about sexual orientation and sexual health: Perspectives of teen young me who have sex with men. *Journal of School Nursing*, [Epub ahead of print].

Reisner, S. L., Bailey, Z., & Sevelius, J. (2014). Racial/ethnic disparities in history of incarceration, experiences of victimization, and associated health indicators among transgender women in the U.S. *Women's Health, 54*, 750–767.

Rice, E., Barman-Adhikari, A., Rhoades, H., Winetrobe, H., Fulginiti, A., Astor, R., Montoya, J., et al. (2013). Homelessness experiences, sexual orientation, and sexual risk tasking among high school students in Los Angeles. *Journal of Adolescent Health, 52*, 773–778.

Richie, B. (2012). *Arrested justice: Black women, violence, and America's prison nation*. New York, NY: New York University Press.

Rowan, D., DeSousa, M., Randall, E. M., White, C., & Holley, L. (2014). "We're just targeted as the flock that has HIV": Health care experiences of members of the house/ball culture. *Social Work in Health Care, 53*, 460–477.

Samuelson, A. (2014, August 22). Black transgender women face highest suicide rates. [Weblog post]. *Annenberg Media Center: Health*. Retrieved from http://www.neon-tommy.com

Schmadeke, S., & Gorner, J. (2015, April 20). Anger follows acquittal in rare trial of Chicago cop. *Chicago Tribune*. Retrieved from http://www.chicagotribune.com/news/local/breaking/ct-chicago-police-detective-manslaughter-trial-0421-met-20150420-story.html#page=1

Singh, A. A., & McKleroy, V. S. (2011). 'Just getting out of bed is a revolutionary act': The resilience of transgender people of color who have survived traumatic life events. *Traumatology, 17*, 34–44.

Singh, A. A., Hays, D. G., & Watson, L. S. (2011). Strength in the face of adversity: Resilience strategies of transgender individuals. *Journal of Counseling & Development, 89*, 20–27.

Sontag, D. (2015, April 20). Judge denies transgender inmates' request for transfer. *New York Times*. Retrieved from http://www.nytimes.com/2015/04/21/us/judge-denies-ashley-diamonds-a-transgender-inmate-request-for-transfer.html

Steinmetz, K. (2014, June 9). America's transition. *Time, 183*(22), 38–46.

Strangio, C. (2015, January 28). Hope and resilience for transgender people: Monica Jones victory. ACLU American Civil Liberties Union of Northern California. [Web log post]. Retrieved from https://www.aclunc.org/blog/hope-and-resilience-transgender-people-monica-jones-victory

Sue, D. W., & Sue, D. (2013). *Counseling the culturally diverse: Theory and practice (6th ed.)*. Hoboken, NJ: John Wiley and Sons.

Trans Women of Color Collective (TWOCC). (n. d.) [Web log post]. Retrieved from http://www.twocc.us

Vincent, A. R. (2014, September 16). State of emergency for transgender women of color. Stop the unjust arrests of TWOC, #Free Eisha. [Web log post]. *Huffpost Gay Voices*. Retrieved from http://www.huffingtonpost.com/addison-rose-vincent/state-of-emergency-for-tr_b_5792722.html

Interview with Angela Davis

Tony Platt, interviewer*

TONY PLATT (TP): FIRST OF ALL I WANT TO THANK YOU AND I APPRECIATE THE fact that you made the time to be here. I think you know this is a group of people from several different countries. We have people from graduate programs in law, sociology, social work, and justice studies. We have people coming together for the first time, with state college students and UC students taking the same class and having conversations. So we welcome you to this conversation.

And also on a personal note, I want to thank you for setting a model of being an academic, an intellectual, and also an activist, which is not an easy thing to do. You set that model for many, many people and we appreciate it.

To begin, I noticed that you were fired in 1970 from UCLA for what they called "inflammatory language."

Angela Davis (AD): That was the second time, I think.

TP: But then you came back.

AD: The first time I was fired for being a communist.

TP: Then they rehired you.

AD: Then I took the case up through the California Supreme Court and the case was overturned. The second time was "inflammatory language" and conduct unbecoming of a professor.

TP: All I can say is, congratulations. But here you are a respectable emerita professor from UC Santa Cruz invited back to the university.

AD: I don't know how respectable. I try not to be too respectable.

TP: But you've always been someone who has tried to bring together intellectual work and writing and research with your activism. That has always been an important part of your life.

AD: Yes.

TP: I'd like to start off by asking you something about the earlier part of your life. You grew up in the segregated South, in Birmingham, Alabama, as a young child and a young teen. But you came from an unusual family in that they were politically active. You grew up in that atmosphere. Would you say that obviously race was important to you in that political time and in your family? Was also class and economics an important part of your political training, so to speak, as a teenager?

AD: Absolutely. Because I grew up in what was at that time the most segregated city in the South—Birmingham, Alabama—I couldn't avoid thinking about race. Race was literally everywhere. My mother had become involved before I was born in an organization called the Southern Negro Youth Congress (SNYC). It was an organization created by Black communists who had come down from the Northeast, primarily from New York, to organize in the South. Have any of you seen that film called *The Great Debaters* (2007)? Do you remember the scene when Melvin Tolson, the character played by Denzel Washington, is organizing black and white tenant farmers? Apparently that was based on the work of the SNYC. I found this out because Dorothy Burnham, my mother's best friend (whose daughter is my closest friend), was one of the people who came down to the South. She saw that film and asked me if I knew the history behind it. I said, "Well, not really." She said, "That was our organization. That was the SNYC. That is the work that we did." So class was always involved as well.

TP: So was that unusual among the other young people and teenagers who you knew to take class and economic issues, as well as racial issues, as seriously as you did? We're talking about the 1950s in the South in Alabama.

AD: Probably, but you know, when I think about it I don't think about a discrete position on class and race. I think about them as being connected in a way that makes it impossible to talk about them separately. Of course, years later when we began to talk, write, and organize around the intersectionality of these various categories, I remembered that this is actually what was being done then. But of course, not having the same categories with which to work at that time I did not think about it in the same way.

TP: Did you think of yourself as doing political organizing when you were a teenager?

AD: The first organization I can remember being involved in was an interracial discussion group that took place at the church I attended. I didn't think of myself as an organizer, but I knew there was something very different about doing that work because the church got burned as a result of our meetings.

TP: What year was that?

AD: I was eleven, so...

TP: Was it 1955?

AD: I guess it was. So you know my age! It was probably in the year before the conclusion of the Montgomery bus boycott.

TP: So not just class and race, not just economics and race, but also an interracial politics early on in your life is something you were used to.

AD: Oh, absolutely, yes. I was fortunate because my mother stayed in touch with the Burnham family and other people who had come from New York to Birmingham to organize. Because a number of them were communists, at some point they were forced to leave the city by police commissioner Bull Connor, who is most notorious for violently confronting civil rights activists. My mother actually did her graduate work at NYU during the summers. So she would take all us children to New York and we would stay with the Burnhams, who had an equal number of children in the family. Now when I try to imagine her studying with six and then eight children in the house, it seems impossible. But she got her Master's degree in that way. She also made friends, white friends, who sometimes came to visit us in the South. I remember those as being particularly tense times because it was literally illegal to engage in any kind of interracial intercourse that was not economic in nature. That is to say, a black person could work for a white person, but a black person could not be friends with a white person. I can remember very tense moments when her friends would visit us. She would drive them somewhere and they had to lie down in the back of the car so nobody saw a black woman driving a white woman.

TP: In your junior year, when you got a scholarship from the American Friends Service Committee and you had some choices of places to go, you had already been to New York with your mother. Is that why you chose New York as the place to go?

AD: Yes, I really fell in love with New York when I was six years old.

TP: The Village, right?

AD: Well, it just so happened that Greenwich Village was the location of the Little Red School House/Elisabeth Irwin High School (LREI). This school was a cooperative run by teachers, many of whom had been kicked out of the public school system because of their politics during the McCarthy era. I very much looked forward to going to New York, although I was tempted to go to Fisk. I had it all worked out. At that time I wanted to be a doctor and received early admittance to Fisk University. I'd graduate from Fisk at 19, because I was 15 at the time. Then I would attend medical school, do my specialties, and be a doctor by the time I was 23 [laughter]. But I decided instead to finish high school in New York.

TP: So then, instead of ending up at Fisk, a historically black college, you ended up at a predominantly Jewish college like Brandeis? You must have been one of a handful of African American students on campus when you went there.

AD: Yes. The high school I attended was also predominantly white, with a few black students here and there. I was interested in a school in the northeast and thought about Mt. Holyoke. The choice was between Skidmore, Mt. Holyoke, and Brandeis. Brandeis gave me a really nice scholarship, so that helped.

TP: Then began an extraordinary intellectual period in your life. You were at Brandeis, studied in Paris and Germany, and eventually received a PhD in philosophy in Germany. There you came to know Herbert Marcuse and became one of his graduate students. While this was happening, the movement was erupting and diversifying in the United States. Without going into the long, interesting history of your education, when you finally returned to live in the United States and joined the political movement here, did the black movement view your education and training, as well as the exposure to French, German, and other colleges, as an asset or a deficit? What kind of situation did it create for you?

AD: No one has ever asked me that question before. It's complicated, because I was seen as an anomaly, I guess. When I first attempted to get involved in black movements in San Diego, people thought I was an agent. It took me a while to figure out why no one was responding. They said, "Well, she just came from Europe and she did this and she did that, so she must be an agent."

TP: There was a lot of that in those days.

AD: Yes. I went to the World Youth Festival in Helsinki in 1961, just after my first year in college. Gloria Steinem was there, and other people. It turned out that Gloria Steinem was working for a student organization that had ties to the CIA. So it wasn't unusual. Now I totally understand why people assumed that.

TP: Have you seen your FBI record?

AD: Yes, some of it. It's too long.

TP: Do you know what year they started observing you and reporting on you? Was it that trip to Helsinki that they are reporting on?

AD: Well, that, but actually I think it begins before that, because when I was very young and a number of my parents' friends were underground during the McCarthy era, we would sometimes be followed by the FBI.

TP: Could you explain the McCarthy period and what it meant to be underground? Some people might be unfamiliar with this.

AD: I am referring to people who were fleeing the consequences of the Smith-McCarran Act. According to the McCarran Act (or Subversive Activities Control Act of 1950), a communist is defined as someone who wants to violently overthrow the government. The Smith Act required communists to register. So if you registered under the Smith Act, then immediately you would be charged under the McCarran Act. Quite a number of people went to prison during that period. Some people decided that instead of turning themselves in, they would work underground. A number of my parents' friends were underground—James Jackson, for example. We were often followed by the FBI, which apparently believed that we might be in touch with him. One of the most important lessons I learned as a child was never to talk to the FBI. You didn't talk to them, because you had no idea what kind of information they were actually seeking. They often lured you into a conversation that you assumed was about one thing, but as a matter of fact, you ended up giving them precisely the information that they wanted. So when I was arrested in 1970, I did not say a single word to the FBI. I am very proud of that.

TP: So, talking about communism, you were an active member of the Communist Party from the 1970s?

AD: Actually, from the late 1960s. I had been involved in a number of organizations, including the Los Angeles Student Nonviolent Coordinating Committee (SNCC) and the Black Panther Party (BPP). It's very complicated. But for reasons you can research if you want, there were major problems within SNCC, especially around the role of women. The same thing happened with the BPP. It was in that context that I joined the Communist Party, precisely at that time.

TP: Because of gender and sexism and other internal problems going on in these other organizations?

AD: Yes, but also because I felt the need to be a part of an organization that addressed class as well as race and gender.

TP: You were a public member of that organization, ran for national office on the vice presidential ticket, twice I think, and left the party in 1991. So a big part of your life was as an active organizer in the Communist Party and in communist circles. Reflecting back on that training, history, and participation, how do you talk about it now given the collapse of the communist world and the debates going on about what we were fighting for then and how we understand that today.

AD: My relationship is still good with what remains of the Communist Party (CP). In fact, last Friday I spoke at an election rally in Detroit that was organized by the Communist Party, the Democratic Socialists, and a number of church people. When I think back on that era, what I treasure most about my involvement in the Communist Party was the sense of collectivity and the arena the party provided for engaging in discussions about a range of issues. I never belonged solely to the CP, and was never a functionary. I was always involved in other organizations: for example, the National Alliance Against Racism and Political Repression and the Black Women's Political Caucus, when Shirley Chisholm was in Congress, as well as a number of organizations like that. I've always done my political work primarily in broader organizations.

TP: At that time, a variety of communist and socialist nations existed around the world. We could point to them and ask whether they fit our model or aspirations, what we agreed or disagreed with, and so on. Now we live in a very different world, one lacking real places where such experiments are occurring. Has this profoundly changed your life, as it has those of many other people on the Left? Are you a "recovering communist"?

AD: I don't want to throw the baby out with the bathwater. I want to be critical of communist parties while holding on to what was good and important. I look at Cuba now and am still very much a supporter. Look at the healthcare system there. In the United States, we cannot even begin to meet the challenge that a healthcare system like that poses. So, I don't simply assume that because a particular version of communism or socialism did not work because of the failure to incorporate economic and political democracy, then we must completely let go of the prospect of socialism or communism.

TP: Perhaps we can now shift the conversation to criminology and prisons and the work that has occupied you for a long time. First, you were held in detention. While you were awaiting trial and during your trial, for about eighteen months, you were held in a women's detention center in Marin and then in Palo Alto. Is that right?

AD: The first jail was in New York.

TP: When you were arrested for the first time?

AD: I was there from October until December of 1970. Then I was extradited to Marin County and spent about a year in the Marin County Jail.

TP: Were you held in Palo Alto during your trial?

AD: Yes. We obtained a change in venue to San Jose, in Santa Clara County. I was held in a very, very bizarre detention center in Palo Alto. It was a jail that was meant to hold people for a few days, but I was there the entire time.

TP: Did the eighteen months you spent in those three different institutions change your views in any way about the justice system? Did that give you an impetus to start doing political work later on around justice issues and prison issues?

AD: Actually, I was already doing that work. One reason I was arrested was because of the work I was doing to free political prisoners. Among a number of cases were the political prisoners within the Black Panther Party, and especially the Soledad Brothers—George Jackson and the Soledad Brothers. Through my involvement with the Soledad Brothers and George Jackson I began to think about prison repression in a much broader context. Initially, I was thinking only about political prisoners. I was familiar with political prisoners both here in the United States and around the world. As I grew up, people were talking about the Rosenbergs and Sacco and Vanzetti. During high school, I will never forget that Carl Braden and Anne Braden were two of the most courageous white civil rights activists in the South. Carl Braden was sentenced to five years in a federal penitentiary because he and his wife Anne bought a house for a black couple in a white neighborhood. He was convicted of having instigated a riot or something like that. I talked with him just before he entered prison, so I had a sense of political imprisonment, but not yet that the prison institution constitutes a mode of racist repression.

TP: During your incarceration, were you able to have conversations with imprisoned people who were not political prisoners?

AD: In New York, I was in solitary confinement almost the entire time. People from the outside could visit me, but I did not have much contact with prisoners. The National Conference of Black Lawyers, W. Hayward Burns, and many others came and filed a suit to get me out of solitary confinement. I managed to live in the main population for three weeks, perhaps a little bit longer.

TP: That experience must make you very knowledgeable about what prisoners in Pelican Bay and other similar places are going through in terms of solitary confinement. Did being in solitary affect you?

AD: It did. Normally I wouldn't joke about something like this, but it occurred to me that having been a graduate student for so long really prepared me [laughter]. Because you spend a lot of time reading and writing, often in a solitary situation, and that is basically what I did. I did a lot of reading and writing. I also exercised. I taught myself how to do yoga and since I had already learned karate, I practiced my katas. I had a way of dealing with solitary confinement that people in other situations probably did not. But I do not mean to minimize the importance of political campaigns against long-term solitary confinement.

TP: So you could get the books you wanted as long as they were sent to you in the right way?

AD: I was my own co-counsel. This is one of the things that law students might be interested in. At the time, I wanted to represent myself, but had not studied the law. Thus, I needed to have lawyers. Apparently, no one had ever claimed the right to represent oneself and the right to counsel simultaneously. So we had to file a special brief that I wrote with the assistance of Margaret Burnham—the daughter of Dorothy Burnham, the woman I mentioned who went down to the South in the 1930s as a communist organizer. Judge Richard Arneson agreed that it didn't have to be either/or. That was the issue. You could either represent yourself, or you had the right to counsel, but not both. So I said, "I want to represent myself and I want counsel with me." We successfully made that argument, so I could get whatever books I wanted since the jail authorities had no right to tell me what would or would not be useful for my case. Interestingly, some of the guards considered paperback books to be storybooks. The rule they wanted to impose was that I could get hardback books, but not paperbacks.

TP: Graduate or law students looking for a paper topic, a research topic, or master's thesis might look at your experience as a co-counsel. It would be very interesting, don't you think? Has it been done?

AD: The problem is that it took place at the trial level. So it is not in any of the books. I think perhaps something has been done on it. Margaret Burnham, my attorney from the beginning and now a professor at Northeastern School of Law, should know.

TP: In 1975, when I conducted the interview with you that this class read, you said that the movement had a tendency to forget the sisters in prison, and that the prison movement focused mainly on men. Not that their struggle was unimportant, but women tended to be neglected. When did your political work begin to emphasize women's issues, gender, and sexuality? Was this from the beginning? When did you first seriously take this on as a political project?

AD: Interestingly, I hadn't really thought about the fact that there might be differences that one could attribute to gender. It hadn't occurred to me.

TP: Are we talking about 1975 or 1970?

AD: I'm talking about 1970, which marks the beginning of the women's liberation movement. At that time, we didn't even use the term "gender." It was a process. After I had been in jail a few days, it occurred to me that we were missing so much by focusing only or primarily on political prisoners, and then primarily on *male* political prisoners. Ericka Huggins was one of the few women political prisoners of that era.

During the few weeks that I was in jail in New York, I was in the main population. We actually did some organizing that corresponded to work that was being done on the outside—a bail fund for women in prison. At that time, many women, if they had had access to a hundred dollars, would not have had to spend so many months behind bars. People were on the outside raising money and on the inside we would decide who would benefit from those funds. Women released on bail in this way had to make a commitment to work with the organization to raise more money so that more women could get out on bail. Most likely, that is the first organizing around prisons I did that specifically focused on women.

TP: For the last thirty years, this has been a central part of what you write about, do research on, and talk about: issues of sexuality, sexism, and gender differences. This has been a central concern for a large part of your life.

AD: Yes. And here we are today addressing what Michelle Alexander has called mass incarceration and what many of us have called the consequences of the prison-industrial complex. Because of the number of people behind bars, almost 2.5 millions, we tend to assume that given the relatively small percentage of women in prison, it is a male issue. Beyond the question of forgetting those who don't correspond to the male gender, a feminist approach offers a deeper and more productive understanding of the system as a whole. Many of us have argued that if we look very specifically at the situation of women in jails and prisons, we understand the workings of the system in a much more complicated way. We must address issues that otherwise might not come up, such as the link between intimate violence and institutional violence. Of course, we can see that connection with respect to men, but if we look at the relationship between the kind of violence women suffer from in the world, we get a deeper sense of how the punishment system works and of the connections — or what I often call the circuits of violence — that move from intimate settings to institutional settings. For me, that is the question, rather than simply a focus on women. It is important to focus on women, but it goes beyond that.

Student: Could you elaborate on the connection between violence against women and institutional violence in the prison-industrial complex and how the feminist movement relates to those two issues?

AD: An organization emerged out of the work Critical Resistance and others were doing. It is called Incite!

TP: They have read the dialogue with Critical Resistance.

AD: If you look at Incite!'s website, you see how their work attempts to address intimate violence without relying on law enforcement and imprisonment. If we are serious about prison abolition, we have to ask what criminalization of the perpetration of violence against women has accomplished. It is very interesting that vast numbers of men and others who have engaged in violence against women over the last 30 years or so have been arrested. It used to be that domestic violence was not a matter for law enforcement. Invariably, their response was, "This is a domestic matter." I take that to mean that the state delegated the authority to punish women to the men in their lives, whether their husbands or fathers. But what I want to emphasize now is that with all the work that has been dedicated to the ending of violence against women over the last three decades, the incidence of violence against women has remained the same. All the people arrested, all the organizations and crisis lines around the world have not had an impact on the pandemic of violence that is suffered by women. That means that we must think beyond imprisonment as the solution to violence against women. I am trying to restrain myself, because I could speak about these topics for several hours.

Student: Does the institutional violence people experience in prison affect the way they treat women when they leave prison?

AD: Are you referring to male prisoners?

TP: Prisoners are victimized or learn how to victimize others in prison, then in a sense come out and re-victimize women they have relationships with.

AD: Yes, I think so. It is a question of how we might eventually eradicate violence against women and children. Where do people who engage in that conduct learn that women can be targeted in that way? For those of you who are law students, it is important to learn the law well. Simultaneously, you must be critical of the law and recognize that it compels us to think about these issues as individualized. The subject of the law is an individual, a rights-bearing individual. How do we move beyond the notions of individual culpability and individual responsibility? Where do people learn this conduct? Where does it come from? Certainly, since we live in a violence-saturated society, there is a connection between violence occurring in intimate relationships and violence in the military, in war, on the street, and by police and vigilantes. In this context, last year's discussion about Trayvon Martin was really instructive. For a few months, newspaper articles, television programs, and everyone talked about him so long as George Zimmerman remained at large. As soon as Zimmerman was arrested, it all died down as if the arrest of one individual were sufficient to address an issue that affects individuals, but has an historical dimension and certainly concerns entire communities, not just individuals.

Student: I am taking a constitutional litigation class and would like to add to what you are saying. To have standing in front of the court, you must show injury in a way that is highly individualized. For example, third parties cannot bring a suit simply because they have seen injury, the issue really touches home for them, or affects their neighborhoods. Causality must be very direct and the injury must be to the plaintiff. It is all about the individual. Barriers exist in cases where plaintiffs are trying to change larger schemes, or the way the law is applied, as being unlawful. We cannot even make those cases in front of the court. This I find to be incredibly frustrating. As you are saying, it is a man-made phenomenon, but that is how we are allowed to litigate, and only in that way.

TP: Now that we are discussing more recent issues around prisons and violence, I want to note that in the 1970s you were very active in the National Alliance Against Racist and Political Repression and were focused on political prisoners. About 11 or 12 years ago, you were among the founders of Critical Resistance and started being very active, talking and writing about as well as organizing around issues concerning the long-range abolition—or hopefully the short-range abolition—of prisons, making prison abolition an important part of your political life and being. I will ask Jonathan Simon for specific questions on this.

Jonathan Simon (JS): One theme that has engaged us here is the relationship between grassroots movements and elite opportunities for change, such as Supreme Court decisions or the recent national crisis. I would like to call on your remarkable experiences and observations to consider two moments in time. The first is the relationship between the radical prison movement of the late 1960s and early 1970s, which failed in some ways, and what some have called the mass incarceration that followed. The second seems to be perhaps the line of success between reopening a grassroots struggle in the mid-1990s around this and what seems to be a gradual turn away from mass incarceration at the elite and popular levels today.

Among the letters George Jackson wrote to the *New York Review of Books* in 1970 before the publication of *Soledad Brothers*, one, dated June 10, 1970, stated that "black men born in the US and fortunate enough to live past the age of eighteen are conditioned to accept the inevitability of prison." It is remarkable to read that now, knowing that according to Bruce Western's research in *Punishment and*

Inequality in America, of the black men of George Jackson's generation who did not finish high school, approximately 18 percent went to prison, or nearly one out of five, which nobody is talking about. For that same cohort in 1975, two-thirds of them went to prison, representing a shocking escalation. This represents a remarkable regression in racial justice during these years. Michelle Alexander and others have written about this.

Against that background, I would like you to reflect on two things as an activist and one of our most observant scholars of social change and social movements. First, from a critical perspective, do you see flaws in the direction of the movement around prisoner rights in the early 1970s? Did a combination of the demonization of George Jackson after his death and the state-produced imagery after Attica help to persuade white America that lockdown was necessary to bring peace to the country? In rethinking the strategies of that period, would another approach have been more effective? Second, by 1996 why did you believe it was an opportune time to start a grassroots movement again centered around prisons?

AD: First of all, whenever we attempt to organize radical movements, we must recognize that in a sense we can never predict the outcome of our work. As Stuart Hall said, "There are never any guarantees." At the same time, you have to *act as if it were possible to change the world*; I am rewriting the Kantian categorical imperative here. I don't know whether I would say that the radical prison movement of the late 1960s and 1970s was a failure. New conditions had emerged. For example, we were involved in the campaign against indeterminate sentencing—George Jackson was sentenced to from one year to life for his involvement in a gas station robbery, in which $70 was taken. He was 18. We thought that by organizing against indeterminate sentencing we could arrive at something more just. We all assumed that. We could not imagine mandatory minimums. We could not imagine Three Strikes. That was not the fault of the activists. Perhaps we as activists could have recognized more rapidly what was going on. Often, when we are involved in movements, we have a goal and we assume that we will know when we get there, right? Often, the changes we make are not necessarily the changes we thought we were going to make. So how do we recognize that fact and that we have also reconfigured the whole terrain of struggle? The way in which the movement brought about unexpected changes became very helpful because it made it possible to think about issues today in a way that would have been previously impossible.

Over the last few years, I have thought extensively about past union organizing and the legal efforts to legitimize union organizing among prisoners. In an amazing 1977 case, *Jones v. North Carolina Prisoners Union*, what was at issue was the right of the prisoners union to organize. The warden of one of the main institutions refused to allow recruiting and organizing to take place and was ordered by a lower court to allow the organizing to proceed. Then the North Carolina department of corrections appealed to the Supreme Court, which overturned the lower court decision. One of the most interesting dissents was by Thurgood Marshall, who strongly favored the right of prisoners to organize unions. In California, the United Prisoners Union called for all of the rights union members enjoy, including vacation pay. If you look up United Prisoners Union Bill of Rights online, a manifesto outlines all the rights for which they fought. So, here we are, 40 years later, and the labor movement writ large has suffered enormous assaults within the context of the globalization of capital. Today, it would be very interesting if some of the major unions were to take up the demand to organize prisoners and prisons. Prisoners continue to do work, are paid practically nothing, and have no rights. This situation seems analogous to the position of labor unions toward black people early in the 1920s and 1930s, when white labor unions refused to allow black people to join, while treating them as if they were all potential scabs. A similar situation exists with prison labor. The labor movement totally opposes prison labor, but only because of its effect on labor in the free world. If they were to take up the call to organize — and I have held discussions with some unions on this — it would be amazing. It could begin to address some problems the labor movement faces given the erosion of the unions in context of deindustrialization.

Questions and Comments

JS: Looking back on the history of Critical Resistance, 1996 does not look like a promising moment to start a movement for prisoners who are in some ways at a high-water mark, the high noon in the arc of penal severity that began in the 1970s. This is the moment of Three Strikes, the Prison Litigation Reform Act of 1995 (Eastern District of Pennsylvania), with the state and federal governments becoming just as comfortable as they can be with severely punishing people. It does not look like a promising moment for a grassroots movement about prisons.

AD: Why wouldn't it be promising?

JS: The whole country appears to be mobilized to think about the war on crime as a patriotic duty. Perhaps the best thing the Left could do would be to forget prisons or that we ever talked about prisons. A cynical perspective on that moment would be to move on to a different topic.

AD: Yes. Precisely because of what you articulated, we decided to attempt to bring together people who were doing this work. In 1996, it was very difficult to talk about prison issues. We did not have a public discourse that allowed us to talk about anything except crime in relation to prisons. Those of us who tried found ourselves to be constantly under attack. So a number of us decided to see what we could do to create a new discursive framework. We thought that a few hundred people were doing the work across the country. In Santa Cruz and in the Bay Area, we formed an organizing committee of about twenty-five to thirty people. We decided to hold a conference in the fall of 1998 on the UC Berkeley campus. Since Mike Davis had written an article in *The Nation* on the California prison-industrial complex, on the transformation of agribusiness into prison business, we thought we should try to popularize the term "prison-industrial complex." That would at least help people think about the soaring numbers of people being imprisoned in a context that is different from crime. You know, "Do the crime, do the time." We consciously took up the term to transform popular thinking about prisons. We had no idea that we would succeed, relatively speaking—that it would catch on.

JS: Is it accurate to say that 5,000 people showed up to that conference? It was much bigger than you expected.

AD: Yes, we were expecting about 500 people. That was going to be an amazing conference. We had no paid staff; it was volunteer work. We did it all, including typesetting the program. We initially hoped that 300 people would show up. When more interest was shown, we revised that number to 500 people. Yet some 3,500 people registered and many more people came. It was an eye-opener that people from all across the country and other parts of the world wanted to experience community in doing this work. Many people were working in their own communities, in their towns. People from Europe and Australia came.

TP: Quite a few ex-prisoners came to the conference?

AD: A lot of ex-prisoners came. It was an amazing organizing experience. We wanted to undo the hierarchy that normally asserts itself when prisoners work together with people in the so-called free world.

TP: Could you explain that further?

AD: We wanted prisoners to play an equal role. We wanted to attempt to create an egalitarian relationship between people who were doing the work in the "free world" and people who were imprisoned, so as to address the "missionary problem"—e.g., we're going to help these poor, poor, prisoners. So at the conference we set up telephone numbers that prisoners could use to make collect calls. We amplified that system so that prisoners could talk in the sessions we held. We also looked very carefully at each of the nearly 250 panels and workshops. We sought to avoid all academic panels or all lawyer panels, instead attempting to assure that we had a mix and diversity that could create conversations. We especially encouraged people to move beyond their own language boundaries. Some said that academics like to use big words and so forth, but we pointed out that even organizers often speak a specialized language. If you have never been involved in the movement and hear the word "struggle," what does it mean to you? We therefore asked everybody to be self-reflexive about their manner of expressing themselves. As a result, there were quite amazing cross-talks in the panels.

TP: Did you take on homophobia from the early days of Critical Resistance or was that later?

AD: It began in the early days.

TP: So that was a remarkable change for the movement around prison issues.

AD: Yes, and later transgender issues were addressed, beyond homophobia and issues of gender within a binary framework. Trans people have a greater likelihood of going to jail or prison than is the case for any other group in the country. You must look at the reflections in the institutional framework. How does the prison system itself consolidate a binary notion of gender? How does the prison system contribute to all of the prejudices that people have about those who do not correspond to this binary construction of gender?

Student: You are the first person to speak to us from the perspective of a self-identified abolitionist. What does an abolitionist vision look like today? Would prisons vanish completely or have a greatly reduced role? Also, what is an appropriate response to crime, even if its definition were to change dramatically?

AD: I first encountered the possibility of prison abolition in the 1970s, or perhaps it was in the late 1960s. During the Attica rebellion, which you have discussed, the prisoners in the leadership self-identified as abolitionists. Not long afterwards, a book entitled *Instead of Prisons: An Abolitionist Handbook* appeared. (Critical Resistance republished it, so it is available today.) That book was largely produced by Quakers, who, interestingly, were partly responsible for the emergence of the prison in the United States. The move from capital punishment to imprisonment was supposed to be a humane alternative.

TP: Next week, we are reading *Struggle for Justice: A Report on Crime and Punishment in America*, which was also published by the Friends.

AD: Good. It is interesting that the Quakers introduced this new mode of punishment, which was supposed to allow people to engage in reflection on themselves and establish a relationship with God. Imprisonment and solitary confinement were based on that concept. When it became clear that it did not work, they introduced the notion of the abolition of imprisonment.

There are several ways to talk about this. First, it is helpful to acknowledge the degree to which imprisonment has become naturalized in and through ideological processes. We assume that punishment can only be addressed by imprisonment, forgetting that other forms, such as transportation and the various corporal punishments, preceded it. The history of this institution has been characterized by pendulum swings in terms of reforms. Michel Foucault's *Discipline and Punish*, of which you have read excerpts, points out that reform is at the heart of the history of the prison. We think about calls for reform once the prison had emerged, but actually the prison itself was a call for reform. Throughout its history, calls for prison reform have helped to consolidate the prison, which is not conceivable outside the context of these reforms and calls for reform. Unfortunately, over the years many people assumed that reforms would make the prison better. In actuality, attempts to improve prisons have so thoroughly entrenched them in our institutions and our ways of thinking that they become the only possible approach to addressing crime. Boundaries are erected and you cannot go beyond the boundaries of the prison. For instance, it does not matter whether rehabilitation works or not within the context of prison. You still must observe those boundaries and talk about rehabilitation. Rehabilitation may be perceived to work in one moment, but then there are calls for more repressive modes of punishment. The pendulum swings back and forth from rehabilitation to repression. In the past few years, we have seen this pendulum effect in California. Nothing changes; it just becomes worse. So how do you imagine ways of addressing harm that do not rely on imprisonment and, in the United States, on the death penalty—for the two are inexorably linked here?

We must imagine solutions that do not respect the boundaries of the prison. If we think that crime or harm should be eradicated, how do we go about doing that? We can't just throw people in prison, since that often reproduces the very problem that you think you are solving. I believe the prison serves as a material institution that hides the real problems, while allowing us to conceptually render those problems invisible. With respect to violence against women, by imprisoning those who commit such violence, you don't have to deal with the problem anymore. In the meantime, it reproduces itself. After being released, as was noted earlier in this conversation, a person will probably be even more inclined to commit violence against others.

How do we find solutions that are not prison based? In Critical Resistance we often talk about moving beyond the footprint of the prison. That institution is so powerful that even the alternatives we propose arise within a context created by the prison itself. Thus we try to talk about education or health care as alternatives—especially those services that should be available to people but have been removed during the era of the dismantling of the welfare state and the rise of the carceral state.

The value of abolitionist approaches are most clearly visible in the global South, which has suffered structural adjustment. Have you seen that amazing film, *Bamako*, directed by Abderrahmane Sissako? The International Monetary Fund (IMF) and the World Bank are placed on trial in a compound in Mali. The film reveals the costs to people's lives when pressure from the IMF and the World Bank led to the forcible removal of capital from human services and redirected it into profitable arenas. More prisons are being built to catch the lives disrupted by this movement of capital. People who cannot find a place for themselves in this new society governed by capital end up going to prison. In many countries, such as South Africa and Colombia (which I visited last year), deterritorialization is underway to allow agribusiness to expand, thus producing surplus populations. In Colombia, people have been removed from their land to make way for sugarcane production for the biofuel consumed by us in the West who wish to minimize our carbon footprint. All the people ejected from that land, who had protected its biodiversity, are being pushed into slums. It is most intense near Cali, in the western part of Colombia, where they are building the largest prison in South America—in part to catch those people who have been deprived of their land and have no source of cash. Thus, the value of abolition is clear in places now acquiring US-style prisons due to shifts in the economy.

Student: At a personal level, I have a political soul fueled by outrage, which often prevents me from living the life I want to and seeing the humanity in everyone—the brotherhood and sisterhood of everyone. Has your political self ever taken over your life, making it difficult to balance the two? That is, to be the person who sees the connection and is hopeful for a difference or change in our society versus the person who is outraged and propelled by that outrage?

AD: Outrage is not the only emotion that political people should experience. Joy is a political emotion as well. Because I grew up the way I did—and I'm just realizing this now—I have never felt that I could engage in the process of severing the political person from whatever else is left of the self. Of course, I have different desires at different times. I also become exhausted, but I think that imagination is a political process. I don't express my political aspirations through rage. Perhaps sometimes it is important. For instance, the general elections tomorrow [laughter]. Make sure you vote for the right candidate!

If one is going to engage in this collective struggle over a period of years and decades, one must find ways to imagine a much more capacious political self—in which you experience rage, as well as profound community and connections with other people. The humanity you mentioned is something we often lack because we have been persuaded that we are first and foremost individuals. We are in community and we are, I hope, connected with people across various racial, gender, or national boundaries. I don't have that problem. Sometimes I have to do other things; for instance, before coming to speak to you, I had to figure out a way to meditate and breathe in my yoga class as well.

JS: Is hope one of those political emotions? How hopeful are you? You talked about the elections tomorrow. A proposition on the ballot to repeal the death penalty has been leading in some polls. Another proposition would reform Three Strikes, though it is inadequate. For the first time in decades, populist movements may be moving the other way. Is this a time of hope for you, either in terms of prisons or more broadly?

AD: I think it is a time of hope. But I keep having a nightmare. You might be too young to remember when Al Gore was running against George W. Bush. We went to bed thinking that Gore had won the presidency and discovered the next morning that he hadn't. So, I'm not going to go to sleep tonight [laughter].

It is a hopeful period, but we should be wary of why some people are coming toward the anti-prison movement. We must always be prepared to move one step further. In April 2011, the NAACP released a remarkable report, *Misplaced Priorities: Over Incarcerate, Under Educate*. It draws upon Michelle Alexander's book, which shows that more black men are in prison, on parole, and under the control of correction agencies today than there were enslaved in 1850. Newt Gingrich and Grover Norquist supported the report. Their belated opposition to mass incarceration is based on their opposition to big government, and, by extension, its big prisons. You have to stop and think: Do you really want them as allies?

If we wish to address the crisis of mass incarceration, the government will have to play a much larger role in creating programs and helping to develop the educational system, recreation, and mental health care. This is definitely not what conservative opponents of mass incarceration are seeking.

TP: That's why you chose the name Critical Resistance, which is a fairly unusual name, right? Resistance we understand; but it is critically minded and wary of different kinds of coalitions and political traps.

AD: We mean critical in two senses: it is critical that we resist; we must be engaged and understand the implications of our resistance. We must be critical in our resistance.

TP: We very much appreciate your critical resistance. [Applause]

Credits